ROADMAP TO
RESTRUCTURING

ROADMAP TO RESTRUCTURING

POLICIES, PRACTICES AND THE EMERGING VISIONS OF SCHOOLING

DAVID T. CONLEY

ERIC CLEARINGHOUSE ON EDUCATIONAL MANAGEMENT
UNIVERSITY OF OREGON
1993

Library of Congress Cataloging-in-Publication Data

Conley, David T., 1948—
    Roadmap to restructuring : policies, practices, and the emerging visions of schooling / David T. Conley.
      p. cm.
    Includes bibliographical references (p.).
    ISBN 0-86552-120-4 : $19.95
    1. Educational change—United States. 2. School management and organiza-tion—United States. 3. Education—United States—Aims and objectives.
4. Education and state—United States. I. Title. II. Title: Road map to restructuring.
LB2805.C616 1993
371.2'00973—dc20   93-13439
                                                      CIP

Design: LeeAnn August
Type: 11/12.5 Times
Printer: Cushing-Malloy, Inc., Ann Arbor, Michigan

Printed in the United States of America, 1993
Second Printing, May 1994

ERIC Clearinghouse on Educational Management
    University of Oregon
    1787 Agate Street
    Eugene, OR 97403-5207
    Telephone: (503) 346-5043 Fax: (503) 346-2334
ERIC/CEM Accession Number: EA 024 472

This publication was prepared in part with funding from the Office of Educational Research and Improvement, U.S. Department of Education, under contract no. OERI-R 188062004. The opinions expressed in this report do not necessarily reflect the positions or policies of the Department of Education. No federal funds were used in the printing of this publication.

The University of Oregon is an equal opportunity, affirmative action institution committed to cultural diversity.

MISSION OF ERIC
AND THE CLEARINGHOUSE

The Educational Resources Information Center (ERIC) is a national information system operated by the U.S. Department of Education. ERIC serves the educational community by disseminating research results and other resource information that can be used in developing more effective educational programs.

The ERIC Clearinghouse on Educational Management, one of several such units in the system, was established at the University of Oregon in 1966. The Clearinghouse and its companion units process research reports and journal articles for announcement in ERIC's index and abstract bulletins.

Research reports are announced in *Resources in Education (RIE)*, available in many libraries and by subscription from the United States Government Printing Office, Washington, D.C. 20402-9371.

Most of the documents listed in *RIE* can be purchased through the ERIC Document Reproduction Service, operated by Cincinnati Bell Information Systems.

Journal articles are announced in *Current Index to Journals in Education. CIJE* is also available in many libraries and can be ordered from Oryx Press, 4041 North Central Avenue at Indian School, Suite 700, Phoenix, Arizona 85012. Semiannual cumulations can be ordered separately.

Besides processing documents and journal articles, the Clearinghouse prepares bibliographies, literature reviews, monographs, and other interpretive research studies on topics in its educational area.

DEDICATION

To the Conleys: Frank, Genevieve, Judy, Robyn, Laurel, Gene, Mike, Karen, Ellen, and Julia.

CONTENTS

FOREWORD xiii
ACKNOWLEDGMENTS xv

INTRODUCTION 1
Purposes and Limitations of This Book 1
Difficulty of Describing Restructuring....................................4
Structure and Use of the Book...5
What Is Restructuring? 7
Thinking about Change 10

PART 1 RATIONALE AND CONTEXT..13
INTRODUCTION TO PART 1 14
CHAPTER 1. HISTORICAL BACKGROUND 15
Educational Restructuring in the 1890s..............................17
Educational Restructuring in the 1990s..............................18
The Evolution of the American High School 19
A Fundamental Difference 24
CHAPTER 2. THE WHYS OF EDUCATIONAL RESTRUCTURING 26
Societal Forces for Change...27
Performance of American Students on International Comparisons 30
Changing Values within Society 33
CHAPTER 3. CREATING NEW HABITS OF HEART AND MIND.................43

PART 2 CHANGING ROLES AND RESPONSIBILITIES 55
INTRODUCTION TO PART 2 56
CHAPTER 4. FEDERAL AND STATE GOVERNMENTS 58
The Federal Government 58
State Governments..61
CHAPTER 5. SCHOOL DISTRICTS 68
Boards of Education 68
Central Administrators 71

CHAPTER 6. SCHOOL SITES 79
    Principals 79
    Teachers 83
    Students 86
CHAPTER 7. PARENTS AND THE COMMUNITY 89
    Parents 89
    The Community 94
    Summary 98

PART 3 DIMENSIONS OF RESTRUCTURING 101

INTRODUCTION TO PART 3 102
CHAPTER 8. PREVIEW OF THE TWELVE DIMENSIONS 104
    Central Variables of Restructuring 107
    Enabling Variables of Restructuring 108
    Supporting Variables of Restructuring 110
CHAPTER 9. LEARNER OUTCOMES 113
    Efforts to Develop Performance-Based Standards 114
    Content-Related Standards 121
    Process-Related Standards 122
CHAPTER 10. CURRICULUM 125
    Depth Versus Coverage in the Curriculum 126
    Balancing Content and Process 128
    Curriculum Integration 130
    Changes in Curriculum Development 132
    The Role of National Curriculum Reports 133
    New Structures for Vocational Education 135
    Challenge for Traditional Core Courses 138
CHAPTER 11. INSTRUCTION 142
    What Is Constructivism? 142
    Constructivism and School Restructuring 145
    Examples of Constructivist Instructional Practices 148
CHAPTER 12. ASSESSMENT 151
    Some Limits of Current Assessment Approaches 151
    Some Early Attempts to Develop New Assessment Tools 153
    Examples of Assessment Strategies 156
    The Challenge of Changing the Central Variables 163
CHAPTER 13. LEARNING ENVIRONMENT 165
    Mixed-Age or Nongraded Grouping Strategies 166
    Schools within Schools 168
    Creating Learning Communities 171
    Community-Based Learning 174

Alternatives to Tracking 177
Untracking Schools 179
Inclusion of Special-Education Students 183
Conclusion 187

CHAPTER 14. TECHNOLOGY 188
The ACOT Project 189
Some Often-Overlooked Technologies 191
The Evolution of Integrated Learning Systems 193
Emerging Multimedia Technologies 196
Issues to Consider When Developing Technology Plans 198
New Assessments 199

CHAPTER 15. SCHOOL-COMMUNITY RELATIONS 201
The Role and Expectations of the Business Community 203
Cooperation with Social-Service Agencies 208
New Expectations for Parental Involvement 213

CHAPTER 16. TIME 217
Redesigning Time in Secondary Schools 217
Extending the School Year 222
Caution: Change in the Enabling Variables Is Not Necessarily
  Restructuring 225

CHAPTER 17. GOVERNANCE 227
Two Strategies for Change 228
Decentralized, Participatory Decision-Making 228
Charter Schools: Bridge Between Site-Based Decision-Making
  and Choice 233
School Choice: The Ultimate Change in Governance 235
Is Decentralization the "Magic Bullet" to School Restructuring? 242

CHAPTER 18. TEACHER LEADERSHIP 245
Why Develop Teacher Leadership? 245
Creating a Range of Options for Teacher Leadership 248

CHAPTER 19. PERSONNEL 257
Creating New Definitions of Teacher 257
New Conceptions of the Paraprofessional's Role 260
The Changing Role of Certified Support Staff 261
Enhancing the Performance of Newly Hired Teachers 262

CHAPTER 20. WORKING RELATIONSHIPS 265
Roots in Industrial Unionism 265
Unionism vs. Professionalism 268
Can Conflict Be Avoided? 270
Restructuring Requires Flexibility 271
Collaborative Bargaining and Policy Trust Agreements 275
The Importance of Faculty Collaboration 280

CHAPTER 21. DISCONTINUOUS RESTRUCTURING 281
    Some Examples 282
    Threats to Change 297
    Need for Congruence of Goals 298

PART 4 PROCESS OF RESTRUCTURING 301

INTRODUCTION TO PART 4 302

CHAPTER 22. THE DIFFICULTY OF CHANGE IN EDUCATION 306
    Ambiguous and Confusing Policy Toward Education 306
    Equity of Finance Systems 308
    Bureaucratic Nature of Educational Organizations 311
    Failure vs. Success of Reforms 313
    Nine Pitfalls of School Restructuring 316

CHAPTER 23. CULTURE, LEADERSHIP, AND READINESS 321
    Understanding Culture and Organizational Frames of Reference 321
    The Critical Role of the Principal 326
    Creating Readiness for Restructuring 329
    The Ten Commitments: Prerequisites to Restructuring 333
    Key Questions to Frame Restructuring Efforts 337
    Looking for Models by Visiting Other Schools 341

CHAPTER 24. THE ROLE OF VISION AND SOME
REPRESENTATIVE VISIONS 345
    Vision-Building: A Potentially Powerful Component
      of Restructuring 346
    Some Prerequisites for Successful Vision-Building 348
    Some 'How To's' of Vision-Building 350
    A Vision of a Restructured School System 354
    Principles of the Coalition of Essential Schools 358

CHAPTER 25. SOME TOOLS FOR TAKING THE NEXT STEPS TOWARD
RESTRUCTURING 361
    Systems Thinking and Total Quality Management 362
    Implementing the Vision: Outcome-Based Education 368
    Lessons from Oregon's "2020" Schools 375
    Finding the Time to Restructure 377
    Note to School Leaders 382

CHAPTER 26. EMERGING VISIONS OF SCHOOL
RESTRUCTURING 384
    Contradictions of Restructuring 384
    Emerging Visions of Educational Restructuring 389
    Are the Visions Being Implemented? 395

BIBLIOGRAPHY 400

ABOUT THE AUTHOR

Davidid T. Conley is an associate professor in the College of Education's Division of Educational Policy and Management at the University of Oregon. He teaches courses on school restructuring, school improvement, educational leadership, teacher leadership, and supervision and evaluation. Conley has conducted studies of schools involved in restructuring and served as a consultant for schools and districts pursuing fundamental change. He frequently gives presentations on restructuring and has published extensively on issues integral to restructuring.

Conley contributed to the development and implementation of Oregon's recent landmark school restructuring bill, the Oregon Educational Act for the 21st Century Act. Currently, he is facilitator for a two-year U.S. Department of Education grant that is enabling nine schools to take "the next step" in restructuring.

Before joining the faculty at the University of Oregon, Conley spent eighteen years serving as a school administrator and teacher in Colorado and California.

FOREWORD

Most of us realize that schools must change. The central issue is this: How should schools change? What changes will provide the United States with the work force and citizenry to fill the needs of a transformed world? Perhaps no challenge is more important to our future economic and social well being. All groups of children and youth must be prepared with basic skills, thinking skills, and the ability to process information and create new knowledge. Adults of all ages must be involved in lifetime learning and creative thinking activities. We know the scope of our task, but what are the steps for change?

David Conley has provided us with an accurate and reliable roadmap for the restructuring of schools. The comprehensive view of restructuring presented in this book is based on the premise that the central variables for restructuring are those involved in the teaching-learning process. Much of the dialogue on restructuring has focused on structural changes or on the expanded role of schools in the community. Important as these changes are, they do not replace the need to rethink our basic understanding of teaching and learning.

Much of our understanding of teaching and learning is based on outmoded beliefs that must be changed—that learning is a passive process of exchange of information from teacher to student; that academic studies do not need to include skills development; and that one form of instruction will meet the needs of all cultural groups. The beginning point of restructuring must be a thorough examination of every area of education along with an updating of our past beliefs. This process of beliefs and paradigm shifts must provide the foundation for restructuring.

Roadmap to Restructuring recognizes that information is the key to change and transformation of schools. The information Professor Conley provides is a synthesis of research and practical knowledge. This book contributes a substantial knowledge base that will be read and then used as a reference book by practitioners and policy-makers alike. It is a guidebook that can be used by district or building planning teams struggling with the difficult problems of developing their own change plans.

Far too much of the "restructuring" that is under way in schools is fragmented, incremental change that is unlikely to produce systemic change or substantial gains in student learning. *Roadmap to Restructuring* provides us with a vision of the level of change that is required to achieve the transformation of schools in ways that meet the needs of individuals and our nation.

There are other works on restructuring and there will be more in the future. Conley's work will remain as one of the seminal publications that can both inspire and guide those who are serious and committed to the essential task of school restructuring.

Shirley D. McCune
Senior Director
Mid-Continent Regional Educational Laboratory
Denver, Colorado

ACKNOWLEDGMENTS

This project began as an expansion of a fifty-five page monograph* I had written outlining a framework within which to understand the phenomenon of school restructuring. Somehow it evolved into a full-fledged book on the topic. Had I known this was going to happen, I might have had the sense to be a bit more daunted by the challenge that faced me. And without the support and assistance of the people I acknowledge here, I'm quite certain that the volume would not have emerged in this final form.

Stuart Smith, director of publications, ERIC Clearinghouse on Educational Management, has been key to the development of this book. His insightful comments and supportive manner made it much easier for me to examine my work self-critically. His editing makes this a book that is much easier to read and is more clearly organized and conceptually consistent than it would have been otherwise.

Other staff at the Clearinghouse have also been very helpful. Linda Lumsden, associate editor, performed valuable editing on an earlier version and shepherded the numerous versions and drafts of this manuscript, helping shape its creation. LeeAnn August, word processor and designer, showed extraordinary patience and persistence in dealing with various technologically based challenges that emerged. She also receives credit for the very readable layout, the cover design, and the succession of proofs that let me see that this was eventually going to be a book, after all.

I am indebted to Philip Piele, director of the Clearinghouse, for his openness to this project and his willingness to nurture this manuscript through to its final inception. His perspective on the publishing process, born of experience, served as a tempering and guiding force in the development of this work.

---

* *Restructuring Schools: Educators Adapt to a Changing World.* Trends and Issues Series, Number 6. Eugene, Oregon: ERIC Clearinghouse on Educational Management, University of Oregon, 1991.

Two people enabled me to examine and consider more critically what I was trying to accomplish with this book, and to them I am particularly indebted. In particular, I am thankful to Fred Newmann for his very thorough and thoughtful review of an earlier draft. Many changes (for the better, I believe) were made as a direct result of Dr. Newmann's critique. Shirley McCune, who graciously consented to write the foreword, also offered many insights and observations that caused me to reflect upon, add to, or alter sections of this book.

Many others offered suggestions and ideas, including students in several classes on restructuring at the University of Oregon, who read early versions and offered comments, and my colleague and friend, Jaye Zola, whose enthusiasm encouraged me to feel I was on the right track. Steve Goldschmidt offered a number of helpful suggestions for the section on working relationships. Paul Goldman reviewed a draft and offered ideas for the title. And, finally, I would like to thank Karin Hilgersom, who has worked truly above and beyond her responsibilities as my graduate assistant to check all the citations and quotations that appear in the book, a particularly challenging task, given my filing system.

INTRODUCTION

I lived briefly in southern Maine, long enough to become familiar with some of the folk tales of New England. One of these stories is of a traveler, hopelessly lost on the back roads of Maine. He stops at the house of an old woodsman who is sitting on his porch and asks directions. The old man begins telling the traveler directions several times, but stops each time midway through and begins again with a different set of directions. Finally, as the traveler becomes more exasperated, the old man strokes his chin thoughtfully and says, "Come to think of it, you can't get there from here."

In many ways school restructuring may be an attempt to get "there" from "here." Many states, as well as school districts and individual schools, are pursuing different paths toward the goal of a restructured public educational system. Some paths may prove to be more fruitful than others. What is becoming clear is that there is no one route all schools will follow. Reports from the field indicate a profusion of strategies and approaches to restructuring. This book explores the paths down which states, districts, and schools are traveling.

PURPOSES AND LIMITATIONS OF THIS BOOK

A tremendous amount has been written about school restructuring during the past half-dozen years. Writers and researchers have investigated, discussed, and debated the need and rationale for change in public education, the various strategies being attempted, their relative effectiveness, and the difficulty of bringing about change in public schools.

This wealth of information has not been easily available to practitioners. It is widely dispersed in journals, papers, and unpublished, hard-to-find documents. When school people begin to consider restructuring, it is not easy for them to assemble the resources that might aid their discussions and decisions.

This book is designed to help address this need, at least in part. It is an attempt to assemble many of the salient works on school restructuring

1

that have appeared in print since discussions on the topic began in earnest in the mid-1980s. But this book goes beyond simply summarizing the writing in this area. Its goal is to provide a conceptual framework within which restructuring activities and processes can be considered; to provoke thinking, discussion, and questions regarding restructuring; and to enable readers to go beyond this text to many other sources that will deepen their understanding of ideas presented here.

The book draws from more than 600 sources across a wide spectrum of perspectives and beliefs regarding restructuring. It incorporates and builds upon several of my earlier works on this topic,* along with information I gleaned from discussions and interviews with practitioners. Additional insights have come from my role as a school restructuring consultant and as a site facilitator for nine elementary, middle, and high schools participating in a U.S. Department of Education grant designed to enable schools to take the "next step" in restructuring.

This book provides a picture of many of the trends and issues in school restructuring and attempts to place these issues into a context that helps explain where schools have come from and where they might be going. The book is designed to serve as a tool to help faculties develop their vision of school restructuring and their strategies for pursuing the process of restructuring. It might also be used profitably as a resource for principals, administrators, and boards of education who are trying to understand in greater detail this concept and its implications.

My goal in writing this book is to help educators, community members, and policy-makers understand more clearly why many educators are trying to restructure education, what people may mean when they talk about restructuring, what a few select schools are doing, and how the process of attempting fundamental change in education is being played out. It is not my intent to adopt the stance of cheerleader or cynic. This choice is left to the reader. Rather, it is my hope that this book will enable the reader to have a more informed opinion on school restructuring, and to be more aware of the causes, issues, techniques, and strategies that are associated with this movement.

The scope of the book is both a strength and a weakness. Because it deals with all the activities being labeled as restructuring, along with the process of restructuring, I have had to exclude many important sources. Others may be oversimplified or given inadequate presentation. A reader with a high degree of expertise in one of the dimensions of

---

* See, for example: D. Conley (March and September 1991); Conley, Dunlap, and Goldman (1992); Goldman, Dunlap, and Conley (1993).

restructuring might take issue with the conclusions reached about the relative importance of particular techniques or trends within that dimension, or with the omission of a particularly important or significant source.

These reactions would be justified. I have made a series of conscious decisions to trade off depth for breadth in many cases. I hope to have avoided superficial treatment of key issues and to have captured the main or representative points of view for all the dimensions discussed. Although I have limited the depth of investigation of each topic, the reference list will direct the reader to sources that could serve as the foundation for a more thorough investigation of topics of particular personal interest.

Rather than try to write the definitive book on all aspects of educational restructuring, I have designed this book to be an accessible, user-friendly guidebook or "roadmap" to allow the reader to develop a better understanding of restructuring from a "big picture" perspective.

This book also does not attempt to demonstrate or prove the effectiveness of the various techniques being prescribed under the rubric of restructuring. When appropriate, I cite or discuss relevant research as it relates to a particular dimension or activity. However, this is not a review of the research in the formal sense. It is an exploration and systematic analysis of the literature on a number of closely related topics designed to help identify and label the key issues and ideas embedded within the topics being examined.

This is not a book about *school* restructuring alone. It considers changes that are occurring in central offices, boards of education, state departments of education, and the federal role in education. At the same time, much of the information presented about restructuring strategies is focused at the level of the individual school site. The school site, while the nexus for restructuring, does not exist in a vacuum. For that reason, I also consider the school's relationship to other levels of organization that have an impact on its ability to reshape itself.

Is this book about elementary, middle level, or high school restructuring? Is it about urban, suburban, or rural schools? While there are many examples from secondary schools, much, perhaps most, of what is discussed here applies to all levels of education. For that reason there is no systematic attempt to divide the text into sections addressing different grade levels. While the unique challenges and needs of urban and rural schools are not addressed separately, an effort is made to consider the impact many of these issues have upon these schools. To address these distinctions adequately would require another book. Once again, this book strives to identify common patterns and themes that might have implications for educators regardless of the location of their school.

Finally, two topics are not addressed directly as dimensions of restructuring but may be thought of as overlays to all dimensions. These are multiculturalism and the presence of a caring staff.

Issues of multiculturalism in American schools will ultimately pervade the reconceptualization of schools, as they are currently reshaping our society. Although multiculturalism is not included as a separate dimension, I emphasize that this concept will have far-reaching implications for schools. The concept will have a significant effect on decisions made in nearly every area listed among the twelve dimensions of restructuring. In that sense it transcends and pervades all the dimensions. Many sections of the book argue for enhanced success for all learners and other manifestations of the concept of equity that implies that all students will be able to succeed in public schools. Underlying these points is the assumption that enhanced student learning for all is unlikely to occur in the absence of a truly multicultural school program and community, one that incorporates and respects the culture, history, beliefs, and values of diverse groups present in the school community and American society.

The other topic that is important but not stated explicitly elsewhere is the notion that effective schools are invariably staffed with competent, caring teachers and other adults who work with children. Let it be noted that almost none of the activities discussed on the coming pages will be possible without highly trained, dedicated, caring people in schools. Let it also be noted that it is not enough simply to hire the best people and let them go their own way. The organizational context must support them. Much of this book is about how the organizational context can support competent, caring staff.

DIFFICULTY OF DESCRIBING RESTRUCTURING

What is it possible to say about restructuring? What is it? How is it interpreted? How many schools are involved in it? How is it being put into practice in schools? There probably is no one set answer to these questions, in part because restructuring is a dynamic, evolving concept that means many things to many people. Newmann (1991b) highlights the difficulty of defining this term and suggests some of the term's relative advantages and disadvantages:

> Restructuring joins a lexicon of other memorable slogans in the history of educational reform (e.g., back to basics, community control, effective schools, choice, cultural literacy). Much of a slogan's appeal rests in its capacity to embrace multiple meanings that draw diverse constituencies together in an apparently common cause. While a slogan galvanizes

attention and energy, thus offering new possibilities for action, its ambiguity brings the risk that energy will be dissipated in scattered, and even contradictory, directions. The danger here lies not in multiple meanings and approaches, but in the failure to clarify the means and ends of different approaches to "structural" change. (p. 1)

In attempting to describe restructuring, writers face a chicken-and-egg dilemma: Should they use the best evidence available to discern patterns that are fluid and still emerging, knowing that these will be subject to constant revision? Or should they wait until there is an adequate research base that verifies what has occurred and how well it has worked? The second strategy, while of great value, is constrained by the current lack of adequate empirical data from which to draw generalizations that can be substantiated. The first is riskier and more prone to error. It involves making "best guesses" based on reading of the literature, emerging descriptive and case studies, interviews and observations of those who define themselves as being involved in restructuring, and analysis of the actions of policy-makers at all levels. It can have some value in moving forward the discussion and understanding of a concept that has meaning *de facto* for many educators and policy-makers.

This book is based on the first strategy, with all its attendant limitations. When trends are suggested or generalizations offered, every attempt is made to provide the justification or basis for the statement. This does not mean that every observation offered in the pages that follow can be supported by empirical data. Many are "best guesses" based on a weighing of the evidence from a variety of sources. At the same time, I have made a conscientious effort to ensure that the empirical data that do exist have been referenced where appropriate. I hope that this method of treating the topic of restructuring may serve as a useful contribution to the evolving understanding of this complex, multidimensional phenomenon, and that it might provide some support or assistance both to those considering and those actively engaged in restructuring.

STRUCTURE AND USE OF THE BOOK

The book is organized into four major parts. Part 1, Rationale and Context, presents a historical context within which restructuring can be considered, as well as a summary of the current motivations for and implications of educational restructuring. Part 2, Changing Roles and Responsibilities, examines the evolution of new roles for essentially all the groups that participate in public education directly or indirectly. These first two parts help provide the policy context within which the specific activities of school restructuring that are discussed in part 3 can be better understood. Part 3, Dimensions of Restructuring, explores the concepts of incremental and discontinuous change, then proceeds to an extended discussion of current activities in school restructuring along twelve dimensions. Part 4, Process of Restructuring, captures the lessons being learned about the process of restructuring schools and presents examples of strategies and techniques for restructuring.

I have not designed this book to serve as a cookbook or a "how-to" guide. Quite the contrary. My presupposition is that, for restructuring to succeed, each school must redefine itself individually and allow each teacher, administrator, student, and parent to create a sense of ownership. To help accomplish this, many schools have adapted techniques from strategic planning to develop a *vision* of where they are going. The vision identifies the gap between the school's current practice and an ideal state. Each individual in the school then interprets and translates the vision personally, determining its implications and meaning.

The process of developing a vision—of creating a framework for discussion of the purposes, values, and methods of education—is enhanced when participants can draw upon a wide range of points of view, conduct their own systematic investigations, and learn from the experiences of others who have attempted to implement their vision. The use of such data helps move the process beyond assertions of personal belief by each participant to a broader framework within which personal perspectives can be weighed and analyzed. As will be discussed later, some common elements are beginning to appear in many of the visions for education's future.

This book can be used in a variety of ways to facilitate the process of restructuring. It can be divided into sections, with different individuals given the responsibility to read and summarize the key points in each section and identify their implications for the school; or a group may choose to focus upon one section and have all members read and discuss the section. Similarly, a team might analyze a section, identify the key sources cited in that section, and then find and reproduce them for the faculty or committee charged with investigating restructuring options. A related technique involves assigning source articles to each faculty or committee member and having them be responsible for preparing a written abstract of the key points in the article. These abstracts might then be copied and assembled in notebook form to allow others easier, quicker access to the literature base on the topic being investigated.

The structure of this book also lends itself to use as a resource book for workshops or courses on restructuring and change in education. Many of the activities described in the previous paragraph might also be used in such settings.

No matter how this book is employed, its purpose is to provide the reader with the broadest possible overview of this complex, multidimensional topic, and to structure the presentation of information on this topic in a manner that triggers the generation of ideas and the identification by the reader of possible problems and potential solutions. The goal is a better-informed reader who is able to make more sophisticated analyses and reach more thoughtful conclusions on this topic of critical importance to the future of education.

WHAT IS RESTRUCTURING?

In education, the term *restructuring* is as notable for its ambiguity as for its meaning. In the private sector the term has come to mean a process of rapid adaptation prompted by the need to maintain or regain competitiveness. The restructuring process has been called a "radical reaction to product or market changes" (Enderwick 1989, pp. 44-45). Employment and work assignment patterns within a company are usually disrupted by this process, and layoffs frequently occur as a result. This is not the meaning for this term as educators apply it to change in schools. In fact, educators often do not distinguish very carefully among possible conceptions of change.

It may be useful to distinguish among three levels of change occurring sometimes simultaneously in public schools: renewal, reform, and restructuring, what might be referred to as the "three R's" of change in education. This differentiation can be important, particularly given the fact that almost every school at some point embarks on a change effort of some sort, and that most attempts to change are serious events in the life of schools.

Renewal activities are those that help the organization to do better and/or more efficiently that which it is already doing. Most school improvement projects fall into this category, as do many of the staff development programs districts offer. It is very easy for faculties to assume that if they are undertaking a number of important renewal activities they are "restructuring," since these activities take a great deal of energy and are capable of yielding positive results. This type of program, however, does not cause schools to examine any of their fundamental assumptions or practices, except by implication. For many schools, renewal may be the most appropriate way to proceed. For others, renewal efforts cloaked as restructuring will lead to frustration and will not achieve the goals for which they were initially intended.

Education has a well-documented tradition of improvement efforts. The pace of systematic improvement has quickened over the past two decades as a research base and models of improvement have been developed (Clarke 1984, Cohen 1982, Edmonds 1982, Joyce 1991, Mortimore and Sammons 1987, Purkey and Smith 1983, Purkey and Degen 1985, Stedman 1987, Vickery 1990). Systematic school improvement may contribute to the ability of a school to attempt more fundamental change. Many models of school improvement help teach educators the skills of data collection and analysis necessary for developing a profile of current practices and identifying areas in need of improvement (Blum and Butler 1985), of determining key shared values and goals (Cook 1988), and of developing the sense of collegiality that allows teachers to talk with one another about practices in their schools (Little 1982). These skills can be important in terms of creating an internal capacity to manage change within the school. Indeed, the existence of this capacity can enable schools to consider change of a more fundamental nature (D. Conley, March 1991; Goldman, Dunlap, and Conley 1993).

Reform-driven activities are those that alter existing procedures, rules, and requirements to enable the organization to adapt the way it functions to new circumstances or requirements. Two important points help to identify and define reform-oriented efforts: First, changes center on procedural elements, the policies and procedures that determine the basic "rules of the game" for all participants in the system; and, second, the impetus for reform almost always comes from some external force, such as a board of education, a state department of education, or even educational reformers. This impetus results in the appointment of committees to examine current practice and to bring the school into conformity with the new expectations or requirements.

Clearly, reform-oriented change cannot be overlooked. At the same time, such activities are as unlikely to result in an examination of fundamental practices or assumptions about schooling as they are likely to produce a new set of rules or procedures. Many externally originated programs of change for schools do not seem to be very successful, in part because teachers are less likely to develop ownership of the program, or to adapt it to their needs (Berman and McLaughlin 1974, Fullan and Pomfret 1977, Fullan and Stiegelbauer 1991, Goldman and Smith 1991). As in the case of renewal activities, schools can devote a great deal of energy to reform-based improvements and never realize that they have not engaged in a consideration of issues related to restructuring the educational environment.

Restructuring activities change fundamental assumptions, practices, and relationships, both within the organization and between the organization and the outside world, in ways that lead to improved and varied student learning outcomes for essentially all students. The important elements of this definition are the idea that fundamental assumptions must be challenged for change to occur and the emphasis on student learning as the key variable being addressed. *Learning* here refers to student learning outcomes as identified and defined by the state, district, and/or school site. The conception of learning contained in the terms *improved* and *varied* is different from that held today by many students, teachers, administrators, parents, and policy-makers. It implies not just brief memorization of factual material, but the ability to retain, synthesize, and apply conceptually complex information in meaningful ways, particularly as such application demonstrates understanding of challenging content, intricate concepts and systems, sophisticated learning strategies, real-world problems, and natural phenomena. The definition highlights the need to consider a variety of learning outcomes and to examine all current assumptions, practices, and relationships in the light of a single overarching goal: enhancing students' learning. It also draws attention to the needs of *all* students attending school, not just those students who are currently succeeding.

Far too often, the emphasis on improved student learning becomes obscured when schools define restructuring as changes that focus on or result in enhanced working conditions for adults. While the needs of adults should not be overlooked, it is important to remember that any change that fails to result in improved student learning doesn't ultimately affect the fundamental purpose of schooling. Clearly, there are many dimensions of life in schools that have an equal impact on the students and adults in the school, and there are excellent opportunities to create improvements that benefit both. Such opportunities can be pursued productively and vigorously. However, many of the ideas for school restructuring being considered currently are unlikely to have much impact on the lives of students unless they are explicitly linked with other activities more closely related to student learning.

Many educators seem to view restructuring as a way to create the appearance of change without necessarily confronting the harsh realities that fundamental changes suggest. These educators seem to say: "I'm all for change—as long as I don't have to do anything differently." This unwillingness to look at underlying assumptions, values, beliefs, practices, and relationships can prevent schools from coming to grips with the profound and disturbing implications of true restructuring.

It seems likely that any district or school that adopts the definition of restructuring presented earlier would find itself in the position of examining almost all its practices. For most schools such self-examination is too difficult and threatening. Fullan (1991) makes this point: "The incentive system of public schools with abstract and unclear goals, lack of performance scrutiny, and a noncompetitive market makes it more profitable politically and bureaucratically to 'innovate' without risking the costs of real change" (p. 28).

Schools should not feel so alone in this respect. In the corporate world as well, it is rare for a company to look very closely at itself in the absence of some external challenge or threat, which precipitates an internal crisis. The more clear and pressing the threat is, the more fundamental the examination, and the more drastic the response is likely to be. Without such external pressure, it may be even more difficult for schools to remake themselves voluntarily, particularly when such a process could involve dislocation, reassignment, and retraining for numerous members of the organization.

THINKING ABOUT CHANGE

There are many ways to think about the type of change required for schools, or any large, complex organization, to adapt rapidly to changing environmental conditions. In general, change can be thought of as occurring along a continuum: At one end the organization is very much in control of the goals and processes of change; at the other it is not. In this conception of change, the key distinction is the rapidity and magnitude of change the organization faces in order to realign itself with a swiftly changing or evolving external environment.

Meyer, Brooks, and Goes (1990) analyzed the strategies organizations employ when confronted by rapid change, or "environmental jolts." They differentiate between *incremental* and *discontinuous* change:

> Almost everyone who spends much time thinking about change processes seems to conclude that the world changes in two fundamentally different modes (Watzlawick, Weakland, and Fisch, 1974). Continuous, or first-order change, occurs within a stable system that itself remains unchanged. Indeed system stability often *requires* frequent first-order change, such as the myriad of small compensatory steering movements that permit a bicyclist to maintain his or her equilibrium. Discontinuous, or second-order change transforms fundamental properties or states of the system. The distinction between first- and second-order change has been likened to that between simple motion and acceleration (Watzlawick et al., 1974). Some compelling examples of social systems plunging from first-order to second-order change are afforded by the sociopolitical upheavals in eastern Europe in late 1989. (p. 94)

Meyer, Brooks, and Goes (1990) state that "as the pace of technological, socioeconomic and regulatory change accelerates, organizations' survival depends increasingly on devising entrepreneurial responses to unforeseen discontinuities" (p. 93).

Meyer and colleagues then offer a conceptual framework for understanding how these changes occur and the responses at individual work sites and at the industry level. They identify four reactive strategies:

1. *Adaptation*: Incremental change within an individual organization

2. *Evolution*: Incremental change within an established industry

3. *Metamorphosis*: Frame-breaking change within an individual organization

4. *Revolution*: Emergence, transformation, and decline of entire industries

They conclude that there is no guarantee organizations will choose a successful or appropriate change strategy. In the late 1970s and early 1980s, San Francisco Bay Area hospitals pursued various strategies in response to decreasing regulation and increasing pressures for cost containment—a pattern of discontinuous change. Historically, protected organizations such as hospitals have had a difficult time responding to second-order change, in part because managers are unprepared for it:

> Discontinuous change is enigmatic and paradoxical for managers caught up in it. It breaks the frame in which they have been operating, a frame which they probably have come to take for granted. The events triggering discontinuous changes can appear so inconsequential, and the onset can be so sudden, that managers often are forced to act before they understand of (sic) the consequences of acting. When turbulence subsides a new equilibrium may be achieved that is partly a product of those actions. In this sense, managers in the throes of revolutionary change assume the role of entrepreneurs reinventing both their organizations and their environments. (p. 108)

Educators find themselves in a similar situation. They may well be on the verge of being confronted with sudden, unpredictable jolts, whose significance will be difficult to discern; incremental responses may be disastrous. Whether, or to what degree, educators can assume the role of entrepreneur to reinvent their organizations and environments may be the key unanswered question upon which the fate of the restructuring movement hinges.

Cuban (1988) makes the same distinction between changes, using the terms *first-order* and *second-order*. First-order changes improve the efficiency and effectiveness of what is being done already "without disturbing the basic organizational features, without substantially altering the way that children and adults perform their roles" (p. 342).

Second-order changes "alter the fundamental ways in which organizations are put together, including new goals, structures, and roles" (Fullan 1991, p. 29). Educators have been largely unable to implement second-order change successfully in schools. The difficulty of this type of change should not be underestimated. A more detailed discussion of the problems and challenges associated with fundamental change in education will be presented in part 4, Process of Restructuring.

Renewal and reform can be thought of as incremental forms of change in most situations and manifestations. They do not disturb organizational features substantially, nor do they necessarily alter the ways adults perform their roles. Restructuring, on the other hand, implies second-order change. However, as will be considered later, many schools that claim to be restructuring appear reluctant in practice to engage in second-order change. They may develop documents replete with the language of such change, but an examination of the nature of their workplace often leads an observer to conclude that little in practice is different, and that those differences that do exist would better be categorized as first-order, rather than second-order, changes. The reader is encouraged to analyze changes occurring in her or his organization and consider whether (or to what degree) they are renewal, reform, or restructuring, and to what degree the organization is conceiving of change as entailing first-order versus second-order alterations of practice and structure.

PART 1

RATIONALE

AND

CONTEXT

INTRODUCTION TO PART 1

The restructuring movement has sprung up in the educational community with such rapidity that it is difficult to place it into a context. Is it old wine in new wineskins? Is it merely another fad? Who wants it? When is it renewal, when is it restructuring? What is it, anyway? Is it a movement at all?

The term *restructuring* means many things to different people. The fuzziness about what constitutes restructuring has been, perhaps, one of its more attractive elements: almost anything qualifies. The term may have to acquire a more precise meaning, as educators and community members come to understand not just what they choose to change about schools, but why in a broader sense they are altering the structure, methods, and content of public schooling. As this focus becomes defined, it is possible to put restructuring into context, both as a change strategy and as a historical phenomenon.

Chapter 1, Historical Background, explores the relationship between contemporary restructuring and earlier attempts at large-scale reform of education. Chapter 2, The Whys of Educational Restructuring, summarizes some of the reasons presented to justify large-scale change in public schools. Finally, chapter 3, Creating New Habits of Heart and Mind, explores some of the values that are embedded in the goals of educational restructuring.

CHAPTER 1

HISTORICAL BACKGROUND

Many people involved in restructuring have heard skeptics utter phrases such as "I know I've been in the business a long time when I see the same ideas coming around for the second and third time," or "Here we go again," or "The more things change, the more they stay the same." These sayings express the idea that if educators try a particular innovation once, they should either incorporate it into educational practice for all time or abandon it categorically. In reality, educational innovations come and go, not necessarily or solely because of their relative effectiveness alone, but at least in part because of societal assumptions and values regarding the methods and purposes of education that influence the perception of an innovation's effectiveness. As these values change, today's success may be defined as tomorrow's failure.

This chapter explores the historical context of school restructuring over the past century. It also traces the values and goals that have driven change in public education at various times and explains how these shifting goals have led to periodic efforts to reshape schools. This brief treatment is not meant to serve as a substitute for a careful reading of the history of education generally or of educational reform specifically. Authors such as Tyack (1974), Cremin (1988), Cuban (1984a), and Callahan (1962) have chronicled these events in much greater depth and detail. My goal is to provide some perspective on current efforts to restructure schools, since historical perspective seems to be lacking in many reform and restructuring conversations and projects.

The restructuring movement appears to lack a sense of history. There seems to be little awareness that significant change has occurred at other periods, or that there is much to be learned from previous attempts to solve educational problems. Few of the spokespeople for today's reforms have identified the link restructuring seems to have with the Progressive school of thought in education, for example. And few analyses note the similarities between concerns emanating from the business community during past phases of fundamental educational reform and those being heard today.

Similarly, few of the advocates of basing curriculum and instruction on the needs of students acknowledge the link their thinking has with other reformers from previous eras. They do not seem to be aware that many of the changes they advocate have been examined by researchers previously and found to lead to greater student learning. One of the best examples is the Eight Year Study, which examined the success that students from "progressive" public schools of the 1930s had when they subsequently entered college. It demonstrated very clearly and power-fully the effectiveness of many techniques being discussed by today's reformers. Ralph Tyler (1986/1987), the director of the study, describes several of its most significant outcomes:

> The Progressive Education Association developed the Eight Year Study in which 30 schools and school systems from Boston to Los Angeles demon-strated the effectiveness of curriculums designed by each school to meet the needs of its own students....
>
> Perhaps [the] most significant [outcome of the study] in terms of current practices in curriculum development was the widespread accep-tance of the idea that schools could develop educational programs that would interest a large proportion of their students, help to meet some of the student's needs and, at the same time, provide students with the prepara-tion essential for success in college. Because of that project, most state departments of education and most colleges and universities greatly re-duced their specific requirements for the high school curriculum and relied more upon each school's taking responsibility—although recent trends have been in the opposite direction.
>
> A second outcome of the study was the recognition by colleges and universities that they could find among high school graduates who had not met specific subject requirements many who would succeed in college work. They learned that they could select successful candidates for admis-sion on the basis of their ability to read, write, solve quantitative problems, and show evidence of strong interest in further education. This led to the wider use of entrance examinations, such as the SAT, that did not test specific content but appraised general skills....
>
> ... [An additional] outcome was the wide acceptance of educational evaluation instead of testing.... The Eight Year Study... demonstrated that it was possible to appraise the progress of students toward [achievement of course objectives] by using questionnaires, observations, and samples of products as well as tests. (p. 38)

Tyler's work on the Eight Year Study is just one example of the lessons that have been learned regarding educational practice, lessons that appear not to be acknowledged in many conversations about and programs of restructuring. The brief discussion of selected historical events that follows serves only to illustrate this point by suggesting other parallels that might be drawn between previous attempts at fundamental change in education and what is occurring now.

EDUCATIONAL RESTRUCTURING IN THE 1890S

Change in public education is nothing new. Although change may be difficult to detect on a year-to-year basis, the educational system has been evolving since the arrival of the Pilgrims. What is more difficult to discern is that education has undergone fundamental change in relatively short periods of time. It has happened before. During the period from the early 1890s through roughly 1920, changes of virtually unimaginable proportion washed over the system with regularity. These changes shaped the system that exists to the present.

The combined forces of urbanization, industrialization, and immigration put tremendous pressure on education during this period. High school enrollments increased twenty-fold from 1875 to 1900 as the right to finance public education through broad tax support was established (*Stuart and others v. School District No. 1 of Kalamazoo* 1874). The legitimization of public funding enabled schools to develop new programs and serve more students.

And more students there were. The tidal wave of immigration peaked at roughly eight million in the 1890s and continued during the next two decades. This influx created pressure for standardization of an educational system that had truly been community controlled and decentralized. While educators took the lead in designing and implementing the reforms of the era, they were clearly influenced by the values, philosophies, and techniques prevalent in the private sector. In addition, higher education exerted a powerful influence in the direction of standardizing educational practice. It was during this period that grade-level organization, the Carnegie unit, the notion of intelligence and of IQ tests, the use of standardized achievement tests, the content and structure of the high school curriculum, the junior high school, and the professional superintendent and principal, among other major reforms, were implemented.

The notion that the purpose of an education was to prepare youth for the labor force in addition to attaining the traditional goals of the liberal arts curriculum also gained respectability and credence. High schools were to be *comprehensive* institutions; they would educate *all* the youth, though in different ways and toward different ends. Previously public education had been viewed primarily as a way to enable students to read the Bible, as a form of socialization necessary in a democratic society, and as a vehicle for the transmission of local community values. A grade school education was generally sufficient to serve these purposes.

It was around this same period that the Progressive movement in American education was born. Although the roots of progressivism can be traced back at least to Rousseau, it was John Dewey who did more than any other individual to give voice to the thinking of the Progressive movement and bring it into the public eye.

The Progressives believed not only in the involvement of the learner in the construction of knowledge through structured experience, but in the use of public education as a tool for social reform (Sewall 1983). Public education came to be seen as the means by which one might improve one's lot in life.

The last state to pass a compulsory school attendance law, Mississippi, did so in 1918. At the same time, many other states were increasing the minimum "leaving age," thereby increasing the number of students going on to higher grades and the challenges associated with instructing them. Public education was to be the key for new immigrants and other city dwellers to establish the foothold that would allow them to climb the social and economic ladder.

Two forces, the Progressive educators and the business community, while not necessarily in agreement on the general goals of school restructuring, ended up being able to advocate or support many reforms that blended together in practice. Progressives favored reform to humanize education and use it as a tool for social reform and economic opportunity for the less advantaged. The business community supported fundamental change in education designed to prepare young people to enter the labor force with the proper attitudes and habits necessary for factory work. For very different reasons, these two groups, one internal to the educational community and the other external to it, supported a series of reforms that served to rationalize and systematize public education and strengthen its links to the economic system.

It is clear, based on Callahan's (1962) interpretation, that the business community was clearly the more powerful of the two forces. However, it is important to remember that strong voices advocating change from both within and outside the educational community had powerful effects, even if their messages were not always the same.

EDUCATIONAL RESTRUCTURING IN THE 1990S

How do the events of the past century and those from earlier in this century help us understand the forces that favor fundamental change in education today? Once again, there appear to be two distinctly different groups, who, for very different reasons, are advocating radical transformation of public education. On the one hand, educational reformers such as Theodore Sizer and John Goodlad promote changes that can be viewed as consistent with the Progressive tradition of education. These reformers emphasize active construction of knowledge by students, demonstration of skills through exhibitions rather than tests, allocation of time based on the needs of the learner rather than on the needs of the school schedule, and alteration of the student-teacher relationship to student-as-worker, teacher-as-coach.

A teacher in a school that is a member of Sizer's Coalition of Essential Schools describes this change in emphasis:

> Since I've moved to this school, my teaching has really changed. I used to feel as if I were the quarterback in the classroom. I carried the ball and made touchdowns with my best lectures. Somewhere along the line, I realized that I was doing all the work. Now I stand off to the side, and the kids do the running. (Wasley 1991, p. 35)

The influence of present-day educational reformers should not be underestimated. They are highly visible within the educational community; their articles appear in journals that practitioners read; and they speak regularly at large educational conferences and conventions. They also have had the ear of many state legislators who have significant power to implement educational reform.

At the same time, a possibly stronger force for change has emerged— the business community. As business has been forced to abandon the traditional factory model in the face of a rapidly evolving world economy, its needs for workers have changed. It is clear that the American economic system must adapt quickly to its changing place in the international economic system, from Goliath to partner. There is compelling evidence that the United States will never again dominate the world economy as it did in the period immediately following World War II. Its new role is still being defined (Reich 1988 and 1990). Business is viewing education and public schools as more important than ever before to its success.

Another way to compare and contrast restructuring is to examine the high school, which was a focal point for fundamental change at the turn of the century and appears to be in such a position once again. The next section takes a closer look at this process.

THE EVOLUTION OF THE AMERICAN HIGH SCHOOL

One clear trend in the restructuring movement is that high schools appear to be quite difficult to change, and at the same time appear to be in need of an examination of assumptions and practices. More so than any other level of education, the high school adopted the factory model of organization with its reliance on standardization, efficiency, task specialization, and batch processing. Ironically, the high school's success in adapting to previous calls for change has made it the level facing the greatest challenge today. The high school also finds itself being the institution where the largest proportion of children fail. A high dropout rate has been acceptable until now for a variety of reasons. However, as will be argued later, it may no longer be acceptable for one of every four or five students to leave school without a diploma. The pressure on high schools to change radically and fundamentally continues to increase.

Why is the high school under such pressure to change? A brief examination of its evolution will help put into perspective its philosophical assumptions and historical role.

The intellectual roots of the American high school can be traced back at least to the 1700s and the Renaissance, and, for some elements, to the ancient Greeks. The structure of knowledge based on empiricism and classical studies still is present in high schools in slightly altered form and comprises the intellectual core of the high school. History, science, mathematics, English, and, to a certain extent, foreign languages (formerly Latin) are still identified as "core" subjects.

In the 1700s, these were the topics of interest to a landed aristocracy and members of a newly emerging business class. They formed a curriculum that helped students understand the universe in a philosophical sense. It was not the purpose of an education to prepare a student for a job, since only the privileged were able to attend secondary schools to begin with. This tradition of secondary education as an opportunity to reflect on one's place in the universe remained essentially unchanged through the mid-1800s.

In the 1890s, enrollments increased sharply as pressure was put on schools to socialize immigrant children, public taxes were used to fund universal education, and new laws held young people out of the work force. Only then did the role of the secondary school come under examination.

The primary "master" of the secondary school was the university. Since the central purpose of a secondary education was to prepare students to attend college, this relationship was a natural one. Beginning in the 1890s, the colleges launched a series of reforms designed to (1) make high school programs more uniform through the use of common course titles; (2) enforce some form of quality control through the imposition of the Carnegie unit, which set standards for the amount of credit to be granted based on the amount of "seat time" in a course; and (3) standardize grading procedures through the use of gradepoint averages and official transcripts. The recommendations of the Committee of Ten, convened in 1892, resulted in a much closer alignment between high schools and colleges.

By 1911, pressures for the high school to change were increasing rapidly. That was the year the committee on the articulation of high school and college submitted its report to the National Education Association. A direct outgrowth of that report was the appointment by the NEA of the Commission on the Reorganization of Secondary Education, which went on to develop the Cardinal Principles of Secondary Education. An excerpt from the commission's report provides insight into the perceived need for change in public education:

> Secondary education should be determined by the needs of the society to be served, the character of the individuals to be educated, and the knowledge of educational theory and practice available. These factors are by no means static. Society is always in process of development; the character of the secondary-school population undergoes modification; and the sciences on which educational theory and practice depend constantly furnish new information.... Failure to make adjustments when the need arises leads to the necessity for extensive reorganization at irregular intervals. The evidence is strong that such a comprehensive reorganization of secondary education is imperative at the present time.
>
> 1. *Changes in society*—Within the past few decades changes have taken place in American life profoundly affecting the activities of the individual. As a citizen, he must to a greater extent and in a more direct way cope with problems of community life, State and National Governments, and international relationships. As a worker, he must adjust himself to a more complex economic order. As a relatively independent personality, he has more leisure....
>
> The responsibility of the secondary school is still further increased because many social agencies other than the school afford less stimulus for education than heretofore.... In connection with home and family life have frequently come lessened responsibility on the part of the children; the withdrawal of the father and sometimes the mother from home occupations to the factory or store; and increased urbanization, resulting in less unified family life. Similarly, many important changes have taken place in community life, in the church, in the State, and in other institutions. These changes in American life call for extensive modifications in secondary education....
>
> 3. *Changes in educational theory*—The sciences on which educational theory depends have within recent years made significant contributions. In particular, educational psychology emphasizes the following factors:
>
>   *a) Individual differences in capacities and aptitudes among secondary-school pupils....*

b) The reexamination and reinterpretation of subject values and the teaching methods with reference to "general discipline"....

c) Importance of applying knowledge....

d) Continuity in the development of children....

The foregoing changes in society, in the character of the secondary school population, and in educational theory, together with many other considerations, call for extensive modifications of secondary education. Such modifications have already begun in part. The present need is for the formulation of a comprehensive program of reorganization, and its adoption, with suitable adjustments, in all the secondary schools in the Nation. Hence it is appropriate for a representative body like the National Education Association to outline such a program. This is the task entrusted by that association to the Commission on the Reorganization of Secondary Education. (Commission on the Reorganization of Secondary Education 1928)

The commission recommended changes that began moving the high school toward meeting the needs of a much broader range of students. It recommended the inclusion of vocational courses, the provision of guidance for students, and attention to the education of the "whole child" through subjects such as health, ethics, the worthy use of leisure time, and citizenship. The high school had now moved from one central mission, college preparation, to possibly three: college prep, vocational education, and general education.

The proportion of students completing high school increased steadily, so that by 1953 half of all American youths were graduating. The high school struggled to provide a meaningful education for all of them. This massive increase in graduation was accomplished at least in part by an expansion of the general education track—less challenging, less focused courses that were designed primarily for those not necessarily going on to college nor preparing for a profession.

The Russians changed this in 1957 with the launching of Sputnik. Alarm bells sounded, particularly in Congress. A series of federal programs were legislated to improve the quality of American education, but with particular emphasis on math and science. James Conant, president of Harvard University, undertook a two-year study of the American high school. His report (Conant 1959) became "the most authoritative design for secondary education in the postwar era" (Sewall 1983). The report emphasized traditional academics for nearly all students, minimum requirements in "core" subjects, and use of ability grouping with particular attention to the academically gifted. These recommendations helped lead to the addition of a new track in high schools—the "Advanced Placement" track. Now there was the college-bound student and the "truly college-bound."

In the sixties issues of equity began to receive greater attention in response to the civil rights movement and the school desegregation process. The high school was under pressure to produce more world-class scientists to compete with the Russians; at the same time, it was expected to educate the less privileged to higher levels so that they might participate in the American Dream. The result was the gradual development of the "at-risk" track, which encompassed a broad array of strategies, including special tracks, alternative schools, and programs within high schools.

The passage of the Education for All Handicapped Children Act (P.L. 94-142) in 1975 led to the creation of the most recent track, special education. Consisting of a bewildering array of acronyms, these programs function within and independently from the high school, sometimes overlapping the at-risk track, often not. Their relationship with the rest of the high school program is problematic at best in most schools, particularly in regard to determining the level of academic achievement special students must attain to earn a diploma.

What emerges is a picture of the high school in the 1990s as an institution that has struggled to adapt during the past hundred years through the sequential introduction of additional tracks to address both equity and excellence goals while accommodating an increasingly diverse student body. Its core, however, is still firmly rooted in intellectual traditions from a time when mass education was not the established practice. This heritage of adaptation creates a constant tension within high schools since some elements of the curriculum are deemed more "legitimate" than others. The tradition of a liberal arts education as "discipline for the mind" confronts a school population that is not motivated to pursue activities simply as "disciplines" or mental exercises. Thus the debate over the role of a liberal education (Bloom 1987, Hirsch and others 1987) overlooks reality; if students are not and cannot be motivated to participate in this model, it matters little what ultimate virtues the model possesses in theory. If society wants all students to become educated to some relatively high level of intellectual functioning, a classical liberal education may not present the most promising foundation if it continues to be the only "legitimate" intellectual basis for secondary education.

This is not the same thing as saying there is no place in high schools for the best elements of liberal education; rather, as will be explored throughout the remainder of this book, new models are emerging that consider a variety of intellectual approaches and instructional strategies to be more or less equal and permit students to follow a variety of paths to meet common standards. This flexibility allows the transmission of a wider range of knowledge in a manner that helps more students to achieve higher degrees of success.

One effect of the restructuring movement has been to stimulate discussion of the role and purpose of high schools, particularly their ability to educate nearly all students to some relatively high level of functioning. It seems clear that the high school must be considered the new "common school," the level of education that all children are expected to attain. This level of common education has risen consistently throughout the history of the country, from a primary education in the 1700s, to an upper-elementary education by the late 1800s, to a junior high school education by the late 1930s. In the postwar era, the expectation that nearly all students would obtain a high school education developed rapidly; this expectation is becoming firmly institutionalized in the postindustrial society of the 1990s. From this perspective, changes that must occur in high schools will need to be more fundamental than those in middle and elementary schools, though those levels face serious challenges as well.

A FUNDAMENTAL DIFFERENCE

It is worth noting that many of the ideas being considered for restructuring in the 1990s were most recently attempted in the late sixties and early seventies. Innovations such as flexible scheduling, team teaching, integrated curriculum, individualized education, schools within schools, and many others were common twenty years ago. Many teachers who are old enough to remember this say, "Here we go again," when they hear discussion of these ideas.

There is at least one major difference in the way these innovations might affect schools now versus then. In the sixties and seventies, various advocates for social change were attempting to use schools as a vehicle to remake society. Many of the people who entered teaching at this time agreed with the notion that schools could be vehicles for social change. The average age of teachers was much younger then, as school officials engaged in several years of frantic hiring to keep pace with the arrival of the baby boom in schools. This younger, perhaps more idealistic, teaching staff tended to make more of a connection between education and issues of social justice. There was a belief that schools could promote the ideals of democratic participation and individual self-worth that the civil rights movement and the "counterculture" represented. These were times when freedom was emphasized and accountability downplayed.

The business community (and many, perhaps most, parents) never truly supported many of the changes that were occurring in schools. In addition to lack of fundamental support, there was lax accountability to determine if these reforms produced tangible improvement in student learning. By the late seventies, a more general repudiation of the idealism of the sixties helped contribute to a swing of the pendulum in the other direction, and the "back to basics" movement emerged.

The situation in the 1990s is quite different in many respects. It is the business community that is leading the call for basic reforms in education and the educators who, in many cases, are resisting. The roles have reversed. Rather than educators attempting to change school in order to change society, it is society (in the form of business and government) that is attempting to change schools. Teachers are the ones advising caution and urging that the pace of change be more deliberate. The teaching profession is now older, more experienced, and perhaps more cautious or wary (some might say cynical) in responding to calls for fundamental reform than it was two decades ago when the last wave of massive experimentation took place. Many from the current generation not only saw those reforms (and what became of them), but have subsequently spent the better part of their lives in public schools. It is difficult for adults at midcareer to be convinced that all they have done throughout their careers might have been wrong or ineffective.

Parents are only now becoming aware of this need for change, but they are likely to become more aware of the need as they come to understand the arguments emanating from the business community and, increasingly, from national and state politicians. The emphasis in the call for school restructuring is not lofty social goals; it is economic and societal survival. The emphasis is not on freedom, but on accountability. Restructuring, in this context, represents a reordering of society's priorities for education. Because many educators are not enthusiastic about this reordering of priorities, the most powerful forces for change in education will continue to come from outside the education profession, at least in the immediate future.

One other important difference between the current era of reform and previous eras is the notable absence of higher education as a driving force. In the 1890s, for example, some of the most important reports of the period were authored either by university personnel or by committees on which higher education was well represented. Similarly, in the wave of curriculum development that followed in the wake of Sputnik and the calls for high school reform in particular, higher education was the leading voice. Colleges and universities have been peculiarly silent to date on school restructuring, except to indicate concern that educational reform not result in the lowering of standards. In part this is a reflection of the fact that current reforms are not necessarily focused tightly on the college-bound, but on the total educational environment and on the improvement of the performance of all students.

CHAPTER 2

THE WHYS OF EDUCATIONAL RESTRUCTURING

Not everyone agrees that schools need to be restructured. Many teachers and parents, in particular, believe that things are about as good as could be expected in schools, and that there is little to be gained by attempting large-scale change in education. At the same time, the world within which schools exist continues to change in many ways. Social, political, and economic systems are evolving (and in some cases imploding) at an ever-increasing rate. Old institutions, beliefs, assumptions, and behaviors no longer seem adequate to explain and cope with the problems and issues that present themselves to citizens in complex societies. Technological developments also create an ever-changing environment in which human behavior and relationships are altered, and new skills are needed to prosper or to survive.

This chapter is based on the assumption that the reader is at least somewhat aware of the shortcomings of the current system of education as they have been described over the past several years by many writers. Therefore, the discussion offered here of the forces underlying the need to restructure education is general in nature. There have been many excellent summaries of the statistical data that demonstrate how students are poorly prepared in schools, how particular ethnic and racial groups are poorly served, and how the number of at-risk students are growing rapidly and schools are not prepared to cope with their needs.* This chapter will look at broader trends that serve to create the imperative for schools to change. These trends have influenced the thinking of some policy-makers as they have considered the types of changes necessary for schools.

---

* See, for example: Anrig and Lapointe (1989); Lapointe, Mead, and Phillips (1989); Beck (1990); Benjamin (1989); Broder (1991); Carlisle (1988); Carnevale (1992); Cetron and Gayle (1991); Cetron, Rocha, and Luckins (1988); Dumaine (1989); Frymier and Gansneder (1989); Hodgkinson (1988); Pennar (1991); Szabo (1990); Wanat (1991); Weisman (December 11, 1991); and Commission on the Skills of the American Work Force (1990).

SOCIETAL FORCES FOR CHANGE

In an earlier work I analyzed the rationale for restructuring by considering changes occurring throughout society in terms of three broad and somewhat overlapping categories: economic forces, social forces, and technological forces (D. Conley, February 1991). The basic points from that analysis are presented here. However, the reader is advised to consult the original work for a more detailed treatment of the topic. A brief summary of these forces, with an additional dimension, Performance of American Students on International Comparisons, follows.

ECONOMIC FORCES

The economic system is transforming in ways that have implications for all social institutions, including schools. Some of the elements of the transformation that have the greatest potential impact upon the schools include the following:

- The transition from a work force composed predominantly of low-skilled workers and a small, highly educated managerial elite who made decisions to a highly skilled work force in which front-line workers are key decision-makers (Reich 1988, 1990).

- Increased economic competition from Asia and Europe that has led to an accelerated rate of change in the business world and the necessity for teamwork in the workplace ("The New Industrial Relations" 1981, Mandel and Bernstein 1990).

- Less access to "guaranteed" jobs for high school dropouts through the old means such as trade unions, one major employer in a community, or use of "old boy" network; more racial/ethnic/ gender diversity in the workplace and concomitant equal employment provisions for hiring that make what one knows more important than who one knows.

- A global economy where companies function throughout the world, workers may have to travel or live outside the U.S. to progress in the company, and almost every business needs to understand its relationship to foreign competitors (Baker 1990, Hoerr and others 1990).

- A federal deficit that exploded during the 1980s and continues unabated in the 1990s, guaranteeing that there will be few additional federal monies available to support education, or any other social programs, and that pressure for tax increases at the federal level combined with decreased rates of personal income growth will tend to inhibit the ability of state and local governments to raise taxes (Hollister 1990).

- A stable to shrinking work force that will be composed increasingly of women, minorities, and immigrants, groups traditionally not served well by public education, combined with the expectation that all new entrants into the work force be educated to some relatively high level of functioning (Hoachlander, Kaufman, and Wilen 1989).

- The elimination of middle-management positions throughout the economy during the late eighties and into the nineties, which results in responsibility for decision-making being pushed downward, requiring workers who are more able to think and managers who are more able to adapt.

SOCIAL FORCES

Some of the important social forces operating to produce change that will have an impact on public schools include the following:

- The changing structure of the family in the era of the "post-nuclear family," the increase in single-parent families, the concomitant disintegration of extended support networks for families; the tendency for any crisis to throw a family off balance for an extended period unless some sort of external assistance is available (Wanat 1991).

- The increase in the number of children who are living in poverty (Moynihan 1988, Pennar 1991).

- The apparent failure of social welfare and social service programs nationally to address the escalating needs of families; a lack of interagency cooperation, which results in duplication and overlap among social service programs and many programs offered by schools (Liontos 1990).

- The failure of schools as vehicles for desegregation or for equal educational performance for minority students (Olson, October 17, 1990; Stockard and Mayberry 1992); the increasing polarization along economic and racial lines, particularly in urban areas (Bates 1990).

- A decreasing sense of civic responsibility, of social tolerance, of a social contract among citizens for the benefit of all; a lack of understanding of the principles of democratic rule by majority with respect for the rights of the minority; decreasing participation in the electoral process and in decision-making at the local level (Boyer 1990).

TECHNOLOGICAL FORCES

Technological forces include a broad array of new techniques for organizing, communicating, and disseminating information that raise some of the following issues:

- Knowledge is becoming more accessible to more of the population. Therefore, the teacher's role as gatekeeper must change. Information need no longer be stored in memory for it to be useful; the ability to access information will be as or more important than the ability to store information in one's memory (Bugliarello 1990, Sheingold 1991).

- Schools are neither organized nor funded in a way that enables them to keep up with changes in knowledge or changes in technology used to store and present such knowledge (Elmer-Dewitt 1991, Levinson 1990).

- Textbooks are an obsolete technology, yet they continue to be central to the way schools conceive of teaching and learning.

- The structure of knowledge is rapidly evolving. The division of academic disciplines is no longer appropriate for understanding or solving the problems that exist in the world, yet schools cling to the old structure.

- Information is seen less as an end in itself than as a means to an end, an essential ingredient in problem-solving. Curricula that focus on information as an end in itself (fact-based rote learning) can be counterproductive, extinguishing the curiosity and inquisitiveness of the learner and providing little practice in applying information to solve problems.

- Schools have defined technology as computers. There are many types of technology in addition to computers that will have an equal or greater impact on learning (D. Conley, February 1991, pp. 8-10).

- Schools arc not moving to intcgratc tcchnology, nor arc thcy keeping up with the latest developments; in fact, they are falling farther and farther behind as the equipment they purchased in the 1980s becomes obsolete and they are unable to purchase new equipment (Elmer-Dewitt 1991).

- Statistics such as the number of computers per teacher are worse than useless as a measure of progress to determine effective use of technology in schools; careful examination of schools' attempts to use computers yields results that are dismaying and disheartening (Borrell 1992).

PERFORMANCE OF AMERICAN STUDENTS ON INTERNATIONAL COMPARISONS

The performance of American students on international comparisons continues to be an area of concern. The results compiled below, combined with studies that compared performance to standards American educators agreed were reasonable, indicated gaps in performance between American students and those from other countries:

- Husen (1967) reports results from tests conducted in 1964: "The International Study of Achievement in Mathematics compared achievement in twelve countries: Austria, Belgium, England, Finland, France, West Germany, Israel, Japan, the Netherlands, Scotland, Sweden, and the United States.... Japanese students excelled all others, regardless of their socioeconomic status, while the U.S. students ranked near the bottom."

- A 1974 study of science achievement found that although the brightest American students fared well in reading, they did not perform as well in science: "Assessments reveal that, while 10 percent of the top United States students excelled similar groups in all other countries in reading, in science they occupied seventh place" (Hechinger and Hechinger 1974).

- The National Assessment of Educational Progress report released in 1989 (Lapointe, Mead, and Phillips 1989) contains a great deal of evidence to suggest that American schools have not improved much during the past decade and that they do not educate the vast majority to high levels. While noting improvement in basic skill acquisition from the midsixties to 1980, Anrig and Lapointe (1989) observe that most of the improvement took place before 1980. "The trend line stopped moving up in 1980 and has remained virtually at the same level for the past eight years" (p. 5). The report goes on to present some of the following information:

  - While 40 percent of American thirteen-year-olds could regularly solve two-step problems in mathematics, close to 70 percent of Canadian students at the same grade level could do so.

- While only 9 percent of American thirteen-year-olds could understand certain mathematical concepts, 40 percent of Korean thirteen-year-olds could do so most of the time.
- The decline in mathematics achievement continues through high school, so that by age seventeen far fewer than 10 percent of American youth have mastered algebra, geometry, and the ability to solve multistep problems.
- In writing, only 25 percent of seventeen-year-olds can write an adequate analytic paper from given information.
- Only 20 percent can write a persuasive letter to the principal.
- Only 28 percent can write an adequate essay in the imaginative area.
- In the opinion of the hundreds of people who served as NAEP advisors, it seemed reasonable to assume that at least 80 percent of thirteen-year-olds could do the following tasks:
  - answer four factual questions about a simply written single-page description of the development of a game of basketball—*only 6 out of 10 can do so;*
  - select, from four options, the correct answer to the question, "Which is true about 87 percent of 10?": "It's greater than, less than, equal to, or can't tell"—*only 2 out of 10 can do so;*
  - recognize that different soils affect plant growth—*only 5 out of 10 can do so;*
  - write an adequate informative report about a simple personal experience—*only 2 out of 10 can do so* (Anrig and Lapointe 1989, p. 9)
- Ravitch and Finn (1987) found in a study of the nation's seventeen-year olds "abysmally low levels of general knowledge about common facts, events, people, authors, and ideas in history and literature" (McDaniel 1989).
- Stevenson and Stigler (1992) developed "culture-fair" tests to compare the performance of American and Asian students in mathematics and reading. Their conclusion was as follows:

    A close examination of American children's academic achievement rapidly dispels any notion that we face a problem of limited scope. The problem is not restricted to a certain age level or to a particular academic subject. Whether we look at the average scores for schools or at the scores for individuals, we find evidence of serious and pervasive weakness. In mathematics, the weakness is not limited to inadequate mastery of routine operations, but reflects a poor understanding of how to use mathematics in solving meaningful problems.

> Nor is mathematics the only subject in which American students do poorly. We have presented evidence of the overrepresentation of poor readers among American children, and American students have fared badly in international studies of achievement in science. (p. 50)

The performance of American students on international comparisons, and on achievement tests, is a complex and emotion-laden issue. Bracey (1991, 1992) and others (Hodgkinson 1991, Berliner 1992, Carson, Huelskamp, and Woodall 1991) have criticized the use of test data and international comparisons as the basis for judging the performance of American students. For example, Bracey questions the value of the International Assessment of Educational Progress, which uses scores from 9- and 13-year-olds:

> Is a multiple-choice test the most appropriate measure of a nation's achievement? Even if it is, is there any relationship between test scores at ages 9 and 13 and later accomplishments by individuals or by nations? Is it wise to give weight to the scores of 13-year-olds... [who] might well rank next-to-last—ahead of only the seniors [in terms of groups that] don't take tests seriously. (p. 108)

There is widespread concern among these writers that the media are focusing on negative test scores. Bracey (1992) states that *Newsweek's* coverage of the results from the International Assessment of Educational Progress (IAEP-2) released in February 1992 "reflects the perverse attention that education gets from the media—when it gets any attention at all" (p. 108). The net effect of such attention seems to have been to foster public opinion that there is a crisis in education. Such perceptions must be acknowledged, whether accurate or not, and factored into any analysis of the motivators for change in American schools.

It is not my intention to impugn the efforts of American educators or to suggest that schools are intellectual disaster areas. Quite the contrary, many educators are exerting superhuman efforts to sustain a system that appears to be having great difficulty adapting to the changing needs of students. Frymier (1992) emphasizes this point in a description of his national study of at-risk students:

> The data collected in the Phi Delta Kappa Study of Students at Risk underscores the point that teachers and others in schools are working hard—very hard—to help children who hurt and children who fail. Whether or not these efforts are effective cannot be determined from these data. The fact that general concern about the problem of children at risk is so widespread in America suggests that such efforts are insufficient, ineffective, or both. But the efforts are real. Anyone who wants to fault schools for not trying has not studied these data carefully.
>
> Still the crucial question remains: How effective are the programs and practices being used today to help students who are at risk? (p. 259)

Issues pertaining to the performance of American students, as well as the societal changes outlined in the preceding section, have received wide exposure and discussion through the media and in educational journals and conferences. There is, however, another set of issues that may have as profound an impact on education ultimately as those listed above. These emerging issues reflect changing values within society, changes that have been occurring gradually for perhaps fifty years or more. In combination with the factors listed previously, these issues suggest that change in education is inevitable, if only to bring schools into closer alignment with societal values.

CHANGING VALUES WITHIN SOCIETY

The data and trends presented in the previous sections are tangible and compelling in making the case for substantive change in school organization and content. Other, less tangible forces may also serve to influence the types of changes that are to occur in schools. These forces can be thought of as value shifts that are occurring at the societal level. In some senses these shifts are more difficult to perceive than those present in demographic data. Often they are best observed in hindsight. As one looks back on a decade or more, these shifts become more apparent; in day-to-day life they may be less apparent.

Why is it important for educators to take these value shifts into account when considering change in schools? The primary reason is that these value shifts often form or influence the context within which policy decisions are made in a representative democracy such as exists in the United States. Policy-makers at the local level (school board), state level (legislature and governor), and federal level (Congress and the President), along with various lobbying and special interest groups, are influenced, consciously or otherwise, by large-scale trends in this society, and, increasingly, the world at large. The ideas that are proposed and the solutions that are entertained are shaped by this value framework, which suggests the desirable goals of public policy and the most appropriate means by which to attain these goals.

While changes are occurring in many different constellations of values, there are four interconnected values in particular that public education does not necessarily reflect well: (1) the increased value placed on the individual and individual rights, (2) the triumph of the marketplace as an economic model, (3) the rise of democratic systems of government, and (4) the changing needs of the work force. These sets of values are not likely to be useful as outlines for particular strategies to be employed at the school site. But they are worth examining as ways of thinking about the solutions policy-makers are likely to entertain or value. These values do help explain why one program or strategy might be more or less attractive to decision-makers, all other things being equal. They also suggest the type of language and rationale that might be used to justify or undergird a program of school restructuring.

INCREASED VALUING OF THE INDIVIDUAL

Robert Bellah and others (1985) have written eloquently about the strong tradition of individualism in American society and its effect on our social institutions:

> Individualism lies at the very core of American culture.... There is a biblical individualism and a civic individualism as well as a utilitarian and an expressive individualism. Whatever the differences among the traditions and the consequent differences in their understandings of individualism, there are some things they all share, things that are basic to American identity. We believe in the dignity, indeed the sacredness, of the individual. Anything that would violate our right to think for ourselves, judge for ourselves, make our own decisions, live our lives as we see fit, is not only morally wrong, it is sacrilegious. (p. 142)

While Bellah and others also note the importance of collective action and its role in American society, the trend over the past thirty-five years appears to have been to define more clearly the rights of individuals, particularly those less able to compete on an equal footing in society. It began with the civil rights movement of the late fifties and sixties, which was designed to ensure that every individual had an "equal opportunity" to succeed in American society, both economically and socially. This is not to deny the importance of collective action, but only to note that from a policy perspective, significant effort has gone into ensuring the rights of individuals. This has an effect on the ways institutions come to be organized and to function, particularly bureaucratic institutions that are sensitive to laws and regulations.

Following on the heels of the civil rights movement were several other pieces of legislation that emphasized the value of the individual. Title IX, which guaranteed equal access by women to athletic opportunities, is only one example of a flurry of legislation designed to ensure equal treatment for women. The Education for All Handicapped Children Act (P.L. 94-142) opened the door for many students who had been denied a public education. It also required schools to provide programs on an individualized basis for students with demonstrated special needs and guaranteed the rights of parents to participate in the placement of their children with special needs. More recently, legislation to ensure the rights of HIV-positive and AIDS-infected students to an education has been enacted in various states. Most recent of all, the Americans with Disabilities Act extends protections to individuals with a wide range of limiting conditions.

Schools have seen a dramatic shift in their ability and latitude to discipline students. Beginning with the 1969 decision *Tinker v. the Des Moines School District,* the rights of students were more firmly established. Corporal punishment, common throughout the nation thirty-five years ago, has been severely curtailed. Students' rights of free expression through dress and speech have been expanded and codified. Teachers are now charged with reporting suspected child abuse to authorities. The Education for All Handicapped Children Act limits the ability of educators to discipline special education students for behaviors related to their handicapping condition.

It is interesting to speculate about the reasons underlying the growing emphasis on the value of the individual. Smaller family size and lower infant and child mortality rates led parents to value each child more and to appreciate each child's individual characteristics. The increasing education level of each succeeding generation enlarged its members' world view and sense of efficacy and worth. The rational-bureaucratic institutions of the early 1900s may have reached (or exceeded) the limits of their economies of scale, and large institutions in general are perceived increasingly as dehumanizing and inefficient. And, as mentioned earlier, the complexity of the economic and social systems are such that individuals are being called upon to make more decisions of an increasingly complex nature, which inherently augments the importance of each person.

In all the examples cited above, the impetus for validating individual rights and recognizing unique differences and needs has come from outside the educational community. While educators do many things to meet the needs of students as individuals, schools and districts are not generally organized in a manner that views each student as a client with unique needs, characteristics, and circumstances. The model upon which much of secondary education is based, what Shedd and Bacharach (1991) refer to as the Factory Management Approach, is designed to minimize differences in order to maximize efficiency. They contend this model is based upon the following assumptions:

- The purpose of a public school system is to provide students with training in a common, basic set of academic skills.
- Teaching is a relatively straightforward process. The situations that teachers face can be anticipated, and appropriate behaviors for handling those situations can be specified in advance.

- Except for age differences, students are a relatively homogeneous group. Differences in their needs and abilities within age groups are minimal or irrelevant. (p. 52)

Much of the difficulty in changing the model under which public education operates will stem not from the specific programs schools propose to undertake, but from the implicit value structure embedded in the Factory Management Approach, a value structure in which the needs of the individual are clearly subordinated to the efficient functioning of the institution.

The increasing emphasis on the value and worth of the individual can easily be confused in American schools with individual isolation. Classes and schools are organized in ways that define instruction and learning as something that occurs on an individual level. They tend to reinforce some of the worst aspects of individualism, while doing little to develop the capacity for behavior and action of a collective nature. Stevenson and Stigler (1992) describe the organization of American classrooms:

> Americans emphasize individuality, an emphasis that has both emotional and academic costs for children. Teachers often leave children to work alone at their desks, and frequently divide the class into small groups, separated according to the children's level of skill. Teachers spend a good deal of time working with these groups and with individual children, and the class operates as a whole only part of the time. So each child spends relatively little time in direct interaction with the teacher. Children spend most of the school day in the classroom, with little time for play and social interaction. As a result, one senses that American children often feel isolated and lonely. Partly for this reason, they are less enthusiastic about school than their Chinese and Japanese peers. Until the school day is reorganized so that there is time for more than six subjects and a fast lunch, it is unlikely that school will assume a central place in the lives of American children. (p. 69)

The increasing emphasis on the individual holds the potential to be both a blessing and a curse. If American schools continue to attempt to define most learning as an individual, isolated process, the majority of students will be less likely to affiliate with schools. At the same time, the reliance on batch processing models, the factory approach, will likely not be successful as a means to develop skills in group and collective action that appear to be important both for learning in school and for functioning successfully in the future. As coming chapters emphasize, there is an increasing recognition within complex postindustrial societies of the importance and value of the individual as a critical contributor to the collective good, and of individual initiative and affiliation as key components of both societal strength and economic competitiveness.

Schools have a long way to go to take into account this changing conception of the individual and of the individual's rights in an organizational context.

THE TRIUMPH OF THE MARKETPLACE

The triumph of the marketplace worldwide affirms a preference for individual decisions over the forces of bureaucratic central planning. In marketplace economies it is the microdecisions made by myriad individuals that in theory determine prices, products, markets, employment patterns, and the ultimate structure of communities. The pronouncements of faceless bureaucracies are to be avoided to the maximum degree possible.

Whether this is how free market economies actually operate is not the point. The perception in much of the world that such an economic system provides the best hope for individual and collective prosperity is what matters. This is particularly important for educators to consider, given that key elements of the marketplace philosophy are choice and competition, two concepts that are troublesome to public education.

When public policy-makers have a particular set of values in the forefront of their thinking, as they tend to have now when it comes to the marketplace, those values have a powerful influence on the solutions offered for social problems. It's a case of the old adage: To a carpenter who loves hammers, everything looks like a nail. Educators can expect policy-makers to explore the concepts of choice, competition, and deregulation as possible remedies for the ills of public education. These remedies have been applied during the past decade to such protected sectors of the economy as airlines, trucking, hospitals, and telephone companies; and these were businesses that were doing well in delivering their services! After nearly a decade of more or less nonstop criticism of public education, and little in the way of concrete improvement from the perspective of policy-makers and the public at large, pressure is mounting to try something more radical to reshape education. Given the symbolic power of the image of the free market, it is likely that policy-makers will look toward choice and competition as concepts to "rescue" public education.

The perceived failure of "big government" worldwide to solve complex problems will push private-sector ideas and experiments in education to the forefront of discussions. The effort by Whittle Communication Corporation to open a string of 200 schools nationwide is only an early manifestation of this phenomenon, as was former President

Bush and former Education Secretary Alexander's call for a new generation of "break the mold" schools that could serve as models and alternatives to the existing system.

In California, comments from a businessman who believed there was a need to change the system of public education through an initiative on school choice illustrate this thinking: "It's a top-down system. It's a rule-driven system. And any rule-driven system, as evidenced by what's happening in Russia and Eastern Europe, just stifles creativity and innovation and is not attuned to the market" (Olson, September 18, 1991, p. 19). This statement is a good example of the type of logic that may underlie proposals for overhauling education during the coming years.

THE RISE OF DEMOCRACIES

The growth of democratic institutions throughout the world clearly goes hand in hand with the development of the marketplace. However, the spread of democracy has some additional implications for educators. Once again, this trend reflects thinking in broad terms about the role of the individual in organizational contexts. Not only in political institutions, but in work settings and even family relationships, coercive measures and behaviors are not viewed as a legitimate means of achieving compliance. Taking a cue from the Japanese, the language of the workplace is moving from one of coercion to consensus ("The New Industrial Relations" 1981, Port and others 1990).

Ironically, in the face of the breakup of the traditional extended family, schools have in many cases increased their use of coercion and control to enforce compulsory attendance policies and to maintain order in the classrooms and halls. These measures are not necessarily Draconian, but they are being pursued by educators as the solution to problems of attendance and discipline. In schools throughout the nation, discussions of "improvements" in discipline and attendance policies are on the top of the list. This emphasis on refining the tools of control and coercion is quite logical in the context of the Factory Management Approach. It is the most appropriate strategy to enhance efficiency. Smith and O'Day (1991) discuss the relationship between the goals of the reform movement and the focus of many schools on discipline and attendance as solutions:

> If the school is to be successful in promoting active student involvement in learning, depth of understanding, and complex thinking—major goals of the reform movement—its vision must focus on teaching and learning rather than, for example, on control and discipline as in many schools

today (McNeil 1986). In fact, the very need for special attention to control and discipline may be mitigated considerably by the promotion of successful and engaging learning experiences. (p. 235)

When educators step back and examine their implicit values, they are more likely to recognize that, while these measures have their role in a system of compulsory education, values held by society as a whole have moved away from accepting the validity of such measures. The challenge in this situation may be not how to develop a "perfect" attendance or discipline system, but how to engage students actively in an education that has some intrinsic meaning and value to the student, and how to enlist parents and community members as equal partners in the process of determining the goals of education. The inconsistencies become highlighted more clearly when teachers and parents demand greater involvement in decisions. They want participatory decision-making and democracy for adults. But it is hypocritical to propose that adults should work and interact in less coercive environments and then turn around and use this enhanced freedom to coerce children more effectively.

THE INFLUENCE OF WORK FORCE NEEDS

As noted earlier, the influence of the business community on educational restructuring is not to be discounted. To understand how the argument for greater economic productivity and adaptability is translated into calls for educational reform, it is useful to examine some of the key documents that describe businesses' agenda for education in broad terms. Whether one believes that businesses' influence on educational purposes and programs is a good thing or not, it is neither reasonable nor realistic to discount the influence that the organized, systematic efforts launched by various business-related groups have had on policy-makers throughout the nation.

Three reports from organizations outside education indicate the direction the private sector wants education to take to adapt to changing economic realities. In 1990 the Commission on the Skills of the American Work Force published *America's Choice: High Skills or Low Wages*. American workers, the report says, are at a crossroads: They must develop higher skills to produce goods with high value on the international market or face decreasing wages as they compete with low-wage Third World workers in the production of low-value, mass-produced items. According to the commission, America must resolve these fundamental questions regarding public education:

- Do we continue to define educational success as "time in the seat," or choose a new system that focuses on the demonstrated achievement of high standards?

- Do we continue to provide little incentive for non-college-bound students to study hard and take tough subjects, or choose a system that will reward real effort with better pay and better jobs?

- Do we continue to turn our backs on America's school dropouts, or choose to take responsibility for educating them?

- Do we continue to provide unskilled workers for unskilled jobs, or train skilled workers and give companies incentives to deploy them in high performance organizations?

- Do we continue in most companies to limit training to a select handful of managers and professionals, or choose to provide training to front-line workers as well? (pp. 8-9)

A second report, which also has been widely circulated among educators, indicates more specifically the types of skills that employers desire in employees in the 1990s. Entitled *Workplace Basics: The Skills Employers Want* and produced jointly by the American Society of Training and Development and the U.S. Department of Labor's Employment and Training Administration, the report was the result of interviews with employers throughout the nation. The report concludes that employers are looking for seven different skill strands:

- Employers want employees who can learn the particular skills of an available job—who have "learned how to learn."

- Employers want employees who will hear the key points that make up a customer's concerns (listening) and who can convey an adequate response (oral communication)....

- Employers want employees who have pride in themselves and their potential to be successful (self-esteem); who know how to get things done (goal setting/motivation); and who have some sense of the skills needed to perform well in the workplace (personal and career development).

- Employers want employees who can get along with customers, suppliers or coworkers (interpersonal and negotiation skills); who can work with others to achieve a goal (teamwork); who have some sense of where the organization is headed and what they must do to make a contribution (organizational effectiveness); and who can assume responsibility and motivate co-workers when necessary (leadership). (Carnevale, Gainer, and Meltzer 1990, p. 8)

A third report that has also been reviewed and discussed by many school faculties, superintendents, boards of education, state legislators, and departments of education interested in reform was commissioned by the U.S. Department of Labor and entitled *What Work Requires of Schools: A SCANS Report for America 2000* (Secretary's Commission on Achieving Necessary Skills 1991). It identifies five competencies and a three-part foundation of skills and personal qualities that the commission described as necessary "for solid job performance." These competencies and skills are as follows:

COMPETENCIES—effective workers can productively use:

- *Resources*—allocating time, money, materials, space, and staff
- *Interpersonal Skills*—working on teams, teaching others, serving customers, leading, negotiating, and working well with people from culturally diverse backgrounds
- *Information*—acquiring and evaluating data, organizing and maintaining files, interpreting and communicating, and using computers to process information
- *Systems*—understanding social, organizational, and technological systems, monitoring and correcting performance, and designing or improving systems
- *Technology*—selecting equipment and tools, applying technology to specific tasks, and maintaining and troubleshooting technologies

THE FOUNDATION—competence requires:

- *Basic Skills*—reading, writing, arithmetic and mathematics, speaking, and listening
- *Thinking Skills*—thinking creatively, making decisions, solving problems, seeing things in the mind's eye, knowing how to learn, and reasoning
- *Personal Qualities*—individual responsibility, self-esteem, sociability, self-management, and integrity (p. vii)

In even a cursory examination of these three reports, readers will be struck by the degree of congruence between what the business community says it wants from workers and the qualities many educators might say they want to cultivate in students. One interesting aspect of the current move to restructure public education is the degree to which the agendas of many neo-Progressives and elements of the business community overlap, albeit in an inadvertent manner and for very different reasons. Both groups tend to advocate the following ideas:

- Curriculum that moves from a primary emphasis on rote learning and factual information to a greater emphasis on problem solving, application, and integration of knowledge and higher-order thinking.
- Students who are actively engaged in learning, who are not being trained simply to do what they are told.

- Learning that is best assessed in terms of outcomes, not processes; the inadequacy of seat time as the primary means to demonstrate mastery; the ability to apply or demonstrate a skill or set of knowledge as the best way to assess whether learning has really occurred.

- Education that extends beyond the walls of the classroom; students who apply knowledge and acquire new skills, information, and insights in the larger community.

- Teachers who facilitate learning, not control it; one of the key goals of education being to create lifelong learners, to develop a student's learning skills, not merely to transmit a body of information in a way that leaves the student with negative attitudes about learning.

- Students who learn to work in groups and as members of teams, not solely as individuals, and learn to work with students who are very different from themselves.

- The belief that each learner is valuable; no "expendable" students; students who have positive self-images and the ability to define goals for themselves.

- "Process" skills considered as important as knowledge of specific content.

This unspoken commonality that exists between progressive educational reformers and business leaders is unusual, not well understood or articulated, and perhaps fleeting. There is an inherent tension when the business community becomes involved in determining the goals and methods of education. It should be recognized at this point that what is occurring is a reexamination and refocusing of the basic purposes and goals of education, not merely the adaptation of existing practices and procedures within an unquestioned structure of values and goals.

The issue of the goals and values of education is taken up in more detail in the next chapter, which suggests new ways of thinking about schooling that may be developing today and that have implications for the ways in which educational experiences are constructed, how schools are structured, and how people relate to one another within the institution of school.

CHAPTER 3

CREATING NEW HABITS OF HEART AND MIND

C hanges in the values of society inevitably have profound effects on education. Although schools profess to attempt "neutrality" on issues of values and morals, all schools possess implicit value and moral structures. These structures generally mirror the community in which the school exists. Such an arrangement makes perfect sense. What happens, though, when value and moral systems are in flux? The compass does not point north with consistency. What are schools to do in an environment of conflicting signals?

Much of the restructuring movement has concerned itself with changing the structures of education rather than examining its values. However, structural changes carry with them implied moral and ethical assumptions. It is worthwhile to examine some of these implicit assumptions embedded in the goals of school restructuring. Each of the six statements that follow was gleaned from a reading of the restructuring literature, what some have called the "new conventional wisdom" (Olson, August 5, 1992). The list reflects values positions and social goals for schooling, in addition to specific structural changes. Educators and others can clarify their own goals for restructuring by carefully examining these statements and the values embedded in them.

1. Essentially all students can be educated to some relatively high level of functioning.

During the previous thirty-five years there has been a tendency by policy analysts to interpret change in education as the movement back and forth between forces favoring equity (equality of educational opportunities for all groups) and those demanding excellence (high levels of performance by the most capable), with the additional dimension of efficiency being applied periodically (Lutz 1978, Marcoulides and Heck 1990). This model has been a useful construct for comprehending the turbulent forces to which public education has been subjected in the postwar era.

It may be that the polar relationship between these values is no longer the only or even the primary framework that should be applied to understand societal expectations for schooling. There is every indication that schools are now being expected to address both equity and excellence simultaneously, that schools will be expected to educate essentially all students to some relatively high level of functioning.

Exactly what such a level might be, or what students will be able to do upon completion of such an education, is only now becoming the subject of heated discussion and painstaking work by policy-makers, state departments of education, university and school faculty, and the public at large.

It is becoming increasingly clear, however, that dropout rates of 25 percent will not be acceptable, nor will rates of 20 percent, 15 percent, or even 10 percent in the long run. Nor will it be sufficient merely to keep students in school, to "warehouse" them until they are old enough to work. How will schools retain and educate students who have abandoned education because they feel it has little meaning or value for them? How will schools adapt if there can no longer be "winners" and "losers"?

For starters, the notion of intelligence as a unidimensional construct that is distributed throughout the population in a way best described by a bell-shaped curve is being challenged (Gardner and Hatch 1989). So long as this assumption is accepted as the basis for educational practice there must be winners and losers *by definition*. Much of generally accepted educational practice is based on this deep, unspoken, unquestioned assumption. Practices such as tracking, standardized testing, grading on a curve, talented and gifted, and remedial education are all based on the notion that some are more able, others less able.

It is difficult to overestimate the pervasiveness of this mode of thinking or the difficulty of challenging its acceptance by educators. Gardner (1983) offers one alternative way of thinking about intelligence when he suggests that there may be (at least) seven intelligences: verbal, logical-mathematical, musical, bodily/kinesthetic, spatial, interpersonal, intrapersonal. These notions help educators rethink what it means for students to be successful; success can occur in many different arenas yet still be validated by the school.

Alternatively, there is the Japanese model. It is with trepidation that this model is even mentioned, given the strong reaction it engenders in American educators, who evoke images of distraught teenagers committing suicide, driven over the edge by pressure to succeed on examinations. There is, however, a lesson to be learned from the Japanese system. This is a system in which 97 percent of the students graduate from high school, apparently at high levels of intellectual functioning. If this is true, then it presents an alternative to the notion of the normal distribution, or at least calls into question the level of performance most students are capable of achieving in public education. Denis Doyle

(1991) states that "depending on whose data sets you use, the top 5 percent of the Americans are at the Japanese average (by about grades 5 or 6)" (p. 16).

There are (at least) two possible conclusions: one, that the Japanese are genetically superior, a rather unpalatable and wholly unsubstantiated assumption; or, two, that somehow they are able to avoid the phenomenon of the normal curve. The notion that the Japanese, or any other Asian culture, is superior genetically is refuted by the research of Stevenson and Stigler (1992):

> The hypothesis that the academic weakness of American children is due to deficiencies in innate intellectual ability is without merit. American children obtained scores highly similar to those of the Asian children on a culturally fair test of intelligence, and we have found no sound evidence that American children's academic problems stem from a deficiency in handling abstract concepts. (p. 50)

Certainly there are cultural differences. However, at a time when many are expressing profound frustration with the American educational system, it would seem logical to reexamine every aspect of educational practice in this country, rather than simply conceding that Americans cannot duplicate the performance of Japanese students. Stevenson and Stigler (1992) summarize this issue in these terms:

> The puzzle lies in trying to understand the poor performance of American children. If explanations that rely on innate endowment are unsatisfactory, then we must look to children's everyday experiences. The most likely locales are those where children spend most of their time: home and school. (p. 51)

The lesson to be considered from the Japanese system is that it is *possible* to educate essentially all students to high levels of academic functioning (even with class sizes much larger than those in most American schools). The impact on student achievement of the teacher's expectations in American schools is well documented (Alderman 1990, Patriarca and Kragt 1986, Smey-Richman 1989, Whelan and Teddlie 1989). Sincerely believing that all students can learn and designing schools in which this occurs may be the greatest challenge ever faced by the American educational system.

2. Learning is what students can do at the conclusion of education, not simply the processes to which they have been subjected.

As mentioned in chapter 1, the Carnegie unit was established to ensure consistency and to institute some form of quality control among high schools for the purpose of college admissions. The Carnegie unit created consistency of process; all students spent the same amount of time in a classroom for the same amount of credit. It did not address outcomes—what students could do after spending that time in a classroom. Now the emphasis has shifted from the courses taken or grades received to what the student is able to do at the conclusion of his or her education.

For educators this emphasis on outcomes translates into a movement away from evaluation (reaching some sort of summary judgment) to assessment (providing ongoing feedback based on the application of skills). Assessment involves more public demonstrations of skills. Currently schools use public demonstrations in certain areas, primarily to entertain (music assemblies, sports events), not to show public accountability for student learning.

Interestingly enough, such public demonstrations were part of public education in the 1890s when, at the end of each week, students recited their lessons to an audience of parents. It quickly became apparent which students knew their lessons and which did not. These types of demonstrations of rote learning would be replaced by more meaningful and complex demonstrations, but the fact remains that there likely will be a much higher degree of public accountability for student performance.

As teachers' conceptions of the goals and purposes of assessment change, they may come to view the process both as a component of learning and as the culmination of learning, in contrast to viewing evaluation as a digression from the learning process, something standing separate from learning. To accomplish this integration of learning and assessment, greater emphasis in teaching is placed on diagnosing and educating each student in a more personalized manner. This process is not synonymous with individualized instruction, in which each child moves through workbooks at her or his own pace. Instead, the system adapts instruction to the interests and abilities of students and uses demonstrations designed to showcase students' strengths as well as weaknesses.

3. Education has economic utility for essentially all students and for society.

Educators often express resentment toward those who state that the purpose of education is to prepare students for the work force. Many, perhaps most, educators believe that education has purposes other than preparing people for employment, and that public schools should maintain a healthy distance from business.

Without discounting the validity of this perspective, it is important for educators to acknowledge that education plays a critical role in determining students' economic future. Gone are the days when a student could drop out of high school and enter a high-paying job with a secure future. Given this reality, the linkage between the needs of the private sector and the structure, content, and outcomes of a public education is becoming more and more tightly intertwined. One can argue the appropriateness of this linkage. However, it appears that this trend will continue for the foreseeable future, in part because education, in the form of training and retraining, is becoming such an integral part of the workplace. As mentioned earlier, it appears that knowing how to learn will be as important as the specific factual information one possesses.

Pennar (1991) summarizes current thinking on the economic importance of education:

> Today, economists agree that the widespread competitive and technological changes that occurred during the 1980s induced a sharp increase in the rewards for skill and education, thereby widening the gap in incomes. From 1980 to 1990, men with four years of high school saw their median incomes fall 15.5% in real terms. During the same period, men with four years of college experienced a gain in median income, after inflation, of 1.6%....
>
> ... "We have to ask ourselves whether the macroeconomy is becoming permanently hostile to less-skilled workers," says [Northwestern University economist Rebecca M.] Blank. If so, there will be considerable costs. First, there are the costs of having to support a population that is barely making it economically. Next, there's the potential cost of possible social disruption resulting from worsening income inequality and a population of persistently poor individuals. Finally, there's the cost of consigning people to low-productivity jobs when they and society could do better. (p. 88)

The challenge for educators centers on the way schools define and teach work skills. Since the 1920s, this has been done through a vocational track that taught specific trades to students. These trades either no longer exist or now demand skills that schools are not able to provide. As the results from the Workplace Basics survey indicate (Carnevale, Gainer, and Meltzer 1990), the line between a "vocational" and an "academic" education is beginning to blur, as all students are expected to acquire the skills of problem solving, inquiry, team building, and oral and written communication. In addition, all students are expected to have high self-esteem, a love of learning, and a strong sense of personal efficacy. Compartmentalized or tracked programs of education will not be a productive strategy for achieving the outcomes.

Schools can be expected to be influenced by other concepts associated with the private sector as well, such as choice, service, niche marketing, and competition. Whether (or how) schools adapt internally to oblige the press for greater accommodation of private-sector needs is a critically important question for the nineties, with significant implications for the social structure of the nation as well as the structure of schooling.

4. Learners participate actively in their own education in a variety of ways. Learning cannot be passive.

One often hears from teachers and administrators that today's students are not like those in previous generations. Although this lament can be traced back literally thousands of years, there is evidence to suggest that the perceptions of today's educators are accurate. They are accurate in part because kids have changed—and because schools have not.

Clearly, today's student must be motivated in fundamentally different ways from children whose parents never questioned school authorities. In the 1950s, when corporal punishment was much more a normative form of behavior management, it would not be unusual for a student to receive a whack at school, notify his parent of the event, and receive two more. Fast-forward to the 1990s, when the same student now notifies his parent, and the parent's response is, "Contact the lawyer!"

While few people yearn for the "good old days" of the paddle, it is illustrative of the changes that have occurred between teacher and student, school and home. The school is fairly isolated from the home and community, the result of a series of insulating barriers established during the past eighty years to "depoliticize" education. These reforms were successful; one of their byproducts was to "professionalize" education at the expense of community involvement and ownership. Educators now find themselves trying to redefine how to involve parents and community members in educational decision-making.

Motivation comes largely from the child, though the social context in which the child exists is also an important factor in determining the child's interest in learning. In fact, writers on motivation argue that a teacher cannot "motivate" students, that motivation is internally controlled. Today's student seems less willing to perform tasks that lack clear meaning or purpose, that lack an inherent joy or sense of accomplishment. The 20 percent of the school population with clear sights on a college education still subscribe to the notion of delaying gratification and of doing the tasks that are asked of them. This creates the illusion for teachers that the system could still work, if only the other students had the right attitude. In the meantime, the other 80 percent may just go through the motions, frustrating teachers, creating discipline problems, and expending as little effort as possible. These differences in motivation often reflect different social, economic, racial, and ethnic backgrounds as well. In effect, certain groups are being disenfranchised from a public education in large measure because it is very difficult for them to become motivated to do the things teachers ask in the absence of any clear reasons to do so (other than receiving the teacher's approval).

This system is kept running by the teacher's input of energy. Teachers come to perceive themselves in Sisyphusean roles—pushing boulders up hills for most of the semester, only to watch them come rolling back down with depressing regularity. It is little wonder that teachers in such an environment are tired, frustrated, and often cynical.

Active participation in learning suggests more individualization of instructional goals and strategies for students, a greater use of instructional techniques such as project-centered learning, inquiry learning, simulations, cooperative and team learning, apprenticeships, internships, and real-world experiences. Teachers will need to become diagnosticians and planners, tailoring and modifying educational experiences to student needs and interests. Constraints on time, content of the curriculum, location of learning experiences, and methods of assessing learning will have to be relaxed to accommodate diverse student interests and the challenges of motivating students who see little purpose in the classic liberal arts curriculum.

It is important to realize that this is not an argument for permissiveness, lowered standards, or a "do-your-own-thing" educational experience akin to the 1960s. To the contrary, such experiences are more demanding for both teachers and students. They require more hours, more work of a higher quality, and more accountability than many current classrooms, which feature endless worksheets, reading assignments, and tests, the contents of which are quickly forgotten (Goodlad 1984). Teachers do not subsidize this learning environment through their own energy. Instead, they often see their energy magnified as students respond to the guidance and direction provided. Teachers serve as catalysts, and their interventions energize learners, rather than frustrate them.

5. Education is a responsibility that extends beyond schools: Parents, employers, community members have responsibilities for the education of the community's young, along with a right to be included as partners in important decisions about education.

As mentioned in the previous section, the partnership between school and the broader community either is or probably soon will be in the process of seeking a new equilibrium point. Structural safeguards against arbitrary community intervention, such as tenure, curriculum and text adoption policies, and formalized communication channels have been highly successful in constraining community influence on educational practice. The new challenge may be to define the proper relationship among various constituencies in schools and in the community. A balance must be struck between the professional rights and prerogatives of teachers and administrators and the inherent rights of parents and community members to see that their children receive a quality education consistent with their values.

Some educators note that many communities are laden with pathologies—abusive parents, drugs, crime, lack of respect for authority. Other educators point to their community and warn of obsessive parents who push their children to achieve, special interest groups supporting any number of programs, and a majority that cares little about what happens in school as long as it fulfills its warehousing function. The degree to which these perceptions are accurate vary considerably from community to community. However, when educators feel they are incapable of success with students because these conditions exist, such beliefs can have the effect of self-fulfilling prophecy (Rosenholtz 1989a). Even if such perceptions are accurate, they may imply more about the need to reorganize schooling and schools than they do about the inability of children to learn.

Changing the relationship with the community takes time and occurs incrementally. It requires trust and effective two-way communication. Both sides are called on to abandon old stereotypes and suspicions. Such changes do not take place overnight. However, the increasing importance of education and the complexity and difficulty of raising healthy children compel a reexamination of the roles and responsibilities each group has assigned to itself. This is a process of social reconstruction in addition to educational restructuring. The institutions of an industrial society do not appear to be adequate in a postindustrial, global society. New ways of meeting the emerging needs of people in such a society are developing. In essence, the concept of community is evolving and being reinvented. As this process occurs, the role of school in the community—and its relationship with the community—also evolves.

New governance structures and new methods of demonstrating accountability to the community will need to be considered. Involving parents and community in activities such as goal-setting will be meaningless unless goals are subsequently achieved and the results reported to the community. Conversely, when a school fails to reach its goals, this information would also be shared with the community.

Educators will continue to have a key role in this process, by virtue of their knowledge, expertise, and high interest level. They will not, in all likelihood, be unchallenged in these areas. It may be difficult for educators to relinquish their control over decision-making. It appears likely that participatory models of decision-making will be around, at least for the immediate future, and that noneducators will expect to be taken seriously when they participate in such models.

Many employers are beginning to understand that the link between education and productivity is much more direct than they had assumed in the past. They are showing a willingness to do more than simply donate money, but are not always certain what to do (Segal and others 1992). Parents, often frustrated by their inability to influence their own children, are looking for help; they may not always know how to ask for it, but many are becoming more aware of the need to be open to help and support. These attitudes may facilitate the establishment of new relationships focused on mutual concern for young people and their role in the community.

The transition from the world of school to the world outside school may be more gradual. Some students will be ready before others. Even young children will be able to gain from experiences with a broader range of adults than those whom the student encounters at home and at school. Having experiences with other adults provides children with new understanding about themselves and their relation to a larger world. Such experiences also help young people develop the skills and self-knowledge necessary to make decisions about career paths and to develop the motivation and discipline to fulfill their goals.

In an increasingly complex world where resources for education are likely to remain relatively constant, it is clear that partnerships between schools and other segments of society can be very important in keeping education relevant and exciting for students. Those partnerships can also help sustain support for public education at a time when the proportion of families with children in the schools may be 25 percent or less.

6. Schools may be the only place where a sense of genuine community can be developed for young people. They might better function as communities, not factories.

As the communities within which schools exist continue to crumble, it becomes apparent that educators are faced with (at least) two choices: (1) to lament the decline of support for education from home and community, and wash their hands of the responsibility to educate students who do not come to school with the desired background and attitudes; or (2) to accept that schools may be the only place in the student's life where he or she is safe, valued, and supported, and embark on the process of redesigning schools based on the needs and realities of the clients they serve.

The first response leads to a dead end. There is little schools can do directly to affect the societal context within which education occurs. The existence of such a response within a school can help explain high levels of teacher frustration. Nothing could be worse than to be unable to teach successfully, and unable to effect the changes necessary to be successful. Stockard and Mayberry (1992), in a review of the research on effective learning environments, describe them as places where "students and teachers have positive feelings about their work setting. High morale appears to bolster the self-confidence of both teachers and students and promote positive attitudes and expectations about teaching and learning ability" (p. 34). Other researchers (Fuller and others 1982, Lanier and Sedlak 1989, Rosenholtz 1989b) have stressed the importance of teacher efficacy—the sense by teachers that they make a difference and that they have some control over their ability to be successful—as an important component of effective instructional environments.

Alternatively, if educators accept that the first response is self-defeating, then they may wish to examine the degree to which their own school is a genuine and healthy community for young people. In many cases, what they will discover may not be pleasant. Most schools are organized after one or a combination of three models: the Factory Management Approach, which was described in chapter 2; the Bureaucratic Approach; and, to a lesser degree, the Craft Workshop Approach (Shedd and Bacharach 1991). The Bureaucratic Approach is characterized by its

> emphasis on tailoring whole programs to groups of students.... [With this approach,] the key question becomes how much specification is needed to guarantee that students are placed in appropriate channels and moved at appropriate speeds through the system as a whole. (Shedd and Bacharach 1991, p. 56)

The Craft Workshop Approach represents a third way of thinking about how schools are organized. Shedd and Bacharach describe the assumptions and practices associated with the model:

> The more teaching is perceived as a craft,... the more likely it is that students will be assumed to be sufficiently homogeneous to justify their placement in classes and curricula that are *not* tailored for those with particular needs or abilities (Bacharach and Conley, 1989). Heterogeneity of students' needs and abilities is a manageable problem, according to this line of thinking....
>
> Thus, the craft model is most often associated with the pursuit of some relatively coherent, singular (some would say narrow) notion of excellence, rather than with the pursuit of either efficiency or equity. (pp. 58-59)

Shedd and Bacharach express concern over the effect of these three models on teachers and students:

> Research on schools as organizations provides ample evidence of the apathy, passivity, minimal expectations, avoidance of responsibility, lack of innovation, and (what is most troublesome) impersonal treatment of

students/clients that are typically associated with bureaucracies (Anderson, 1968; McNeil, 1986; Goodlad, 1984; Sizer, 1984). (p. 65)

Schools are based on structural designs adopted in an era when students were expected to have their needs for affiliation fulfilled primarily through other institutions in the community, including extended family, church, and various social groups. In many cases, these institutions no longer meet these needs for young people. Youth are left to identify with the mass culture created by retailers and the media or, of greater concern, with gangs or cliques that embrace antisocial values.

A large part of the problem is the decreasing presence of positive adult role models in the lives of young people (Stevenson and Stigler 1992). Schools with hundreds of students, where a child can attend several years and be known by only a handful of acquaintances and teachers, create conditions that support student alienation or identification with youth culture of varying types. Not only are the young deprived of role models, they are held in very narrowly bounded age cohorts and thus do not have an opportunity to view the behavior of older or younger children as a yardstick against which to gauge their own development.

One strategy is to restore schools to a human scale. Assumptions about economies of scale can be productively reexamined, with true economies retained and false economies abandoned. How "economical" is it to house 2,000 students in one building if hundreds of them are dropping out each year due to feelings of alienation and a sense that no one cares about them? Each of them represents not only lost opportunities, but lost resources for the school.

Smaller schools, schools-within-schools, schools in various locations in the community, more adults in schools in various roles, more events at school that have meaning and interest to people in the local community—these are all strategies that can contribute to a stronger sense of genuine community within schools. Stockard and Mayberry (1992), in a review of studies on school size, conclude that "the most extensive and complete analyses... suggest that students benefit most when they study in smaller classes and in smaller schools." They state that "studies of elementary students suggest that small schools provide a more humanistic learning experience," and that "several studies suggest that students in small high schools are involved in a greater number and variety of activities, assume a greater number of positions of responsibility, arc lcss alicnatcd, and havc a grcatcr 'scnsc of bclonging' to thc group than students in larger schools." Other strategies include partnerships with community agencies to provide services on school grounds and programs that place more children in contact with positive adult role models outside school.

Extending this sense of pervasive caring and community to the faculty as well is an important consideration, since they will be modeling community through their interactions with each other. Can they develop positive interreliance, identify their common beliefs and values, define what it is about their school as a community that makes it unique or gives it character, and unite to defend the school when it is under attack from external forces? These are behaviors that allow parents and students to understand what it means to be a member of the school community, that help them define their roles and responsibilities, and that enhance their sense of identification and affiliation.

Through such strategies schools may become places where many diverse adults interact with a modest number of students (perhaps 150-300) in ways that allow each student to feel part of some group with meaning, purpose, and direction, and to develop an identity within the group at least in part by observing the behaviors of competent, healthy adults.

These six new "habits of heart and mind" illustrate changes that educators may need to make in their underlying assumptions, given changes that have already occurred in society. As these assumptions change, it will become much more feasible to develop new programs and structures within public schools that respond to the needs associated with these values. Energy can then be focused primarily on resolving implementation and logistical issues, rather than being consumed in political battles and in dealing with passive-aggressive behavior from those who see no need for change.

The chapters in part 1 have presented an overview of many provocative ideas regarding the reasons for changing schools. These ideas provide the grounds for thoughtful discussion and analysis of the rationale and need for remaking schools. They offer a series of possible perspectives on these issues, but are not exhaustive in their content or breadth.

There does not appear to be one compelling set of statements that serves to motivate faculties in all schools to perceive a need for fundamental change in education. Individual school sites may find that one or two of the concepts presented here are all the reason needed to change; other sites may feel that none of the factors presented for consideration has great relevance to them. As will be considered later in part 4, the process of changing schools appears to hinge on the ability of each school site to construct meaning and responses appropriate for that site. The materials presented here may help school personnel determine whether there is a need to examine current practice in greater depth. The chapters in part 2 discuss the ways in which the roles of a number of educational constituencies may be changing.

CHANGING

ROLES AND

RESPONSIBILITIES

INTRODUCTION TO PART 2

Large-scale change alters the ways in which people define their roles within an organization. Change also alters the ways in which those outside the organization define their relationship to the organization. Herein lies one of the most difficult tasks of restructuring. Adults develop their roles over time and, in professions such as education, come to equate their identity with their role. Periods of rapid change bring about restructured roles. The chapters in part 2 are based on the assumption that the roles of *everyone*—those outside as well as those inside schools—are changing, both as cause and result of educational restructuring.

There has been a tendency during the past eight years of educational reform for all the participants to stand in a large circle and point the finger of blame at whomever is standing next to them. It can be the high school teacher blaming the middle school teacher for sending students with inadequate study habits and poor content knowledge, who then can blame the elementary teacher for not developing basic reading and mathematical skills adequately, who then can point to the parents and lament their lack of preschool preparation for their youngster. Or it might be the parents who can blame the schools for shoddy teaching and outdated curriculum, who then can blame the universities for producing inadequately trained teachers. Or one may hear legislators who bemoan the quality of test scores only to hear educators excoriate first the test makers for providing biased, irrelevant tests, and then the lawmakers for not providing adequate funding or flexibility to allow schools to succeed.

It is a ritual that is becoming tiring and frustrating for all who participate in it or observe it. Clearly, responsibility for success or failure of the educational enterprise cannot be affixed easily and unambiguously. This does not mean that there can be no accountability for student performance, however.

What seems to be occurring is discussion and reconsideration of roles and responsibilities from the federal government to the classroom, and all levels in between. Joseph Murphy (1991) summarizes the tendency to rethink roles along with the rationale for what he describes as "work redesign":

> One of the key ingredients of school restructuring is a redefinition of the roles and responsibilities of professional staff.... This includes the redesign of work relationships between the superintendent (district office) and the principal (school) and between the principal and the teachers. In

56

general, restructuring work signals "a major shift in how people in school systems think about roles and relationships. The shift is from a system characterized by controlling and directing what goes on at the next lower level to guiding and facilitating professionals in their quest for more productive learning opportunities for students" (David, 1989, p. 28). (Murphy 1991, p. 22)

These changing roles and responsibilities, and the accompanying changes in accountability that are implied, are examined in the following chapters, first at the broad level of federal and state involvement in education, followed by the local school boards, central administration, principals, and teachers, and concluding with the supporting level occupied by parents, community members, and students.

CHAPTER 4

FEDERAL AND STATE GOVERNMENTS

There can be little doubt that the role of federal and state government in the local educational process has changed significantly during the past decade. Every indication points to a continuing evolution during the 1990s. Long a political backwater, education-related issues, not just education budgets, are receiving attention from legislators, governors, Congress, and the executive branch of the federal government. Education is less a bipartisan issue than it has been historically. Its movement into the partisan political arena signals its emergence as a significant national policy issue. As presented in this chapter, the relationship between school districts and other levels of government is changing, perhaps profoundly and permanently.

THE FEDERAL GOVERNMENT

The federal government had very little involvement in public education before the 1960s. At that time, the federal government began to intervene primarily in an attempt to provide equality of opportunity through programs such as Head Start and Follow Through, and equality of achievement through Chapter 1 programs.

The traditional "hands-off" role of the federal government toward education may change significantly during the coming decade if the linkage between educational achievement and international economic competitiveness is more firmly established and reinforced. This linkage may provide a more compelling rationale for a heightened federal role in the name of "national security," an area of legitimate federal interest.

A prime example of movement in this direction is the effort to develop a system of national education goals and standards. Although many will see this as the beginning of a national curriculum, it has been argued that such a curriculum exists de facto already, as a result of textbooks, standardized achievement tests, and college entrance requirements (Tye 1987).

The national education goals proposed by former President Bush and the nation's governors, including then-Governor Clinton of Arkansas, at a meeting in March 1990 are as follows:

1. All students will start school each day ready to learn.
2. The high school graduation rate will increase by the year 2000 to at least 90 percent.
3. Students will leave grades 4, 8, and 12 with demonstrated competency in challenging subject matter.
4. American students will be first in the world in mathematics and science.
5. Every adult will be literate and will possess the knowledge and skills to compete in a global economy.
6. Every school will be free of drugs and violence and will offer a disciplined environment conducive to learning.

To accomplish these goals, the administration proposed that each community in the nation declare itself an "America 2000" community, committed to the achievement of the six goals through locally developed responses and programs. The federal government would provide guidance and encouragement to these communities, publicize their projects, put them in touch with one another, and provide them with a certain legitimacy and prestige that surrounds such efforts.

The federal role may continue to emphasize education as a tool for the enhanced ability of the United States to compete internationally and, to some extent, to monitor the quality of education from state to state. When the National Education Goals Panel released its recommendations for a system to measure progress toward the national education goals, it included these types of measures:

a national assessment system to measure student achievement in key subject areas, a "child-development profile" to gauge children's readiness for schooling, and a student-identification system to track students across districts and states. (Rothman, April 3, 1991, p. 1)

The panel recommended creation of a "curriculum-related national assessment system," as opposed to a national curriculum. The distinction may be a fine one, since the panel envisioned "an examination system, for which students could prepare and toward which teachers could teach." This assessment system, according to the panel, would be linked to the national standards. In theory the purpose of such examinations, likely based on the National Assessment of Educational Progress (NAEP), would be to inform the nation whether the goal of improved student performance nationally is being achieved and also to improve teaching and learning, thus making achievement of the goal more likely. These actions suggest there is the sense that the American educational system needs "steering" or "guiding" in a particular direction and that state and local control cannot be counted on to provide consistent direction. Initial attempts by the National Assessment Governing Board to set achievement levels for NAEP proved difficult, illustrating how contentious this process is likely to be (Darling-Hammond 1992).

Indicator systems reflect "each historical era's predominant political and social ideologies, and [such] measures have been developed in response to (or occasionally in reaction against) prevailing political, social, and economic goals for schooling" (Darling-Hammond 1992, p. 237). As federal officials become more interested in the ways in which schools are performing in relation to indicators, their interest in indicator systems may increase:

> If policy makers really want to understand what is going on in an educational system, they will need not only a comprehensive system of indicators (much more comprehensive than what would be determined by an immediate set of perceived "policy needs") but a full research portfolio examining teaching, learning, and policy implementation in schools. (Darling-Hammond 1992, p. 241)

A second example of heightened federal interest and leadership, at least in the short run, was the creation of what George Bush described in his America 2000 strategy as "a new generation of American schools." During his administration the federal government proposed to act in partnership with business leaders and state governors on:

- Improving existing schools
- Creating "a new kind of school"
- Fostering continuing education for adults
- Challenging Americans to "cultivate communities where children can learn" (Miller 1991, p. 26)

To address these goals, the America 2000 strategy proposed to establish 535 experimental schools by 1996—one for each House district and two more for each state. Such schools would be "expected to set aside all traditional assumptions about schooling and all the constraints conventional schools work under."

These schools would be expected to serve two purposes: (1) provide new models of public education that educators can use to improve existing schools, and (2) provide serious competition to public education. Former Secretary of Education Lamar Alexander stated that he could envision profit-making schools participating, and others in the Department of Education indicated that religious groups might be eligible for funding as well. One likely goal of the New American Schools process was the creation of a number of models for schools that would receive the "blessing" of the federal government. These models might then have served as templates for school choice programs in states or districts so inclined. Even though it does not appear likely that the program will be implemented, it nonetheless represents a radically different conception of the federal role in education. In comparison, the last federal intervention of this magnitude into educational innovation, the Experimental Schools Program of the early seventies, funded local school district initiatives and was focused on making public education better by means of experiments within the system.

The executive branch of the federal government can, at least for the short-term foreseeable future, be expected to continue to exert pressure on public education to improve or change, for a variety of ends and purposes, not all of which have been clearly articulated. This pressure, begun by former Secretary of Education William Bennett's use of the "bully pulpit" and the Wall Chart, with its state-to-state comparisons, is likely to be one of the key tools in the arsenal of the executive branch. The use of rhetoric is an inexpensive but relatively effective strategy (politically speaking) to show concern and demonstrate "leadership" in an area where the federal government has little statutory authority, particularly as long as the majority of Americans believe, as polls indicate they do presently, that the public educational system is in a state of crisis. In this type of climate the federal government can be expected to continue to support the establishment of national education goals and the collection and publication of information that evaluates school performance relative to national goals and international standards.

The national political scene is far beyond the control of local districts and individual school buildings and is an arena in which most educators are not used to playing. It appears that it, too, will have to be taken into account to an ever greater degree when educators consider how they are to respond to calls for improvement and fundamental change.

STATE GOVERNMENTS

The past decade has seen a major increase in the willingness of states to use their power over their public education systems (Wirt and Kirst 1989). Ravitch (1990) describes this phenomenon as being "a shift of major proportion (in which) the locus of educational policy-making moved from the federal government and local governments to the states" (p. 48). Mazzoni (1991) summarizes this shift in greater detail:

In the 1980s, the "entrepreneurial states" made improving schools their principal target for policy innovation (Van Horn, 1989). Their intense and pervasive activism, building on previous decades of more gradual state involvement—notably in the 1970s (Campbell and Mazzoni, 1976; Kirst, 1984; Mitchell, 1988), resulted in the "full-fledged emergence of state educational leadership." (p. 115)

It is important to be aware of the important role that state government is likely to play in restructuring. While much of the literature on restructuring focuses on the school site and the school district, there is evidence that for restructuring to succeed there must be consistent educational policy that is initiated and coordinated at the state level. Smith and O'Day (1991) argue that "what is needed is neither a solely top-down nor bottom-up approach to reform, but a coherent *systemic* strategy that can combine the energy and professional involvement of the second wave of reforms with a new and challenging state structure to generalize the reforms to all schools within the state." They envision a more proactive role for the states in the process of restructuring—a role that "can set the conditions for change to take place not just in a small handful of schools or for a few children, but in the great majority" (pp. 234-35).

Most of the current restructuring literature focuses exclusively on the school and district levels of the system. When states are mentioned at all, it is usually in the context of providing waivers from various regulations currently in force.... [D]uring the past 20 years, most states have gradually amassed greater authority and responsibility over their educational systems as their share of the educational budget has risen, as the economy and productivity of the state have been seen to be more and more dependent on its educational system, and as issues of equity and fairness in the distribution of resources and services among districts became an important part of the nation's agenda.

... [T]he states are in a unique position to provide coherent leadership, resources, and support to the reform efforts in the schools. States not only have the constitutional responsibility for education of our youth, but they are the only level of the system that can influence all parts of the K-12 system: the curriculum and curriculum materials, teacher training and licensure, assessment and accountability. (Smith and O'Day 1991, pp. 245-46)

State government is where the statutory responsibility for education resides, based on the implied powers doctrine of the U.S. Constitution. The role of state government has varied considerably throughout the nation, in terms of the amount of state versus local control that existed. State involvement has generally been proportionate to the amount of funding for school districts that comes from state revenues versus local property taxes. As funding authority and responsibility accrue to the state level, so do influence and control over the instructional program and all other aspects of local school districts.

States have generally satisfied their need to establish standards for local districts through accreditation procedures, implemented by state departments of education or regional accreditation agencies. These procedures usually involve examination of a series of input measures (number of books in the library, minutes devoted to required elements of the instructional program, proper teacher certification for classes taught, and so forth) but do little to ascertain the quality of the outputs of education in forms such as observable or demonstrable student performance.

Although some states have had programs of statewide testing for many years, the majority have not. Testing has been optional and has been conducted at the district level. It was not uncommon for a half-dozen different standardized achievement tests to be used by different districts throughout a state, thereby making state-level summaries or district-to-district comparisons difficult or impossible.

The reform movement of the 1980s brought about an upsurge in the number of states with formal, mandated programs of statewide achievement testing whose purpose was to provide comparisons of some sort, either to other states, among districts in a state, or even between individual school buildings. In many cases these tests were lawmakers' first systematic attempt to assess educational effectiveness within their state. Given the reluctance of legislators to fund large programs without some form of evaluation, it is interesting that public education has escaped scrutiny for as long as it has. Traditions of local control have contributed to an attitude that student performance in schools was not the concern of the legislature, but of local boards of education. This tradition is gradually being abandoned.

The Education Commission of the States, a nonprofit, nationwide interstate compact comprising forty-nine states and the District of Columbia, has as its primary purpose helping governors, state legislators, and state education officials develop policies to improve the quality of education in their states. Its publication *Exploring Policy Options to Restructure Education* (1991) outlines strategies for state-level policy-makers to follow in their attempts to restructure education. The report states that "the focus must be shifted to student learning outcomes instead of predominantly on the process of schooling." Policy-makers should be actively engaged in establishing a vision "of what students should know and be able to do, and how the education system should work." Six policy categories needing attention by policy-makers are presented with recommendations for the types of policy changes needed:

I. *Leadership Policies....* Policies that support and encourage broad-based leadership are needed. Four particular types of policies needed are those that encourage the development of (a) shared vision and comprehensive strategic plan, (b) expectations that roles and responsibilities need to be open to change, (c) exemplary practices from which others can learn, and (d) waivers to remove barriers.

II. *Learning Policies.* Current learning policies—those related to curriculum, instruction, assessment and student learning goals—frequently focus on number of hours spent on a subject, amount or type of material to cover in a course, use of specific textbooks, credits earned and attainment of minimum skills and knowledge.

Learning policies need to shift from these focal points to a commitment to: (a) **prepare *all* students,** (b) **set high expectations measured by performance of desired outcomes** and (c) **establish instructional approaches that best teach essential skills.**

III. *Inclusion Policies.* Policies are needed to prevent certain groups from being underserved and to involve people traditionally excluded from significant roles in the education system.

The policy options [must] address the need for (a) **parental and community involvement,** (b) **interagency cooperation** and (c) **business partnerships.**

IV. *Organizational Policies.* Organizational policies must support greater responsibility and accountability by people at all levels in the system. In particular, more accountability and responsibility for learning by those closest to the students are needed to handle the diversity and complexity of student learning. Shared decision making among representatives of all groups in the school community is important if schools are to reach and implement the best decisions to improve student learning. Accountability processes must be in place to monitor the results of improved teaching and learning practices.

Thus, policies that redefine (a) **decision-making roles** and (b) **accountability** are needed.

V. *Finance Policies.* In the past, regulations and mandates tied to education processes have dominated finance policy. Attention now is being given to transforming finance policy to focus on outcomes and cause change.

Finance policies need to recognize that restructuring involves upfront costs as well as reallocation of resources based first and foremost on higher student outcomes while maintaining equity. Finance policies need to (a) **provide funding for restructuring,** (b) **encourage innovation,** (c) **promote a focus on learning outcomes,** and (d) **address federal involvement.**

VI. *Renewal Policies.* Given the increasingly rapid rate of change, states and districts need policies specifically designed to encourage renewal. Such policies need to support the continual growth and development of individuals and the system itself by effectively bringing the best knowledge, technology and ideas into the system. Barriers to renewal, such as contractual language, must be changed to promote focusing on student achievement. New ways to promote professional growth and recruitment of high-quality teachers and administrators must be identified. There must be an ample number of competent, culturally diverse teachers and administrators.

Renewal policies (a) **promote growth, development and renewal of individuals and groups,** (b) **ensure availability of quality future educators,** and (c) **encourage ongoing evaluation of progress toward the shared vision.** (pp. ii-iv, emphasis in original)

These model policies suggest the newly emerging role of state government as a change agent, standard setter, and judge of the efficacy of public education. At the same time, states retain the ability to set the basic groundrules for the system through means such as funding, teacher licensure, structure of the curriculum, requirements for teacher staff development, and methods by which schools must report their progress to parents and the community.

States are increasingly providing the impetus for local districts to experiment. On the West Coast, for example, there are programs in Washington ("21st Century Schools" program involving thirty-three sites), Oregon ("2020 Schools" program with over 100 schools participating during the past two years), and California (300 to 400 restructuring grants worth $6.5 million), all designed to provide seed monies to selected schools in the hope that they will develop innovative programs that can serve as models for other schools.

Examples of other state projects include Arkansas' Restructuring for Higher Order Learning pilot, Indiana's Schools for the 21st Century, New Mexico's 21st Century Schools program, and Utah's site-based management grants.

Arizona supported sixteen schools to pursue restructuring efforts. The state provided these schools complete regulatory flexibility and encouraged them to emphasize ungraded classrooms in grades 1 through 8. These schools are making changes in the following areas: integration of technology, parental involvement, year-round schooling, and interdisciplinary education.

Colorado has identified fifty "creativity schools" that are commissioned with promoting innovation and partnerships (National Governors' Association 1991).

New assessment programs are under development in numerous states. In California, for example, twenty-five districts were selected to field test new methods of student testing authorized by the state board of education under the Alternative Assessment Pilot Project ("Schools

Selected for Testing Pilot Project" 1991). The intent is for school districts to develop local performance-based assessments. Such locally developed tests will serve in tandem with a new statewide assessment program as the "linchpin" of reform efforts in California. These efforts will tie into the curriculum frameworks being developed at the state level, providing a content and assessment framework within which districts can make choices about instructional materials and techniques and can compare their progress to that of other districts in the state. The 1990 Science Framework is cited nationally as an example of how states can provide conceptual frameworks within which local curriculum decisions can be made (National Governors' Association 1991).

In June 1991, Oregon enacted the Education for the 21st Century Act, a far-reaching law that will require fundamental change in schools and schooling. Key requirements in the law reflect the state's changing role. The act imposes extensive accountability and reporting requirements on schools and establishes public standards all students will be expected to meet at certain points in their education. Such information must be announced publicly and made available to parents. The law establishes checkpoints at which student performance must be assessed using a variety of means, and it mandates the creation of statewide standards. To receive their Certificate of Initial Mastery by approximately age sixteen, students must demonstrate mastery in a number of areas and through a variety of methods, including work samples, portfolios, tests, and a culminating project or exhibition. Schools must provide alternative means of instruction to students who are not making adequate progress toward attaining a Certificate of Initial Mastery. After attaining Certificates of Initial Mastery, students pursue Certificates of Advanced Mastery at public schools, community colleges, or other institutions of higher education. These advanced mastery certificates begin directing students toward various career options.

The Oregon law says very little about the processes schools are to employ to achieve the stated goal of success for all students in achieving a Certificate of Initial Mastery, and it does not specify the content of the strands for the Certificate of Advanced Mastery. In fact, there are provisions for schools to request waivers from restrictive rules and regulations, as well as a grant program to fund innovative strategies, techniques, and structures of education to encourage districts to experiment. Furthermore, the implementation process will be accomplished by developing pilot demonstration sites around the state that offer a variety of approaches and strategies for satisfying the goals of the law.

This law illustrates a changing relationship between the state, school districts, and school sites. In this new relationship, the state establishes standards and encourages innovation and experimentation. It creates accountability for the achievement of standards but allows schools considerable freedom to decide how best to meet the standards. The local school board and central administration are limited in their ability to set the local educational program independently from the state, since the statewide outcome standards tend to drive each school's instructional program. Enhanced accountability through reporting of school-by-school performance is likely to cause schools to demand greater flexibility so that they can adapt their program to the unique needs of their constituency and achieve greater success. Local boards and central administrators will be less able to create standardized instructional programs within a district. Their roles, too, will evolve, as suggested in the following chapters.

SCHOOL DISTRICTS

In the U.S., local school districts, about 15,500 in all, are accustomed to being able to operate with relative independence (when compared to educational jurisdictions in other countries). While some are more accountable than others, either to boards of education, an active community, or a regulatory-minded state department of education, few are prepared for the type of scrutiny to which they are likely to be subjected during the coming decade. Expectations for improved student performance will likely increase, as will involvement by all groups in decision-making.

The implications are profound for all groups that have a role in the delivery of public education. This chapter explores the impact on boards of education and central-office administrators. Subsequent chapters focus on changes at the site level in the roles of principals and teachers, and on changing roles of students, parents, and the broader community.

BOARDS OF EDUCATION

The local board of education is a cherished and unique institution in the American educational system. It embodies the principle of local control of education and facilitates the close relationship that is supposed to exist between home, school, and the community at large. However, the challenges it faces are such that its goals, purposes, procedures, and even its continued existence may be called into question.

The school board was designed initially as a guarantee that the values of the community would be transmitted effectively to the young and that tax monies, raised locally, would be spent properly. The political role of the school board has gone through several transformations. That role has evolved from being an extension of church and local values, to becoming highly political in a partisan sense in the 1890s as cities grew, to reflecting the best of the Progressive movement's ideals for reforming government shortly after the turn of the century when much reform of boards occurred, to becoming increasingly political again as it comes under siege by constituencies organized into highly effective interest groups. This evolution continues, as local boards see their power and discretion being challenged from both the top and bottom.

Wirt and Kirst (1989) attribute this "squeeze" on school boards' power to three trends that have occurred during the past twenty years. Parents, who once loyally supported school professionals, now challenge their authority and widely regard them as "failing." Also challenging traditional authority inside the school are teachers, whose success in collective bargaining has further constrained school officials' authority. Finally, according to Wirt and Kirst, the increase in state control over education has been the "most striking feature of state-local relations in the last twenty years" (p. 24).

This politicization of education, combined with the tension between boards and state government, may be leading to a redefinition of the role of board member. From a job that was almost symbolic in nature, board members are now subjected to extreme pressures from organized groups of parents, teachers, taxpayers, and various special interest groups. Today's board members operate in a highly charged environment in which they are subject to intense criticism and receive little reward for their efforts. Thus it has become more difficult in many cases to attract competent people to a position that has not been coveted historically and seldom is a stepping stone to higher office.

At the same time, the board is expected to provide leadership for change. The impetus and rationale for this change frequently emanate from the state, not the local, level. These often conflicting forces are exacerbating tensions in what Wirt and Kirst (1989) describe as

> an ongoing basic problem in the governance of American schools; that is the tensions between the community's need for school leadership that can lead and be trusted and the same community's desire to have its own will carried out by that leadership. (p. 10)

Boards of education increasingly may be expected to be sophisticated and knowledgeable and to possess a perspective on education that extends beyond the borders of their school districts. They may be called upon to influence state policy decisions in areas other than funding. They may be challenged to be seen as part of the solution to the challenges facing education by developing unique responses locally, not viewed as part of the problem by erecting barricades to change.

Given that school sites will probably continue to gain decision-making authority, along with greater accountability, boards of education might increasingly serve as "boards of directors," who help set a general direction for the organization, then review the plans, goals, and outcomes of the various organizational units. Such a role suggests that school boards would spend less time in their meetings on administrivia, on detailed reviews of the methods of instruction, and on supervision of decisions that should be made by the professional administrative staff. In contrast, school boards that serve as boards of directors might pay more attention to the "strategic direction" of the district, to the performance of students, and to the development and periodic review of the types of behaviors students should be able to demonstrate at various points in their education. School sites consistently unable to meet their goals (goals appropriate to their circumstances) would be held accountable by the "board of directors."

One intriguing notion, following the metaphor of school board as board of directors, is to have the board meet only two times a year, once to review and comment upon proposed goals for the district and individual buildings, and once to assess the degree to which school and district goals were achieved. Obviously, such meetings would have to be longer than regular board meetings, perhaps taking up a Friday evening and all day Saturday. And perhaps there still needs to be a meeting in which the budget is formally reviewed and approved. Most other decisions would be reallocated to management, augmented by the types of community appeal processes that have been developed by most districts.

Such an arrangement might even attract more high-caliber candidates to school board races. It might free the superintendent to run the district on something other than a crisis management basis, and it might change the manner in which organized special interest groups interact with the district. It could be one more step toward loosening schools from constant oversight, bureaucratic control, and micromanagement, which many identify as a source of organizational inflexibility and resistance to change.

Given the increasing involvement of states in establishing outcome measures and accountability requirements, the role of boards may move naturally toward issues of internal coordination and quality control. If decision-making continues to be decentralized, as many states are causing to happen by creating school site councils with considerable authority, boards may not mandate so much as coordinate, set parameters, and enforce consequences for a district's failure to achieve performance goals. This could be a very difficult transition for many board members, accustomed to viewing themselves as the final authority. To act as extensions of the will of the state government on the one hand and the desires of school site councils on the other may be a very challenging balancing act for boards of education in many districts throughout the nation.

CENTRAL ADMINISTRATORS

There may be no other group whose role could be affected more profoundly by the coming changes in education than central-office administrators. Some administrators seem to recognize the enormous challenges they face; others appear not to acknowledge the profound ways in which their role may be altered.

The size of school districts' central administrative staffs soared during the sixties and seventies, particularly in urban areas, where the number of administrators continued to increase even as the number of students decreased.

The administrative structure of school systems has drawn its inspiration from private-sector models and the military, which employ familiar concepts of "line" and "staff" authority to describe positions and relationships within the "chain of command." This structure led to a significant increase in the centralization of authority in school districts in the fifties (a time during which many small districts were consolidated into larger ones), the sixties (with an interruption for many incidents of decentralization and experimentation that tended not to outlast the decade by much), and the seventies (with its emphasis on "back to the basics"). This trend was in step with the basic belief of the scientific management school of thought in economies of scale. It also fit the general notion that educational processes could be directed and controlled in much the same manner as manufacturing processes.

Just as school districts seemed to be mastering the implementation of centralized authority systems, the rules of the game within the society at large began to shift. As early as 1981, the private sector began to adopt and extol the virtues of decentralized decision-making, worker involvement, and participatory management ("The New Industrial Relations" 1981). Meanwhile, education was putting the final touches on systems of "teacher-proof curriculum," behavioral objectives, standardized and criterion-referenced tests, and collective bargaining.

Many central offices are inhabited by people who were groomed in this old system of management. They are used to having their ideas and orders carried out. They are not evil people; they simply have a single way of thinking about how an organization should be run in a time when the rules of the game are changing dramatically.

Central administrators may be faced with a twofold challenge: (1) redefine their roles so that their contribution to the organization becomes clear in the context of a different notion of educational governance, and (2) develop the skills necessary to succeed in these newly defined roles.

If trends of increasing decentralization coupled with assessment for outcomes at the building level continue, central administrators may come to possess a new mixture of skills and responsibilities, some of the components of which might include the following abilities: assist in the development and implementation of an organizationwide vision and mission; plan and coordinate those aspects of the organization best conducted centrally; facilitate change and all the interactions that surround it; build linkages across institutional boundaries; communicate effectively in a variety of ways; resolve rather than sublimate conflict and disputes; and enhance the efficiency of the organization. These and other responsibilities are explained in greater detail below.

VISIONARIES

One of the unanswered questions of decentralization is: How will people decide to do anything other than what they already know how to do in the absence of a vision of clearly superior alternatives? One of the key roles central-office administrators might occupy in decentralized systems is to help in the development of a vision of vastly improved, or different, educational outcomes and the transformations of the system necessary to achieve these outcomes. This role requires that administrators be aware of current trends and issues in education, to discuss, debate, and analyze on a regular basis key educational issues. Rather than becoming overwhelmed by the administrivia that currently seems to occupy their lives, these people would also be expected to function as educational visionaries. The difficulty of assuming both of these roles simultaneously should not be underestimated.

Perhaps staff meetings might become places where the merits of the latest ideas in education are carefully discussed and critiqued, rather than environments devoted primarily to reactive crisis management. Perhaps notions of reflective practice (Schön 1983, 1989) can be incorporated into the culture of the central office to a greater degree. Perhaps the ability to articulate a vision of education may become a key consideration in the appointment and retention of central administrators.

PLANNERS

Central-office administrators may expect to have more responsibility to guide the organization through systematic planning activities designed to establish the organization's direction and purpose. In the absence of a common plan that establishes shared vision, mission, and goals, there is little reason for schools to remain in an organization such as a district, other than to obtain certain conveniences of scale.

Identifying a common sense of purpose, or mission, and the unique roles the different elements of the organization have in accomplishing that mission are important skills for central administrators in environments where systematic planning is practiced and institutionalized (Bryson 1988, Bryson and Roering 1988). To conduct such a process successfully requires knowledge of and skill with various planning models and with the interpersonal and political issues that surround planning.

FACILITATORS

To a greater degree, central administrators may become facilitators of change, of planning, of implementation, of dispute resolution, of interactions among organizational entities. Facilitation is the skill of supporting or enabling others to act on their own to solve problems or achieve organizational goals, as opposed to doing it for them (or to them). Facilitation works best when conducted within an environment where organizational goals are known and shared (Rosenholtz 1989a, Saxl and others 1987). Central-office administrators have many opportunities to function in a variety of ways that facilitate change by individuals or school sites toward the achievement of organizational goals.

BOUNDARY SPANNERS

Central-office administrators will continue to be able to move among the organizational units more freely than most of the people assigned to any one unit. They also have more opportunities to interact with a broader cross-section of the community at large. They may be more able to take advantage of the potential presented by the unique insights and opportunities such a perspective provides. They may be critical agents in building political consensus within the community for change, and be the early warning system that identifies possible problems or reactions that changes in the school are engendering in the community. This knowledge enables them to move the process of change forward in a productive manner.

COMMUNICATORS

The need for central-office administrators to communicate effectively, through the written and spoken word, seems likely to increase. While it is already an important ability for some central administrators, it may become even more important as these roles involve greater communication of a vision, resolution of problems, spanning of boundaries, and many of the skills outlined above. Aspiring leaders may need to demonstrate their competence and knowledge through verbal and written forms of communication as one of the key ways by which others may judge their fitness to lead.

DISPUTE RESOLVERS

Rather than mandating behaviors and then manipulating people to create desired outcomes, central-office administrators may be called upon to mediate among different units of the organization where friction exists, between the organization and the outside world, and within individual units of the organization. They may take on the role of "objective" external arbitrator, rather than as a player with a clear vested interest.

Particularly with the development of shared decision-making and participatory styles of management, increased conflict at individual work sites can be expected, as people begin to interact with one another around issues of power and resource acquisition and allocation. It is likely the organization will need people who can help move the process of self-governance along. This role, akin to an organization developer, exists now in a few districts. It may be needed in many more districts in the immediate future if current trends toward greater involvement and empowerment continue.

EFFICIENCY ENHANCERS

Since central-office administrators have presided over the establishment of a bureaucracy, there have been few incentives for them to make their organizations more efficient. In a bureaucracy, more attention may be given to empire building than to efficiency. Education, with its lack of clear outcome measures, is vulnerable to self-justifying and self-perpetuating organizational behaviors. This can lead to decreased efficiency and loss of organizational focus.

Since it is hard to envision a scenario in which the amount of inflation-adjusted funding available to schools increases significantly during the coming decade, it is likely pressure will continue on central administrators to improve efficiency so that resources can be freed up and transferred to the school site and the classroom. Not only does this streamlined efficiency mean the loss of jobs from central offices, but it means that fewer resources will be available for performing many of the district's functions. A central administrator in this role would have to be an expert on alternative forms of service delivery and organizational analysis in order to present options for making the bureaucracy less cumbersome while ensuring that the needs of school sites are met.

COORDINATORS

As suggested earlier, the different levels of the organization, such as elementary, middle, and high schools, need to develop some method of coordinating their efforts if school districts attempt to move toward integrated outcomes that are the result of cumulative educational experiences from kindergarten through grade 12, as a number of states are now beginning to legislate. In many, perhaps most, districts there is precious little coordination currently between different levels.

Central-office administrators can expect to be challenged to maintain a balance between the needs for some order and internal consistency, on the one hand, and for individuality and adaptation for school sites on the other. Decentralized decision-making tends to pull organizations apart, while cumulative outcomes and accountability for achieving them necessitates cooperation across levels and school sites. Such a balance will be difficult to strike.

STANDARD SETTERS

One of the elements driving coordination is standards or outcomes. Central-office administrators can play a key role in the identification of standards, stated in the form of key learner outcomes and skills, for which different units of the district will be responsible.

Once these standards are set, central administrators are in the ticklish position of assessing the degree to which the standards are met. While most districts currently have testing programs of one form or another, many forces tend to make it as difficult as possible for this information to be used to assess the performance of individual buildings against any preestablished standard or outcome. As standards and outcomes are established, it may become easier (or at least possible) for the public to measure the performance of schools against those standards. Given the increasing demands of state legislatures for accountability and a general public perception that schools are not "getting the job done," it seems likely that accountability will be measured in more specific terms than current measures. Standardized achievement tests, for instance, have lost credibility in part because of what has been called the "Lake Wobegon Effect," where all the children are above average.

Because it makes little sense for each school to develop its own program of accountability independent from all other schools and from the state's program, the central office is in the position of coordinating and integrating accountability methods and standards, with the understanding that such programs might need to be adapted to the special or unique goals of each school. Central-office administrators are uniquely situated to play a key role in developing and implementing districtwide accountability programs.

It is this sort of justification of the role of central-office administrators that can create greater legitimacy for the allocation of resources to central-office positions. The individuals who fill the positions can benefit by employing a new set of skills and attitudes as they define their relation to school sites. The previous hierarchical model of management may be evolving to include elements of a matrix style, where various decision-making "nodes" in the organization report to or collaborate with other nodes. The nodes relate to each other sometimes as equals, sometimes in subordinate-superordinate relationships, sometimes with elements of both, depending on the specific task or responsibility. The central office is one more node, with its own areas of authority and responsibility, but it is not necessarily the top of the pyramid to which all information flows and from which all decisions emanate.

The Vancouver, Washington, school district provides an example of how this role transition might take place and of some of the issues associated with the transition (Parsley 1991):

> The central office acts as a support agency staffed by facilitators and resource coordinators.
>
> Central-office resource coordinators are selected for their group process skills, problem-solving abilities, curriculum and pedagogy expertise, and communications ability. They frequently serve on building-level or district-level teams and are expected to be generalists with a strong ethic for service beyond their immediate background or span of control....
>
> ... On a human level, central office reorganization has been a difficult challenge.... Traditional centralized administrative structure served as an impediment to change and had to be addressed if meaningful school reform was to be achieved. Nonetheless, interpersonal dynamics associated with this type of reorganization assure a high degree of stress and anxiety as an unavoidable companion throughout the planning and initial implementation phase....
>
> ... The implicit assumption in Vancouver's reorganization is that the central office functions more as a support agency staffed by facilitators and resource coordinators. The district office continues to do those things it can do most efficiently, notably strategic planning, curriculum coordination, transportation, legal services, accountability and research, payroll, and food services, while emphasizing new and expanded roles at the building level. (pp. 13-14)

This description of the newly emerging roles and duties of central-office administrators is very similar to the one offered in a report issued by the National LEADership Network Study Group on Restructuring Schools. This group is composed of representatives from projects in the national Leadership for Educational Administration Development network of federally funded programs to improve educational leadership skills. The report described this new role as follows:

> Restructuring should entail changes in central offices as well as school buildings. District staff need to stress facilitation and enablement and de-emphasize control and compliance. Central offices might retain small troubleshooting staffs, competent in the specialties of plant management, personnel and bargaining, law, transportation, and other technical subjects, who would be detailed to work in trouble spots with administrators in charge. Field administrators might rotate on occasion into these slots, where they would develop and use expertise in the subject matter as well as in facilitation of problems of site administrators. (Mojkowski and Bamberger 1991, p. 51)

A number of urban districts have undertaken reorganizations and downsizing of their central offices to try to accomplish some of the transformation of roles described above. The success of these efforts, which have been arduous, is undetermined at the moment (Ayers 1991, Clinchy 1989, Rebarber 1992).

Rebarber (1992) describes the changes in the relationship between sites and central administration in the Chicago schools occurring as a result of the passage of the Chicago School Reform Act in 1988:

> Formal authority at individual schools was shifted to 540 new local school councils (LSCs)... composed of 10 elected members plus the (non-voting) principal. Six LSC members must be parents, two are teachers and two are from the local community.
>
> Schools were given new authority in all areas of curriculum, budgeting, and personnel. The extent of that authority in many areas is vague, however, and is a frequent source of friction between schools and the district office....
>
> ... [I]t seems LSCs are taking as much authority as they feel they need and struggling with the district when opposed....
>
> Schools also gained limited additional discretionary spending.... The new funds were made available primarily as a result of...the reform act. The Chicago public school district was required to cut hundreds of central office employees; this provided a substantial proportion of the... discretionary funds....
>
> ... The reform act created an entirely new structure of district management whose authority was to flow primarily from the bottom up. New councils at the regional level consist of parent or community representa-

tives from LSCs located in the sub-district. They choose whether to retain or replace the previous sub-district superintendent. Regional superintendents are facilitators of reform in their area and help coordinate improvement efforts where appropriate. With the approval of their council, they also have authority to place schools that fail to improve on "probation."

Rebarber states that "it is too early to judge progress in terms of student outcomes" (p. 13). Although the structures have been implemented smoothly,

> the success of school-level reform by councils and principals is not as clear. Schools have discharged their formal duties to adopt school improvement plans and budgets. There has been a significant degree of friction between LSCs and the superintendent....
>
> On several occasions where the superintendent sought to implement district-wide policies, strong disagreements developed with councils that disagreed and felt such actions were no longer within the superintendent's purview....
>
> Apart from disagreements with the central-office it is not clear how imaginative or successful LSC reform initiatives have been....
>
> Lack of accountability structures may be a significant flaw. (pp. 12-14)

The Chicago experience highlights the challenges and difficulties embodied in any change in power relationships. It also illustrates the need for many of the skills discussed in this section. Changes in the relationship between central offices and school sites occur only with great effort on the part of all involved. The Chicago experiment is particularly informative in that members of the local site councils include few professional educators. Governance of the schools is transferred not from central office to other professionals in the schools, but to lay people who work in concert with professionals at the site but are not subordinate to them. Many of the approaches to decentralization being enacted by school districts and state legislatures are designed to involve more *teachers* in decision-making, not necessarily parents and community members.

CHAPTER 6

SCHOOL SITES

Substantive change in education ultimately means changes in the roles of those at the school site. Teachers, students, and school site administrators create the meaning of education through their daily decisions and actions. Roles define and direct those decisions and actions within schools. Restructuring means changing the roles adults and children occupy in schools. Corbett (1991) contends that "a social system's structure is its pattern of rules, roles and relationships. Restructuring, then, represents changes in these social relationships." Such changes will be difficult for all involved, particularly adults at or beyond midcareer who are now being asked to radically reconceptualize their roles. As this chapter indicates, classical bureaucratic roles may change into relationships based on collaboration, collegueship, facilitative behaviors, and community membership.

PRINCIPALS

In schools where considerable effort has been devoted to restructuring, it has been observed that the role of the principal is quite often very different from the role described in the effective schools research, where the principal was characterized as a strong, forceful leader who provided the impetus for change and improvement within the school by dint of personality alone (Goldman, Dunlap, and Conley 1993; Louis 1992; Prestine 1991). Principals in restructuring schools demonstrate skills similar to those described previously for central-office personnel. They lead through and with others, not by dictating but by facilitating. Cushman's (1992) discussion of the ways in which principals in the Coalition of Essential Schools exercise power highlights the movement away from some of the tenets of the effective schools research:

> Researchers within the Coalition of Essential Schools argue... that the Effective Schools model is less well suited for schools moving away from the existing system. They see that system as flawed, along with the convention of one strong leader it depends on. (p. 2)

An outline of what this emerging role of principal might look like can be gleaned from a study of Oregon's "2020 schools" (Goldman, Dunlap, and Conley 1991; D. Conley, March 1991). The 2020 program (named after the number that the bill creating the program was assigned as it passed through the legislature) is formally titled the "School Improvement and Professional Development Act." Its goal is to create numerous model sites where teachers and administrators together develop site-based programs of staff development and program development that result in improved educational practices.

These schools are selected by the state through a competitive process and are provided additional money to enhance the professional growth and development of staff while they experiment with new methods of education and leadership. Each school has a site committee with substantial responsibility for developing and implementing the school's program of improvement. The site committee develops "a plan to improve the professional growth and career opportunities of a school's faculty" and to improve its instructional program; that plan "may reflect efforts to explore initiatives in shared decision-making" (Oregon Department of Education 1990, p. 4). These schools serve as "laboratories" where insights may be gained on the emerging redefinition of roles occurring for the principalship. A summary of what effective principals are doing in some of these schools follows.

BEHAVIORS OF PRINCIPALS IN SCHOOLS UNDERGOING CHANGE

A clear sense of purpose linked to the vision. Principals' actions and decisions are guided by a vision of education. Vision may reside in the principal as an individual, but more frequently it is created jointly with the staff; in all cases this vision is clearly and repeatedly articulated within the school. All important programmatic decisions are linked to the vision. It serves as a screen through which new ideas, proposals, and programs are viewed and evaluated.

The use of data to inform decisions and create vision. Data are used to develop and implement this vision. These data take many forms, from profiles of the school's performance on dimensions such as student achievement and attendance, to student discipline records and surveys of parents and students, along with information on the latest educational and societal trends gleaned from journals, books, and other sources.

Principals frequently take the role of disseminators of information. They attend conferences, read voraciously, discuss ideas with colleagues, copy articles, and distribute them to the faculty. They encourage an examination of current practices and assumptions and the development of new ideas.

Analysis of data provides a base upon which discussions take place and helps move decision-making about educational goals from the level of anecdote and unquestioned beliefs to examination of current assumptions and practices. This has the effect of helping to neutralize some of the political factions within the school that can be counted on to oppose any substantive change. The appeal to objective evidence also deflects charges that the process is being manipulated by the principal to produce some predetermined outcome.

Allocation of resources consistent with the vision. Having developed and agreed upon a common focus or purpose in the form of a vision, principals facilitate the process by allocating resources in a way that moves the school toward its goals. This replaces a process of resource allocation dominated by political considerations, what is commonly referred to as the "squeaky wheel" method of management (D. Conley, March 1991).

These principals allocate resources such as money, space, scheduling, and personnel in ways that help achieve the vision. These actions are not perceived as being "top-down" when the staff has developed and endorsed a mission. In 2020 schools, principals have created common prep times, team meeting times, and opportunities for peer observations. They have moved personnel around in school buildings to create space for new programs, and they have reallocated staffing to support specific 2020 goals.

Creation of new decision-making structures. As facilitators, principals have to work with existing decision-making structures, recognizing their limitations. What many principals have chosen to do, rather than confront these existing structures and attempt to assign new duties to them, is to create entirely new structures and allow new leaders to emerge. Principals are not necessarily "in control" of this process. In other words, having created a new leadership structure, they are willing to stand back and let people make decisions, and to relinquish personal control to a significant degree. The following quote from a principal in the study illustrates both the excitement and difficulty of letting go:

> I used to work more at getting people to go into positions when I thought they were ready. Now, people choose their own goals and move through the positions and committees with less direction from me. The current group, for example, is not a team I would have chosen for school leadership, but they are working hard to become as informed as they can be—the best informed in the building—and they are doing fine.
>
> I am more comfortable working with whomever comes along. Part of that is the maturity of the process, part is the maturity of the staff as a group, and part of that is me. I've developed. Now I talk with people about the difference between being congenial and being collegial. (D. Conley, March 1991, p. 40)

Another principal described the interaction with these new leaders:

> We try to get them to do the things they say they want to do. Our role has shifted. We're not doing it. We don't own the task any more. We need to constantly remind them because this is new behavior for them. You remind them they have money to manage, suggesting, not telling them, how they might go about this. There's a lot of coaching that goes on with the committees. (D. Conley, March 1991, p. 40)

Provision of information to teachers. Teachers have difficulty being involved in decision-making in any meaningful way if they do not have the information necessary to inform them of their options and the implications of their actions. Principals in this study provided information to teachers that enabled them to make decisions about budget, staffing, building schedules, and the curricular program.

Principals also provide information about how the school functions internally, how money is allocated, what resources are available, and how decisions are made regarding staffing or class load. By moving these issues into the public light, suspicion is decreased. At the same time, the quality of decisions made by teachers is enhanced when they can see the impact of their decisions on other aspects of the school or can suggest solutions that acknowledge the complexity of the institution.

Less direct leadership, more support of teachers. Part of the process of "letting go" required principals to learn how to support decision-making from the sideline. Sometimes this requires them simply to remain silent in a meeting; other times it means trusting teachers to make good decisions and allowing them to do so. This is not easy, even for those principals who are committed to changing. A quote from one principal indicates how specifically these issues were dealt with by this individual:

> I try to do whatever I can do to remove barriers to successful implementation. I'm constantly asking ways to do this. Every agenda of every meeting has [an agenda item from me] on barriers [to implementation]. I also refuse to be deferred to as the principal. If someone wants clarification, o.k., but otherwise I say, "You had probably better talk to the chair of the committee about that." I try to redirect the question so it does not come to me but to the responsible person or committee. That is important. Ego can impede the outcomes. You have to be ready to let go, and keep on letting go, so others know that they are really in charge of something and really take responsibility for it. (D. Conley, March 1991, p. 41)

Prestine (1991) reached similar conclusions in a study of four schools participating in the Coalition of Essential Schools. She states that "significant new demands on principals in schools attempting essential schools restructuring" fell into three categories: sharing power, participation without domination, and facilitation. As schools in this study began planning to restructure, there were clear expectations for the role of principal to change.

Teachers in the schools Prestine observed and teachers in Oregon's 2020 schools appear to share many of the same perceptions of the behaviors principals must demonstrate to facilitate change.

CHALLENGES OF ROLE TRANSITION

The preceding paragraphs illustrate some of the ways in which reformist principals attempt to facilitate rather than control change in their buildings. This new way of doing business can be fraught with difficulties for many principals, in part because many were selected for their ability to be "strong leaders," which has been interpreted to mean someone who is able to impose his or her will on others. Essentially, these people are being asked to modify their personalities. To shift one's conception of the exercise of power and influence 180 degrees is a tremendously difficult thing to expect of any adult, particularly of those who feel that they are currently doing a competent job and see little reason to change.

A second challenge inherent within this role transition derives from the likelihood that principals will bear the brunt of responsibility for the achievement of goals as schools become more accountable for student performance. Many may worry about ending up in the position of a manager of a baseball team that is losing; in most cases, the manager goes and the players stay. Those principals who adapt their behavior to the changing rules may see the advantages of working through others and may reap considerable reward. This outcome, however, is far from guaranteed.

TEACHERS

When restructuring is attempted with some success, there is a strong likelihood that the role of teacher also undergoes redefinition. Schools that define themselves as being involved in restructuring generally operate in ways that tend to "professionalize" the role of teacher (Lieberman and Miller 1990). Teachers are often charged with making many more decisions and are given the wherewithal to implement programs based on these decisions. They spend more time discussing the goals, purposes, and methods of education as colleagues, and they interact around issues of instruction to a greater degree.

Rosenholtz's (1989a) study of teachers' workplace concluded that a number of factors were associated with schools where teachers were more effective, more satisfied, and more amenable to change and improvement. These factors included high consensus on shared goals, significant teacher collaboration, ample opportunity for teacher growth and learning along with an abundant spirit of continuous improvement, some certainty or agreement about what constitutes effective practice, and a strong sense of the possible along with a commitment to make things happen and to solve problems. When teachers have an organizational environment with these characteristics, changes in the way they approach teaching are much more possible and likely.

It appears to be almost impossible for teachers to transform their teaching in isolation or in the context of the current factory/bureaucratic model of schooling (Lieberman 1990, Lieberman and McLaughlin 1992, Little 1982). Obviously, structural changes are needed to allow teachers to work together and to have adequate time to develop and practice new skills. At the same time, teachers need structures that provide opportunities to become more involved in teams of varying compositions—sometimes with other teachers, perhaps with paraprofessionals of differing levels of technical skill, often with volunteers from the business community as well as the home—if they are to develop the interaction patterns that accompany collegial environments.

Rosenholtz (1989a) makes clear that in schools that are meeting the needs of a wide range of youngsters, teachers cannot do whatever they define personally as effective teaching and operate in isolation from their peers. Opening up the classroom and the instructional process may not be easy for many teachers.

If teachers are to have greater decision-making authority, they will need to be able to use human-relations skills such as communication, negotiation, consensus, goal-setting, and conflict resolution to a greater degree than they do currently. The old norm of isolation, which allowed a teacher to reject new ideas and decisions, is challenged by such behaviors (Rosenholtz 1989b, Rosenholtz and Kyle 1984). The development of more professional environments will support or necessitate greater teacher discussion about what constitutes effective practice and what practices are detrimental to children.

Administrators have an important role to play in this process; they help to implement the decisions of the group and assist in overcoming obstacles mounted by individuals by referring to the decisions of the whole, rather than to the dictates of the administration. They help teachers deal with situations that are beyond their control or that are particularly complex or conflict-laden, but attempt to do so without taking total control. They enable teachers to continue to develop necessary group-process skills successfully (D. Conley, March 1991).

When restructuring efforts are successful in helping teachers develop new roles, the organizational structure changes in ways that support teachers' ability to develop a broader perspective on their role in the organization (David 1989, 1991; Lieberman, May 1988). As they begin to make more complex decisions, they come to grips with the implications these decisions have for the organization as a whole. They deal with issues such as the allocation of resources within the system, legal and contractual constraints, the political effects of their decisions, and the reactions of their colleagues (Goldman, Dunlap, and Conley 1991). For many teachers this broader view is new and somewhat uncomfortable. What seemed so simple before suddenly becomes very complex. This challenges teachers to remain involved, to address the ramifications of their decisions, and to direct decision-making to issues that have the potential to have a positive impact on student learning.

Along with greater authority over learning conditions can be expected to come greater accountability for results. Such a change can cause considerable consternation among teachers, accustomed to closing their doors and doing more or less what they please without responsibility for any particular outcomes. Meadows (1990) points out the conflict that exists as decision-making responsibility is shared more widely:

> I have discovered that, as long as decisions are successful, a leader runs little risk in sharing decision making. However, if a decision proves unsuccessful, the leader will be held accountable; the leader, not the group, must accept the blame for failure. (pp. 545-46).

If teachers come to accept more authority for decisions that affect student learning, they will have to be prepared for increased expectations that these decisions will result in improved learning. This linkage between decision-making authority and outcomes does not yet exist in many of the initial attempts at shared decision-making. If such linkages begin to develop, there will be significant implications for the ways in which teachers interact with one another and how they define their roles, both within their classrooms and within the larger school.

The partnership between teacher and parent also changes in the context of a restructured school (Davies 1991b; Henderson 1987; Moses and Whitaker 1990; Oakes and Lipton 1990). Many schools limit the role of parents today to doing what they are told to do by the teacher, who wants parents to support whatever activities and behavior system the teacher may have established for the class and for each student. While parental support for teacher decisions is important, there are additional dimensions to this relationship that develop or are enhanced as schools move toward partnership models.

In effective schools, parents may become partners in more meaningful ways (Mortimore and Sammons 1987). To facilitate this partnership, teachers share more information with parents on what the teacher is trying to accomplish. The teacher's expectations for the parent are spelled out more clearly. In addition, the teacher solicits information on the student's interests, personality, and other factors that might affect performance. The ritualistic parent-teacher conference may be replaced with more genuine interactions, perhaps in the home of the student, that lead to an exchange of perceptions and a greater understanding of the goals of each party (Love 1989). A true partnership requires teachers to be willing to modify their instruction to some degree based on the realities of a child's support system and to validate and respond to the views and concerns of parents. Parents, and students, have additional implied responsibilities that will be discussed in more detail. The changing roles of parents are the subject of chapter 7, and the responsibilities of the student are considered next.

STUDENTS

Sizer (1991) has described the role of the student as worker and the teacher as coach. In the restructuring school, students undergo a role transition—it may be implied or stated explicitly—from passive to active participants in their own learning (Beane 1991; Brooks 1990; Brophy 1992; Leinhardt 1992; Newmann 1991a). This shift will not be easy, particularly for those students who have already spent many years in the system and have developed successful coping strategies. Newmann discusses this challenge:

> Teachers face the persistent difficulty of engaging students in serious academic work in schools as we know them. Except for a few highly motivated students, most young people complete school only as a ritual. This pervasive disengagement creates massive problems of crowd control for educators and wastes the time of students and staff members alike. (1991a, p. 459)

To engage students more effectively, Newmann states,

> more time will be needed for teachers to communicate with individual students through sustained talk and writing and for students to talk with one another. Substantive conversation also entails major shifts in the roles of teachers and students. Teachers will function more as mentors and coaches, less as depositories of static knowledge to be reproduced. Students will function more as constructors and producers of knowledge. They will rely on teachers for help, but they will not be mere absorbers or consumers of everything the teacher says. Students will also have to take

on the new roles of seeking help from and giving help to one another as they learn. (p. 462)

To become actively engaged in learning, students need to have some control over and input into what they learn. They need opportunities to make more decisions about their learning. They need structures that ensure that they accept the consequences of those decisions. With choice comes accountability. The extensive use of personal-learner goals, coupled with public assessments and demonstrations, is one strategy that helps promote this linkage. Such a method can create personal accountability in front of parents, peers, teachers, and community members. This removes the anonymity most students are able to maintain in schools today. In addition, students need opportunities to collaborate, to work together to solve real problems, to demonstrate what Newmann (1991a) calls "authentic student achievement." To do so, students will need to exercise "some control over the pace and procedures of learning; over opportunities to ask questions and to study topics deemed important; and over constructing and producing knowledge in one's own language, rather than merely reproducing the language of others."

Students who are now drifting through school will need to be challenged to become much more aware of their personal strengths and weaknesses. They will have to be willing to accept, even demand, formative feedback that enables them to assess their skills more accurately against any of a number of external standards. They will need to be willing to set longer term goals, longer than "pass the test," and to think about how the skills they are choosing to develop relate to one another. They will start to think about the relationship between what they are doing in school and what they will be doing when they leave school. They will begin to think of their behaviors in terms of their life goals. And having made these linkages, they will have to be willing to work much harder and produce much higher quality work than they do currently. Their expectations of themselves will need to rise, along with teachers' and parents' expectations of them.

College-bound students will be called upon to reexamine the cynical transactional relationship they frequently develop with teachers, counselors, and administrators, wherein every activity is judged according to its utility as a means to college admission. Newmann (1991a) describes the reaction to restructuring of those who may be on the college-bound track: "Teachers, parents, and students who have experienced only the conventional version of education—especially those who have been successful—cling tenaciously to it, even when they have the opportunity to make substantial changes."

While these students surely should be encouraged to pursue their ambitions, they should also be involved in educational experiences that enable them to learn more about themselves; they, too, need to participate actively in constructing their own learning in addition to following the advice of teachers and counselors. They should be able to take courses that are challenging and that help them develop their intellect, even if there is risk of not getting an "A." They should see experiences in the world of work as valuable. Thus they would welcome opportunities like internships, apprenticeships, shadowing experiences, and other chances to understand how what they are learning relates to the world they are entering, to see that cooperative teamwork is as important as individual achievement, to understand what quality work is, and to be more aware of the need to think critically, solve problems, and develop skills to make themselves successful lifelong learners. These are all skills identified by many as being associated with success in the workplace of the future. College-bound students may inadvertently neglect the development of these skills if they remain in an educational environment that stresses individual achievement and conformity to teacher-structured and -initiated activities as the primary criteria of success.

Furthermore, high school students in particular can benefit from a learning environment that causes them to reassess the appropriateness of holding a job that has no relation to their program of study while attending school full time. The jobs, often for minimum wages, offer little future for most students, while detracting substantially from the time they have to devote to school work. If schools become more successful in offering students a range of experiences in the world of work, these experiences, though not necessarily paid positions, could help displace students' short-term needs for money, if they were structured so that they ultimately lead to higher-paying jobs for students, particularly during summers and after graduation.

The role of principal, teacher, and student changes in schools where restructuring is attempted. The ultimate effect of these changes of student learning is still to be determined, since few schools have gotten to a point where the roles described here have been successfully institutionalized on a widespread basis for enough time to enable the results to be assessed systematically. Anecdotal evidence, particularly from teachers and students, is encouraging (Hayes 1992, Meier 1987, Ratzki and Fisher 1989/1990, Richmond 1974), along with studies of learning environments (Stockard and Mayberry 1992) and particular teaching techniques that involve students actively and allow them to make choices (Joyce, Showers, and Rolheiser-Bennett 1987; Rothman, October 30, 1991; Slavin 1988, 1991).

CHAPTER 7

PARENTS AND THE COMMUNITY

There is a growing realization that a school cannot educate children in isolation from the community in which it exists. As forces cause educators to move from "closed systems" notions and perspectives on schooling toward more inclusive "open systems" conceptions, the role of parents and of the larger community as well changes substantially. Many schools are already moving actively to rethink the ways in which they involve parents and community members. This chapter provides a rationale for such changes and describe these new roles and relationships.

PARENTS

Over time the responsibility for educating the young has gradually been transferred from the parent, the extended family, and the community at large to professional educators, what Seeley (1989) has called the "delegation model" of education. The structure of public education has evolved over the past 150 years based on much the same rationale used to develop common fire, police, sanitation, and public-welfare systems. Once government creates a system, citizens have only to pay taxes and hold elected officials accountable for the efficient and effective delivery of the services. Well-trained professionals are to make the day-to-day technical decisions that drive the system and ensure provision of high-quality services to all.

The limits of this delegation model seem to have been reached in many areas other than education. Police protection, for example, once relied on strong neighborhoods that enforced behavioral norms for most residents. With the breakdown of such neighborhoods and the social institutions associated with them, local police departments have discovered the same thing that educators have: The safety of the community cannot be delegated to a few trained professionals who are not a part of the neighborhood or community.

Many rural communities function in ways that acknowledge the importance and necessity of community involvement in and responsibility for civic survival, often because there is no other alternative. Volunteer fire departments are only one example of how lay people acknowledge they must participate actively in the maintenance of their community. It is clear that interdependence and a strong sense of personal responsibility are essential to civic viability.

One other example of how the delegation model has begun to be replaced or redefined is in the arena of health. It was not so long ago that many people would ascribe responsibility for their health to their doctor. This has changed. Now more people accept greater personal responsibility to be knowledgeable about health-related behaviors and to alter their behaviors based on the information they have. In this conception of individual wellness, doctors are seen more often as resources who help confirm or question the individual's own tentative diagnosis, who have access to specialized knowledge and equipment, and who deal with extraordinary cases or situations where expert training and knowledge are truly needed. Health is based on personal decisions; doctors are there to help when something goes wrong or when support is needed. They are not solely (or, in some cases, even primarily) responsible for personal wellness.

Public education is nowhere near this point, if the anecdotal evidence from teachers who describe their interactions with parents is to be believed. When a principal or teacher contacts a parent regarding a problem his or her child may be having, it is not unusual for the parent to reply, "You're the educator. You deal with the problem." This attitude is very frustrating to educators, yet they may have contributed inadvertently to its development. The public school system has put into place over the past fifty years a series of protective buffers, including teacher tenure laws, restricted access to classrooms, due process for teachers, the tendency of teachers (especially in urban areas) to live outside the communities in which they teach, the emergence of the principal (and the central office) as a barrier and buffer between teachers and parents, and a whole series of measures to "professionalize" teaching, many of which also served to create more of a gap between parents and teachers.

Since many parents have in essence relinquished the education of their children to professional educators, and since the schools have put in place many of the barriers to parental involvement, it appears that schools will need to begin the process of reaching out. Educators can provide information to and foster communication with parents, as well as involve them in setting goals for their children that the school and home can jointly attempt to achieve.

There is evidence that student learning will be enhanced if parents see education as a shared responsibility (Henderson 1987, Stevenson and Stigler 1992, Watson and others 1983). Just as the health care community has come to emphasize the importance of the patient as a partner in maintaining personal health, the educational community may well benefit from a reexamination of the parent's role as partner in the education of the young.

Parents who devote more time to their children's education—not just helping them do their homework—have a positive impact on the children's attitude toward school and their subsequent achievement (Stevenson and Stigler 1992). In many places, parents now are invited to school primarily to be entertained or to contribute money. The development of new parent roles would be enhanced by their having many more opportunities to participate in their child's education. Here are some examples of possibilities: coming to school to see their children demonstrate their skills; assisting in the development of student projects; receiving briefings on the status of school goals and student performance; assisting in decision-making and goal-setting; and coming to perceive the school as a focal point for their social activities and as a center of newly developing conceptions of community. These methods of involvement can be made as applicable in the innercity as in the suburbs with adequate attention to the different contexts and challenges of each environment.

Several examples of ways in which the role of parents can be redefined follow.

Becoming knowledgeable about learner outcomes. As schools move to programs designed around the things a child can do and around the learning outcomes they have mastered, parents need to know what these outcomes are. They will then be in a position to monitor student performance on these outcomes and to support their development. When parents review student work or attend a demonstration by their child, they will be able to determine the level of performance they are seeing.

Setting learning goals with the teacher and child. Education that is personalized to the child's needs and interests allows parents to have a means to participate more actively in the learning process. For example, they can be involved in the development of individual learner programs that specify learner goals. Use of such goals is one strategy that creates a focus for dialogue among parents, student, and teacher. The goals build on the child's interests, while allowing the teacher to keep the activities within the context of general learner outcomes.

Communicating with teachers about child's interests and learning style. Most parents feel comfortable talking about their children's interests. This topic provides a natural starting point for the development of a helping, supporting relationship, but only if the teacher is capable of showing how the school's educational program will incorporate or build upon these interests and strengths. The validation of parental perceptions and knowledge about the child can serve as a springboard to develop the skill of parents as diagnosticians. They can be taught about learning styles (and learning disabilities), and they can communicate with teachers in these terms, providing examples of how their child learns or how the child copes with learning disabilities outside school. Through this interaction, they will become more sophisticated in their knowledge of the learning process generally, and of their child's strengths and weaknesses as a learner specifically.

Becoming involved in site-based decision-making. There will be many new opportunities for parents to be involved in decision-making at the school site. For such a process to work effectively, parents will need to be provided enough information to follow the process and form opinions on crucial issues.

Parent involvement of this type has tended to be carefully controlled by educators (Malen, Ogawa, and Kranz 1990; Malen and Ogawa 1988). When there is an opening on a committee or decision-making group, principals may be tempted to select from among what Louie, the corrupt police chief in the movie "Casablanca," described as "the usual suspects." The "safe" parent from the PTA or the parent who has volunteered in the library for some time and is not likely to challenge the professionals is often the one appointed to serve on the new governance council. This type of hand-picked compliance is unlikely to create new opportunities for parent involvement or a new sense of the relationship between school and home. Parents and educators together will need to take some chances with one another, as new voices enter the decision-and-influence process.

Advocating and supporting change in schools. Most parents are unaware of what is occurring in their child's classroom, or of the need to change education to bring it into the 21st century sometime very soon. The first reaction to change by many parents is to be concerned or opposed. They may have little faith in educators, who they view as being subject to fads and too willing to experiment on their children.

Such attitudes can be overcome only by providing parents with much more of the information they need to be aware that change in education is necessary. Educators are often reluctant to offer such information, since it implies that schools are doing something wrong. If parents are ever to become advocates, they will first need to be given the opportunity to become knowledgeable, both about the need for change as well as the options available to the school.

For their part, parents will have to be more willing to spend the time necessary to understand the myriad changes that must occur in education if it is to adapt to the changes that have already taken place in the world that surrounds schools. Given the demands on parents' lives currently, this is a difficult challenge for all involved.

Schools need to be flexible in the options and strategies they employ to increase parent involvement. Many programs under way currently explore these options in a variety of neighborhoods and settings (Bauch 1989; Chrispeels 1991; Cross, LaPointe, and Jensen 1991; Davies 1991b; Dornbusch and Ritter 1988; Jennings 1990; Lueder 1989; Olson, April 4, 1990; Silvestri 1989; Williams and Chavkin 1989; Wolf and Stephens 1989).

Finding time to become involved in their children's education. As busy as most parents have become, current involvement options are nonoptions for many of them, who find it difficult to attend meetings at the school during the day or evening. To deal with this problem, the school can set parental involvement as an expectation and provide a menu of options for parental involvement. Parents then can be given support and assistance in choosing from among these. Those parents who do not choose to participate can be contacted to determine the reason for their noninvolvement, and provisions can be made to find times or activities that are suitable to them. These ideas require obvious, significant changes in the structure and organization of the school day and the teachers' contract.

Expanded use of videotape can allow most parents to see their children in action at school in many settings. Outlines of expectations for parental involvement in assignments and projects throughout the year can be sent home for review. In a followup meeting, the specific skills necessary to assist on the project or task (along with necessary materials and equipment) can be explained and reviewed.

The home visit, once a fixture of most social-service agencies and now nearly nonexistent, can be revived as an option. Parents will need to know how and when to request a visit in situations other than crises resulting from inappropriate behavior. A home visit can and should be a time to show the parent how to be involved in the child's education.

Accepting education as a shared responsibility. Education and parenting are two intertwined activities. Teachers and parents can support, but not replace, one another. This message cannot be sent if educators lecture parents as if they were children and restrict involvement to narrowly defined arenas controlled by the educators. At the same time, parent behaviors that abdicate the responsibility for child rearing and nurturing cannot be ignored or condoned. Parent apathy, however convenient politically, cannot be allowed to be the institutionalized norm of the school community. Educators are the ones who will need to take the lead in redefining this relationship, but parents will be called upon to rethink their expectations and assumptions for public education, as well. This is a dialogue that, if successful, will spread beyond teachers and parents to include the broader community.

Perhaps choice will be a mechanism by which parental involvement is created. As parents consciously select a school or program, it is possible to establish clearer expectations beforehand for them and their children. But even if choice is not employed, schools can expect much more of parents than what they do currently and can provide them with information that supports the new expectations. If schools provide varied opportunities for parents to be involved, they can begin to expect greater involvement. If educators are persistent and patient, they can institutionalize this expectation for involvement over time. Involvement is a critical first step toward redefining the roles and responsibilities of parents in the educational process.

THE COMMUNITY

Educators often take a somewhat calculating perspective on the community's obligations to the public schools. Members of the community with no children in school have traditionally been viewed as a commodity to be managed by schools from a public-relations perspective: How can they be encouraged to vote for bond and other tax elections? Other community institutions, such as businesses and governmental agencies with responsibilities for the young, have often been perceived from an equally transactional perspective: How can donations be procured from businesses, and how can community agencies provide services the public schools deem supportive of the schools' mission? The future role of these groups is likely to be much more substantive.

Schools have great difficulty succeeding in dysfunctional communities, though success in such environments is not impossible (Purkey and Smith 1983). Many schools attempting to restructure are developing more interdependent relationships between themselves and the institutions that surround them (Davies 1991b; Liontos 1990; MacDowell 1989). Although schools cannot make communities functional, they can serve as a nucleus for the development of new conceptions of community. For schools to adapt to changes in their communities, they will need to be involved during this period when many places in the country are attempting to redefine, even reinvent, their communities. Schools will be challenged to participate in the process of making communities more functional. Perhaps they can provide more opportunities for people to affiliate with one another in ways that satisfy their mutual self-interest and that motivate them to work together for an enhanced common good.

Admittedly, this prescription for the involvement of schools in the reinvigoration of communities is perhaps a bit overoptimistic. How can schools bring about change in environments where issues of economic deprivation, racism, substance abuse, and lack of resources and opportunities are the dominant themes? Nevertheless, many schools are embarking on just such an exercise because they perceive no other alternative if they are to be successful with young people. They are not attempting this alone; they are working in close concert with public and private community agencies, governments, and business groups (Chrispeels 1991; Cohen, January 23, 1991; Payzant 1989).

Several suggestions of how different groups might be involved in education and in the redefinition of community follow.

Providing learning experiences in the world of work. To succeed with all young people, particularly with those who have been disenchanted with traditional academic environments, schools may have to extend learning beyond the school site and bring many more adults into classrooms (Glatthorn 1991). For this to occur, the community must become an active partner in education. *Community* here is defined broadly to mean all institutions, public and private, that have a stake in a well-educated citizenry and that may contribute to the educational experiences of young people.

Many community agencies and businesses may be asked to mentor students in their workplace, often as interns or observers, rather than as work-study students. They may be expected to help students learn, not just put them to work. This will be a new and, for some, a problematic responsibility. Support, guidance, and financial incentive will need to be offered to those in the private sector to induce large-scale participation.

The movement to provide learning experiences outside schools may have to be developed gradually. But such programs offer a potentially powerful strategy for making school more relevant to students and for easing the transition from school to work while simultaneously enabling the community to reexamine its involvement in education.

Recent reports and writings from the business community show a much greater awareness of the difficulties involved in changing public schools. Many of these reports are beginning to outline in much more specific language the kind of involvement business will need to be prepared to commit to if it is to influence public education (Akers 1990, Cowan 1989, Nancy 1989, National Alliance of Business 1989, Segal and others 1992, J. Smith 1991, Weisman 1991, Widell 1991). These writings suggest that it may be possible to begin the very basic and difficult changes in the relationship between schools and the community suggested here.

Providing loaned expertise to schools. Community members can assist in education within schools on a more regular basis. Many citizens possess content knowledge that is much more up-to-date than that of the teacher. They can bring real-life problems into the school for students to solve. And they infuse greater diversity into the school, making it more likely that a student will connect with an adult.

Letting teachers and administrators work in noneducational settings in structured ways. Many educators have spent their entire lives in schools of one sort or another. They may have difficulty relating student learning to the world outside schools. There need to be many more opportunities for teachers to leave their schools for periods of time to participate in and come to understand other work environments.

There are many examples of such programs where students are provided opportunities to learn about the world they will enter when they leave school (see, for example, Waltner 1992). There are fewer designed to provide teachers with similar experiences. Schools and noneducational organizations can work together closely to provide structured programs of visitation and internship for teachers, both during the school year and the summer. Such programs invigorate teachers and enable them to align their curriculum and teaching methods more closely with the needs of society.

Sharing, coordinating, and combining resources. One example of an area where resources can be shared is facilities construction. Currently, each agency that serves young people constructs its own facility, at great expense. These facilities are scattered throughout the community and may be located inconveniently for the clients to be able to move among them. A first step is to begin to construct these facilities collaboratively, or at least in a coordinated manner.

Other opportunities for sharing resources exist. Sometimes personnel can be shared among agencies, as between schools and parks and recreation departments. Similar arrangements with social welfare agencies are possible, though infrequently explored.

Releasing workers to support education. Business owners can be encouraged to support education by allowing employees to be released from work, perhaps once a month, to visit the public schools, to adopt a school, to provide tutoring, or to visit their children's classrooms more regularly. Such adjustments in work schedules (not additional vacation time) can often be accomplished with relative ease and minimal expense. Among the many benefits of such programs is that many more people can experience the positive feelings associated with helping children to learn. A growing number of employers, large and small, have already adopted such programs.

Creating pressure for fundamental change in education. Educators cannot be expected to transform schools without support and leadership from those outside schools. The role of parents as supporters of change has been mentioned. The larger community has a responsibility as well to be aware of the changes that are needed to transform schooling. A great deal of written material has been prepared that would help employers and employees understand the implications of educational change, or the lack of it, for the business community. Employers can make such materials available in the workplace. Business Roundtables in many states have such materials available.* Chambers of commerce and civic service clubs can devote time not just to understanding the crisis in education, but to becoming aware of its possible solutions and the role they can play. Leaders of local government can be given the opportunity to understand schools in terms other than viewing them simply as another governmental unit competing for resources.

The net effect of these efforts can be to create broad-based awareness and acceptance of the need for educational change. Such a climate makes it more possible for local boards of education and school administrators to support, sustain, and be encouraged to initiate programs that radically reshape education and its relationship to the community.

Being involved in site-based decision-making. Qualified members of the community can be valuable participants in processes such as decentralized decision-making. Site-based decision-making will tend to have less impact on the basic assumptions and practices of schools if energetic, diverse, and imaginative voices from outside schools are not included.

Serving as judges for student demonstrations and assessments. For those not inclined to participate in governance or other formal structures, there can be many more opportunities to contribute to schools without making a long-term, formal commitment. As more alternative assessment practices are instituted, and as the movement to outcome-based education continues in many states, there will likely be more widespread use of senior projects, capstone experiences, portfolio review, public demonstrations of skills, and other techniques that require students to demonstrate publicly their ability to meet certain standards

---

* See, for example: Zimmerman and others (1990), Associated Oregon Industries and The National Association for Schools of Excellence (1992), National Alliance of Business (1989), National Business Roundtable (1988), Berman and others (1988), Melaville and Blank (1991), Segal and others (1992).

and to apply certain skills successfully and competently. These can be judged by others in addition to educators, partly to lend added credibility and gravity to the activity and partly to help keep educators "honest," in the sense of helping them maintain their perspective and standards.

Becoming more aware of education as a shared responsibility. If businesses and corporations continue to believe that there is a relationship between the educational level of their employees and their ability to succeed in the marketplace, more partnerships and working relationships are likely to develop. It behooves both groups to explore ideas such as donations of equipment to schools, movement of school programs to work sites, provision for workers or executives to be "on loan" to a school district, and other innovative ways of strengthening the knowledge and ownership of public education within the total community. Many programs of this type exist and will need to be expanded. Many more will likely be created. This redefinition of roles and responsibilities will take place gradually, in much the same way that the reinvention and redefinition of community are occurring.

SUMMARY

This chapter brings to a close the discussion of the new roles and responsibilities that educational restructuring will require of the most important groups of people both inside and outside schools. Chapters 1-7 describe a framework within which these new roles and relationships may change in a fashion that enables schools to function more effectively and successfully with broad-based support in an environment of clear expectations for all. Is this portrait of change idealistic, unrealistic? Perhaps it is to some degree, particularly if the reader interprets this discussion to be a prescription for new roles or a "how to" that should be put into practice. However, this book is designed to present the emerging *visions* of educational restructuring, and these are the kinds of changes in roles and responsibilities that are, in fact, being actively discussed and pursued in various places throughout the nation. Changes of this magnitude do not take place easily or smoothly. They are uneven in their emergence and impact on practice. They are not necessarily amenable to direct control, particularly by school people.

Then why present them? There are two reasons. First, educators who attempt to change their schools need to be aware of the complexity of the changes facing schools as institutions that exist within a broader social context. And second, people's assumptions about the role of institutions and their relationships to them are powerful forces in determining their behavior in the institutional context. This interplay between education's role in the broader social context and the specific views that individuals hold regarding their relationship to public education will tend to limit and guide restructuring efforts at the school, district, state, and national levels. Perhaps this interaction cannot be controlled, but it can be acknowledged and understood. And perhaps such awareness can enable educators to help guide, channel, or direct the development of these new roles in relationships to some degree.

The discussion now turns from the broad context for educational restructuring to the more specific programs being attempted by schools, what might be thought of as the "content" of restructuring. In part 3, I describe these strategies for restructuring schools in twelve areas. It should be borne in mind that without a reconsideration of the roles and responsibilities of all those associated with the enterprise of schooling, it is unlikely that any of the structural or programmatic modifications described in the next part will, in and of themselves, transform schooling. Many of the ideas and strategies discussed in the coming chapters can provide the impetus for teachers, parents, administrators, and others to alter their view of education, but only if the implementation of these programs is accompanied by a reconsideration of the roles and responsibilities as discussed in the preceding chapters.

P A R T 3

DIMENSIONS

OF

RESTRUCTURING

INTRODUCTION TO PART 3

As educators approach the task of restructuring, the first question many ask is: Where do we begin? Parts 1 and 2 help to establish the broad context for restructuring. Parts 3 and 4 provide more detailed and specific description of the projects, programs, and processes that are being undertaken in the name of restructuring. The chapters in this part, Dimensions of Restructuring, outline many of the activities and programs schools are defining as restructuring.

The activities described in this part fall into two broad categories that I refer to as incremental and discontinuous attempts at change in schools. Incremental change results in gradual adaptations to the existing system. Discontinuous change implies activities that reinvent the way the organization functions. By far the majority of so-called restructuring activities being instituted in schools today belong to the first category of change, and the number of chapters devoted to these activities reflects this imbalance. Chapters 9-20 elaborate on these more prevalent incremental change efforts. The more isolated and infrequent examples of discontinuous changes being attempted in public schools are featured in chapter 21.

Although the distinction between these two types of change becomes somewhat arbitrary after a certain point, the concepts are useful as frameworks within which restructuring activities can be analyzed. This distinction also helps raise and define an important question: Can schools engage in discontinuous change? Can they, in fact, restructure themselves by means of radical transformation? This distinction also raises the inverse question: Can schools transform themselves through incremental change? Will a series of incremental adjustments be adequate to enable schools to retain their institutional legitimacy and the funding that accompanies it? Do schools that take the incremental route have the capacity to sustain the large number of separate, independent projects that will be necessary to achieve the types of radical improvement in student learning being called for from many quarters?

Not every trend or approach to restructuring is included, for obvious reasons. Nor is there an attempt to distinguish elementary from middle-level and high school efforts. This stance is taken in part because many activities and strategies spill across levels (alternative assessment, project-centered learning, teacher leadership, technology, and interdisciplinary curriculum are a few examples). Similarly, while the agendas of urban, suburban, and rural schools are not necessarily the same, the activities presented in the following chapters are possible in all settings and are being discussed by at least some schools in all three environments. It is still too early to define completely an urban or suburban or rural restructuring agenda completely separate from the others.

It should be noted that these varied activities in and of themselves do not necessarily represent or cause restructuring in schools. Whether these activities result in restructuring depends on the ways in which they are implemented and conducted. For example, cooperative learning can be used as a strategy to practice the old math curriculum or to help children develop team problem-solving skills in science; a site-based governance council can simply replicate the inept decision-making of an administrator whom the council replaced or it can make decisions of higher quality and broader ownership.

The reader should bear in mind that the examples of trends and activities presented in the following twelve areas are not necessarily individually or in total "restructuring." Rather, they are a synthesis and summary of the range of strategies educators are considering to respond to external demands and pressures for change. They should be considered tentative and possibly transitory responses. A number of public schools are in a period of rapid and extensive experimentation. No doubt the ideas and trends described here will develop and permutate. It is also critical to note that many schools are talking about these innovations more than they are implementing them, and in the cases where schools implement them, they may be doing so without changing basic relationships and structures.

Restructuring is simultaneously exciting and a bit terrifying for educators. Given the tendency of school personnel to look to one another for models or programs before launching any new effort themselves—what DiMaggio and Powell (1983) call "institutional isomorphism"—this rapidly changing landscape offers little comfort to the faint of heart who are looking for "the answer" or "the restructured school" to emulate. Meaning is being created at the level of the individual school site based on needs and goals defined within a particular school. In this context, the twelve dimensions of restructuring are offered not as a manual but as a "roadmap" of restructuring.

CHAPTER 8

PREVIEW OF THE TWELVE DIMENSIONS

A ctivities and programs designed to bring about changes of one type or another are proliferating in schools today. This burst of energy has led to a remarkable amount of discussion, self-examination, planning, and projects in many schools. Keeping track and making sense of all these projects is difficult for the average educator. The twelve dimensions introduced here and described more fully in chapters 9-20 provide a convenient roadmap to many of the major trends and themes in each of these areas.

Much of what is occurring under the banner of restructuring can be categorized as first-order restructuring, or what Lindblom (1959) described as *incrementalism*—the gradual process of changing dimensions of organizational functioning to improve goal achievement. In theory, the net effect of these myriad small adjustments would be to remake the institution of schooling over time—and without the political disruption associated with more fundamental, rapid change. Kirst (1991) has called this approach to restructuring "project-itis," because schools generally respond by developing a new program or project that becomes defined as the "restructuring project." Upon its completion, the school is considered "restructured."

This notion that schools can be improved incrementally toward some ultimate ideal has been described by Tyack (1990) as "tinkering toward utopia." Implicit in this strategy is a desire to avoid the upheaval and conflict that inevitably accompany second-order change. Also implicit is the idea that schools should pursue improvement for moral, idealistic reasons, rather than in response to shifting market conditions, economic realities, or customer expectations. While the vision of a restructured educational system that schools pursue may be idealistic, the motivation and support for change may derive from shifts in the surrounding social and economic systems. The question to be asked is as follows: Can schools remake themselves (and retain control of the process) in an incremental fashion quickly and profoundly enough to remain in sync with the environment within which they exist, and to respond to the needs of the clients they serve?

It is difficult to make sense of the multitude of activities being undertaken by schools in their attempt to tinker toward utopia. A previous publication (D. Conley, February 1991) offered a framework designed to make some sense of the myriad projects occurring in public education. This framework grouped restructuring activities into eleven broad dimensions, ranging from curriculum to personnel. Although there is considerable overlap, the act of identifying some distinct categories seems to be a useful way to help people understand what might best be described as "incremental restructuring" in public education.

If the term *incremental restructuring* sounds a bit like an oxymoron, that's because it is. This phrase highlights the challenges faced by public schools in their attempt to bring about fundamental change with this approach. Can schools remake themselves fundamentally through a series of projects or programs, however radical, that allow the basic structure and culture of the organization to remain intact? Do schools have the political will and the resources necessary to sustain these incremental changes until the point where cumulatively they have redefined the school as an institution? The evidence at this point has not been encouraging, as one reads descriptions by practitioners and researchers of the difficulty schools have had putting relatively simple programs or changes into place (Brickley and Westerberg 1990; David 1991; Dwyer, Ringstaff, and Sandholtz 1991; Glickman 1989; C. Murphy 1991; Strauber, Stanley, and Wagenknecht 1990; Westerberg and Brickley 1991).

It is worth restating that the act of presenting this framework should not be confused with an affirmation of its use as the sole means or model by which to restructure schools. Rather the framework is designed to make sense of the multitude of activities that schools call restructuring. The model leaves unanswered the larger question of whether schools can, in fact, restructure incrementally. This question will be revisited in part 4, Process of Restructuring.

The twelve dimensions are grouped into three subsets—central, enabling, and supporting variables—to identify their relative importance and the relationship between and among them. Four dimensions that focus directly on student learning are categorized as *central variables*: learner outcomes, curriculum, instruction, and assessment/evaluation. Four dimensions that enhance the learning process are categorized as *enabling variables*: learning environment, technology, school-community relations, and time. Four additional dimensions hold the potential to restructure education but are more removed from the classroom. This final set of dimensions are categorized as *supporting variables*: governance, teacher leadership, personnel structures, and work-

FIGURE 1

DIMENSIONS OF RESTRUCTURING

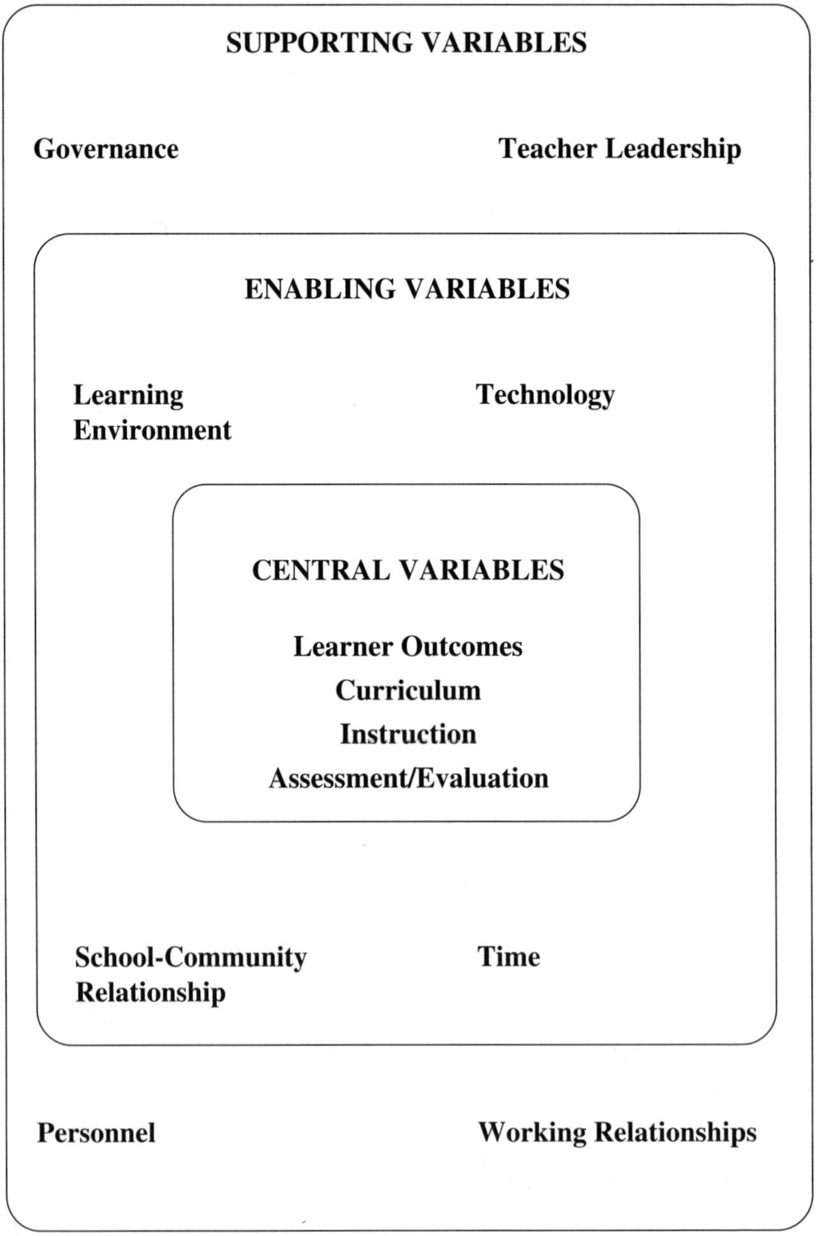

SUPPORTING VARIABLES

Governance   Teacher Leadership

ENABLING VARIABLES

Learning   Technology
Environment

CENTRAL VARIABLES

Learner Outcomes
Curriculum
Instruction
Assessment/Evaluation

School-Community   Time
Relationship

Personnel   Working Relationships

ing relationships. Figure 1 portrays the relationships among these three sets of dimensions.

This chapter presents a general introduction to these dimensions and their three categories. The next twelve chapters offer a more detailed discussion of each dimension.

CENTRAL VARIABLES OF RESTRUCTURING

Learner outcomes, curriculum, instruction, and assessment comprise the central variables of this framework. Changes in these areas are at the heart of teaching, what Elmore (1990) describes as the "core technology" of teaching. These dimensions include everything teachers do that relates to the instructional process: what they teach, how they teach it, how it is measured and evaluated. These activities are, after all, supposedly the raison d'être of public education. If it is possible to bring about change in these areas, then it will be possible to say that education really is experiencing fundamental change.

As might be expected, change at this level is the most difficult to achieve, and this is one place where incremental changes are more difficult to employ. Examination of early restructuring strategies (Lewis 1991, David and others 1990, Lewis 1989) reveal that they rarely reach these central variables, since this is where teachers "live." Teachers' identities are often closely associated with what, who, and how they teach. When developing "restructuring" strategies, most educators appear to prefer to look first at change in almost anything other than these variables.

When educators identify *learner outcomes* they are determining what it is that students should be able to do as a result of the education they receive. Outcomes are statements that delineate those behaviors, knowledge, and skills most valued in the learning process. They indicate the goals students and teachers should pursue and provide a reference point against which student performance can be measured. Outcomes can be stated in terms of the existing curriculum, or they can be phrased in broader, more integrated terms of attaining higher cognitive levels. Outcomes suggest a new relationship of teacher to learner and learner to learning; it is not enough simply to offer learning experiences if the learner cannot demonstrate the ability to apply the learning at some point in a meaningful way. Failure cannot be built into school systems; the system is designed to ensure mastery of outcomes by essentially all students.

Changes in *curriculum* call into question what is worth knowing and how knowledge should best be organized. Much of the traditional structure and content of the curriculum is being closely reexamined, from the national to the state to the local level. Many national subject-matter organizations and state departments of education are issuing new curriculum guidelines. Teachers are becoming more involved as curriculum developers. There are substantial changes occurring in the general education and vocational tracks of high schools. Even the traditional core curriculum for the college-bound is being reassessed. Curriculum change is difficult, given the conflicting policy signals schools receive and the material they use. Such signals are often not congruent with the goals schools pursue.

The variable *instruction* entails all the strategies used to engage students in learning and the assumptions educators have regarding the relationship of the child to the learning experience. Instructional strategies are beginning to include the learner to a greater degree. Learners construct meaning from the experiences presented to them; not everyone learns the same thing from the same experience. There is a greater emphasis on developing the ability to think, reason, and solve problems, rather than simply to memorize information. Moreover, the unique needs of at-risk students are being considered to a greater degree as instruction is reconceptualized.

Assessment encompasses the strategies by which teacher and learner determine the results of the learning process. The goal of assessment is to ascertain the student's performance in relation to outcomes and to enable learners to take more control over their learning. The trend is toward holistic, integrated forms of assessment that serve the primary purpose of improving student performance and the secondary purpose (if at all) of passing a judgment on students or ranking them relative to one another. Assessment may be linked to outcomes, so that everyone knows what is expected of students in any given learning setting. By almost any measure, the range of methods and techniques for assessment is increasing tremendously beyond traditional paper and pencil tests.

ENABLING VARIABLES OF RESTRUCTURING

The ability to bring about changes in the central variables often requires, or is aided by, alterations of other practices closely related to instruction. These variables, called the enabling variables, are *learning environment, technology, school-community relations,* and *time.* This is not to suggest that, in practice, schools proceed to plan for changes in the central variables, then consider how to modify the enabling variables in a way to support changes identified in the central variables. Quite the contrary: In many cases it appears that schools are limiting their focus to these enabling variables and hoping that changes here will ultimately lead to changes in the central variables. The assumption seems to be that if these structural dimensions within which learning occurs are altered, it will cause the methods and content of teaching to change as a result. While this may, in fact, occur at times, there is no guarantee that alterations in the structure and organization of the school automatically translate into changed behavior within classrooms by individual teachers.

The *learning environment* encompasses ways in which the relationship between learner and teacher is structured, such as the number of years an elementary teacher remains with a class of students, the grouping of students by ability or otherwise, the use of schools-within-schools, or the extension of learning beyond the four walls of the school.

Technology is considered as a separate dimension, since it can be used in any number of ways, some of which support restructured learning, others of which do not. In this sense, technology can enable restructuring to occur if used in ways that empower learners and enhance the quality and quantity of student learning. Technology is defined broadly to include many different forms of information-transition and-processing devices. Some of these devices, such as computers and video equipment, are commonly associated with restructuring, but others, such as the telephone, are often overlooked.

School-community relations includes the role parents have as partners in the educational process, as well as the ways the broader community generally and the business community specifically can be involved in the education of young people. Various organizations from the business community have proposed remedies or models to transform public schools. This dimension also encompasses the newly emerging collaborative relationships between schools and social-service agencies. Finally, educators in restructuring schools are experimenting with strategies to involve and communicate with parents.

The dimension *time* refers to altering the school schedule in some way, either in terms of the way time is allocated within the school day or in terms of the length of the school day or year. A variety of options and models have been proposed. Some educators have succumbed to the temptation of thinking that by making changes in this single dimension, they are engaged in restructuring.

A great deal of energy is being devoted to programs focused on these variables. Programs in these dimensions can have the appearance of being significant changes without engendering the political opposition that changes in the central variables tend to arouse. In secondary schools in particular, changing the scheduling of time is especially popular, but it is not necessarily accompanied by the changes in classroom teaching that must occur for any new schedule to affect student learning. Elementary schools may favor the introduction of a computer lab to demonstrate that they are keeping up with the times. Closer examination may reveal that the lab is staffed by an aide and that teachers drop off their classes at the lab; because the technology has not penetrated the classroom, it has not had an impact on the central variables.

Apparently, some reform-minded educators hope that by changing the schedule, developing schools-within-schools or multiage elementary classrooms, creating technology labs, or involving parents more in the education of their children, sufficient pressure will be created to induce change in the central variables. The assumption—a big one—is that teachers will be compelled to alter basic practices in the face of changes in the structures that surround their classroom. It is worth noting that there is little evidence at this point to support this assumption.

SUPPORTING VARIABLES OF RESTRUCTURING

There is another level at which changes are occurring that are being labeled as "restructuring." By and large, these address organizational conditions of teaching and schooling. These variables are the furthest removed from classroom life in their immediate impact and are, paradoxically, being touted by some reformers as the prerequisites to any change in classroom behaviors. These variables include *governance, teacher leadership, personnel structures*, and *working relationships*.

All initiatives to decentralize decision-making in schools fall under the category of *governance*, be they site-based management, participatory management, school-based decision-making, or any of the variations on this theme. These attempts were among the initial remedies offered to restructure schools (Clinchy 1989, David 1989, Elmore 1988, Guthrie 1986, Mertens and Yarger 1988). They are threatening and difficult to implement successfully because they force administrators to redefine the ways in which they exercise power, and they are often greeted with suspicion and cynicism by teachers who may be particularly concerned about new governance models that require significantly more time on their part.

Many site-based management schemes do not require all teachers to do anything new or different. Other than being asked to attend a meeting of a "site council," the teacher may continue in his or her isolation, and change can be left to those who have an interest in it. Not surprisingly, the focus of such site-based decision-making structures often becomes teacher working conditions, not teacher performance in the classroom or student learning outcomes, since there are no parameters that clearly focus the process on teaching and learning.

Issues of choice in public education are also included in this category. There are at least three types of choice: choice within a school, choice among schools in a district, and choice between public and nonpublic educational options. Choice continues to surface in many policy proposals and appears to be gaining credibility among policymakers at the federal and state levels. Among the public, broad philosophical agreement regarding choice is reflected in the 1991 Gallup Poll, which found supporters outnumbered nonsupporters by nearly a two-to-one ratio among virtually every major segment of the population, including parents of public school children (Elam and others 1991). Nevertheless, the specific programs offered to operationalize this emerging support of choice continue to disappoint.

The evolving sense of teacher professionalism has led to a proliferation of new programs of *teacher leadership*. Some of the new roles being created are familiar, such as the role of mentor teacher; others, such as site team leader or teacher researcher, are less familiar. Many schools are experimenting with roles for teachers such as teacher-as-reflective practitioner, in-building staff developer, lead teacher, or team leader. Many of these roles blur the boundary between "labor" and "management." Teachers are undertaking many tasks that have been considered at least quasi-administrative. They are also exercising more control over working conditions through site committees and other governance structures. These new leadership roles can threaten the existing leadership (and social) structure present in a school, as new leaders emerge and traditional ones are displaced.

The way *personnel* are employed to staff schools is another dimension along which restructuring may occur. The current personnel structure has two categories: (1) professional, or certificated, staff in the form of administrators and teachers; and (2) classified staff, generally in roles such as instructional assistants, secretaries, custodians, and food service workers. In terms of education, training, salary, and responsibility, the gap between certificated and classified staff is generally quite large. Given a future that seems to indicate no major increases in funding for public education, it seems likely that public schools will need to consider reallocating existing resources as part of any attempt to restructure. Since between 70 and 90 percent of a typical school district's budget is allocated to personnel costs, it seems clear that an examination of how these resources are employed will occur.

The dimension *working relationships* refers primarily to contractual relationships between teachers and administrators and boards of education. Changes in contracts can support change in classrooms and schools, but rarely cause it. Many changes in this dimension involve the addition of what is called permissive language; individual sites are permitted to receive waivers from the contract if certain procedures are followed (such as a majority vote of the faculty), but, once again, no site is required to do so. Other changes include the development of Policy Trust Agreements and the use of collaborative-bargaining techniques to build trust, improve problem-solving abilities, and enhance communication. The intent of changes in working relationships often appears to be to create a more "professional" working relationship between leaders of the teachers' organization and the administration, which is considered a precursor to more substantive change.

These twelve dimensions help capture and categorize the thicket of projects and programs currently under way in schools. Some of these ideas have originated in schools or districts; others have come about as the result of state mandates. In either event, they offer a picture of the daunting challenges facing schools attempting to remake themselves. Where and how schools can be expected to get the resources and energy necessary to attempt changes of this magnitude and complexity will be examined in a later chapter devoted to the process of restructuring. For now, suffice it to say that schools involved with restructuring face a Herculean task, described by Schlechty (1990) as akin to changing a flat tire on a car that is moving down the highway at sixty miles per hour, or rebuilding an airplane while it's in flight.

CHAPTER 9

LEARNER OUTCOMES

A s educators at school sites begin to explore different approaches to education, they find themselves asking what it is they want students to know and be able to do, not just what learning experiences educators want to offer. Educators are challenged to define what they want to measure and to establish the standards against which success is to be determined. Such a process can easily lead to a reconsideration of the entire curricular and instructional program, both its structure and relevance. These are difficult topics for teachers to discuss; the very nature of what they teach and how they teach it is called into question.

To their credit, some schools and school districts are beginning to identify learner outcomes that are not merely restatements of the traditional curriculum: They are identifying outcomes that will require an integration of the traditional curricular structure and could conceivably lead to an abandonment of it.

This step, the identification of learner outcomes clearly stated in ways that can be assessed, is a watershed activity in the process to refocus education. Historically, schools have not been committed to producing outcomes, only to conducting specified educational processes. Courses have the proper titles, include the proper objectives, and are taught by someone with the proper certificate for the proper number of minutes. When students are subjected to these routinized processes, learning, *by definition,* is said to have occurred.

The movement to outcomes, what Finn (1990) describes as the "biggest reform of all," has the potential to reshape the face of public education. The old saying, "Hey, I taught it: If they didn't learn it, that's their problem," would be replaced with "Hey, they can't demonstrate they learned it: What should we be doing differently?"

EFFORTS TO DEVELOP PERFORMANCE-BASED STANDARDS

Several states are switching from Carnegie units to outcomes as the standard for determining educational achievement (O'Neil 1992a, Pipho 1992). The Pennsylvania State Board of Education adopted new assessment and curriculum regulations that had the effect of abolishing Carnegie units as the standard for high school graduation. These are to be replaced by "learner outcomes," which require students to demonstrate mastery. Pipho (1992) describes Pennsylvania's "quality education goals":

> The primary goals include specific outcomes in such areas as communication, mathematics, science and technology, environment and ecology, citizenship, appreciation and understanding of others, arts and humanities, career education and work, and wellness and fitness, along with personal, family, and community living. The board also adopted a common core of learning that includes developing a sense of self-worth, acquiring information and thinking skills, learning independently and collaboratively, adapting to change, and making ethical judgments. (p. 663)

In Oregon, legislation passed in June 1991 mandates the creation of the Certificates of Initial and Advanced Mastery, to be awarded at approximately ages 16 and 18. To obtain these certificates, students must also demonstrate mastery on outcomes. The general areas for mastery stated in the law include the ability to read, write, problem solve, think critically, and communicate across disciplines; and to exhibit the capacity to learn, think, reason, retrieve information, work effectively alone, and work effectively in groups. Methods of demonstrating mastery include work samples, tests, portfolios, and a culminating project or exhibition that demonstrates attainment of required knowledge and skills. Work is under way to develop more specific indicators that define what mastery in these areas means.

Minnesota required all school districts to ensure that each graduate demonstrates achievement in seven outcomes at no less than an adept level, as defined by state regulation. Each Minnesota graduate shall demonstrate the knowledge, skills, and attitudes essential to:

- communicate with words, numbers, visuals, symbols, and global communities
- think and solve problems to meet personal, social, and academic needs
- contribute as a citizen in a local, state, national, and global community
- understand diversity and the interdependence of people
- work cooperatively in groups and independently
- develop physical and emotional well-being

• contribute to the economic well-being of society (Minnesota Department of Education 1992)

The Aurora, Colorado, Public Schools has done extensive work developing learner outcomes. This district began with five general learner outcomes:

• Self-directed learners, who use positive core values to create a positive vision for themselves and their future, set priorities and achievable goals, create options for themselves, monitor and evaluate their progress, and assume responsibility for their actions

• Collaborative workers, who use effective leadership and group skills to develop and manage interpersonal relationships and organizationally diverse settings

• Complex thinkers, who identify, access, integrate, and use available resources and information to reason, make decisions, and solve complex problems in a variety of contexts

• Community contributors, who contribute their time, energies, and talents to improving the welfare of others and the quality of life in their diverse communities

• Quality producers, who create intellectual, artistic, practical, and physical products which reflect originality, high standards, and the use of advanced technologies (Aurora Public Schools 1992)

The district then created additional outcomes in the following specific content areas:

• Arts and Humanities

• Career Management

• Communication

• Environmental Issues

• International/Multicultural Issues

• Life Management

• Mathematics Proficiency

• Science Literacy

• Social Sciences

• Technology (Aurora Public Schools 1992)

Aurora has continued the design and implementation process necessary to move outcomes to the center of the instructional process.

The district has developed the various performance indicators and levels necessary to enable teachers to develop instruction and assessment tools that are congruent with the outcomes.

Reynolds High School, in Troutdale, Oregon, identified seven general exit outcomes for students based on standards first developed by Aurora, Colorado, Public Schools. These outcomes embody the vision, mission, goals, and operating principles of their community. The Reynolds School District expects its graduating students to demonstrate that they are becoming:

- quality producers

- collaborative contributors

- effective communicators

- adaptable problem solvers/perceptive thinkers

- community contributors

- individual achievers

- lifelong learners

For example, under the "collaborative contributor" outcome, Reynolds High School students will use leadership and group skills to develop and manage interpersonal relationships within diverse settings and to demonstrate conflict prevention and resolution, responsibility, cooperation, and the ability to anticipate, assess, and resolve problems in a group setting. As "community contributors," students are expected to understand and participate in local, state, and federal governments and demonstrate an understanding of and respect for multicultural diversity and global relationships.

The next important step is to identify exemplars of each of these exit outcomes and specify assessment strategies that will be employed to determine mastery.

The Alameda, California, Unified School District has developed a very comprehensive set of outcome statements. These outcomes are combined into a "Graduate Profile" that "represents a broad array of outcomes that should result from the entire K-12 school experience, including academic skills and knowledge, personal and social skills, attitudes and attributes" (Alameda Unified School District 1992). The following elements comprise the Alameda graduate profile:

I. Personal Qualities/Work Habits and Attitudes:

Displays responsibility, self-esteem, sociability, self-management, and integrity and honesty.

II. New Basics/Skills:

Reads, writes, performs arithmetic and mathematical operations, listens and speaks, possesses historical, cultural, geographic and economic understandings, thinks scientifically and applies scientific principles to life, values and appreciates the arts and nurtures one's own health and well being.

III. Thinking Skills and Reasoning:

Thinks creatively, makes decisions, solves problems, visualizes, knows how to learn and reason.

IV. Interpersonal/Collaborative Ability:

Works with others.

V. Technology:

Works with a variety of technologies. (Alameda Unified School District 1992)

A series of subheads corresponding to the various elements stated in the heading were then developed. For example, under IV (Interpersonal/ Collaborative Ability) are listed the following subheadings:

A. *Participates as a Member of a Team*: Contributes cooperatively to group effort with ideas, suggestions, and hard work.

B. *Teaches Others New Skills*: Helps others learn.

C. *Serves Clients/Customers/Colleagues*: Develops work-ready ability and attitude; works to satisfy customers' expectations.

D. *Exercises Leadership*: Communicates ideas to justify position, persuades and convinces others, responsibly challenges existing procedures and policies, motivates others. Argues sensitively in an informed, measured way.

E. *Negotiates*: Works toward agreement involving exchange of resources, resolves divergent interests, chooses non-violent solutions.

F. *Works with Diversity*: Works well with others from diverse backgrounds and accepts and rejoices in diversity. Develops a sensitivity to and an understanding of the needs, opinions, concerns and customs of others. (Alameda Unified School District 1992)

The Alameda model goes one level of detail further by providing indicators for each of these subareas. For example, under A *(Participates as a Member of a Team)* are listed the following defining statements, or indicators:

• Cooperate with others.
• Contribute positively to a group effort.
• Participate in reaching group decisions.

- Interact in a socially appropriate manner.

- "Carry one's own load."

- Appreciate the roles and responsibilities of parents, children, and family. (Alameda Unified School District 1992)

The Alameda school district's model exemplifies some of the issues surrounding outcomes. First, the level of detail developed in the outcomes is somewhat arbitrary. In other words, there is no ideal or perfect level of detail. In general, a level of detail adequate to allow for the development of instructional and assessment activities and the identification of performance levels is needed. Different districts will define this level of detail differently.

Second, outcomes specify values in ways that most school systems have not previously attempted. These outcomes state more clearly the behavior and beliefs that are valued in a democratic, pluralistic society. Given the increasing responsibility schools have to socialize children, this greater emphasis on an explicit value system for public education should not be surprising. However, many parents and organized groups in the community will find any mention of values objectionable. In fact, Pennsylvania's attempt to implement outcomes encountered stiff opposition at least in part on this issue (Rothman, September 23, 1992).

Another example of how a district can move to develop new, integrated performance standards is represented by Adams County School District 14, Commerce City, Colorado. This district's exit outcomes, mastery of which is necessary for a high school diploma, comprise four general elements and eighteen demonstration components, which are listed below. Performance indicators have been developed for each component, and assessment strategies will be developed.

General Academic Skills

- Demonstrate the ability to use effectively the communication skills of reading, writing, speaking, and listening

- Demonstrate the ability to understand and apply basic mathematical functions and principles in real-life problem solving situations

- Demonstrate knowledge and understanding of the basic principles, concepts, and language of the natural sciences

- Demonstrate a functional level of computer and technological literacy.

- Demonstrate knowledge and understanding of the history, geography, government, and economic systems of the United States and other countries

Problem Solving Skills

• Demonstrate skills in individual and group problem solving and decision making

• Demonstrate the ability to identify and critically analyze problems

Social Literacy and Responsibility

• Demonstrate an understanding of one's rights and responsibilities in a democratic society

• Demonstrate an understanding of the implications of the cultural diversity of this country

• Demonstrate knowledge and understanding of world cultures

• Demonstrate the knowledge and understanding necessary for environmentally responsible behavior

• Demonstrate an understanding of the arts as an expression of culture and personal creativity

Personal Effectiveness

• Demonstrate the interpersonal skills necessary to be personally and professionally effective

• Demonstrate the ability to develop and implement plans for achieving personal and career goals

• Demonstrate knowledge of effective employment skills

• Demonstrate knowledge and understanding of maintaining personal emotional and physical health

• Demonstrate an understanding of the personal and economic responsibilities of adulthood

• Demonstrate the skills necessary to be an effective life-long learner (Adams County School District 14, 1991, p. 3)

Littleton High School in Littleton, Colorado, moved to a dramatically new system of schooling for freshmen who entered in fall 1991. Education at Littleton High School is driven by performance-based graduation requirements. Graduation will be contingent on demonstrations of what students actually know and can do, not on the number of credits earned or the amount of time spent in class. Students become eligible for graduation when they demonstrate mastery of nineteen performance-based graduation requirements through portfolios and exhibitions before a graduation committee. Portfolios include samples of students' work, essays, special projects, tests scores, and grades. Exhibitions are opportunities for students to demonstrate knowledge and skills to the graduation committee. Students' instructional plans are personalized through a Program Advisor based on individual student's strengths, weaknesses, goals, and aspirations.

Several years of planning and development preceded the implementation of Littleton's performance-based system in fall 1991. The plan was directed by a steering committee made up of the principal, nine teachers, and seven working subcommittees. Topics of the subcommittees were graduation requirements, curriculum, K-12 articulation, postgraduation articulation, public relations, staff development, and project evaluation.

The curriculum committee drafted thirteen integrated learner outcomes for the ninth-grade class of 1991-92, the first cohort of students who will graduate under the new system. The ninth-grade performance-based curriculum is structured around thirteen integrated learning outcomes. In addition to communication skills of speaking, writing, reading, listening, and facility with another language, the Littleton High School Class of 1995 will be required to demonstrate proficiency and/or understanding in the following areas:

- community involvement
- consumer economics
- critical thinking
- ethics
- human relations
- literary arts
- mathematics
- personal growth
- sciences
- social and world relations
- technology
- visual and performing arts

In many school districts across the country, educators are beginning to integrate discussion of assessment strategies with identification of performance outcomes. If old outcomes are retained while new assessments are adopted, the result will likely be old wine in new skins: Changing measurement techniques will not alter outcomes if teachers still believe implicitly that they are seeking to achieve existing educational goals (Roemer 1991). The development, *first* of newly defined outcomes, and *then* of assessment strategies, is one way to ensure that the instructional program is driven by the desired outcomes, rather than vice-versa.

Most of the preceding examples of outcome-based systems that are being developed by states and school districts either do not explicitly mention content-related standards or mention them in very general terms. Considerable discussion is occurring about how such standards might be developed and what they would look like, nationally and at state and local levels (Who's Who, October 23, 1991; Viadero, April 1,

1992). It is difficult to conceive of process-related standards separate from content. Students must learn *about* something in order to practice the processes, and, in any event, the public currently defines education in terms of what students know, the content they have mastered. The following sections provide examples of an integrated set of standards that addresses both content and process goals of education.

CONTENT-RELATED STANDARDS

These standards form the functional core of the curriculum and reflect the minimum expectations of society for schools. They guarantee to society that traditional core competencies will be taught and assessed systematically. It is important not to overload the standards with too much detail; at the same time, it should be emphasized that these are absolute minimum expectations. Individual districts, schools, and teachers must decide what needs to be added to these minimums, and how they must be combined with meaningful learning activities in order to lead to mastery.

A *content standard* comprises an information base along with rules, laws, or principles in enough specificity to form a generally recognized discipline or body of knowledge. It is assessed through demonstration of mastery of the structure and content of desired knowledge and by its application to real-world problems. Note that it is quite possible to construct standards and indicators that dictate integrated, cross-disciplinary teaching and application of learning. Some examples of content-related standards follow:

- *Reading*

  Functional literacy skills

  Knowledge of literature

- *Writing*

  Functional literacy skills

  Mastery of various writing styles

- *Mathematical computation and concepts*

  Computational mastery

  Addition, subtraction, multiplication, division

  Conceptual mastery

  Topics where it is important to understand the mathematical concept, but not as critical to demonstrate automaticity in computation (fractions, percentages, algebraic concepts)

Problem-solving ability (application to genuine problems and real-world situations)

Additional mathematical concepts

Statistics, estimation, logic

- *Historical/geographical information*

Historical and geographical facts that can be agreed to be of general importance

- *Democratic principles*

Information about traditions, processes, and values critical to functioning as a citizen in a democracy

- *Cross-cultural awareness and communication*

Mastery of foreign language(s) as a tool for understanding of others

Ability to understand, communicate with, and relate to peoples from differing cultural backgrounds, both within the United States and from other countries.

- *Scientific principles*

Basic principles and knowledge fundamental to the understanding of the natural world

- *Aesthetic techniques*

Methods of understanding and participating in art, music, drama, crafts, creative expression

- *Physical coordination/stamina/wellness*

Small and large-motor coordination and the ability to possess stamina adequate to complete common life tasks, principles of wellness.

PROCESS-RELATED STANDARDS

These standards reflect the concern expressed by many critics of schooling, both within education and in the private sector, that the focus of public education is no longer relevant to the world in which children will live. These standards will be the ones that cause schools to examine their curricular and instructional programs and bring about the types of radical transformations that will lead to enhanced student learning.

A *process element* is an intellectual or affective process consisting of attitudes, behaviors, beliefs, skills, or techniques that may be applied in a wide range of situations and to a wide variety of learning situations in ways that help in the comprehension and processing of information. Process elements are generally (though not always) assessed in their application to content, not independently from it; generally they can be assessed in several different content areas. Some commonly mentioned process standards include the following:

- *Teamwork*—Working with others to create products, solve problems, or reach conclusions in ways that utilize all members of the group

- *Problem solving*—Applying information to a real-world problem in ways that demonstrate understanding of both the information and the problem

- *Use of information*—Selecting and evaluating from among diverse information sources to reach a conclusion, to include the use of technology

- *Self-esteem*—Demonstrating positive sense of self through actions and decisions

- *Goal-setting*—Creating and achieving realistic personal goals

- *Community involvement*—Functioning as a contributing member of a community

- *Career awareness*—Demonstrating awareness of career options as they relate to personal strengths and interests

- *Creativity*—Creating original pieces of work, combining existing works to create new products

- *Communication*—Using language in all its forms along with other forms of visual communication to convey complex ideas, solve problems, express feelings

- *Quality work*—Producing work of a high quality consistently; understanding the elements of quality

- *Systems awareness*—Demonstrating understanding of social, organizational, and technological systems and the relationship of the individual to such systems

- *Integrative thinking* Using information from a variety of disciplines in an integrated fashion to demonstrate understanding of the world or to solve problems

These examples of learner outcomes reflect the changing purposes of education and the emerging assumption that it has economic utility for nearly all students. Schooling is not seen simply as an end in itself, as a way to "get into college," or as a means to keep children off the streets and out of the job market. Instead, education, as now conceived, leads to demonstrable changes in student behaviors, changes that can be assessed using agreed-upon standards.

These standards have various roots; it is apparent that the educators who write the standards pay attention to the reports released by organizations outside the educational community. Standards adopted by schools represent a synthesis of many of the current documents that specify stated expectations for American students, including the America 2000 goals (Miller 1991), Workplace Basics (Carnevale, Gainer, and Meltzer 1990), and the SCANS Report (Secretary's Commission on Achieving Necessary Skills 1991), among others. In addition, they attempt to reflect the unique educational goals that different communities choose to pursue, while also emphasizing things that are generally valued by society at large.

This notion of standards as expressions of values is central to understanding this movement. Although many of the standards, or outcomes, may not look terribly different from existing activities, there is a valuing process going on here nonetheless. In many cases, educators, boards of education, and parents are affirming for the first time what is most important, what must be mastered by all students, what the core values of the school as an educational institution are. Some lists of outcomes attempt to capture everything that is currently taught in schools, but most do not. They at least imply that some things may, in fact, be more important than others. They also emphasize that the habits of thinking and attitudes toward learning that are developed are as important as the specific content that is taught.

CHAPTER 10

CURRICULUM

The importance of changes in curriculum may seem to be self-evident, but there is evidence that restructuring in many schools has yet to have much impact on this core area of schooling. Smith and O'Day (1991) discuss the centrality of changes in curriculum and instruction as a component of any systematic program of restructuring and the challenges that accompany attempts to restructure curriculum:

> Although restructuring literature stresses the critical importance of developing complex problem-solving and higher order thinking skills in our youth, achieving this goal requires a major reorientation in *content and pedagogy* as well as in the structure of the educational enterprise. Perhaps more importantly, it requires a reconceptualization of the knowledge and skills we expect our children to learn, and of the teaching and learning process. This in turn will require that existing elementary and secondary teachers learn, and learn to teach, considerable amounts of new material in the physical and social sciences, humanities, and mathematics. (p. 234)

Meaningful, long-term change in education does not occur without curriculum reform. Lewis (1991) reports results from a study of urban middle schools involved in reform or restructuring. She uses the following excerpts from an interview with Joyce Epstein to make the point that curricular reform is central to school restructuring. As Epstein points out, reform of the curriculum is a challenging, critical component necessary, but often lacking, for the transformation of urban schools:

> The hard work of making urban middle schools successful lies in the curriculum. This is not where schools usually begin when they consider reforms. Too many never get to this point at all and instead become enmeshed and discouraged with organizational change. Joyce Epstein of The Johns Hopkins University, studying the effects of curriculum offerings on eighth graders, observes: "The core—the essence—of any school is its curriculum and instruction. No matter what else is improved in the name of school reform or restructuring, if the curriculum does not challenge the students or if the instructional approaches are inappropriate, the students will not learn as much as they might, nor will they develop a love for learning.... Schools usually work first on mechanical changes that are

immediately visible, such as creating teams of teachers who work in wings of schools; or establishing seven-, or eight-, or 16-period days; or scheduling a teacher-group advisory period to discuss students' concerns and development. These are important but not sufficient reformations for improving middle grades education and increasing the success of early adolescents." (Lewis 1991, p. 61)

Underlying many of the changes in curriculum are changing assumptions regarding knowledge itself (Murphy 1991). One basic assumption underlying much curriculum—that knowledge is objective and exists independent of human thought and action—is being reexamined. "Learning is a social phenomenon," argues Murphy:

> New views about what is worth learning are emerging in restructuring schools. In these classrooms, the traditional emphasis on content coverage and rote learning of basic skills is being challenged by more in-depth treatment of topics and a focus on higher order thinking skills....
>
> ... The teacher-centered instruction that is at the heart of the factory model of classroom instruction is giving way to growing demands for learner-centered pedagogy. (Murphy 1991, pp. 19-20)

An examination of modifications being undertaken in each curricular area is beyond the scope of this book. However, it is possible to discuss some general trends. These include attempts to strike a new balance between depth versus coverage in the curriculum; changes in curriculum development; efforts to achieve greater balance between subject area content and intellectual processes through infusion of tasks that generate higher-level thinking; extensive experimentation with curriculum integration; changes in the way curriculum is developed; the role of various national reports suggesting new conceptualizations of particular subject areas or disciplines; new structures for vocational education; and the challenge for traditional core academic courses.

DEPTH VERSUS COVERAGE IN THE CURRICULUM

Perhaps the major problem that will have to be addressed in curriculum restructuring is the issue of depth versus coverage. The current view of the curriculum present in most American schools holds that it should expose all students to as much important knowledge as possible. Teachers often talk of "covering" the curriculum, perhaps not noting that "to cover" is defined as "to hide from sight." As long as curriculum is designed to cover as much as possible in as little depth as possible, it will be very difficult to achieve the depth of understanding envisioned by many who are calling for educational restructuring.

The debate over depth versus coverage begins with the crucial, and controversial, issue of what is worth knowing and what is the school's rightful role in the intellectual development of the learner:

> The aim of precollegiate education is not to eliminate ignorance. The view that everything of importance can be thoughtfully learned by the 12th grade—notice I did not say "taught"—is a delusion. Those who would treat schooling as designed to educate students on all important subjects are doomed to encounter the futility that faced Sisyphus: the boulder of "essential content" can only come thundering down the (growing) hill of knowledge....
>
> ... The inescapable dilemma at the heart of curriculum and instruction must, once and for all, be made clear: either teaching everything of importance reduces it to trivial, forgettable verbalisms or lists; or schooling is a *necessarily* inadequate apprenticeship, where "preparation" means something quite humble: learning to know and do a few important things well and leaving out much of importance. The negotiation of the dilemma hinges on enabling students to learn about their ignorance, to gain control over the resources available for making modest dents in it, and to take pleasure in learning so that the quest is lifelong.
>
> An authentic education will therefore consist of developing the *habits of mind and high standards of craftsmanship* necessary in the face of one's (inevitable) ignorance....
>
> ... The task is to *reorganize* curriculums more than to add or subtract from them. The aim is to establish clear inquiry priorities within a course, around which facts are learned. (Wiggins 1989, pp. 44-47, emphasis in original)

Wiggins goes on to point out that if high standards are applied consistently, not all students need to learn exactly the same thing. He also asserts that an understanding of the outcomes sought by the teacher, rather than the material to be covered, must be the starting point for determining essentials, and that "the essentials" are not synonymous with "the basics." The essentials recur in different guises and levels of difficulty within a course of study and over the term of a child's education.

Wiggins also points out challenges that are arising as the goal of the curriculum changes and teachers exercise more control over curriculum development:

> The implication for curriculum design in all of this is profound: if the students' questions partially determine the direction of the course, it will no longer be possible to write scope and sequence lesson plans in advance. The teacher and the students must have the intellectual freedom to go where essential questions lead, within bounds set by the general questions, themes, and concepts of the syllabus. The teacher must have access to

material that offers a variety of specific inquiries to pursue, with suggestions on how to deepen student responses and to use the text as a more effective resource. *The textbook, instead of being the syllabus outline and content, would be a reference book for student and teacher questions as they naturally arise.* (p. 47, emphasis in original)

If curriculum reform means injecting more higher-order cognitive tasks into the existing fact-based, basic-skills curriculum, this may result in even greater gaps in achievement between the "haves" and the "have nots":

> What is particularly disturbing is that, with regard to the higher-level cognitive goals now proposed,... basic skills models may further disadvantage those students already at risk in our schools. While an emphasis on isolated facts and skills is unlikely to foster complex thinking skills among students generally, less-advantaged students often lack a surrounding environment that helps them fill in the gaps and draw the connections necessary to construct complex meaning in such situations (Peterson, 1986). (Smith and O'Day 1991, p. 240)

It is difficult for many in education to rethink their assumptions about the curriculum (and their role in delivering that curriculum) at the level Wiggins and Smith and O'Day suggest. Curriculum reform is made all the more difficult by the "fragmented policy system [that] makes substantial, widespread change in instructional practice and curriculum virtually impossible" (Smith and O'Day 1991). However, there are a number of attempts at significant curriculum revision already under way in several subject areas (see, for example: Commission on Standards for School Mathematics 1989; West, April 1991; National Center for Improving Science Education 1989; National Science Teachers Association 1989; Curriculum Task Force of the National Commission on Social Studies in the Schools 1989). These projects will be discussed briefly later in this chapter. Their effect on practice is yet to be determined, but their impact on policy discussions has been substantial in many instances (Viadero, September 23, 1992).

BALANCING CONTENT AND PROCESS

Many schools have already been struggling for some time to create a balance between transmission of content and development of intellectual processes. Public schools have been criticized for failing to produce students who think. Most of the existing curriculum developed during the seventies and early eighties, the heyday of behavioral objectives and "back to the basics," is heavily oriented toward discrete, observable, measurable behaviors and competencies. This focus, combined with measurement technologies and techniques that are more amenable to capturing information about low-level cognitive skills, helped ensure that classroom teaching in the eighties emphasized short-term retention of information in an unconnected manner by students. Lewis (1990) explains the impact on the curriculum of the educational reforms of the early eighties and quotes Clune and others to support her assertion that the addition of more required courses did not necessarily lead to enhanced student thinking:

> The cheap, easy policy of requiring students to take more core academic subjects passed over the nation's classrooms with hardly a ripple. Higher requirements resulted in more students, especially middle- and low-achievers, enrolling in basic academic courses, according to William Clune and others [1989] in a study for the Center for Policy Research in Education. However, higher requirements "failed in getting students into the most rigorous possible courses, in producing a reasonably uniform education for all students, and, probably, in conveying the higher-order skills necessary for a competitive economy." (Lewis 1990, p. 534)

The conception of knowledge as a tool for intellectual development, emphasized in the sixties perhaps to the neglect of more specific content knowledge, tended to be downplayed. The abilities to think critically, solve a problem, present a rationale for a choice, argue convincingly for a point of view, or research an issue were skills that were not necessarily emphasized or tested extensively in the program of instruction offered to the vast majority of students in the late seventies and throughout the eighties. (A subset of students, generally those who were college-bound, did receive a program of instruction that encouraged them to develop these abilities.) This neglect of process skills led to the inevitable fragmentation of knowledge into "infobits," and to graduates who appeared unable to apply much of what they had learned to real-world situations.

The results from the National Assessment of Educational Progress (NAEP) seem to verify this conclusion. A report on the NAEP results states:

> The curriculum is treated as a collection of discrete content areas in which teachers move from one topic to another in lockstep fashion. As a result, lessons are often developed in isolation from one another and fail to help students relate their new learnings to what they already know. (Applebee, Langer, and Mullis 1989, p. 33)

Lewis (1990) elaborates on the lessons the NAEP reports teach about the content and structure of the curriculum:

> The NAEP reports have been consistent in their findings about the inability of students to go beyond basic skills—their inability to elaborate, to synthesize, and to solve problems. While this failing is certainly related to uncreative instructional strategies, dull content is considered equally at

fault. The pattern begins with the minimalism of basal readers, say the curriculum reports, and continues through secondary texts and the minimum competency testing that emphasizes discrete, unelaborated skills. (p. 535)

One of the challenges facing curriculum developers in the nineties is how to restore (or create) a balance between content and process. How can students be motivated, first to identify the information they need for the particular learning at hand, and then to apply that information in ways that result in the information being retained and integrated into more general thinking strategies? This will be a formidable task in schools where students have fared quite well simply by reciting a minimal amount of factual information.

CURRICULUM INTEGRATION

Perhaps the strategy that is being explored and enacted in the most schools currently is curriculum integration, particularly in elementary schools, and in middle schools where traditional academic subjects such as English and social studies or math and science are combined. Numerous permutations exist. In fact, the combinations being attempted to breach the boundaries of the disciplines are too numerous to mention. Almost any association of subject areas can be found if one looks at enough schools. The vigor and creativity behind this movement to develop integration of knowledge at the school level is impressive.

Integrated curriculum can take many different structural forms. Vars (1991) identifies three distinctly different strategies: all-school themes, interdisciplinary teams, and core curriculum. These strategies exist along a continuum of increasing collaboration among staff on teaching duties and consensus on core elements of the curriculum itself. As agreement is reached about what students should know in broad terms, collaboration and integration can increase. If a school allows each teacher to determine individually what his or her students should learn, integration is nearly impossible.

Fogarty (1991), providing even greater detail, describes ten ways to integrate curriculum:

Beginning with an exploration *within single disciplines* (the fragmented, connected, and nested models), and continuing with models that integrate *across several disciplines* (the sequenced, shared, webbed, threaded, and integrated models), the continuum ends with models that operate *within* learners themselves (the immersed model) and finally *across* networks of learners (the networked model).

The *fragmented* model, the traditional design for organizing the curriculum, dictates separate and distinct disciplines....

... The *connected* model... provid[es] a close-up of the details, subtleties, and interconnections within one discipline. While the disciplines remain separate, this model focuses on making explicit connections within each subject area.... The key to this model is the deliberate effort to relate ideas within the discipline, rather than assuming that students will automatically understand the connections....

...The *nested* model... takes advantage of natural combinations. For example, an elementary lesson on the circulatory system could target the concept of systems, as well as facts and understandings about the circulatory system in particular....

...[In] [t]he *sequenced model*..., [a]lthough topics or units are taught separately, they are rearranged and sequenced to provide a broad framework for related concepts. Teachers can arrange topics so that similar units coincide....

... The *shared* model... [uses] overlapping concepts as organizing elements, [and]... involves shared planning or teaching in two disciplines....

... The *webbed* model... usually use[s] a fertile theme to integrate subject matter, such as Inventions. Once a cross-departmental team has chosen a theme, the members use it as an overlay to the different subjects.

... The *threaded* model... threads thinking skills, social skills, study skills, graphic organizers, technology, and a multiple intelligences approach to learning throughout all disciplines. The threaded model supersedes all subject matter content.... Using the idea of a metacurriculum, grade-level or interdepartmental teams can target a set of thinking skills to infuse into existing content priorities....

... The *integrated* model... [uses] a cross-disciplinary approach [to blend] the four major disciplines by finding the overlapping skills, concepts, and attitudes in all four. As in the shared model, the integration is a result of sifting related ideas out of subject matter content. The integration sprouts from within the various disciplines, and teachers make matches among them as commonalities emerge....

... The *immersed* model... filters all content through the lens of interest and expertise. In this model, integration takes place *within* learners, with little or no outside intervention. [For example, A]fficionados, graduate students, doctoral candidates, and post-doctoral fellows are totally immersed in a field of study. They integrate all data by funneling them through this area of intense interest....

The *networked* model..., [l]ike a three- or four-way conference call, provides various avenues of exploration and explanation. In this model, learners direct the integration process. Only the learners themselves, knowing the intricacies and dimensions of their field, can target the necessary resources, as they reach out within and across their areas of specialization. (pp. 61-65)

Curriculum integration is not without its problems. Particularly at the secondary level, it generally requires collaboration between two or more adults who are expert in specific content areas. This collaboration includes joint development of curriculum (or translation of an existing curriculum into appropriate lesson format), joint planning of instructional activities, agreement regarding what students will be expected to know from each discipline individually and in combination, coordinated assessment strategies, and, in some cases, joint instruction within the classroom.

Creating the conditions for this level of collaboration to occur requires many adjustments in the organizational structure of most schools. It also requires adults who are inclined to operate in close collaborative relationships. This may be why there is more integrated curriculum in elementary schools, where one teacher generally delivers most of the instructional program, thereby eliminating some of the need for collaboration. The differential expectations of teachers for the level of specialized content knowledge in elementary versus secondary schools may also be a factor.

CHANGES IN CURRICULUM DEVELOPMENT

More players are becoming involved in curriculum development. Once the domain primarily of textbook publishers, federally funded projects, universities, states, and large school districts, restructuring efforts have helped stimulate renewed interest in developing and adapting curriculum locally to meet the needs of students as perceived by their teachers. Rather than relying solely on textbook publishers or national efforts, such as the National Science Foundation programs of the sixties, state departments of education, small publishers, and school districts are embarking on curriculum development projects large and small. The scope of some of these projects may turn out to be beyond their reach; however, a tremendous amount is likely to be learned about curriculum development as a result.

Smith and O'Day summarize some of the problems associated with today's textbook-based curriculum:

> Diffuse authority structures and multiple goals within the system foster mediocrity and conservatism both in the publishers' supply of curricular materials and in the demand generated by local educators. On the supply side, publishers respond to the lack of consistency and the market-driven approach to materials development in two ways. First, they attempt to pack all the topics desired or required by different locales into the limited space of the typical textbook. As a result, in content areas like science, literature, and social studies, textbooks end up merely "mentioning" topic after topic, covering each so superficially that the main points and connections among them are often incomprehensible to the student. In addition, and...particularly in history and social studies texts, publishers deal with conflicting de-

mands and controversial issues by watering down content, evading sensitive areas, and choosing the least common denominator among the various viewpoints. This approach often leaves the student with so little information or context that he or she is unable to construct his or her own analyses or form his or her own judgments (Tyson-Bernstein 1988, Newmann 1988). (Smith and O'Day 1991, p. 239)

California and Texas signal the changing role of the textbook publishers, though each state takes a different approach. Both states have at one time or another rejected all the books submitted by publishers for adoption (Viadero, January 22, 1992). In Texas a conservative watchdog group uncovered numerous errors in texts. The mistakes ranged from incorrect dates to more serious errors. For example, Sputnik was described as "the first successful intercontinental ballistic missile." After the text publishers reviewed their books and certified them as error-free, reviewers found an additional 160 errors, including statements that the Emancipation Proclamation took effect in 1963 and that Britain owned parts of Mexico in 1753. "It is disheartening," said Lionel (Skip) Meno, state education commissioner.

California has relied on the development of curriculum frameworks to cause publishers to adapt their offerings to the needs of the nation's largest state. These frameworks serve a centralizing function by guaranteeing the general outline of the state's curriculum, while at the same time allowing for local adaptation and interpretation of curriculum.

THE ROLE OF NATIONAL CURRICULUM REPORTS

Within the past several years, there have been many national reports on the need to reform core subjects. These reports have stimulated a great deal of discussion among policy-makers and others in education, but most seem to have had little impact so far at the school-site level. A notable exception is the *Curriculum and Evaluation Standards for School Mathematics,* issued in 1989 by the National Council of Teachers of Mathematics, which is being adopted in many states as an outline for curriculum development or frameworks. This report is also beginning to have some influence among schools that identify themselves as restructuring, particularly in the primary grades. Other examples of these reports include:

- *Report Card on Basal Readers,* National Council of Teachers of English, January 1988

- *Democracy Through Language*, English Coalition Report, 1989

- *Everybody Counts: A Report to the Nation on the Future of Mathematics Education,* National Research Council, 1989

- *Science for All Americans: A Project 2061 Report on Literacy Goals in Science, Mathematics, and Technology* , American Association for the Advancement of Science, 1989
- *The Reform of Science Education in Elementary School*, National Center for Improving Science Education, 1989
- *Essential Changes in Secondary Science: Scope, Sequence, and Coordination,* National Science Teachers Association, 1989
- *Charting a Course: Social Studies for the 21st Century*, National Commission on Social Studies in the Schools, 1989
- *American Memory: A Report on the Humanities in the Nation's Public Schools*, National Endowment for the Humanities, 1987

All these reports have one thing in common: They recommend reconceptualization of the organization and presentation of key curriculum elements of the various disciplines. Some go further and hint at new models for structuring the knowledge base of traditional disciplines, and most assume different goals of teaching that suggest vastly different skills teachers would be expected to master. They are significant partly because of the discussion they have helped generate among subject-area specialists in education, and also because of their linkage to discussions about national standards for content knowledge. These reports or others like them may serve to provide the conceptual framework within which new standards for student performance will be developed.

These examples are only indicative; there have been many other reports and critiques, particularly by organizations outside the educational community, detailing the need for fundamental curricular reform. For example, the National Geographic Society and National Science Foundation have developed initiatives that suggest the need for extensive curriculum revision in their respective areas. Lewis (1990) notes that these "two subjects were the only curriculum-related topics on the standard-setting agenda of the National Governors' Association and the White House." In other words, where reports exist that make concrete recommendations regarding what students should know and how knowledge might be organized in ways that allow students to learn the desired material, such reports are being taken seriously and are having an influence on policy-makers.

As might be expected, it has taken some time for this flood of reports to begin to be noticed at the school level, let alone have an impact on educational practices. These documents have been disseminated through professional meetings and publications in the content areas. Subject area specialists in particular, along with more reform-minded teachers, may be beginning to encourage their colleagues to examine the recommendations contained in these reports. The reports present justification and support for those curriculum specialists and teachers who believe change is necessary. They help provide a platform and framework for grassroots curriculum development.

These activities stand in sharp contrast to the dominant strategies for curriculum development prevalent in the mid- to late-sixties, when, for example, the National Science Foundation sponsored major curriculum development programs in physics and biology, the School Mathematics Study Group program was being implemented, and *Man: A Course of Study* was developed and disseminated widely in social studies. These approaches generally employed university-based personnel to define and interpret what essentially all students should know and how they should know it. Implicit in this approach was the notion that learning experiences valid for all types of students in all areas of the nation could be designed centrally, and that teacher involvement in curriculum development was not necessary and might actually be a hindrance. These recent reports imply much more decentralized curriculum development, within broadly defined parameters, and much greater teacher involvement in constructing and interpreting curriculum as key strategies to improve student performance, particularly in terms of enhancing the quality and quantity of student thought.

NEW STRUCTURES FOR VOCATIONAL EDUCATION

One area fully involved in curricular upheaval is vocational education and industrial arts. The traditional programs in business; home economics; wood, metal, and auto shop; electronics; welding; and related subjects are under intense pressure to change. Theirs is a challenge fundamentally different from that faced by "core" academic courses. Vocational/technical courses must transform themselves to survive; they are not able to change incrementally. It will not be enough simply to develop an "improved" wood shop curriculum, for example. It is the relevance of the subject itself that is being called into question.

Gray (1991) describes the challenge faced by traditional vocational education programs:

> If enrollments are any indication, high school vocational education faces an uncertain future.... [T]he numbers peaked in 1984. Enrollments in vocational education are now suffering widespread decline.
> It seems like a strange time to suggest that vocational education may be in trouble. Global economic competition has focused attention on the need to improve the quality of the American work force.... However, the very economic forces that should be creating a rosy outlook for vocational education have led to increased graduation requirements and changing

student aspirations. Ironically, these forces have put vocational education curriculum at risk. (p. 437)

Gray elaborates on the growing belief that vocational education must be reformed if it is to survive:

> A consensus seems to be developing about the directions such reform should take, starting with a new mission and a new relationship with the total high school program of study....
>
> ... Many of us in the field are proposing that the new mission for vocational education should involve a somewhat radical departure from the past by de-emphasizing preparation for full-time employment and emphasizing instead "tech/prep"—technical preparation for two-year postsecondary technical education—along with the role of vocational education as an important instructional modality for all students....
>
> ... The curricular structure in vocational education has remained virtually unchanged for 80 years. Programs are typically organized around specific occupational titles; the content is determined by observable competencies (typically manipulative in nature) that are determined by a panel of experts to be related to employment in the field. While these competencies have changed over the years in response to changing technology, the basic structure has not. It is time that it did. Two issues seem to transcend all others: instruction should be organized around a broader occupational structure, and the emphasis on academic and workplace literacy skills and content should be increased....
>
> ... The vocational education curriculum should be reorganized around broader—clustered—definitions of work. For example, students interested in technical careers are better served by broad instruction in electromechanics than by narrow instruction in electronics....
>
> Obviously, in an increased emphasis on tech-prep calls for an increased academic emphasis. Likewise, there is growing consensus that a loosely defined set of skills—termed "workplace literacy"— may actually be more important than manipulative occupational competencies. (pp. 443-44)

Business courses, with their traditional emphasis on technical skills instruction, find themselves increasingly unable to keep pace with changes in the workplace. It is difficult enough to respond to the constantly changing technologies employed in the world of work, let alone to deal with the changing roles of workers. While it was once possible to train students in the basic use of a typewriter and calculator, instruct them in dictation and bookkeeping, teach them to write business letters and answer telephones, business teachers now find themselves confronting a workplace where secretaries may be expected to be "executive assistants" with considerable decision-making responsibility, where voice mail takes over a significant amount of the responsibility of a receptionist, where computers directly link executive-level workers, and a letter may be written and delivered without a secretary ever seeing it. These changing roles and technologies present profound challenges to traditional business teachers, some of whom continue to insist that students learn to type first on electric typewriters.

Shop teachers face a similar challenge. Their classes have been a refuge for students who do not perform well in traditional academic courses, with their emphasis on language skills and mastery of abstract concepts. "What will become of these students without the shop?," they ask. Shop teachers can make the case for their programs on other grounds as well. Students can apply math, solve problems, work in teams, be judged on the actual products of learning. All of these points are true, and shop is not a bad experience for children. In a world of unlimited resources, such programs might be retained somewhat longer. The issue facing educators is not the absolute worth but the relative worth of a program. Given the resources allocated to a program in terms of staffing, space, and materials, what is the return on investment? Traditional shop classes do not produce workers with marketable skills. And even as avocational experiences, their emphasis on obsolete, esoteric, or expensive equipment limits their value for the hobbyist.

Some schools are choosing simply to eliminate these programs, sometimes gradually, sometimes suddenly, rather than reform them. In other places, these teachers are developing new curricula and being retrained to offer hands-on instruction that is academically challenging at the same time. The movement away from specific skills instruction and toward more general technological principles is often described as *applied academics.* One new curriculum in this area, "Principles of Technology," is being adopted widely as a replacement for shop programs. In this curriculum, students must master mathematical and scientific principles and apply them to technological problems.

Rosenstock (1991) presents several examples of how such programs might be structured:

> Students in an automotive program, rather than learning only repair skills, can learn to establish and operate an automotive shop, study the history of the automobile, examine the transportation industry at large (including public transportation in the community), learn the underlying scientific principles of engine design and artistic principles of body design, and examine the effect of fuel economy on the environment.
>
> Instead of merely learning how to join wood, students in a carpentry shop could consider why a 2" by 4" is actually 1 1/2" by 3 1/2", study the impact of wood harvesting on the economy of underdeveloped countries and—perhaps—learn about the effects of deforestation on global warming. Carpentry students could also study weatherization of homes, redlining practices of banks, community revitalization, workers' rights, zoning regu-

lations, building permits, and all the other aspects of running a construction business. (p. 436)

Home economics classes often employ a similar strategy, incorporating chemistry into lessons on cooking, or sociology into studies of families. They teach about early childhood education and, in an increasing number of high schools, offer day care on campus as a "lab" for students to apply their skills. Business programs begin to emphasize "communication" strategies over training in the use of one type of machine. They create "executive internships" that allow students not traditionally drawn to business courses to spend time in the community as an intern to a lawyer, architect, or other professional and receive academic credit for it.

O'Neil (1992a) describes what he calls the "erosion of the long-standing wall separating academic and vocational programs." Academic and vocational teachers create new courses jointly in areas such as algebra, geometry, chemistry, and physics through applied, "hands-on" techniques.

The inevitable result of these curricular adaptations by vocational educators is an overlap between what they do and what is taught in the "core" subjects. Science and mathematics are taught in shop; writing is taught in business; sociology and psychology in home economics. How are issues of credit and curricular continuity resolved when this begins to occur? Which courses should count toward college admission? Particularly with the movement toward applied academic courses, the distinctions between academic and vocational, between core and elective, between thinking and doing, become much less clear. The result of such changes is a challenge to the underlying structure of the high school curriculum in particular, and to the notion that academic classes are the "legitimate" intellectual core of the institution.

CHALLENGE FOR TRADITIONAL CORE COURSES

Those who teach mandatory courses find themselves in an awkward position. Because students must fulfill program requirements, they are less able to express their dissatisfaction with curriculum in core courses by declining to enroll. Consequently, teachers are less likely to discern a problem with their curriculum. On the contrary, there is a tendency to locate problems in core required courses with the learner. At the same time, as their colleagues who teach electives begin to modify their programs, introducing relevance, problem-solving, integration and application of knowledge, and real-world experiences, the limitations of the core curriculum as it is taught in many schools stand out more clearly in the contrast.

Wiggins (1991) cites an example from the private sector that illustrates the challenge faced by core curriculum teachers:

Specifications should define what it takes to satisfy the customer.... Quality is the customer's perception of excellence. Quality is what the customer says he needs, not what *our* tests indicate is satisfactory....

This is old news in most vocational programs, athletic departments, and many art, music, and debate classes, but it is unfortunately a novelty in the traditional academic subjects. (p. 24)

So much instruction within the core subjects has been based on the transmission of basic factual information that students' ability to grapple with concepts is severely limited. Early results from student performance on California's open-ended math assessments indicated that "the most serious difficulty for students was inadequate use of concepts to help communicate the instructions. For a vast majority of students limited use of concepts got in the way of clear explanation" (California State Department of Education 1989, p. 10).

The greatest threat to the traditionally required academic courses may ultimately be outcomes-based education philosophies, particularly the use of integrated exit outcomes instead of course-specific competencies. If districts allow students to pursue any one of many paths to mastery of exit outcomes, the monopoly of the required courses will be broken. In such an environment, extensive integration of curriculum is not only possible but almost mandatory, particularly if complex forms of integrated assessment are employed. Students could attain and demonstrate the necessary exit outcomes through many different types of learning experiences. There would be no guarantee that they would attend courses that had little inherent interest or active involvement.

The last line of legitimacy for the core courses are traditional college admissions requirements. These are indeed a formidable challenge for curriculum reformers, since institutions of higher education have not yet participated in educational restructuring in any meaningful way, particularly regarding curricular restructuring. Individual professors may have done so, along with some research projects, but at an institutional level colleges and universities have tended not to become actively engaged in the policy discussions or issues surrounding school restructuring. Perhaps academicians view restructuring as being linked more closely to work force preparation than to academic achievement.

Ironically, most colleges and universities would maintain that students come to them deficient in many of the precise areas where curricular restructuring is focused. Such deficiencies include students coming to higher education with high gradepoint averages and little basic knowledge, poor reasoning skills, no problem-solving abilities, little intrinsic motivation or initiative, and apparently little love of learning. It will be interesting to see how universities and colleges respond to schools whose students possess these characteristics to a much greater degree but have not followed a traditional academic program of study. Will demonstrated mastery cause colleges to abandon (or soften) their reliance on the nineteenth-century quality-control methods of course title, Carnegie units, letter grades, and class standing, in favor of demonstrations of student mastery of exit outcomes set at high levels of performance?

If curricular restructuring is to succeed, it appears that teachers will need to provide the leadership for a rethinking of the content and structure of the traditional disciplines. Advances in information technologies now make it possible for teachers to be curriculum developers in ways that would have been only a dream as recently as twenty years ago. This new access to a broad array of curriculum sources and resources, combined with an emerging philosophy about the nature of the learning process and the learner's relationship to the curriculum (which are discussed in the next chapter), may drive teachers to rethink and reconfigure the curriculum over the next half-dozen years through literally thousands of small-scale development projects. The challenge will be to create conditions that motivate core-curriculum teachers to examine their content and rethink how they teach their discipline, then support and share the results from these efforts without reverting too soon to the "standardization" of the curriculum that now characterizes American education, what Tyack (1974) refers to as the "one best system."

Teachers will not be able to restructure curriculum without the existence of standards, discussed in the previous chapter on outcomes, and quality assessment strategies, considered in an upcoming chapter. To have any realistic opportunity to succeed, teachers will need to operate in a system that challenges them to enable essentially all students to master complex content and to apply their knowledge to real problems and situations as a dimension of mastery. Schools will need to cease attempts to teach everything worth knowing and concentrate on creating greater depth of understanding among fewer, more universal concepts and topics. Teachers will need to be able to work across disciplinary boundaries, but still retain the essence of the organization of the disciplines. They will need to be able to rethink assumptions about the importance of knowing versus doing, and the relationship between the two. And they will need to work in partnership with institutions of higher education to demonstrate that student learning can, in fact, be demonstrated more effectively through performance than through transcripts and grades. There is little to suggest that such conditions exist currently in many schools. This reality highlights the challenges involved in curricular restructuring.

The dimension of curriculum has been considered early in this discussion, both because of its importance and because of the tendency for it to be overlooked in discussions of restructuring. Closely related in importance and difficulty is the dimension of teacher instructional philosophy and technique, which is considered next.

CHAPTER 11

INSTRUCTION

There appears to be one overarching concept under which most changes in instruction can be subsumed. It is that learners must be more actively engaged in defining and developing responsibility for their learning. Examples of this trend abound. They range from whole language instruction in elementary schools to cooperative learning in secondary schools, community service in high schools, and project-centered and experiential education at all levels. Philosophically, these forms of learning are based on the assumption that learners can and must make decisions about what they learn, and they must process and interpret content individually to make it meaningful.

WHAT IS CONSTRUCTIVISM?

The notion that individuals create personal constructions of reality is known as *social construction of reality* in sociology, *constructivism* in psychology, and *phenomenology* in philosophy (Berger and Luckmann 1966, Giorgi 1985, Luckmann 1978, Thines 1977). Educators borrow from these disciplines when referring to "constructivist" conceptions of student learning.

O'Neil (1992b) describes the influence the constructivist perspective has had on curriculum development and reform during the past several years, then summarizes the key elements of constructivism:

Constructivist views strongly influenced the "whole language" movement in English, the curriculum standards developed by the National Council of Teachers of Mathematics, and new recommendations on effective science practices issued by the National Center for Improving Science Education (NCISE).

The key tenet of constructivist theory, experts say, is that people learn by actively constructing knowledge, weighing new information against their previous understanding, thinking about and working through discrepancies (on their own and with others), and coming to a new understanding. In a classroom faithful to constructivist views, students are afforded numerous opportunities to explore phenomena or ideas, conjecture, share

142

hypotheses with others, and revise their original thinking. Such a classroom differs sharply from one in which the teacher lectures exclusively, explains the "right way" to solve a problem without allowing students to make some sense of their own, or denies the importance of students' own experiences or prior knowledge. (p. 4)

Brooks (1990) describes constructivism as a means for educators to combine two distinct but potentially complementary educational traditions:

(1) the *mimetic*, in which students are expected to acquire facts and skills from drill and practice exercises, and (2) the *transformative*, a type of teaching that seeks to influence the attitudes and interests of the learners, evoking changes in perspective. In the mimetic tradition, teachers disseminate knowledge, and students receive it. In the transformative, the student is the actor, and the teacher is the mediator [Jackson, 1986]....

Alone, either extreme is insufficient preparation for a world that demands specific knowledge and skills, but also attitudes and interests conducive to vision and creativity.

The primary question for the teacher... is how to help students build a foundation of skills and information while they simultaneously use their creative, intellectual abilities to solve real problems and incidentally develop positive dispositions toward such endeavors. The powerful concept of *constructivism* can help us find solutions to this question.

Constructivists believe that knowledge is the result of individual constructions of reality. From their perspective, learning occurs through the continual creation of rules and hypotheses to explain what is observed. The need to create new rules and formulate new hypotheses occurs when the student's present conceptions of reality are thrown out of balance by disparities between those conceptions and new observations.

Constructivism describes an internal psychological process. In the classroom, students and teachers negotiate both their means of acquiring credibility as members of a group and their emerging understanding of the content of the curriculum. These negotiations occur as each participant actively seeks to learn about himself or herself, the other group members, and the content of the course.

In this process, each person is continuously checking new information against old rules, revising the rules when discrepancies appear, and reaching new understandings, or constructions of reality. In psychological terms, the old rules are the existing cognitive structures. When the old rules and the new information collide, the checking process generates cognitive disequilibrium. The revision is the accommodation that occurs when new rules or new internal cognitive structures are required to replace the old ones, which no longer explain reality. The new understandings are stops along the path of learning that occur when equilibrium is temporarily restored. This process occurs in both the teachers and the students, in both academic and social contexts. (pp. 68-69)

Leinhardt (1992) states that when the social nature of teaching and learning are considered, attention must be given to both the knowledge possessed by the individual and the knowledge shared by the group. What kinds and amounts of knowledge students bring to a learning situation cannot be ignored. These factors affect how the student constructs meaning from the material presented. Prior knowledge does not necessarily mean a child's readiness to demonstrate prerequisite skills, but encompasses the depth of understanding and interconnectedness of the knowledge, and the ease with which the child can access it. Knowledge is much more than building blocks of information. It is a complex network of ideas, facts, principles, actions, and perceptions. In the following examples, Leinhardt illustrates the role of prior knowledge and social construction of reality in learning:

> How we read a text is influenced by what we expect (from previous experience) to find there and how that material is parsed. Thus, a headline such as *Vikings Cream Dolphins* has a different meaning depending on whether we are thinking about the eating habits of ancient seafarers or about U.S. football teams. Similarly, if one believes that light emanates from an object (as many naive science students seem to believe), then science textbook diagrams such as those showing dotted lines between the human eye and a perceived object have a different meaning and interpretation than they would if one believed objects are seen because of reflected light. (Leinhardt 1992, p. 21)

Leinhardt explains the core assumptions many modern researchers have about learning and considers the implications of these assumptions for schools as learning communities:

> First, learning is an active process of knowledge construction and sense-making by the student. Second, knowledge is a cultural artifact of human beings: we produce it, share it, and transform it as individuals and as groups. Third, knowledge is distributed among members of a group, and this distributed knowledge is greater than the knowledge possessed by any single member.
>
> One pedagogical problem is how to use knowledge of facts, principles, actions, and representations that is available within the group—or classroom—to help individuals and groups gain more knowledge. Proposed solutions include an emphasis on "authentic" tasks.
>
> Another view on this, though, is to consider a school as having its own social system with its own artifacts and sense of authenticity. In such a culture of ideas and meanings, thought and reasoning are valued for themselves, not only for what they can do in the "real world." Both conceptions, however, suggest powerful changes in the dynamics of classrooms, changes that lead to learning. (pp. 23-24)

Brophy (1992) helps create a linkage between the teacher-effects research of the seventies and eighties and the constructivist thinking of the nineties. As one of the leading teacher-effects researchers in the seventies and eighties, he helped identify many specific teacher behaviors that led to enhanced student achievement as measured generally by standardized or criterion-referenced tests. These behaviors and tests, however, "focused on mastery of relatively isolated knowledge items and skill components without assessing the degree to which students had developed understanding of networks of subject-matter content or the ability to use this information in authentic application situations." He notes the limitations of the notion that such teaching and learning is all that should occur in schools and discusses the shift in the focus of current research on subject-matter teaching from the teacher's behavior to the student's vital role in constructing meaning:

> Current research, while building on findings indicating the vital role teachers play in stimulating student learning, also focuses on the role of the student. It recognizes that students do not merely passively receive or copy input from teachers, but instead actively mediate it by trying to make sense of it and to relate it to what they already know (or think they know) about the topic. Thus, students develop new knowledge through a process of *active construction*. In order to get beyond rote memorization to achieve true understanding, they need to develop and integrate a network of associations linking new input to preexisting knowledge and beliefs anchored in concrete experience. Thus, teaching involves inducing *conceptual change* in students, not infusing knowledge into a vacuum. (Brophy 1992, p. 5, emphasis in original)

CONSTRUCTIVISM AND SCHOOL RESTRUCTURING

Many different approaches to school restructuring contain constructivist elements, either implicitly or explicitly. Sizer's Coalition of Essential Schools lists among its basic principles the notion that the student should be viewed as a worker and the teacher as coach, nonparallel metaphors that conveys the idea that the student must have considerably more control over learning. Students are viewed as active participants, not products. The teacher's role as coach implies guidance rather than control as a primary means of garnering desired performance. There is a greater sense of partnership in the endeavor of learning than is engendered by the image of teacher as boss. Sizer (1991) describes the current state of instruction and some of the tradeoffs of giving students more control over learning:

Today, most of the teachers, rather than the students, "do the work." We present material and expect merely that students will display back to us that to which they had been exposed. Not surprisingly, the kids forget much of what they learned in a matter of months. They were not engaged. They did not have to invent on their own. They saw little meaning to their work.

So,... we must change the curriculum from display-of-content to *questions-that-ultimately-provoke-content*. Press the kids to do the work, to solve the problems presented. The cost? It takes longer to provoke kids to learn for themselves than it does to deliver content to them. The differences among the students become glaringly manifest when each is made to perform. A teacher cannot, thus, easily plan to "finish Mao Tse-tung by Friday"; the kids don't all master the matter at precisely the same rate. (p. 33, emphasis added)

This idea of deriving the curriculum in some measure from the questions or interests of the learner represents a fundamental departure from the thinking that prevailed in the late seventies to mideighties, an era in which behavioral objectives defined the structure of learning and teaching to a significant degree.

McCune (1988) presented similar ideas in her early descriptions of how instruction in a restructured school would differ from instruction in a traditional setting:

- Schools must extend the methods of instruction and provide a significantly greater amount of time in interactive activities.
- Schools must move away from the teaching of facts as the outcomes or ends of the learning process and use facts as the means for developing information processing skills.
- Schools must help students to relate information across subject areas and to real-world issues.

It is important to note that constructivist notions of learning do not imply that students will learn less content, that they will simply play at learning, retaining whatever they might glean from their activities. The goal is not simply to make learning enjoyable, though that can be a frequent collateral outcome. The goal is to cause students to learn and retain significantly more information. The movement toward high-content curriculums can succeed only if instructional techniques that foster the integration and retention of more content are also employed.

According to Lewis (1991), instruction in a school with a high-content curriculum has the following characteristics:

- *Consciously teaches higher-order thinking skills.* [Joyce] Epstein's research on eighth graders concludes that "students generally benefit in skills and behavior in math and English from higher level math instruction and more difficult reading and writing activities."

- *Constructs active learning opportunities.* Students need to be discovering, rather than receiving, knowledge. Teachers need to be coaches and facilitators.

- *Makes greater use of original source materials.* High content minimizes the dependence on textbooks, especially because they do not usually contain rich multi-perspectives on the curriculum for urban students. Using richer resources for instruction also supports the first two points, allowing students to deal with higher order thinking and become active researchers themselves.

- *Integrates and interrelates subjects and disciplines.* Early adolescents' cognitive growth leads them to integrate their knowledge, to get meaning from a whole perspective. Working across disciplines, teachers can match the other three characteristics of high content instruction to the development of their students. (pp. 62-63)

What is interesting about the current movement to reshape schooling is that the recommendations being espoused by educational reformers are in some cases parallel to those being presented by the business community and governmental leaders calling for changes in teaching and learning—both have elements of constructivist notions to some degree.

For example, consider the report *Workplace Basics: The Skills Employers Want,* prepared in 1990 by Carnevale, Gainer, and Meltzer for the American Society of Training and Development and the U.S. Department of Labor's Employment and Training Administration, which was discussed earlier. Its description of the new "basic skills" for American workers is similar to the types of things many progressive teachers have been trying to do for years. It seeks to develop employees who know how to learn and are motivated to do so, who can listen and convey a clear response, who have positive self-esteem and personal goals, who can get along with their peers, and who demonstrate leadership and motivation in their interaction with peers.

These behaviors describe learners in firm control of their own learning, who possess high degrees of initiative, and who are actively participating in the construction of their learning and of their social reality. If students have opportunities to explore and practice such skills during their formal public education, there is a greater likelihood that they will demonstrate those skills in the workplace. The implications are profound for a system of education that for most of its history has been working on perfecting mechanisms for controlling individual behavior and thought. It should be carefully noted that the implications for the workplace, which has had similar goals, are at least as profound, and that many employers may not really want workers who think critically, any more than educators may.

It would be naive to suggest that there is anything approaching complete congruence between the agendas of educational reformers and business leaders. Many business people still value the "practical" dimensions of education and assume the need for a strong emphasis on "basic skills," though the definition of these basic skills is shifting, as noted. However, the potential for significant dialogue between educators and business people regarding what constitutes effective educational practice appears at least possible if not promising.

EXAMPLES OF CONSTRUCTIVIST INSTRUCTIONAL PRACTICES

Many examples of changes in instructional practice that reflect the incorporation of constructivist perspectives could be offered. Cooperative learning represents a case in point. Its popularity has soared during the past decade. It has had to overcome concerns that it would undermine traditional American values of competition, that individual students would not be accountable for their own learning, and that high-achieving students would be dragged down or held back by the group. It appears that teachers who adopt cooperative learning have been able to respond successfully to these concerns.

Cooperative learning is an example of a teaching strategy that helps teachers adapt to more heterogeneous groups of students, and at the same time the strategy produces solid achievement gains and increases in prosocial behavior (Slavin 1990c). Traditional teaching techniques do not seem to have the same potential for enabling essentially all students to achieve successfully in school. If schools want all students to succeed and be able to demonstrate their learning in terms of what they can do, not just what they know, techniques such as cooperative learning will be central to the achievement of this goal.

Slavin (1991), in a review of the research on cooperative learning, presents the following summary of the effects of cooperative learning based on an examination of high-quality research studies:

> Overall, of 67 studies of the achievement effects of cooperative learning, 41 (61 percent) found significantly greater achievement in cooperative than in control classes. Twenty-five (37 percent) found no differences, and in only one study did the control group outperform the experimental group. (p. 76)

These changes in instructional theory and technique have implications for staff development and teacher retraining that have not been addressed adequately by reformers. Slavin suggests that only 10 percent of teachers are employing cooperative learning (Willis 1992). Such a low level of adoption of a teaching technique that has clear power to improve upon current practice, after nearly a decade during which high-quality training in the technique has been available, illustrates the magnitude of the challenge facing education. If the 1990s are to be a decade during which teachers transform their instructional practices to ensure that essentially all students can perform at high levels, how can current practice and best practice remain so far apart?

Whole-language approaches to literacy development are another example of the application of constructivist notions both to curriculum and instruction in an integrated fashion. The organizing principle of whole-language instruction is individual interpretation and meaning-making by the learner. The teacher facilitates learning through the creation of environments and experiences that allow the learner to make choices, construct meaning, create products, and extend understanding, in both individual and social settings. This method can be contrasted to structured approaches to reading instruction, as represented by basal reader series, that define and control the nature and pace of understanding of material for students.

Many other instructional techniques contain constructivist elements, and interest in these techniques appears to be increasing, based on discussions at professional conferences and articles in subject-area journals. Examples of these techniques include *personal goal setting*, where learning is based on the goals of the learner or at least where the learner must describe the learning experience in relation to personal interests; *simulations and role-plays,* which by their very nature engage students actively and are based on student interpretation and meaning-making; *project-centered learning*, a technique that has been popular with gifted and talented students for some time (for example, science fairs and programs such as Odyssey of the Mind) and is based on student-developed projects as the focal point both for instruction and assessment; and *case-study approaches*, where students are presented a body of information that describes a real-world situation and must answer questions and solve problems related to the situation.

These techniques all argue for student involvement and engagement in learning at a much higher level than direct-instruction techniques prevalent in perhaps most American classrooms. Such approaches appear particularly promising (in combination with well-designed and well-implemented uses of direct-instruction techniques) as vehicles to engage at-risk youth and to do more with them than simply retain them physically at school.

The difficulty with a movement toward constructivist notions of learning is not merely the task of equipping teachers with new strategies, though this alone is a significant challenge. The true "restructuring" of teaching and learning comes when teachers reshape their entire paradigm of the relationships of teacher to curriculum, student to knowledge, and teacher to student. Will teachers come to accept the notions that it is all right not to "cover" the entire curriculum, that students will not "know" exactly the same things at the conclusion of a course, that the student is actually in charge of the learning process in a fundamental sense, and that the teacher's most promising role is that of facilitator? These are profound shifts in the world view of people who function within an institution that allows them to maintain relatively stable world views (Pace 1992). The challenge is not just to transform practice, but to restructure basic assumptions about learning and learners. The difficulty of this transformation should not be underestimated.

CHAPTER 12

ASSESSMENT

It may appear a bit jarring to separate the discussion of outcomes from that of assessment by the two intervening sections on curriculum and instruction. A case can certainly be made that there is a very close linkage between outcomes and assessments, which there is. At the same time, the two should not be confused. An assessment determines achievement of an outcome, and there can be many ways to do this. The outcomes themselves, however, serve to drive decisions about curriculum, instruction, and other related processes. The process of identifying outcomes, in this framework, precedes these other decisions, including the choice of assessments. In reality, this is rarely the case, since curriculum, instruction, and assessment already exist.

Once standards have been established and agreed upon, discussions of the proper assessment tools can take place in a more informed environment. Assessment can be altered so that it provides useful information to teacher, student, and parent about performance relative to district (or state) performance outcomes, to district curriculum objectives, and to individual learner goals. This rational, linear approach is rarely followed in such a step-by-step manner, in part because outcomes and assessment practices exist *de facto,* even if they are not written out and adopted formally. The fact they already exist means that any changes in these areas have immediate, direct implications for teaching and learning practices.

If the types of changes in curriculum and instruction that have been described in preceding sections take hold in American education, there will be a concomitant change in the philosophy and technology of assessment and in the outcomes identified as having primary importance for all children. The familiar saying "what gets measured gets done" has significance for school restructuring.

SOME LIMITS OF CURRENT ASSESSMENT APPROACHES

The current testing technology, from the classroom to the national level, is built largely on assumptions about goals of the curriculum and methods of instruction that are being questioned. Most current tests are designed to provide a summation of the factual information retained by students. These methods of testing are based on considerations of efficiency and have close ties to the behaviorist notion that all learning can be disaggregated into a series of measurable units and that the sum of the performance on the subunits accurately measures the full scope of what is known by the student. These tests may have high reliability (that is, perform similarly in different situations) but low validity (they may not measure what those giving the test want to know about the learner); in other words, they tell us a great deal about things that may have very little to do with what students actually know and are able to apply. They provide little insight into the ways in which discrete pieces of information are combined, or integrated, by the learner to solve real-world problems or to serve as the stepping stones to new learning experiences.

O'Neil (1992b) describes how behaviorist notions affected the ways in which instruction has been organized and assessed:

> Popularized by B.F. Skinner and others, the behaviorist view of learning, when translated by schools, was characterized by lengthy lists of measurable behavioral objectives and tightly sequenced curriculums. Knowledge and skills were broken down into smaller and smaller bits, under the assumption that mastering simpler steps would add up, in the end, to complex thinking. These "bits" tended not to be placed in the context of an authentic problem situation, and students had difficulty applying what they had learned in new contexts. Little attention was given, moreover, to the conceptions and misconceptions that learners held about the skills or knowledge being introduced; so misconceptions frequently resurfaced after the learning task concluded. (p. 4)

These concerns are confirmed by the results from a three-year $1 million study sponsored by the National Science Foundation and conducted by researchers at Boston University (Rothman, October 21, 1992). The study reviewed standardized achievement tests and the tests contained in textbooks through the use of three strategies: (1) an item-by-item analysis of the six most widely used standardized achievement tests along with a sample of textbook tests in science and math in grades 4, 8, and high school; (2) a questionnaire administered nationwide to 2,229 math and science teachers in grades 4-12; and (3) interviews with 199 math and science teachers and 90 building-level administrators in six urban districts. The researchers found that those tests emphasized thinking and content at the levels of knowledge and comprehension. Very few questions measured conceptual knowledge, problem-solving, or other forms of higher-order thinking.

SOME EARLY ATTEMPTS TO DEVELOP NEW ASSESSMENT TOOLS

If expectations for student learning shift from measuring what students can repeat to demonstrating what they can do, the technology of testing can be expected to shift or evolve accordingly. This process of developing new methods is still in its infancy and will take a number of years to mature. In the meantime, schools involved in restructuring will be hard pressed to demonstrate improvement. The Saturn School in St. Paul, Minnesota, is an example of one such program caught in the middle (Weisman, July 31, 1991). The heralded model program found its students' scores on the Iowa Test of Basic Skills declined each of the first three times students took the test, including a ten-point drop in math scores over two years.

Since mathematics tests are the most fact-based and decontextualized of all achievement tests, this is the area where test scores would be expected to drop if a curriculum were decoupled from a traditional objectives-based structure and allowed to move more toward student-directed learning. Supporters of the Saturn School note that much of the computer technology necessary for the school's skills instruction program arrived late or was inappropriate for the program and had to be redesigned. Written accounts of the program do not indicate, however, that there was any sustained effort to develop alternative means of assessment to demonstrate what students did know. Schools such as this may well need to identify learner outcomes and develop assessment methods in tandem with creating new curriculum, time structures, or learning environments.

The difficulty of such an undertaking is highlighted by experts in the field of assessment, who suggest that five years may be a minimum period necessary to develop new assessment tools (Rothman, March 20, 1991). Eva Baker, codirector of the federally funded Center for Research on Evaluation, Standards, and Student Testing, believes it will take from five to ten years to develop and implement this new technology. She expresses concern over the ability of teachers to learn and implement new measurement techniques in the context of their existing responsibilities.

This strategy, however, assumes that development must be done by large research centers under the support of multimillion-dollar grants. While this sort of development effort may be valuable, particularly for creating alternatives to standardized achievement tests, it is likely that much, perhaps most, of the development work on new assessment techniques will take place at the state and district levels. The U.S. Department of Education is encouraging this effort through its support of the State Alternative Assessment Exchange, which is housed at the Center for Research on Evaluation, Standards, and Student Testing and cosponsored by the Council of Chief State School Officers. The exchange provides a central database and clearinghouse for alternative assessment strategies developed by states (Rothman, March 13, 1991).

For example, the California Assessment Program (CAP) has traditionally been based predominantly on standardized achievement tests. The new direction for the program "indicates the dedication of the California Department of Education to the development of assessments that challenge students to create performances and products that really matter" ("With Funds Restored, CAP Adds 'More Authentic Measures' " 1991, p. 2).

Plans for CAP in 1992 included the implementation of integrated language arts exams in reading and writing, and of new performance assessments in science. CAP has been employing writing assessments at the eighth-grade level since 1987. The program introduced open-ended math questions in 1989. Some examples of the skills and abilities students are expected to demonstrate through the new assessments include the following:

Language Arts

- Reflect the meaning-centered, literature-based curriculum described in the English-Language Arts Framework.
- Construct their own meanings, integrating new insights with the unique knowledge and experience each brings to the task.
- Integrate reading, writing, speaking, and listening in ways that are natural to good instruction.

Mathematics

- Respond to open-ended questions that:
  - Present students with a situation that is engaging.
  - Allow students at various levels of ability and experience to respond to problems with multiple entry points.
  - Encourage creative responses by permitting students to investigate several paths to a solution or find multiple solutions.
  - Direct students to write for an audience so they can demonstrate their abilities in effective communication.

Science

- Provide opportunities for students to find connections among scientific concepts and principles.
- Encourage students to discover and construct, through inquiry and investigation, the important ideas of science.
- Engage students in science thinking processes embedded in content.

- Enable students to move beyond the activity to apply knowledge and conceptual understanding.
- Allow students to demonstrate understanding by doing—by designing and performing investigations that ask them to observe, measure, classify, sort, infer, detect patterns, formulate hypotheses, and interpret results.

History-Social Science

- Enable students to demonstrate knowledge of history.
- Incorporate multicultural perspectives and interdisciplinary approaches, especially with art and literature.
- Encourage ethical understanding and civic virtue.
- Emphasize democratic values embodied in the United States Constitution and Bill of Rights.
- Promote knowledge and cultural awareness through study of history, the humanities, geography, and social sciences. (Adapted from "With Funds Restored. . ." 1991, p. 2)

The California state system, by virtue of its size, will have an impact on educational practices nationally. Publishers will not ignore changes in California, an important market for texts and tests. At the other end of the spectrum, Vermont is pioneering a statewide assessment program in writing and mathematics. Piloted initially during the 1990-91 school year in forty-eight schools, the assessment was scheduled to become the first statewide test in the state's history. All fourth- and eighth-graders were to be assessed in writing and mathematics in three ways:

- A uniform test, which uses equivalent tasks administered under the same conditions for each student. [The intent is to make these tasks performance-based.]
- A portfolio, which includes material collected during the course of the year.
- A "best piece," which represents what a student considers his or her best effort for the year. (Rothman 1990, p. 18)

Results from the portfolio and "best piece" assessments are to be reported in the form of a "school report day," in which parents and other community members will attend what amounts to a New England-style "town meeting" where the work of students will be reported, displayed, and discussed.

Rothman (1990) describes the content and structure of the writing and math portfolios:

The writing portfolio is expected to contain a poem, play, or personal narration; a "personal response" to a cultural or sports event, book, mathematics problem, or current issue; and prose pieces from classes other than English and language arts.

The material will be evaluated on at least seven criteria, including the degree to which the organization suits the writer's purposes, the writing exhibits a sense of personal expression, and the use of detail adds to clarity, as well as evidence of progress over time and evidence of opportunities for students to revise their work.

The math portfolio is expected to contain a range of materials that "demonstrate the student's ability to learn and understand materials beyond the 'facts and knowledge' level," according to a report by the math committee.

Such materials, the report states, could include: a solution to a problem assigned as homework; a problem made up by the student "with or without solution"; a paper done for another subject that includes math, such as an analysis of data presented in a graph; or entries from a journal. (p. 18)

School districts and schools are experimenting with methods of alternative assessment. This is not as unreasonable as it might first appear; if the results are not to be used for comparison between and among school buildings or districts, that is, if they are not *high-stakes* tests, then there is considerable latitude in the technical standards that need be applied to such development projects. If the data from the tests are going to be used by districts primarily for internal decision-making and for program improvement, then entirely different processes can be employed to develop these tests. Teachers can become much more centrally involved in assessment design to ensure that the results of assessments are of value to teachers.

This is not to say that standards of reliability and validity should be abandoned. In fact, teacher involvement can help improve validity in particular by helping to identify what needs to be assessed early in the design process. In the debate on assessment, it is becoming increasingly clear, however, that slavish adherence to the illusion that current assessment tools are objective and rational can be dangerous. Data from those assessments can be used as the basis for program decisions and, in some unfortunate cases, student academic placements. Test-makers are not necessarily to blame, since they often inform school personnel of the limitations of their instruments. And teachers, for their part, often find themselves in the unenviable position of either using marginally relevant test data or using no test data at all as the basis for making decisions. They cannot be faulted for selecting what often appears to be the lesser of two evils.

EXAMPLES OF ASSESSMENT STRATEGIES

While large-scale projects are being undertaken by states, universities, and large research centers to develop new performance standards and new assessment tools and strategies, many educators at the district and school-site levels are actively involved in creating their own standards and assessment methods. They are not content to wait until the large-scale projects, with their long timelines for development and their tendency to produce a horse by committee, are ready for use.

Two school-based research projects (Rogers and Stevenson 1988) explored a variety of techniques for assessing student work. Assessment on a fifth-grade social studies unit included the following methods:

- *Small-group interviews.* In small group discussions with an adult, students are asked to explain what they have learned. The level of student understanding is probed and explored through these discussions.

- *Situational pictures.* Children view a picture of a situation that illustrates the conflict caused by the application of some right (a nativity scene on public property being taken down two weeks before Christmas), and are asked to discuss its significance and meaning.

- *Card sorts.* Students are provided information about key governmental roles and institutions and are asked to sort them into piles labeled "most important" and "least important," and to provide a rationale for the decisions they make.

- *Learning logs.* Students describe in a notebook the most important thing they learn each day, identify areas where they are confused, and so forth.

- *Leader snapshots.* Students view pictures of key government figures and then attempt to identify them and tell what they do.

- *Open-ended versions of conventional tests.* Students provide extended explanations to more traditional questions. After answering an agree/disagree question, students list examples and provide justification for agreeing or disagreeing. (pp. 69-70)

The alternative strategies used to assess student learning from an eighth-grade unit on the poet Robert Frost were of a very different nature. A series of longitudinal tests and interviews was employed. Beginning with a test given immediately following the completion of the unit, researchers returned periodically throughout the semester and readministered elements of the original test. They also interviewed students. The results of this procedure provided insight into what students actually retained over time from a unit where they scored well on the initial posttest. In addition, the assessment captured student perceptions and motivations related to the learning experience. This type of information is useful, not only to students, but to teachers, who can use the feedback the next time they prepare to teach the same material. Teachers often lack this type of information and mistakenly interpret the posttest results as an accurate gauge of student learning, as do the students.

A strategy that involves public demonstration of work by groups of students is exemplified by the Rural Educational Alliance for Collaborative Humanities (REACH) Program's use of an exposition for students from ten project sites to display their work (Barone 1991). The REACH Program encouraged students to explore their personal and community history and the culture of their rural community to help foster a sense of connection among the students, the school, and the community. Students produced writings, interviews, dramatic presentations, and media productions. These were presented at a two-day "exposition," along with portfolios demonstrating student work such as poetry, stories, and collections of essays that demonstrated the students' progress.

Portfolios of student work have been proposed as a potentially powerful tool for gauging student growth, encouraging self-analysis, and helping students to develop a sense of ownership and pride in their work. Paulson, Paulson, and Meyer (1991) provide guidelines for schools that are interested in using portfolios to reflect student progress:

1. Developing a portfolio offers the student an opportunity to learn about learning. Therefore, the end product must contain information that shows that a student has engaged in self-reflection.

2. The portfolio is something that is done *by* the student, not *to* the student. Portfolio assessment offers a concrete way for students to learn to value their own work and, by extension, to value themselves as learners. Therefore, the student must be involved in selecting the pieces to be included.

3. The portfolio is separate and different from the student's cumulative folder. Scores and other cumulative folder information that are held in central depositories should be included in a portfolio only if they take on new meaning within the context of the other exhibits found there.

4. The portfolio must convey explicitly or implicitly the student's activities; for example, the rationale (purpose for forming the portfolio), intents (its goals), contents (the actual displays), standards (what is good and not-so-good performance), and judgments (what the contents tell us).

5. The portfolio may serve a different purpose during the year from the purpose it serves at the end. Some material may be kept because it is instructional, for example, partially finished work on problem areas. At the end of the year, however, the portfolio may contain only material that the student is willing to make public.

6. A portfolio may have multiple purposes, but these must not conflict. A student's personal goals and interests are reflected in his or her selection of materials, but information included may also reflect the interests of teachers, parents, or the district. One purpose that is almost universal in student portfolios is showing progress on the goal represented in the instructional program.

7. The portfolio should contain information that illustrates growth. There are many ways to demonstrate growth. The most obvious is by including a series of examples of actual school performance that show how the student's skills have improved. Changes observed on interest inventories, records of outside activities such as reading, or on attitude measures are other ways to illustrate a student's growth.

8. Finally, many of the skills and techniques that are involved in producing effective portfolios do not happen by themselves.... [S]tudents need models of portfolios, as well as examples of how others develop and reflect upon portfolios. (pp. 61-63)

Another popular method of integrated performance assessment is holistic assessment. Generally applied to writing samples or student demonstrations in which it is important to consider the learning as a whole rather than as a series of component parts, holistic assessment generally relies on the use of a scoring rubric to determine student performance. The rubric contains specific descriptions of behaviors and evidence of performance an observer can use to analyze and categorize the student's performance along a continuum, usually designated by a numeric scale of 1 to 5, with five representing the highest, most competent, and most complex level of performance. One of the advantages of the rubric method of scoring is that it can be developed and applied by teachers. The behaviors identified as the focal point for observation in most rubrics are ones that can be grasped relatively easily by educators, students, parents, and community members. They also can generate discussion about what it is students should know, and at what levels and by what means they should demonstrate mastery of this knowledge.

An advantage of using rubrics is that they signal the outcomes necessary for success beforehand; learners don't have to guess what they must do to be successful. Furthermore, the rubric can be applied to preliminary drafts or be used throughout a course of study to provide formative feedback to the learner indicating clearly what he or she must do to improve performance. Such feedback can be more valuable and useful than a score of 64 or 72 on a test. The standard for success is identified before the fact, as well. A 3 on a scale of 1 to 5 might be designated as meeting the school's standards for mastery. Schoolwide profiles of student performance that are more descriptive than test scores can be developed and provided to teachers to help them pinpoint deficient areas to be addressed in the future. Schoolwide profiles also enable parents to understand what students can and cannot do as demonstrated by the assessment. This knowledge helps in the process of identifying school improvement goals.

Mark Twain Elementary School in Littleton, Colorado, created a rubric to judge written reports produced by fifth-graders as one element of an assessment process that also required them to research a topic, create a visual presentation relevant to the research topic, and deliver an oral presentation three to five minutes in length. Each element of the process was assessed separately, and a separate rubric was employed to assess the oral presentation as well. The written report was assessed employing the following five-point rubric:

5 - Excellent: The student clearly describes the question studied and provides strong reasons for its importance. Conclusions are clearly stated in a thoughtful manner. A variety of facts, details, and examples are given to answer the question, and provide support for the answer. The writing is engaging, organized, fluid, and very readable. Sentence structure is varied, and grammar, mechanics, and spelling are consistently correct. Sources of information are noted and cited in an appropriate way.

4 - Very Good: The student adequately describes the question studied and provides reasons for its importance. Conclusions are stated in a thoughtful manner, but with less clarity and insight than in an Excellent rating. A sufficient amount of information is given to answer the question, and provide support for the answer. The writing is engaging, organized, and readable. Sentence structure, grammar, mechanics, and spelling are generally correct, and sources of information are appropriately noted.

3 - Good: The student briefly describes the question and has written conclusions. An answer is stated with a small amount of supporting information. The writing has a basic organization although it is not always clear and sometimes difficult to follow. Sentence structure and mechanics are generally correct with some weaknesses and errors. References are mentioned, but with some adequate detail.

2 - Limited: The student states the question, but fails to fully describe it. The answers and/or conclusions given are vague, and basic information may be lacking. The writing generally lacks organization and is difficult to follow. There are many errors of sentence structure and mechanics. References may or may not be mentioned.

1 - Poor: The student does not state the question. No answer or conclusion is given. The writing is disorganized and very difficult to read. Sentence structure and mechanics are consistently weak. References may or may not be mentioned.

0 - No written report is made. ("Mark Twain Elementary: The Peak Performance School," Littleton Public Schools)

The performance demonstration is yet another form of holistic assessment. Walden III, an alternative school in Racine, Wisconsin, with a long history of performance assessment, has developed what they title a "Right of Passage Experience" (ROPE). This process has served as a model for other schools. The model contains the following dimensions:

All seniors must demonstrate mastery in fifteen areas of knowledge and competence by completing a **portfolio**, a **project**, and six other **presentations** before a ROPE committee consisting of staff members (including the student's home room teacher), a student from the grade below, and an adult from the community. Nine of the presentations are based on the materials in the portfolio and the project; the remaining six presentations are developed especially for the presentation process.

The Portfolio: The portfolio, developed during the first semester of the senior year, is intended to be "a reflection and analysis of the graduating senior's own life and times." Its requirements are:

1. *A written autobiography,* descriptive, introspective, and analytical. School records and other indicators of participation may be included.

2. *A reflection on work,* including an analysis of the significance of the work experiences for the graduating senior's life. A resume can be included.

3. *Two letters of recommendation* (at minimum) from any sources chosen by the student.

4. *A reading record* including a bibliography, annotated if desired, and two mini-book reports. Reading test scores may be included.

5. *An essay on ethics* exhibiting contemplation of the subject and describing the student's own ethical code.

6. *An artistic product* or written report on art and an essay on artistic standards for judging quality in a chosen area of art.

7. *A written report analyzing mass media:* who or what controls mass media, toward what ends, and with what effects. Evidence of experience with mass media may be included.

8. *A written summary and evaluation of the student's course work in science/technology; a written description of a scientific experiment* illustrating the application of the scientific method; an *analytical essay* (with examples) on social consequences of science and technology; and *an essay on the nature and use of computers* in modern society.

The Project: Every graduating senior must write a library research-based paper that analyzes an event, set of events, or theme in American history. A national comparative approach can be used in the analysis. The student must be prepared to field questions about both the paper and an overview of American history during the presentations, which are given in the second semester of the senior year.

The Presentations: Each of the above eight components of the portfolio, plus the project, must be presented orally and in writing to the ROPE committee. Supporting documents or other forms of evidence may be used. Assessment of proficiency is based on the demonstration of knowledge and skills during the presentations in each of the following areas:

1. *Mathematics knowledge and skills* are demonstrated by a combination of course evaluations, test results, and work sheets presented before the committee, and by the ability competently to field mathematics questions asked during the demonstration.

2. *Knowledge of American government* should be demonstrated by discussion of the purpose of government; the individual's relation to the state; the ideals, functions, and problems of American political institutions; and selected contemporary issues and political events. Supporting materials can be used.

3. The *personal proficiency* demonstration requires the student to think about and organize a presentation about the requirements of adult living in our society in terms of personal fulfillment, social skills, and practical competencies; and to discuss his or her own strengths and weaknesses in everyday living skills (health, home economics, mechanics, etc.) and interpersonal relations.

4. *Knowledge of geography* should be demonstrated in a presentation that covers the basic principles and questions of the discipline; identification of basic landforms, places, and names; and the scientific and social significance of geographical information.

5. Evidence of the graduating senior's successful *completion of a physical challenge* must be presented to the ROPE committee.

6. A demonstration of *competency in English (written as well as spoken)* is provided in virtually all the portfolio and project requirements. These, and any additional evidence the graduating senior may wish to present to the committee, fulfill the requirements of the presentation in the English competency area.

The above is drawn from the 1984 student handbook, "Walden III's Rite of Passage Experience," by Thomas Feeney, a teacher at Walden III, an alternative public school in Racine, Wisconsin. Preliminary annotations are by Grant Wiggins. (Cushman 1990, p. 10)

The preceding pages provide examples of both issues and techniques in alternative assessment. The process of developing such assessments is complex, yet critical to the success of school restructuring. Without clearly defined outcome standards and assessment methods, it will be difficult, if not impossible to demonstrate accountability in restructured learning environments. Parents, policy-makers, and the public at large appear less likely to tolerate a system of public education that lacks adequate accountability procedures and measures. In fact, public policy seems to be moving toward increasing accountability for public schools. This appears to be due at least in part to the continuing accretion from the local to the state level of the responsibility for financing local school districts as more courts find school financing schemes unconstitutional. Additional impetus for accountability comes from the expectation, held by a growing number of people, that governmental agencies and programs are responsible not just to provide services, but to effect outcomes, to make a difference, and to meet client needs if they are to justify their continued funding.

THE CHALLENGE OF CHANGING THE CENTRAL VARIABLES

Many restructuring schools establish some sort of project or change in school structure and identify this as restructuring. Others take a broader view and develop a vision, mission, and key strategic directions. Missing from both approaches is the development of performance standards and appropriate assessment methods—what its students will be able to do upon completion of an education and how such learning will be judged. As discussed earlier, performance standards can provide a framework within which appropriate assessment strategies can be selected or developed.

Once standards and assessment strategies are identified and agreed upon by a school faculty, the changes that need to be made in the structure of the school and the content and organization of the curriculum and instructional program may become much clearer. This process of working from outcomes to program structure makes it easier to determine which projects should be launched to restructure the school; it also establishes a framework within which all new ideas and proposals can be debated and analyzed by all faculty.

Such a conversation is not an easy one, particularly for faculty members who are not accustomed to discussing substantive issues related to curriculum, instruction, and assessment. Ultimately, such issues are rooted in values. Members of the school community must ask themselves: What is worth knowing? How is it best taught and assessed? If faculties and communities can reach some agreement on what young people should know, and how they should be expected to demonstrate their ability to apply what they know, the work of restructuring moves from a strategic level to a tactical one in which the primary question is: How can the school best be organized to ensure that the desired outcomes are achieved?

Such an approach challenges the traditional isolation of teachers. It suggests that teachers will have to teach in ways that will lead to certain agreed-upon outcomes. As schools currently exist, there are few mechanisms that help or expect teachers to think in terms of how their work relates to what other teachers are doing, have done, or will do. Performance standards arrived at through dialogue and discussion will tend to drive instruction in a school and will require considerable communication, cooperation, and collaboration among faculty to succeed. These norms may not be embraced with enthusiasm by teachers accustomed to working in isolation.

Furthermore, these discussions are difficult because they may call into question the value of a particular area of the curriculum or method of teaching. In some cases the threat goes even further, with certain existing subject areas not being included in lists of outcomes developed and approved. A process such as this is terribly difficult to conduct successfully in an environment such as a school (or school district) where there is a high premium on maintaining harmony, where many administrators pursue this goal over all others. The development of outcomes that result in accompanying changes in curriculum, instruction, and assessment will be very challenging for districts to do on a voluntary basis when motivated only by the goal of professional improvement of practice. Changes of this nature are highly political in nature and require a political context conducive to change. Elements of such a context will be considered in part 4.

The preceding four dimensions—outcomes, curriculum, instruction, and assessment—constitute the core of schooling. They are the areas that must be addressed sooner or later for substantial improvement or change in educational outcomes to be achieved. They are also the areas most difficult to change. This is true in part because many of the changes described in this chapter require teachers (and administrators) to examine many of their assumptions about learning and learners, about what constitutes valid educational experiences, and about how learning should be organized. Change is also hindered by the lack of resources for staff development and release time that would give teachers the opportunity to engage in the type of thoughtful analysis and planning necessary to rethink teaching and learning, and to develop new curriculum materials, teaching skills, and assessment strategies. Lack of adequate vision and leadership by those in administrative positions can make change of this nature much more difficult, or impossible.

CHAPTER 13

LEARNING ENVIRONMENT

Amultitude of projects and experiments seek to change the learning environment. For the purposes of this discussion, the *learning environment* is defined as the ways in which students are organized for instruction, including grouping patterns, grade levels and other organizing strategies, and instructional settings.

For example, many elementary schools are experimenting with multiage groupings of various types, are having groups of students stay with a teacher for more than one year, and are working to integrate students from pullout programs into the regular classroom. Secondary programs are experimenting with schools-within-schools, community-based education, and the elimination of tracking.

Why is it important to examine the structure of the learning environment? As noted earlier, most schools have many elements of a bureaucracy built into their structures. These elements aid in making schools more efficient but can hinder the personal interactions so critical to the learning process. Stockard and Mayberry (1992) summarize the research on effective educational environments and indicate the importance of both cognitive and affective dimensions of the learning environment:

> In effective learning environments, students and teachers have positive feelings about their work setting. High morale appears to bolster the self-confidence of both teachers and students and promote positive attitudes and expectations about teaching and learning abilities....
>
> That is, academic achievement is enhanced when the normative structure of the group integrates high academic expectations with learning processes that emphasize interdependence, cooperation, and an orderly learning environment characterized by warmth, concern, and respect of others. (pp. 34-35)

Many of the efforts to change the learning environment are attempts to achieve a better balance between these sometimes conflicting needs for order and warmth. The challenge is to create an environment in which all students feel valued and challenged simultaneously, where they enjoy being at school but also achieve academically. Stockard and

Mayberry (1992) describe this as attempting to achieve a balance between the expressive, or socioemotional, dimensions of classrooms and schools, and the instrumental, or task-related dimensions. The remainder of this chapter is devoted to a discussion of some of the strategies schools are employing in their attempt to establish (or reestablish) this balance.

MIXED-AGE OR NONGRADED GROUPING STRATEGIES

There is a great deal of experimentation occurring with mixed-age learning environments in elementary schools, particularly at the primary (grades K through 3) level. This approach, often called *nongraded primary*, is based on the premise that it is not useful to organize children into instructional units based on age when the key organizing concept should be the developmental interests, abilities, and readiness of the child. In such environments children are grouped and regrouped based on factors other than age. The curriculum is not merely a simpler version of that which will be offered in the coming grades, but is designed to offer experiences and activities that are inherently interesting to children at this particular developmental stage of their lives.

Nongraded programs are not new. They have seen periods of popularity at different times during the past fifty years. In fact, the one-room schoolhouse may be thought of as the ultimate nongraded program in some respects. In 1963, Goodlad and Anderson expounded the rationale for such programs in *The Nongraded Primary*. This book has since been revised (Goodlad and Anderson 1987), in part due to the interest that has been demonstrated in various places, including Kentucky and British Columbia, which have mandated mixed-age, developmentally appropriate learning environments for primary grades, and Oregon, which has mandated investigation and development of such models. Interest is evident in other states where individual schools or districts are establishing classrooms or schools that demonstrate how nongraded programs work, and at professional conferences for elementary teachers, where presentations on the rationale, organization, and techniques of such programs are increasingly commonplace.

What exactly are the characteristics of such programs? Pavan (1992) provides a definition of the nongraded school:

> A nongraded school does not use grade-level designations for students or classes. Progress is reported in terms of tasks completed and the manner of learning, not by grades or rating systems. A team of teachers generally works with a team of students who are regrouped frequently according to the particular task or activity and student needs or interests. Many times

these are multiage heterogeneous groups pursuing complex problem-solving activities in interdisciplinary thematic units.

Students are active participants in their learning and in the collection of documentation to be used for assessment and evaluation. The continuous progress of pupils is reflected in students' growth of knowledge, skills, and understanding, not movement through a predetermined sequence of curriculum levels. (p. 22)

Studies that compare graded and nongraded schools "provide a consistent pattern favoring nongradedness," Pavan reports. Students in nongraded groups performed better than (58 percent) or as well as (33 percent) students in graded groups on measures of academic achievement. Such performance is "rather remarkable," since nongraded schools do not necessarily teach the textbook in the manner in which traditional classes do. Because nongraded schools adjust learning tasks based on individual differences, students may not be exposed to the same material in the same sequence as students in graded classrooms. "Yet nongraded students performed as well or better than graded students on achievement tests emphasizing mastery of content that is generally not the primary focus of the nongraded school" (Pavan 1992).

At the same time, students in such environments fared better on assessments of mental health. They had more positive attitudes and scored higher in self-esteem inventories. Studies that tracked students over time found that those who spent their entire elementary careers in nongraded classrooms demonstrated superior academic achievement and felt more positive or the same as students in age-graded classes. One study found that nongraded students received fewer discipline referrals when they entered junior high school. Nongraded programs were found to benefit boys, African-Americans, students from low socioeconomic backgrounds, and underachievers.*

Guiterrez and Slavin (1992) present findings that are in general consistent with those of Pavan. They found the most positive achievement effects to occur in plans that were simpler forms of nongradedness evaluated during the 1960s. These programs resembled the Joplin Plan, in which cross-grade groups are used primarily for reading. Positive effect sizes were also noted for programs that grouped across grade level for multiple subjects. Slavin cautions that nongraded education should not be confused with individualized instruction, for which little evidence of enhanced achievement can be found. Based on Guiterrez and Slavin's study (1992) of the effect size (proportion of a standard devia-

---

* For complete information regarding the sixty-four research studies used as the basis for these generalizations, the reader is referred to Anderson and Pavan (forthcoming).

tion by which experimental groups exceed control groups) of nongraded learning environments, Slavin concludes:

> The effectiveness of nongraded elementary programs depends in large part on the features of the program, especially the degree to which nongrading is used as a grouping method rather than as a framework for individualized instruction. (Slavin 1992, p. 25)

Nongraded forms of organization appear capable of creating an environment that engages students positively and allows them to retain positive attitudes about themselves and schooling while developing the basic skills necessary to succeed in school. Nongraded approaches challenge the factory model of organization, where children are labeled based on an arbitrary characteristic (age) to allow for the orderly assignment and flow of students through the institution. Age-based grouping provides many advantages for those who must organize schooling; it may offer relatively fewer advantages for those who are being educated within that structure.

SCHOOLS WITHIN SCHOOLS

There is evidence to suggest that smaller schools lead to greater student success along a number of dimensions. Stockard and Mayberry (1992) offer this assessment of the research on school size and student attitudes:

> Studies of elementary students suggest that small schools provide a more humanistic learning experience....
>
> Several studies suggest that students in small high schools are involved in a greater number and variety of activities, assume a greater number of positions of responsibility, are less alienated, and have a greater "sense of belonging" to the group than students in larger schools (Huling 1980; Barker and Gump 1964; Willems 1967; Baird 1969; Peshkin 1978; Turner and Thrasher 1970; Morgan and Alwin 1980; Wicker 1968, 1969; Downey 1978). These results occur in both urban and rural areas and particularly with students from lower socioeconomic backgrounds (Holland and Andre 1987). Because of their greater involvement, those in small schools report feeling needed and challenged, that they have an important job (Willems 1967; Wicker 1968). Many studies have linked these feelings of involvement with a lower probability of dropping out of school. Students who feel more identified with their schools are much more likely to remain in school until graduation (Finn 1989). (p. 47)

Large high schools and middle schools are experimenting with schools-within-schools to capture the advantages of both large and small schools in one educational setting, to allow students to connect with school, and to expand choice while accommodating the diverse interests and goals present in most communities. Teachers with a unique vision of education have an opportunity to attempt to translate that vision into practice. Such settings create opportunities for affiliation and community-building. They can offer parents a way to have some choice regarding what type of program their child attends within the public schools.

Roderick found that students whose grades fell sharply during their freshman year were more likely to drop out of school. She concluded that "a lot of students simply find it hard to make a good transition from the lower grades, where they're given personal attention, to the large bureaucratic institutions many of our high schools have become" (cited in Hayes 1992).

Sooner or later, however, most schools-within-schools will face the problem of institutional legitimacy, particularly in environments of declining resources. In other words, which school is the "legitimate" school: the school-within-a-school, or the larger school? The experiences of such programs in the early seventies indicate that such programs are very sensitive to declines in resources in the district. Their need for very specific types of staff members comes into conflict with the district's needs to assign or reassign teachers. As cutbacks occur, the contract may dictate that teachers who do not necessarily agree with the basic premises of the school-within-a-school will be assigned to it anyway because of seniority. Pressure to revert to the "legitimate" model of education, as embodied in the remaining traditional structure, will be strong.

If schools-within-schools are attempted, several issues can affect their success. If a school-within-a-school exists in a larger educational structure that continues to be labeled as the "legitimate" or "real" school, the larger school may eventually overwhelm the smaller, more vulnerable school-within-a-school. This danger argues for a complete transition to a series of programs within one building. The new programs should be roughly equal in size and all be distinctly different from a "traditional" program, with no single program able to claim primary institutional legitimacy. One way to accomplish this transition has been demonstrated by District 4 in New York City. The district disbanded an existing school and turned over the site to a series of programs from different grade levels that had little in common other than the shared site.

Another alternative is to officially designate the school-within-a-school as the research and development center for the building or district. Staff within the larger school site (or district at large) agree that new practices developed and tested at the school-within-a-school that prove to be successful will eventually be implemented in the larger school (or the district). Such a caveat is likely to increase staff interest in the goings-on in the school-within-a-school significantly, as well as to establish a clearer relationship between the school-within-a-school and the rest of the educational environment.

The designation of a school-within-a-school as an R & D center has another benefit. It creates a place where teachers can observe and be trained in new teaching techniques before implementing them in their "regular" classrooms. The concentration of resources, such as new technologies or adequate staff development funds, in such a center can allow educators to develop and experiment with new techniques in a cost-effective manner. Such a school also shows parents that new programs are being carefully developed and tested under controlled conditions.

Since enrollment in such a school would be voluntary, it is likely that those involved with the schools would be open to new approaches. The smaller size of the R&D center would allow staff to develop a close working relationship with parents and to solicit parents' feelings about new programs and techniques that may be piloted at the center. This involvement would also provide an indication of the kinds of issues that may be raised by those in the traditional program when the new techniques are implemented there.

One of the dangers of schools-within-schools is that they often become dumping grounds for the unwanted, the difficult-to-teach, or the "at-risk" student. While these students certainly need educational environments in which their needs are addressed, there is little to suggest that concentrating these students in one location is preferable to allowing them to interact with a wider range of young people.

At the other end of the spectrum are schools-within-schools that become elite programs. Experience suggests that when one such program gains a reputation as being "better" than the rest of the school, there is pressure to disband it because of the subtle (or not so subtle) competition for students and the social ranking that begins to occur. The tendency is for some to insist that norms of mediocrity be enforced on all aspects of the school equally and that the "elite" program be disbanded. A better result would be that the program serve as a catalyst for the rest of the school to improve. That will require a remaking of the culture of the school and the incorporation of new norms regarding professional relations. As has been noted frequently throughout this book, the difficulty of such changes should not be underestimated.

CREATING LEARNING COMMUNITIES

The premise behind all schemes for breaking down large, complex organizations into smaller subunits is that such structures will allow more opportunities for human interaction and affiliation to occur. In other words, the potential that a strong sense of community will develop is enhanced. This sense of community appears to be an important dimension of student learning, particularly for at-risk students.

The Holweide School in Cologne, Germany, has been cited as an example of a school in which the conditions of the learning environment have been altered to bring about new relationships between students and teachers and to create a learning community. Group membership is a key concept in this school.

The Holweide School is composed of schools-within-schools of approximately ninety students each. The staff base their organizational model on personalizing education for the fifth- through tenth-grade students in the school. Their two key goals are to diminish anonymity and to allow students of varying backgrounds to work together. The groups of ninety students and six teachers stay together for six years. The groups of ninety are further broken down until ultimately a student ends up as a member of a "table group" comprising five or six students. This group remains stable for a year or more.

Students are trained in the best methods of working together as a team. Twice a year groups consult with their tutors to assess their progress and their personal contributions. These meetings often take place at the tutor's home, over breakfast. The table groups develop common offcampus experiences and projects, which may involve them in social issues in the neighborhoods surrounding the school. Ratzki (1989/1990) describes the learning environment at Holweide School:

> We assign students to table-groups of five or six members integrated by sex, ability, and ethnic origin. Within these "social unit" groups, the children tutor and encourage each other. The difference between our groups and cooperative learning groups is that our children stay in these same groups for every subject, normally for at least a year. The aim is to promote stable groups in which the members learn to work together despite their individual differences. To achieve good group results, each member is responsible not only for his or her own work but also for that of the other members. If the work of one child in the group is unsatisfactory or his or her behavior a problem, then we try to discuss the issue with the individual child as well as the group....
>
> Each table-group meets once a week to discuss any problems or to suggest improvements in their every day working situations.

During lessons, except for free learning periods, the group practices and works things out *together*. Students who are more able are expected to help the other members in their group. Since the teacher's time is limited, this *helper system* is of great benefit. (p. 48, emphasis in original)

Differences among students are recognized through individual learning activities, such as techniques in learning how to learn:

Each school week begins with a discussion circle. For this event, the students move their tables aside, and those who wish to can tell about something special or interesting that happened to them over the weekend. After these remarks, the tutors announce any special events in the coming week. Next, the tutors present the weekly plan, which structures each student's work for the upcoming days. They also write the individual obligatory tasks for their subjects on the board, which the students copy into their plan books. Each student then checks his or her plan for the previous week and copies any unfinished exercise into the new plan. As teachers for other subjects come into the classroom, the plans are added to....

The circular discussion group format is also used for certain lessons. For example, during *tutorial lessons*, students discuss any problems with the tutors and how these can be solved. The students themselves determine the agenda for these lessons; the teacher plays a passive role. Each person in the discussion group who has just spoken in turn chooses the next speaker, irrespective of whether students or teachers have expressed their wish to voice an opinion. Coming from traditional schools, where teachers have an almost absolute right to speak whenever they wish, many teachers find that this format requires some getting used to. (Ratzki 1989/90, pp. 49-50, emphasis in original)

Teachers do not play a passive role in constructing the learning environment. They must make many decisions and take responsibility for creating the structures and content that allow students to engage in learning successfully:

Teachers in Holweide have a great deal of autonomy. Between them, they teach all the subjects and are responsible for the education of three groups of 28 to 30 students. They form their own teams of 6 to 8 members; devise schedules for the coming year; choose who will teach which subjects in which classes; decide how the curriculum will be taught (in a single period or longer block of time, for example); cover for absent colleagues; and organize lunchtime activities, parents involvement, field trips, and many other concerns. They also decide among themselves which two people will work together as *class tutors* (home class, or home room, teachers) in a given class. (Ratzki 1989/90, p. 48, emphasis in original)

Other descriptions of organizational structures designed to increase student affiliation and construction of learning experiences contain similar elements. Nickle and others (1990), in their description of a school-within-a-school, make reference to increased sense of community and affiliation as program outcomes:

> Another aspect of the program that has proved successful is "personalization".... Because the four [teacher] coaches are responsible for a total of only 80 students, the students get to know us and one another better than would be the case in a regular school. An unexpected rapport has developed within the [School-Within-A-School] SWS....
>
> A final beneficial aspect of the structure of the SWS is that students have developed a sense of "ownership" of the program. Those who interfere with learning are prodded into remembering why they are in school. The students usually reprimand and cajole their peers kindly, but such pressure is far more effective than an admonition from the instructor. Students also help one another freely and easily. As one student put it, "We can better explain things to one another because we speak the same language, and we aren't embarrassed to ask one another questions about things we don't understand." (p. 150)

Lewis (1991) describes how one middle school faculty moved to a school-within-a-school structure that would enable its members to create different blocks of time within the school for different subgroups of students. The structure would facilitate teacher planning as well. The goal was to enhance the quantity of content teachers were able to teach:

> Discussions on high content piqued the Frick teachers' interest in interdisciplinary teaching. This led to a decision to go for teaming and to create "castles," in which groups of students stay together all day with a team of core teachers. By dividing the school into castles, teachers obtained common planning time, flexibility to schedule block periods, and closer relationships with students.... Organizing the teams required a massive moving day as teachers regrouped from subject-matter departments to castles. "That ruffled a few feathers," says Donna Blochwitz, perhaps Frick's most enthusiastic supporter of teams....
>
> June Jackson, principal at Frick when the castles were formed, found the process of organizing and starting the teams difficult for teachers at first. "It takes time and training for people to learn to work together," she explains. "Some relish an opportunity to change; for others, it is quite painful, even though they are stagnating." (pp. 50-51)

Descriptions of programs such as these suggest that viable learning communities can be created within larger organizational structures, if careful thought is given regarding their relationship to the larger structure. Such environments can serve to do more than simply retain students in school. They can be places where enhanced social affiliation and greater learning occurs.

COMMUNITY-BASED LEARNING

Another way the learning environment is being redefined is by moving more instruction outside classroom walls. One strategy being considered by several states is the community service requirement, in which all students spend some time outside school working in volunteer positions to improve the community. Such programs help students develop an appreciation of their roles in a democratic society and of their obligations to others through the concept of a social contract. It is interesting that these programs may have more support within the business and social-services communities than among educators and parents of college-bound students, some of whom are cautious about the idea of making such service mandatory for all students (Lawton 1991).

Conrad and Hedin (1991) conclude that school-based community service can have a positive impact on both the academic and social/psychological development of students. Peer tutoring shows evidence of increasing reading and math achievement for both tutor and tutee (Hedin 1987). Conrad and Hedin (1982) found enhanced problem-solving ability. Students who participate in community service programs tend to exhibit enhanced social and personal responsibility, more favorable attitudes toward adults and toward community agencies and the people who work in such agencies (Conrad and Hedin 1982), more positive attitudes toward others, a greater sense of efficacy, and higher self-esteem than do students who do not participate in such a program (Luchs 1981). Participating students also show fewer signs of alienation and isolation and have fewer disciplinary problems (Calabrese and Schumer 1986).

A different strategy is to move learning beyond the classroom and into the community, utilizing the community as the curriculum. Examples of this approach that were piloted in the late sixties and early seventies include the Parkway Program in the Philadelphia School District and Other Ways in the Berkeley School District.

Gardner (1991) describes a type of educational environment he believes is based on how young children approach thinking and learning in the absence of formal schooling. In constructing such an environment, he strives to apply what is known about how the human mind develops:

> Imagine an educational environment in which youngsters at the age of 7 or 8, in addition to—or perhaps instead of—attending a formal school, have the opportunity to enroll in a children's museum, a science museum, or some kind of discovery center or exploratorium. As part of this educational scene, adults are present who actually practice the disciplines or crafts represented by the various exhibitions. Computer programmers are work-

ing in the technology center, zookeepers and zoologists are tending the animals, workers from a bicycle factory assemble bicycles in front of the children's eyes, and a Japanese mother prepares a meal and carries out a tea ceremony in the Japanese house. Even the designers and mounters of the exhibitions ply their trade directly in front of the observing students.

During the course of their schooling, youngsters enter into separate apprenticeships with a number of these adults. Each apprentice group consists of students of different ages and varying degrees of expertise in the domain or discipline. As part of the apprenticeship, the child is drawn into the uses of various literacies—numerical and computer languages when enrolled with the computer programmer, the Japanese language in interacting with the Japanese family, the reading of manuals with the bicycle workers, the preparation of wall labels with the designers of the exhibition. The student's apprenticeships deliberately encompass a range of pursuits, including artistic activities, activities requiring exercise and dexterity, and activities of a more scholarly bent. In the aggregate, these activities incorporate the basic literacies required in the culture—reading and writing in the dominant language or languages, mathematical and computational operations, and skill in the notations drawn on in the various vocational or avocational pursuits.

Most of the learning and most of the assessment are done cooperatively; that is, students work together on projects that typically require a team of people having different degrees of and complementary kinds of skills. Thus, the team assembling the bicycle might consist of half a dozen youngsters, whose tasks range from locating and fitting together parts to inspecting the newly assembled systems to revising a manual or preparing advertising copy. The assessment of learning also assumes a variety of forms, ranging from the student's monitoring her own learning by keeping a journal to the "test of the street"—does the bicycle actually operate satisfactorily, and does it find any buyers? Because the older people on the team, or "coaches," are skilled professionals who see themselves as training future members of their trade, the reasons for activities are clear, the standards are high, and satisfaction flows from a job well done. And because the students are enrolled from the first in a meaningful and challenging activity, they come to feel a genuine stake in the outcomes of their (and their peers') efforts. (p. 40)

The Lowell Public Schools, in Massachusetts, established a variation on this type of learning environment by creating a school structured as a microsociety. Based on the book *The Micro-Society School: A Real World in Miniature* (Richmond 1974), the school opened in the downtown business district in 1981. The goal was to engage students, teachers, parents, and community in the development of a miniature society that would serve as a school:

> The effort began with the introduction of money, markets, and property into the school. The students, advised by their teachers, used these ingredi-

ents to create a microeconomy. The microeconomy, in turn, has led to the creation of numerous organizations and jobs in them. Students fill these positions. Some of the work opportunities have arisen in the business sector; others have developed in government agencies, in the miniature society's fledgling legal system, and in a variety of cultural organizations. As these institutions evolve, so do markets for land, labor, and capital. Interacting with these markets has become a dynamic part of each student's school experience.

Beginning in kindergarten, children attending the microsociety school play with the fundamental building blocks of modern society. As they grow and mature, their miniature society matures with them. Apart from gaining insight into adult experience and adult society, there is no pre-scribed ideological path that the students must follow. With the assistance of parents and teachers, they fashion their own.

The Lowell microsociety school is a living experiment in applied moral development. Children and adults constantly face moral dilemmas that they must solve as they strive to build a "good" society. Do you want a microsociety with the extremes of poverty and wealth? Do you want a state based on law or one based on fear and violence? Should the microsociety's government assist or ignore children who may not be succeeding? Do you want a democracy or totalitarian state? What liberties should students have? And what responsibilities should they shoulder? What kinds of activities should be taxed? When does one put the community's welfare ahead of the rights of the individual? What civil rights should children enjoy in their microsociety? When has justice been done? Children attending the City Magnet School face these dilemmas under the guidance of parents and teachers, many of whom may be struggling with similar issues in the real world.

The City Magnet School provides students with a strong, traditional program in the basic skills.... [T]he students learn basic skills as they legislate, adopt budgets, pass tax measures, administer justice, govern, or simply communicate with one another regarding commercial and legal matters. They read, write, and use mathematics with purpose. In other words, the basic skills have utility. In the tradition of John Dewey *doing* reinforces *learning*. (Richmond 1989, p. 233, emphasis in original)

Another strategy is to relocate the learning environment by moving the school into the community. This method is being attempted in Minnesota by a consortium of districts that have constructed a school in a shopping mall. Five school districts have constructed a facility that will provide educational services from preschool to adult education within a 4.2 million-square-foot shopping center. The mega-mall will employ 10,000 workers, who, along with the children, will comprise a natural constituency for educational services.

Planners of the mall's education facility say the blueprint calls for five separate elements: a preschool with afterschool child care; an early-grade elementary school, also with child care; a learning center for high-school students that could be linked to part-time jobs in the mall; an adult-learning program ranging from vocational training to college courses; and an "exploratorium" component that could provide short-term learning opportunities for visiting students. (Walsh, October 9, 1991)

The preceding examples indicate that it is possible to think of schooling and learning occurring in a variety of settings and structures other than the factory-derived models based on the notions of economies of scale, centralization, and specialization that originate in scientific management. Such alternative settings offer the potential for education to focus on new and varied learner outcomes, rather than be limited to incremental improvement of current learning tasks.

ALTERNATIVES TO TRACKING

Another fundamental change in the structure of the learning environment involves rethinking how students are grouped for instruction. The one grouping strategy that is coming under the closest scrutiny is *tracking*, the practice of grouping students based on some measure of ability. Tracking tailors the curriculum and instruction to each group based on assumptions about what each is capable of learning. Students are retained in such groups over long periods and for a variety of subjects.

The research on ability grouping has not always used the most sophisticated methods, such as randomized experimental designs. Nor has it necessarily taken into account the interaction among the range of variables that have an impact on student learning. Nevertheless, the findings across studies appear to be fairly consistent. Stockard and Mayberry (1992) reached the following conclusions regarding those findings:

A large number of studies from a wide range of years suggest that, when students are in an environment with other high-achieving students, their own achievement tends to increase. In contrast, ability grouping appears to be detrimental for low-ability students. In other words, although ability grouping may sometimes benefit high-achieving students, a good deal of research indicates that it impedes the progress of students in lower groups (see Bridge et al. 1979; Kulik and Kulik 1982; Esposito 1973; Begle 1975; Brophy and Good 1986; Hallinan 1987, 1990; Sorensen and Hallinan 1986). In addition, ability grouping can affect status differences in a classroom with those in lower groups held in lower esteem (Hallinan 1984). Thus ability grouping can actually lead to larger differences between the high and low ends of the achievement and social distribution within a school or classroom.

In general different types of grouping systems may have different effects on learning outcomes. For instance, some studies suggest that various types of ability groupings can sometimes benefit students in mathematics classes (Slavin and Karweit 1985; Dewar 1964; Smith 1960). Other work suggests that the Joplin plan, which calls for cross-grade grouping of students in reading and whole-class instruction (Moorhouse 1964; Kierstad 1963; Skapski 1960), can enhance achievement (Slavin 1987a, b; 1990b). (Stockard and Mayberry 1992, p. 11)

The feelings run strong for and against tracking and ability grouping, both among educators and researchers, who often criticize the methodologies of the research on the topic. At the same time there appear to be areas of agreement among researchers on some points:

Participants in these debates tend to agree that ability grouping does not enhance achievement for the majority of children. In addition, they tend to agree that grouping arrangements that enhance achievement appear to alter the allocation of both instructional and learning time and instructional activities (see Slavin 1987b, 1990a, 1990b; Hallinan 1990; Provus 1960; Morris 1969). In other words,...differential effects in ability-grouped classes appear primarily because the instructional process is altered (see Barr, Dreeben, and Wiratchai 1983; Gamoran 1986; Hallinan 1990). (Stockard and Mayberry 1992, p. 12)

Tracking is usually instituted to help teachers deal with instructional issues related to the range of achievement present within a group of students. However, it has unintended effects on the self-concepts of both high and low-achieving students:

School officials have assumed that, by preventing extensive contact of lower-ability students with their higher-ability peers, the self-esteem and self-concepts of lower-ability students are protected. In fact, exactly the opposite result seems to occur. Instead of feeling more comfortable about themselves, students in lower tracks tend to develop lower self-esteem, lower aspirations, and more negative attitudes toward school (Oakes 1985, 1987).

It is also important to note that the result of higher track placement is not uniformly good. In may enhance achievement but not necessarily increase aspirations or self-evaluations. Students in higher tracks tend to have peers who perform well, thus enhancing group norms regarding performance.... [A] higher-ability context can lead individuals to give more negative evaluations of their own ability than they would in other contexts. (Stockard and Mayberry 1992, p. 14)

Rather than being primarily a tool to enable teachers to deal with the diverse achievement levels present in a classroom, tracking may, in fact, function to reinforce and define social relationships:

Ideally, track placement would only reflect a student's academic achievement, ability, and motivation. In reality, most studies conclude that students' track placements are related to both their prior academic achievement and their social class background (Sorensen 1987) ....

Many scholars suggest that tracking in secondary schools and ability grouping, its counterpart in elementary schools, function as the mediating variable between students' socioeconomic background and their educational achievement, occupational aspirations, and perceptions of themselves and their school.... These studies suggest that tracking reproduces class status by sorting students from different socioeconomic backgrounds into different curricula and providing them with unequal learning environments...[see] Oakes 1985; Schaefer and Olexa 1971; Alexander and McDill 1976; Barr, Dreeben, and Wiratchai 1983; Dreeben and Gamoran 1986; Garet and DeLany 1988; Sorensen 1987).

In general, these studies suggest that students from lower socioeconomic backgrounds receive educational experiences that offer them limited access to high-status knowledge and normative climates that are not conducive to achievement. In contrast, students from higher socioeconomic backgrounds are much more likely to enroll in challenging curricular programs and college preparatory tracks that provide the type of knowledge and normative standards that are essential for higher levels of education and entrance into high-status occupations. (Stockard and Mayberry 1992, pp. 14-15)

Acknowledging that tracking is deeply rooted in the culture of many schools, Oakes and Lipton (1992) suggest a critical examination of basic assumptions about students and learning will be required before a movement away from tracking can begin to take hold. They describe schools that have abandoned tracking successfully and have established a culture of "detracking." Such schools recognize that the norms that support tracking are powerful and must be acknowledged as alternatives are developed; that changes in tracking must become part of a comprehensive set of changes in school practice; that the process of removing tracking is politically sensitive, is idiosyncratic to each school site, and requires broad-scale staff involvement; that it requires changes in adult working relationships and roles; and that certain teachers emerge as the risk-takers whose persistence over the long haul helps institutionalize alternative practices.

UNTRACKING SCHOOLS

Wheelock (1992) describes the work of the Massachusetts Advocacy Center, which, since 1990, has worked to identify untracked middle schools and to document their success in promoting both equity and excellence for all students. Researchers identified some 250 schools engaged in efforts to move away from tracking. Through questionnaires, interviews, and site visits, they discovered clues to the process of untracking, what it takes to begin to move away from tracking. Their search led to identification of nine ingredients of the untracking process:

- A belief that all students can learn, that untracking is merely a means to the end of greater student learning for all within the context of a democratic school community.

- A belief that systems-level change is possible in schools, and that the removal of tracking necessitates changes in curriculum, instruction, assessment, and other areas of the school.

- A belief in high expectations for all students and in inclusive practices in all aspects of school life. Schools develop practices that acknowledge the success of all students and that guarantee that a wide range of students participate in all school activities. They treat students as members of a learning community.

- A partnership between leaders and teachers that leads to agreement on common mission, vision, and goals for the school, which include concepts of equality.

- A commitment to parental involvement throughout the process in genuine ways, such as participation in planning and implementing heterogeneous groups, provision of information to parents, and commitment to institute two-way communication with parents, particularly with those who perceive their children as being "gifted and talented."

- Indications of support from local and state policies that encourage such practices.

- The development of a multiyear plan that allows the numerous steps necessary to prepare for untracking to occur in a systematic, comprehensible manner. Examples of such steps include disseminating research about tracking and alternatives to tracking, visiting other schools with heterogeneous classrooms, developing appropriate curriculum, planning staff development activities.

- A plan to address the multifaceted needs for professional development that accompany this transformation, showing models of how alternatives to grouping can work and providing teachers with general knowledge and specific techniques to facilitate untracking.

- A commitment to phased-in implementation based on what is possible or desirable within the school. Such a phase-in may employ any one of many possible strategies, depending on the specific circumstances and existing organizational structure of the school. (Adapted from Wheelock 1992)

One of the key challenges that must be addressed if schools are to institute learning structures other than tracking is how to meet the needs of gifted students. Johnson and Johnson respond to some of the key objections to cooperative learning raised by advocates for the gifted. They begin by making a distinction between high-ability students (the top 33 percent) and gifted students (the top 5 percent). The needs of these two groups will probably be different, they say, though there is somewhat of a tendency to think of them as one group. These students should not always work in cooperative groups (Johnson and Johnson 1991) and should have opportunities to compete with one another. At the same time, they can benefit from participation in mixed-ability groups. Based on nine studies conducted over the past fifteen years, the Johnsons (1992) have concluded that:

- High-ability students benefit academically from cooperative learning groups. The exchange of ideas within the group is richer, and group discussion enhances the ability to apply information in subsequent situations when working alone.

- Learning cooperatively with lower achieving peers does not decrease the critical thinking and higher-level reasoning of high-ability students. In fact, cooperative learning provides alternatives to drill and practice activities that serve little purpose for high-ability students.

- High-ability students who work cooperatively with others outperform high-ability students who work exclusively in competitive or individual settings. While individual work may lead to quicker mastery of lower-level cognitive tasks, cooperative work results in more higher-level cognitive strategies and reasoning, more sophisticated problem solving, and enhanced retention.

- Low-achieving students do not hinder the learning of high-ability students. By explaining material to others, high-ability students strengthen their grasp of material while they restructure and practice its organization.

- Having high achievers work together does not automatically lead to enhanced achievement. High achievers may not feel compelled to explain their reasoning to one another or to generate alternative explanations or solutions. There is little expectation that one student will teach anything to another in such settings.

- Heterogeneous learning groups are not the best model for transmitting large quantities of material. They are effective for ensuring the quality of thought students develop regarding the material that is presented.

- Heterogeneous groups can have significant social benefits for high-ability students. They can create a setting where academic ability is valued socially, something that rarely occurs in many schools. They can decrease the sense of isolation some high-ability students feel. (Adapted from Johnson and Johnson 1992)

Matthews (1992) suggests six ways to make cooperative learning more effective for high-achieving students, based in part on her discussions with gifted students:

- Design cooperative projects so that all students can interact and contribute equally. Avoid traditional worksheet, "right answer" tasks.

- Use new curricular materials that involve collaborative practices—projects in which students share creative ideas, build on one another's knowledge, and draw on diverse skills (Cohen [October 1990]; Gamoran 1990). Projects might include: writing workshops, oral histories, guided nature walks, ecology projects, discussions of political issues, plays, science experiments, manipulatives-based math explorations, Odyssey of the Mind competitions, Future Problem Solving teams, and foreign language talk shows.

- Encourage successful group functioning by including five conditions: positive interdependence, face-to-face interaction, individual accountability, social skills, and group processing. (Johnson et al. 1986).

- Set authentic group goals that are important to group members....

- Teach students how successful groups work and how to apply this information to their own groups (Johnson et al. 1986). How to ask for assistance, help others, and take responsibility for group members are important skills (Cohen [October 1990]). Roleplay and model these skills with students.

- Group students in flexible ways.... Flexible grouping gives the low achievers the opportunity to realize the positive effects of being the "explainer" and provides gifted students opportunities to get to know and work with a wide range of students. (p. 50)

Alternatives to tracking are being pursued in some schools primarily as strategies to increase the educational success of all students. Interestingly, the goal is to increase both equity and excellence. New practices are not being instituted simply to make students feel better about themselves, or strictly to benefit low-achieving students. The approaches being tested are designed, in most cases, with the goal of providing richer educational experiences for all students and bringing techniques formerly reserved for talented and gifted or accelerated programs to all students.

Successful alternatives to tracking help to steer the curriculum away from highly sequenced courses focused on the lock-step mastery of skills and information. The goal instead is a curriculum rich in complex ideas and opportunities for students to pursue multiple paths to common outcomes. To accomplish this, teachers need many opportunities to develop an expanded repertoire of instructional skills. Additionally, provisions must be made for students with special needs. At the same time, alternative assessment and grading practices have to be developed.

These new assessments provide information to students that allows them to make continuous progress toward common learning outcomes rather than being consigned to failure at arbitrary points in the process.

INCLUSION OF SPECIAL-EDUCATION STUDENTS

Another alteration in the structure of the learning environment that is being seen in some schools is a movement to include special-education students in regular-education classrooms to the maximum extent possible. Along with detracking, this trend represents a major challenge to the organization of the learning environment as it currently exists in most schools.

The complexity and emotion surrounding this topic are such that it is impossible to provide an adequate treatment of it in a work such as this. The inclusion of special-education students into regular-education classes, combined with attempts to eliminate or modify tracking or ability grouping, creates a tremendous challenge for traditional classroom structures and teaching methods at all grade levels. And while efforts are under way to develop models such as consultative teachers and joint planning teams, a tremendous amount of work remains to be done before American classrooms can hope to accommodate wide ranges of student ability successfully.

The National Association of State Boards of Education (1992) produced a report entitled *Winners All: A Call for Inclusive Schools* in which they encourage state boards of education to develop educational systems where students with disabilities are not just mainstreamed, but fully included in classrooms. Full inclusion is different from mainstreaming in that it calls for teaching children with special needs in regular classrooms throughout the entire day, rather than having them spend only part of the day in the regular classroom. This method relies on special-education teachers working in regular classrooms, team-teaching or providing other forms of support for students with special needs. All teachers would need to be prepared to teach all children. To accomplish this, teacher training programs would have to be redesigned to teach more about special-needs students and more about collaboration between regular-education and special-education teachers.

The pressure for inclusion comes in part from democratic principles of equal treatment for all students and in part from the limited success of pullout programs to achieve the goal of enhanced educational achievement for special-education students of some types, particularly learning disabled. This movement applies to all pullout programs, including Chapter 1 and other remedial approaches that remove the student from the regular classroom. Miller (1990) suggests that it may be possible for classroom teachers and special-education teachers to form a partnership to support and benefit from school reform efforts.

Programs of school restructuring may provide the forum within which long-held beliefs about the nature of children and how they learn can be challenged, and alternatives can be explored. Such an environment may be necessary to permit the types of changes that appear to be necessary to support the full inclusion of the entire range of student ability in one classroom. Traditional models of instruction that beam a lesson just above the perceived ability level of the midpoint of the class have little utility in such inclusive environments. Yet the alternatives require not incremental adjustments, but fundamental reorganization of curriculum, instruction, and assessment, and redeployment of resources, including professional staff, reconfiguration of time, integrated use of technology, and redefined parental involvement. The discussions of mainstreaming and full inclusion serve to highlight the challenges the educational system faces in its attempt to meet the needs of all students to function at high levels cognitively and socially.

Case (1992) contends that special education serves to "rescue" the traditional system. Operating from the medical model, special education diagnoses and prescribes treatment based on the needs of each individual. However, the system in which the child exists and to which she or he must return is not examined or affected:

> Problems with the instructional setting have not been analyzed; changes needed in classroom instruction have not been specified; and special education intervention has rarely been targeted to improve learning in the classroom. Children's learning has been jeopardized because the basic system that is ineffective for them is left untouched. Because the child, not the system, is defined as the problem, children remain dependent on special education. We are caught in a self-perpetuating system of dependence on special education and are hard-pressed to break the cycle. (p. 33)

Suggestions are being proposed for how school systems might proceed to modify and adapt, rather than abandon, special services for those students who truly need them, while at the same time improving the quality of instruction all students receive. Danielson and Bellamy (1988) note that between 1976-77 and 1984-85 "the number of U.S. students identified as learning disabled increased 127 percent." Wang, Walberg, and Reynolds (1992) propose several changes that need to occur in the immediate future for special education to better serve students with special needs:

- The enhanced use of effective instructional practices that are based on student achievement needs; materials and procedures that allow students to proceed at their own pace; frequent assessment of student progress;

additional time for those who need it; enhanced student responsibility for monitoring and guiding their own learning; and learner goals that students can work cooperatively to achieve.

- School environments that monitor student progress more closely; are more aware and mindful of student characteristics; assess which programs are working and which are not, which need to be improved, which need to be abandoned, and which need to be extended; use outcomes against which students can compare their individual achievement to a greater degree; and have less need to categorize children.

- More effective use of technology to allow special-needs students to work at home as well as at school, on weekends and during the summer, and that give parents better information about student progress.

- The elimination of separate teacher preparation to deal with special-education students, and in their place programs that train all teachers to deal with all students.

- Increased coordination with and integration of health and welfare agencies and programs into the school.

- Coordination among all levels of government to support coherent programs that serve all students. (Summarized from Wang, Walberg, and Reynolds 1992)

Wang and colleagues suggest that the disjointed nature of educational services generally, and those for special-education students specifically, has led to a loss of focus on the needs of the learner. Improvement might be achieved through the use of "waiver for performance" strategies (Wang, Walberg, and Reynolds 1988). States could allow districts to experiment with enriched regular-school programs in broad noncategorical or cross-categorical programs in return for providing data showing enhanced pupil learning outcomes.

The Winooski, Vermont, school district describes its initial attempts to move away from categorical or pullout programs (Villa and Thousand 1992). A single job description for "teacher" was created. Administrative roles and responsibilities were redefined. Pupil personnel services were disbursed to schools. Central administration retained responsibility for inservice training, observing and assisting teachers with their improvement goals, and managing support service paperwork. The key element of the model was teacher collaboration in the form of teaching teams. Teams must agree to coordinate their work to achieve agreed-upon goals, and to use collaborative principles from cooperative learning. The principles of collaboration extend to students who work together as peer tutors, assist one another with intensive challenges, act as advocates for one another, provide social support by being "peer buddies," and offer coaching to their teachers. Educators in the district believe these collaborative arrangements have promoted integrated education for intensively challenged students, created better conditions for equity and parity among students and adults, and enhanced the spirit of community present in the school.

The Edmonds, Washington, school district restructured its categorical programs to "group and serve students according to their instructional needs, not their labels and funding sources." The intent was not necessarily to eliminate pullout programs, but to create an environment in which schools experiment with different structures and strategies based on the needs of their students and the capabilities of their staffs.

> In their reform efforts, district schools have focused primarily on structural changes and program enhancements. Because teaching positions are now blended, job titles such as Chapter 1 teachers or special education resource room teachers no longer exist. Support teachers—called "learning support"—are funded out of several sources. In addition, teachers are using different grouping strategies such as within-grade, cross-grade, multiage, and in-class services....
>
> Schools have also concentrated on the causes of student failure by attempting to enhance learning opportunities. For example, they are exploring options in cooperative learning, study skills, social skills, learning styles, self-concept, thematic curriculum, guidance support, and peer/teacher tutoring. (Fink 1992, pp. 42-43)

Integrating special-needs students into classrooms represents a unique challenge to educators, since these students represent two distinctly different groups of children. One group is composed of those who have never before been included in public school classrooms with any regularity; among these are students with severe and profound disabilities of a physiological or neurological nature. These children have been in special schools or programs devoted to and organized around their needs. Regular-classroom teachers have little idea of how to cope with such students. Programs of integration for these students will need to be of one type, since teachers have few experiences or reference points to draw upon in responding to the needs of such children.

The other group of students only recently were withdrawn from regular education but are now returning. These include children with learning disabilities and those who are emotionally or behaviorally disturbed. Such students were a part of regular education until the midseventies and the passage of P.L. 94-142. Since that time numerous special programs have been developed for such students, and many regular-classroom teachers have ceased to accept responsibility for the instruction of these children. Teachers whose careers began prior to P.L. 94-142 do have experiences and reference points to draw upon, and for them a different form of training and support is called for.

To be successful, the integration or reintegration of special-education students will require a change in the culture of schools. Inclusion of these students implies teachers will see themselves responsible for the education of *all* students. Such a transformation will be exceedingly difficult to achieve in environments where teachers work in isolation from one another, set different standards of success, and hold differing expectations for appropriate student behavior. Also contributing to the complexity of change will be parent groups that support the rights of special-needs students. These groups are well organized and influential. Some are viewing the movement toward greater inclusion with a cautious eye "because they fear losing the hard-won rights and special education services" they have gained over the past fifteen years (Viadero, November 4, 1992).

CONCLUSION

All these changes in the learning environment hold a common thread. A shift is taking place in which the learning environment is being designed with less attention to meeting the needs of the adults conducting the learning and more attention to meeting the needs of the students engaged in the learning. Carrying out this shift requires a delicate balance between engaging/empowering the learner and simultaneously maintaining standards for performance. Humane environments can become indulgent ones; environments with high standards can become dehumanizing ones. The linkage between changes in the learning environment and those in outcomes, curriculum, instruction, and assessment become clearer within such a framework.

Changing the learning environment can help to reconceptualize relationships between students and subject matter, and between children and adults. By instituting such changes, material can be made more meaningful to students, and the quality of human relationships within a school can be improved for all participants. Such changes are difficult since they require substantial rethinking by all participants in the learning process. Teachers must reexamine their assumptions regarding the distribution of ability among students and the innate ability of all students to learn. Administrators must reconsider the rationale they employ when designing specific structures for organizing schools. And students must take responsibility for and control over their own learning.

CHAPTER 14

TECHNOLOGY

The most striking observation one reaches about technology in education over the past dozen years is not its impact but its lack of impact. Information technologies have been adopted in the central offices of most midsized school districts, particularly in business offices and, to a lesser degree, in school offices where they are used primarily to manage data on students and schedules. But technology has not revolutionized learning in the classroom, nor led to higher productivity in schools.

In an edition of *Macworld* magazine entitled "America's Shame: How We've Abandoned Our Children's Future," Jerry Borrell, editor, describes his magazine's research on the use of computers in schools and the concerns it raised:

> We debated whether we should invest more effort developing a story on how America is using personal computers in schools. Department of Education statistics told us that America made significant progress toward introducing personal computers in primary and secondary schools during the 1980s, that more than 50 percent of all children in grades 1 through 8 use computers at school.... Remarkable findings. Too remarkable....
>
> ... [W]e decided to look further, to visit schools across America, to talk with policymakers in Washington, and to talk with professional associations for teachers and educational administrators. What we found is a false dependence on statistical analysis and a reality so discouraging that it made us question how this situation has remained unremarked on for so long. Antiquated computers; unused computers; computers used for games and not for teaching; schools and teachers unprepared to use computers that they own; mismanaged or misdirected policies; and unknown hundreds of millions of dollars spent over the last decade for little return. (Borrell 1992, p. 25)

The only technologies that have firmly taken root in most schools are the copier (which simply replaced the ditto machine) and the videotape recorder and television monitor (which replaced the 16mm projector and screen). In the vast majority of schools, telephones are still not readily available to teachers. Voice mail systems are just beginning to be seen in some schools. Fax machines are a part of most central offices but are just now appearing in school buildings. It is interesting to note that these forms of telecommunications are often not even a part of a district's plan for technology, because parents, teachers, and community members usually only associate technology with one thing: the computer.

THE ACOT PROJECT

The computer may be the only image that comes to mind when the issue of technology is raised, though this appears to be changing. Much of the evidence on computer use in schools over the past decade indicates the computer will not single-handedly revolutionize teaching and learning. Dwyer, Ringstaff, and Sandholtz (1991) describe the Apple Classroom of Tomorrow (ACOT), one of the most extensive projects for classroom implementation and integration of computers. Even with the benefit of this carefully designed, resource-rich program, teachers took quite a while to move away from familiar ways of approaching teaching.

> What we witnessed during the [first year of the project] was the adoption of the new electronic technology to support traditional text-based drill-and-practice instruction. Students continued to receive steady diets of whole-group lectures and recitation and individualized seatwork. Although much had changed physically in the classrooms, more remained the same. (p. 47)

Dwyer and colleagues describe how the integration of technology brought about gradual changes in the mix of teaching techniques:

> The new technology became thoroughly integrated into traditional classroom practice. Lecture, recitation, and seatwork remained the dominant forms of student tasks; but these were supported 30-40 percent of the time with the use of word processors, databases, some graphic programs, and many computer-assisted instruction (CAI) packages. (pp. 47-48)

The popularity of CAI packages indicates that computers are being used to continue the teacher's control over the curriculum and to impose the structure of the curriculum on the learner via the computer, rather than allowing the learner to create meaning from the wealth of information the computer is able to make available. In the ACOT project, it wasn't until the second year that a cadre of teachers emerged who began to provide instruction that was informed by a comprehensive understanding of the full potential of technology. After they mastered the technical dimensions of the machines, they were ready to experiment with new methods of teaching.

> As teachers reached [the point where they mastered the technology] independently of each other, their roles began to shift noticeably, and new

instructional patterns emerged. Team teaching, interdisciplinary project-based instruction, and individually paced instruction became more and more common at all of the sites. To accommodate more ambitious class projects, teachers even altered the foundation of the traditional school day: the master schedule.... [T]his type of teamed, project-based learning activity opened up opportunities for teachers to step back and observe the results of their own pedagogic shifts. What they saw was their students' highly evolved skill with technology, ability to learn on their own, and movement away from competitive work patterns toward collaborative ones. (pp. 48-49)

The ACOT project serves to demonstrate the difficulty associated with the introduction of any new instructional method or material into classrooms. The researchers themselves admit that they may have underestimated the complexity of introducing change into the classroom:

In the early days of the introduction of computers to classrooms, everyone seemed to focus on the innovation: computers and software. Little thought was given to the elements that would most likely remain the same: instruction, student tasks, and assessment. In many ways the early progress of ACOT repeated the error. Although the sheer number of computers in ACOT classrooms radically transformed the physical environment, for the most part student learning tasks remained unchanged. (pp. 46-47)

Collins (1991) identifies eight major trends that often accompany extensive use of computers in schools, as I have summarized below:

1. A shift from whole-class to small-group instruction. In another study of the ACOT project, Gearhart and her associates (1990) reported "a dramatic decrease in teacher-led activities and a corresponding increase in independent or cooperative activities."

2. A shift from lecture and recitation to coaching. There is evidence of a movement from didactic to constructivist approaches to learning. Schofield and Verban (1988) point to the switch by teachers from second-person grammatical constructions ("You should do this") to first-person constructions ("Let's try this") as evidence of this shift.

3. A shift from working with better students to working with weaker students. There is evidence to suggest that in whole-class instruction, teachers carry on a dialog with the better students in the class. In classrooms where students are utilizing computers individually, researchers have seen evidence of teachers increasing the attention they pay to weaker students by a significant amount (Schofield and Verban 1988).

4. A shift toward more engaged students. In classrooms where computers are accessible to students to use for long-term activities or projects, "researchers have reported dramatic increases in students' engagement" (Brown and Campione forthcoming, Carver 1990, Scardamalia and others 1989).

5. A shift from assessment based on test performance to assessment based on products, progress, and effort. Teachers are beginning to require students to solve problems before they move on to the next level of complexity in the curriculum, and to evaluate projects based on the products that the students produce. Teachers are still developing the standards and skills to assess student work against outcomes and effort, rather than factual knowledge.

6. A shift from a competitive to a cooperative social structure. When students are working on a common database, or on projects which utilize the same database, there is more sharing of information, problem-solving, and communication among students (Brown and Campione, forthcoming, Newman 1990, Scardamalia and others 1989). By contrast, when students work on Integrated Learning Systems, where each is working independently to master factual information, there appears to be an increase in competition (Schofield and Verban 1988).

7. A shift from all students learning the same things to different students learning different things. A curriculum that requires all students to learn the same things naturally ends up focusing upon the things that students have not learned, and directs student effort toward their weaknesses rather than their strengths (Drucker 1989). While there are areas of instruction where this may be quite appropriate, for many students their entire education consists of constant focus on their weaknesses, and no attention to strengths. Access by students to large, diverse databases, coupled with the opportunity for students to make some choices of what is of interest to them allows students to share information and to develop areas of strength and interest (Foster and Julyan 1988, Pea forthcoming).

8. A shift from the primacy of verbal thinking to the integration of visual and verbal thinking. Computers, electronic networks, television, and multimedia educational systems are providing a new type of "electronic literacy" which allows people to think differently than they did when restricted to print material as the primary means for transmitting ideas and thoughts at a distance. Much as the invention of the book changed the way in which people think, so too will the extensive use of electronic, visual information. Schools have yet to adapt their methodologies to this changing reality.

SOME OFTEN OVERLOOKED TECHNOLOGIES

Telephones, fax machines, and video cameras are less glamorous than computers, and for that reason their potential benefits for instruction often go unnoticed. While schools flock to install satellite dishes and to hardwire for computer networks, the most basic form of telecommunications, the telephone, often remains overlooked as a potential tool, both for teacher productivity and student learning. Telephone lines possess the ability to carry voice, electronic, and visual data. The telephone can serve as a tool for better communication between teachers and parents. If phones are available, teachers will use them. If they are inconvenient to use, teachers will be much less inclined to make repeated efforts to reach parents, for example.

Use of the phone goes beyond normal teacher-parent or even teacher-student communication. Some devices enable teachers to leave recorded messages, such as the day's homework assignments, which parents may access by punching a predesignated code for each particular teacher. Soon it will be feasible to assign codes to individual students, if the parents and teacher believe that regular messages are needed. Schools can also use such equipment to provide a verbal "bulletin board" of upcoming events and needs. Such technology pays for itself in reduced mailing costs and increased efficiency in the transmission of important information.

Phone lines also allow students to communicate with others in the local community and around the world. Conference calls allow direct, real-time communication; computer networks, like the National Geographic's Kidnet, allow electronic communication. Online databases can also be accessed through conventional phone lines, putting vast amounts of information at the fingertips of teachers and students. And recent developments in video transmission technologies are allowing phone lines to transmit video images to accompany a conversation.

Access to a telephone line also creates the capability to employ a fax machine in a variety of ways. As these machines become more ubiquitous, new uses for them will surely be found. For now, they allow for the transmission of printed information from school to school almost instantaneously. Using a fax machine, students working together on a network can transmit information (such as writing, drawings, local newspaper articles, and other forms of data that would be cumbersome to transfer to the computer) to one another to enliven discussions or focus investigations. With the capacity to beam messages to predefined groups of users with a single command, a fax machine could allow a teacher to communicate with all parents simultaneously, when or if we reach the point where most parents have such machines. A facsimile of an individual child's work for the day could be quickly transmitted to parents while the original remained at school. Parents could comment on an upcoming assignment or offer a critique of their child's work, which could be returned to the teacher and incorporated into the next day's lesson.

The video camera, a powerful, accessible tool for curriculum development and student expression, is used sparingly and is viewed more as a toy than an educational tool. It is ironic that video is largely ignored at the same time that students spend large blocks of their leisure time viewing information from video sources. Visual images are an increasingly important part of students' lives, and of most workplaces, yet video clearly remains on the fringes of instruction in schools. Low-cost editing equipment and small portable cameras with relatively sophisticated technical features enable children and adults to collect and organize visual information with relative ease. Advances in multimedia technologies are leading to the integration of video and computer-based information.

Telecommunications in the form of satellite transmissions, generally referred to as *distance learning*, along with interactive computer networks, are being employed by more and more schools throughout the country. This combination is especially appealing to rural schools as a source of learning experiences they are otherwise unable to offer. Interactive distance learning also offers a way for students to communicate with other children in very different environments, thereby counteracting the sense of isolation often present in rural settings. While telecommunications may prove to be a powerful tool for restructuring, its use at this point is primarily to expand, not to change, the existing curriculum by offering courses such as physics or French to schools not otherwise able to offer them and by employing traditional instructional strategies.

As educators become more familiar and comfortable with the potential inherent in distance learning and computer networking, and as more schools purchase the equipment necessary to participate fully in satellite uplink-downlink and computer networks, it is likely these technologies will be employed to restructure as well as expand the curriculum. If nothing else, telecommunications allow rural schools to adapt rapidly (sometimes more rapidly than their larger urban cousins). For example, rural schools with interactive capacity are offering courses in foreign languages such as Japanese and Chinese. These courses are taught by highly trained teachers, often native speakers, while urban schools, relying on their own teachers, may have to limit their offerings to the "traditional" European languages.

THE EVOLUTION OF INTEGRATED LEARNING SYSTEMS

The Integrated Learning Systems (ILS) that came into being in the mideighties were often based on the use of computers in a centralized lab as tools for individual student work on a common structured curriculum, generally containing liberal doses of drill and practice. David

Conley (February 1991) describes how these systems were primarily another example of substituting a new technology for an old one without changing the basic dimensions of teaching and learning:

> For some schools, the vision for technology is to move the fact-based, textbook-driven curriculum to a disk, allowing each student to move through this material individually on a computer, with the teacher monitoring on a central machine. These Integrated Learning Systems (ILS), or Integrated Instructional Systems (IIS) are developed by large corporations, many with ties to the textbook market. [Major producers include: Jostens Learning Corporation, WICAT Systems, Wasatch Education Systems, New Century Education, Ideal Learning, Computer Curriculum Corporation, Computer Networking Specialists, and Computer Systems Research.] They are touted as tools for increasing teacher "productivity"; one teacher can monitor several students simultaneously. The curriculum is designed by the corporation based on its conception of what each age group "should know." It is a mastery-based approach, which can be very valuable for certain portions of the curriculum with certain students in certain situations. The danger is that, having made major investments in hardware and software for these centralized labs, there will be pressure to keep them occupied with students. They will come to drive the curriculum.
>
> Programs that integrate math, English, social studies, and science already exist. Their emphasis is on the mastery of factual material at a knowledge and comprehension level. How much time students can spend at these learning stations before "productivity" declines remains to be seen. However, once this technology is purchased, the commitment to use the materials in their current form and for the goals specified is relatively irrevocable.
>
> The appeal of the IIS is evident, particularly to local boards of education, whose members are frequently business people to whom the "efficiency" of such systems generally appeals. (p. 29)

These systems may now begin to experience dramatic changes as manufacturers move to incorporate CD-ROM technologies and to allow teachers to have much greater control over the content and activities delivered to students. The use of CD-ROMs with ILS means that much greater amounts of information can be made available to students and more sophisticated learning tasks developed. "Open architecture" designs allow teachers to combine elements from different programs into more highly integrated and interesting learning experiences and to tailor experiences to individual students with relative ease. They can choose among existing learning objectives or create their own. Teachers have all the elements necessary to design an entire course within the system (Greenfield 1991).

This new generation of Integrated Learning Systems can play an important role in schools attempting to personalize learning while still ensuring that all students learn certain skills. Skillful use of such environments both as centers for student exploration and construction of knowledge and for more highly structured drill and practice offer the potential to allow students to take much greater ownership of their own learning while simultaneously enabling teachers to monitor student mastery of key skills and knowledge. Ideally, such environments could function as resource centers where students go to acquire a skill as needed to complete a project or learning experience successfully. This potential to obtain knowledge or skills "just in time," to be able to see the utility of what was being learned, and to be able to apply it almost immediately creates an opportunity to produce powerful learning experiences, where students are more likely to integrate and retain what they learn.

These examples suggest that technology could have a significant impact on instructional practices and goals, both to improve current practices and to restructure them. As mentioned earlier, the impact of technology to this point has not been significant in most schools either in terms of improvement or restructuring. It has been common to merge technology into the program without disrupting established routines or ways of thinking. Even the computer has been incorporated in a way that allows the current structure of learning to remain intact. Levinson (1990) offers two scenarios of how technology might become integrated into public schools, one suggesting how technology could change learning fundamentally, the other extending current practices out into the next decade:

> Students and teachers with a common interest, though miles apart, meet in a teleconference. Voice mail provides individual contact between teacher and student. An expert in learning styles uses a sophisticated program to diagnose the special needs of children in three school districts on one day. At computer workstations, teachers customize instruction, maintain contact with parents, and handle administrative chores. Networks and groupware allow students to work across classroom boundaries; CD-ROM technology puts huge libraries at everyone's fingertips; videotapes and satellite transmissions encourage multisite instruction, freeing classroom teachers for coaching and small-group work.
>
> Consider a second scenario....
>
> It is the year 2000. Every student has a personal computer linked to a local network; every teacher has a computer workstation to monitor student progress and record grades; every classroom is linked to the media center for video. But the organization of the school and the patterns of student/teacher interaction remain the same—except that now they are computer-mediated, perhaps slightly more efficient, certainly more complex to manage....

Which scenario will prevail? A strong case can be made that elementary and secondary educational institutions will co-opt the complex and central changes necessary to make the vision of technology-mediated education a reality. These institutions may instead use technology to replicate the status quo, supporting or streamlining current modes of operation—or school systems may introduce incremental changes that create more complexity without achieving greater effectiveness. (pp. 121-22)

In other words, technology per se is no guarantee of a better, or even a different, education for tomorrow's students.

EMERGING MULTIMEDIA TECHNOLOGIES

One of the most promising of the rapidly emerging technologies is multimedia. Multimedia combines computer, video, audio, and other sources, such as online data, in a way that allows users to interact with information and make decisions about how and what they learn. Like many recent technologies, multimedia has received considerable hype as the next tool to revolutionize education and schooling. Stansberry (1993) anticipates teachers' response to this hype and explains the potential value of multimedia:

> Try telling teachers that multimedia will revolutionize the American classroom, and chances are that their eyes will roll toward the ceiling. It's a promise that educators have heard before, about everything from the overhead projector to closed-circuit TV....
>
> Educators realize, however, that the new technology is here to stay, like it or not. They know they must prepare their students to survive in a computerized workplace. For many teachers, as well as students, the enticements of the new media are hard to resist. Unlike earlier educational computing efforts, in which rote learning exercises were pretty much moved verbatim from the page to the screen, many new applications introduced to K-12 schools attract students with images and sound, involve them with interactivity and feed their minds with vast stores of hyperlinked data.
>
> Many new applications go hand in hand with constructivist learning theory, which holds that in today's fast-changing world the ability to analyze and solve a variety of problems quickly is more important than applying memorized information. And the best way to teach the conceptual thinking required for these tasks is through a system of inquiry in which the student is immersed in hands-on, real-world situations and asked to provide solutions.
>
> Interactive multimedia—with its potential for engaging the user—may well be the perfect support medium for such a process. The new applica-

tions invite students to navigate their own paths and explore connections among disciplines that might not have been obvious. Many programs encourage students to rearrange provided media objects or generate their own to create original presentations. (pp. 30-31)

Multimedia gives students the opportunity not only to research the written word, but to employ graphic images and full-motion video in combination with text to create an integrated report. Students become much more involved in the decision-making process concerning both what they learn and how they organize and present what they have learned.

In the past two years, California, Florida, and Texas have led the way by creating many more options for the use of multimedia in their school districts. Initiatives are also under way in Utah, Wisconsin, and Minnesota. California in particular had an important impact on the development of multimedia for education when it issued a request for proposals three years ago that asked textbook publishers to integrate multimedia into their science curriculum. This request stimulated many smaller developers. The effect was that a number of titles began to emerge in a relatively short time for use in science.

An example of such a program is *Science Essentials*. This fully interactive program allows students to access information from sixteen laserdisks, a video dictionary, a word processor, and a video editor.

> In one module, students study the complex interplay of light and sound during a thunderstorm. The teacher calls up a storm sequence, which can then be stopped at key points while the students measure the amount of time between a thunderclap and a flash of light. In this way, they calculate whether the storm is approaching or receding, and at what rate and distance.
>
> *Science Essentials'* video dictionary provides visual and oral explanations for key concepts and terms. Students type in a word such as "erosion" and the video monitor displays a picture of a hillside being worn away by wind and water. Simultaneously, the computer screen presents a written definition, which is spoken aloud by a disc-based narrator. Students can cut and paste the video clips to assemble their own multimedia reports. (Stansberry 1993, p. 33)

Changes in textbook purchasing rules are driving much of the initial movement toward multimedia. Texas and California, in particular, have allowed schools to spend state textbook funds on multimedia curriculum materials. The first self-contained multimedia curriculum taught without a standard textbook was recently approved. The program, *Computer Visions,* teaches computer literacy and is in use already in scattered districts throughout the country. Districts seemed more willing to inves-

tigate alternatives to texts in this area (computer literacy) as their first
venture into multimedia curriculum.

The existence of a technology is guarantee neither of its ultimate use
nor of its effectiveness. Although multimedia holds great potential,
teachers will need to be willing to rethink their role along with their
instructional strategies.

> Recent studies by Dr. Dennis Falk and Dr. Helen Carlson at the University
> of Minnesota suggest that the biggest roadblock to multimedia lies in the
> mundane observation that teachers tend to teach in the same way they
> themselves were taught.... [T]his underlies the necessity for teacher train-
> ing in computers and multimedia. (Stansberry 1993, p. 36)

Many teachers and school districts are on the verge of making
decisions to employ multimedia more extensively. Many new titles are
currently available, prices on hardware have come down considerably,
the types of equipment school districts are likely to purchase now are
much easier to use, and there is much more staff development of high
quality available to teachers. In such an environment it is likely that
multimedia will begin to proliferate in public schools throughout the
decade—provided teachers come to embrace it as an ally and not a threat
or nuisance.

ISSUES TO CONSIDER WHEN DEVELOPING TECHNOLOGY PLANS

The introduction of computers into schools has been viewed primarily as a hardware/software project. The ACOT study and others suggest
that the integration of technology requires attention to six variables
simultaneously for any technology plan to have a significant educational
impact. These variables are hardware, software, staff development,
curriculum, instruction, and assessment. Unfortunately, most district
technology plans focus on hardware acquisitions almost exclusively.
This mistake may be avoided with the move to multimedia technologies.
Adequate resources should be devoted to the purchase of laser disks,
CD-ROM discs, or other appropriate software to support new hardware
purchases.

Staff development to support technology usage has been haphazard
at best. While this is often true of the private sector as well, it offers little
consolation to educators who face a newly equipped computer lab that
has been stocked over the summer and readied for students only days
before school begins. Before being expected to share information with
students, teachers need adequate time to learn and experiment with new

software and hardware. Technology acquisition programs often do not address this need in a systematic way.

There is little reason to purchase technology if the curriculum is not modified to take advantage of its unique potential. The purpose of technology is to enhance student learning; it is unlikely that this goal will be achieved if exactly the same curriculum is used after the technology is purchased as was used before the technology was available. There should be an expectation that new curriculum will be developed and modified regularly based on the role technology can play in learning. Similarly, the instructional techniques teachers employ in whole-class instruction are rarely well suited to the inherent potential of technology to personalize learning. Helping teachers learn to move beyond their position at the front of the classroom and to develop new management techniques that allow students to work independently and in small groups while using technology as a learning tool will be essential if teachers are to integrate technology successfully. One out-of-control class that results from the failed use of technology will discourage many teachers from using technology for years to come.

NEW ASSESSMENTS

New technologies, curricula, and instructional strategies imply new assessments, as well. If the measurement of effectiveness for new technologies is limited to standardized achievement test scores, the ultimate uses of those technologies will be extremely limited. Assessment should be designed to capture the unique aspects of learning that occur when technology is integrated thoughtfully into instruction in ways that reshape learning.

Sheingold (1991) discusses in detail the issues related to creating synergy between restructuring and technology. In particular, she identifies four recommendations to speed the process, which I have paraphrased as follows:

1. *Bring technology and learning to the same "table" when restructuring is being planned.* Make certain that those who purchase technology and those who design the learning experiences for which it is used communicate with one another.

2. *Reconsider how technology is organized in the district.* Who makes technology decisions, central office or teachers? What are the advantages of each? Should money for technology be spent on administrative uses of technology (student scheduling, information management), teacher networks and workstations, loaner machines so that

teachers can learn technology at home, new multimedia technologies, or more classroom computers? Such issues must be considered in terms of the needs and goals of each school.

3. *Work toward a critical mass of equipment and expertise.* Once enough educators understand and implement a technology, they can model its use and provide technical assistance and training to those who want to develop proficiency. A critical mass is achieved, at least in part, by having machines that are easy for educators to access. Integrated learning systems for which all lessons are programmed, for example, do not allow teachers to develop much proficiency with technology in a broad way, or to develop new uses for the computers.

4. *Use the media to convey new images and metaphors of schooling.* Technology should ultimately create schools that do not look or feel the way today's schools do. There will be little need for teachers to stand in front of quiet children seated in straight rows and tell students what to do and think. Small-group discussions revolving around data generated from a computer, student interviews and other projects using video equipment, or teacher-student evaluation of student electronic work may be more dominant images of the classroom.

Many long-awaited technologies are now available, and their price is falling. Schools are beginning to experiment with integrating these technologies into instruction. We are perhaps at the crossroads of our relationship with technology. Will it transform teaching, learning, and schooling, or will the "deep structure" (Tye 1987) of schooling overwhelm technology and make it conform to the current practices and goals of schooling (Levinson 1990, Mecklenburger 1990)? Experimentation and decision-making by educators during the next five to seven years should begin to yield the answer to this question.

CHAPTER 15

SCHOOL-COMMUNITY RELATIONS

Schools during much of this century have increased the relative separation between them and their immediate communities. While organized interest groups have certainly made their influence felt on public education, schools have not generally worked in concert with community agencies, businesses, local government agencies, or, in many cases, even parents, in a concerted fashion to adapt to the changing needs and realities of their constituents.

Many of the reforms during the first half of the twentieth century—such as nonpartisan boards of education, a professional managerial class composed of principals and superintendents, tenure and dismissal laws, formal processes for curriculum or book challenges, and the general bureaucratization of school procedures—served to insulate schools from community influence and to give them control over determining the ways and means by which community involvement took place. This separation fostered the perception that education was the responsibility of the educators, that they alone possessed the knowledge necessary to make the proper decisions regarding how schooling should be organized and conducted.

Over time, it appears that educators themselves came to believe that they did, in fact, know best and could work successfully in relative isolation from the communities in which they existed. They tended to view desirable school-community relations as a process of telling parents what they needed to do and when they needed to do it, and of insisting the business community not become involved in education except to provide resources.

This is not to say that there are no avenues open for parental involvement. Many (but by no means all) elementary schools accommodate parent volunteers in a variety of helping roles, but such involvement drops precipitously at the middle-school level and is nearly nonexistent in high schools. Many schools have active parent networks that raise funds (as well as concerns), and some are effective in shaping school policy and practice. States have instituted requirements for more formal parental and community participation in decision-making. At the same time, in most American schools community involvement still translates primarily into volunteer work in primary classrooms; attendance at sporting events, musical programs, and other forms of entertainment; and contributions of money or resources for various school projects or programs.

New fiscal and demographic realities combined with rising calls for accountability are beginning to change these traditional patterns of involvement. School administrators are much more concerned with how they are perceived in the community, and they are coming to realize the gap that separates them from their communities. This new sensitivity becomes particularly evident whenever there is the need to pass a tax measure. The proportion of families with children in school is often less than a third, or even a quarter. Most community members have little connection or communication with schools. Administrators find that business leaders do not understand or appreciate the challenges schools face, but at the same time the business community expects schools to improve dramatically before new funding is committed to them. Such realizations by school leaders have caused them to begin to rethink the relationship between schools and communities and to redefine the needs each can fulfill for the other.

A new relationship may be emerging. Although it may not necessarily be welcomed by all schools, it is one that appears to be necessary for schools to survive and adapt in the future. This new relationship entails both parent and community involvement in the schools. It also involves the movement of children from schools to the community for portions of their education. This alteration of the school-community relationship will be difficult, both because of the attendant expectations that accompany such a readjustment and the strongly ingrained norms regarding parental roles and involvement in schools.

Three aspects of this new relationship are discussed here. One is the emerging role of the business community in shaping, directing, and determining the goals, methods, and content of the education of all youth. Many educators have strong feelings that their central purpose should not be to prepare workers, and yet there are ever increasing indications that the linkages between education and economic viability for individuals and nations are stronger than ever. Another issue is the need to integrate the work of schools with all the social agencies that provide services to young people so that these efforts lead to enhanced student success. Finally, the relationship between parents and schools is changing and being redefined.

THE ROLE AND EXPECTATIONS OF THE BUSINESS COMMUNITY

What does the business community expect from schools and how are corporate leaders beginning to redefine their view of education's role and goals? Four reports provide insight into these questions: the SCANS Report, the Workplace Basics report, an analysis conducted by the National Business Roundtable, and a series of recommendations from the California Business Roundtable. This section examines these documents and considers their potential impact on education. Two of the reports (SCANS and Workplace Basics) were discussed earlier, so are presented in summary form here.

The Secretary's Commission on Achieving Necessary Skills (SCANS) released its report in July 1991 (Harp 1991). The report, a systematic analysis of the skills employers say they need for many broad employment clusters, is one of the first documents to attempt to systematically identify the skills that will be needed by future workers.

The report concludes that "despite a decade of reform efforts, we can demonstrate little improvement in student achievement. One reason for the lack of educational improvement lies in the confusing signals exchanged between the education and business communities." Five competency areas designed to produce the "workplace know-how" needed by employers are identified in the report. The five competencies are defined as "the productive use of resources, interpersonal skills, information, systems, and technology, built on a foundation of basic and thinking skills and well-developed personal qualities" (Harp 1991). The report states that "real know-how cannot be taught in isolation; students need practice in the application of these skills." It also implies that teachers need to employ student portfolios and other performance-based assessment strategies to ascertain "workplace know-how."

A second report, *Workplace Basics: The Skills Employers Want,* was produced jointly by the American Society of Training and Development and the U.S. Department of Labor's Employment and Training Administration (Carnevale, Gainer, and Meltzer 1990), based on interviews with employers throughout the nation. The report concludes that employers are looking for workers who have "learned how to learn," who have the ability to listen and communicate effectively; who have pride in themselves and their potential to be successful (self-esteem); who know how to get things done (goal-setting/motivation); who have some sense of the skills needed to perform well in the workplace (personal and career development); who can get along with customers, suppliers, or coworkers (interpersonal and negotiation skills); who have some sense of where the organization is headed and what they must do to make a contribution (organizational effectiveness); and who can assume responsibility and motivate coworkers when necessary (leadership) (Carnevale, Gainer, and Meltzer 1990, p. 8).

The National Business Roundtable, made up of the chief executive officers of 218 of the nation's largest corporations, has initiated a process to identify the gaps between what each state has done and what it plans to do to conform to the group's ambitious school-reform agenda, developed two years ago. This "gap analysis" has already been conducted for several states. The following nine areas are examined:

> High expectations for all students; outcome-based education; strong and complex assessments; rewards and penalties for schools; greater school-based decision making; an emphasis on staff development; establishment of high-quality prekindergarten programs; provision of adequate health and social services; and use of technology. (Weisman, November 20, 1991, p. 22)

The California Business Roundtable (Berman and others 1988) provides another example of the significant role state-level business organizations are playing in fundamentally restructuring public education. A number of state business roundtables have developed policy recommendations for public education that go beyond recommendations for well-prepared workers. These reports offer models for effective school systems for all students, not just potential workers. In a concisely written summary of its proposal for school reform, the California Business Roundtable outlines the principles for a new education system, followed by six specific recommendations tied to the general principles:

Principles for a New Education System

- *Performance-based.* Students, teachers, administrators, schools, and districts should be evaluated according to their performance and held accountable for results.

- *School Autonomy.* Principals and teachers should have the authority and support to provide quality education attuned to community needs and characteristics.

- *Parental Choice and Flexible Alternatives.* Parents should be able to choose schools and schooling appropriate to their children, including small-school, flexible environments in which parents are actively involved.

- *Incentives and Innovation.* Teachers and administrators should have incentives for high performance, productivity, efficiency, and the use of modern technologies.

- *Professionalism.* Teaching should be an honored, respected, and well-paid profession in which teachers are compensated according to their ability, experience and responsibility.

- *Pluralism.* The learning gap between poor minority and other children should be eliminated, and ethnic, linguistic, and cultural diversity should be treated as a strength.

The Recommendations

1. *Expand and focus schooling.*

   A. Establish primary schooling for all students.

   B. Focus and consolidate elementary and secondary education on core academics.

   C. Institute a post-10 student option of specialized education.

2. *Establish accountability based on performance and choice.*

   A. Set student performance goals, institute state-wide exit tests, and deregulate schooling.

   B. Strengthen school performance reports and intervene in failing schooling.

   C. Support parental choice of expanded school options.

3. *Establish school autonomy, and empower parents, teachers, principals.*

   A. Provide schools with discretionary budget funding and authority.

   B. Involve parents, community members, and teachers in school governance.

   C. Expand teacher responsibilities and promote team approaches to instructional management.

4. *Modernize instruction.*

   A. Redirect staff development to advance implementation of effective practices.

   B. Enable all schools to integrate technology into instruction and management.

   C. Promote adoption of flexible educational programs.

5. *Strengthen the teaching profession.*

   A. Establish multi-tiered teaching system with higher salary rates.

   B. Upgrade process of becoming a teacher.

   C. Assure continuing high professional standards.

6. *Capitalize on diversity.*

   A. Build school capacity to provide English language acquisition.

   B. Assure foreign language proficiency for all students.

   C. Establish critical and minority teacher shortage program. (Berman and others 1988, pp. 2-3)

These four reports are striking in the breadth and depth of the changes they are suggesting. They present an analysis of how schools function, what is wrong with them, and how the system must be redesigned from the perspective of the business community. This is a striking departure from the notion that professional educators should be charged with solving the problems of education in isolation. The reports, and others like them, portray the belief that education is an integral dimension of a nation's well-being, not an activity to be valued primarily for its custodial and social-sorting functions, and that, by extension, the processes and outcomes of education are now, or should be, the concern of everyone, not just educators or parents.

Many of the points contained in these four documents have at least something in common with recommendations coming from educational reformers regarding changes that are needed in curriculum and instructional practices. The difficulty appears not to be so much at the level of general rhetoric, but at the level of specific curricular and instructional responses. It seems evident that the changes schools are contemplating under the banner of restructuring are unlikely to be sustained or institutionalized without some support from the business community. It also appears evident that there is adequate common ground for educators and business leaders to communicate, to explore areas of agreement and disagreement, and to educate one another during this period of intense examination of public educational practices.

Neither the business nor the education community knows exactly how to relate to the other, though awareness of the potentially symbiotic nature of the relationship is increasing (Amster and others 1990, Gordon 1990, Hurwitz 1987, Nancy 1989, Smith 1991). A recent survey released by the National Association of Manufacturers (Weisman, December 11, 1991) indicates an awareness of the need for school-business partnerships but also reveals minimal collaboration.

> Up to 40 percent of the nation's manufacturing firms say their efforts to upgrade workplace technology and increase productivity have been stymied by the low level of education of their workforce, according to a new study by the National Association of Manufacturers.
>
> The study also found that most manufacturers believe the workplace must be more integrated into the schools through such programs as apprenticeships, job shadowing, and other methods of school-to-work transition. Nevertheless, it notes, only a handful of firms are participating in such projects.
>
> The report was based on a survey of 360 small, medium, and large manufacturing companies...
>
> The survey also found, however, that few manufacturing firms are responding to their problems by becoming involved in education. (p. 5)

Attempts are being made by some businesses to become more involved in education through a variety of programs and approaches. Although cooperative efforts between schools and private-sector organizations are not new, the upsurge of interest and activity in this area is being described by some as the "partnership movement" (Merenda 1989). Since 1983 the number of schools reporting that they were engaged in some form of partnership with a private-sector organization has increased from 17 to 40 percent (National Center for Education Statistics 1989). The current interest in partnerships expresses itself in a variety of types of programs and approaches. Merenda (1989) describes five levels of partnership, each closer to the classroom, that I have summarized as follows:

Level 1: Policy Partnerships. These are collaborative efforts among businesses, schools, and public officials to shape the policy debate regarding education, and to develop policy recommendations, including legislation, that address issues raised in this debate.*

Level 2: Partners in Systemic Educational Improvement. At this level, businesspeople and educators work together to identify needed reforms and then work together over the long term to make those reforms happen jointly.

Level 3: Partners in Management. In this type of partnership business provides schools with support and expertise in specific areas of management, such as labor relations, personnel and incentive systems, purchasing processes, plant and equipment management, strategic planning, legal, finance, and tax issues, management information systems, performance standards, productivity, public relations, or any of a wide range of possible areas. Executives on loan are one method by which such partnerships are enacted.

Level 4: Partners in Teacher Training and Development. Businesses involved in teacher and counselor training and professional development provide opportunities for educators to update, upgrade, or maintain skills, or to learn more about the labor market in the community. Activities might include summer internships that enable teachers to learn more about the business world, or specific courses for teachers in areas such as science and math.

Level 5: Partners in the Classroom. In these partnerships, volunteers from a business bring their expertise directly into the classroom, or bring the classroom to the business. Engineers might demonstrate design techniques to students, or serve as tutors and mentors.

The high level of interest in (and perhaps unrealistic expectations for) partnerships is illustrated by the response of national magazines that cater to the private sector, such as *Business Week*, which featured an

---

* The report from the California Roundtable presented earlier is an example of the product of a Level 1 partnership.

issue with the headline: "Education: Can the Private Sector Save Our Schools?" The lead article, entitled "Saving Our Schools: With America's Classrooms Besieged on So Many Fronts, Here's How the Private Sector Can Help" (Segal and others 1992), described ways partnerships could be developed, paralleling those presented above by Merenda.

Ahead lie many pitfalls to the development of new relationships between businesses and public education. Many business leaders—results-oriented people—are driven to distraction by the pace at which change in education is pursued, even in those schools identified as being on the leading edge of reform. They cannot comprehend the lack of a sense of urgency for change in most schools. Businesspeople may become impatient when educators insist that they cannot be held responsible for producing a product, and that there is no equitable way to measure performance of teachers. Those in the private sector tend not to accept the argument of educators that little more can be done without additional resources; after all, most radical change in business occurs only after a company loses money. Financial rewards come as the result of a higher quality product, not in response to mediocre performance.

Many educators, for their part, tend to view "business" as a monolith, not making distinctions among large and small employers, progressive and conservative businesspeople, or the corporate cultures present in every business. They are certain businesspeople do not understand or appreciate the difficulties educators face attempting to teach the current generation of children without the resources they feel are minimally necessary. They believe that only they, the educators, are truly concerned about the development of the whole child. They believe the methods of business will not work in schools; businesses are places to secure resources and little else.

Neither side finds it easy to view the world through the perspective of the other. At the same time, it appears as if the evolution of social and economic systems will force these two groups to reach much greater understanding of one another and to identify their true areas of common interest and potential mutual support.

COOPERATION WITH SOCIAL-SERVICE AGENCIES

In addition to developing a new relationship with the business community, educators will likely strengthen their ties with social-service agencies. It is becoming increasingly clear that schools cannot deal with the complex social and emotional needs demonstrated by more and more students without help. Guthrie and Guthrie (1991) summarize the current state of the services provided by social-service agencies:

A wide assortment of social service agencies has been organized to serve children and youth at risk; but the services often overlap, agencies are compartmentalized, and children are incorrectly referred (Fantini and Sinclair 1985, Heath and McLaughlin 1989, Hodgkinson 1989, Kirst and McLaughlin 1989, Melaville and Blank 1991, Schorr 1988)....

... Now is the time to look at the full range of functions that schools are being asked to perform and identify which of those the school is best suited to handle, which can best be provided by other institutions and agencies, and which can best be accomplished by joint efforts. The challenge is not simply to divide up responsibilities, but to reconceptualize the role of the school and relationships among the school, the community, and the larger society. The new arrangement must be designed so that it shifts the emphasis of each agency away from itself and toward the client: the child. (p. 17)

There are many difficulties inherent in coordinating and integrating services between different public-service agencies to provide more comprehensive service delivery. The Education and Human Services Consortium, a group of twenty-two agencies that offer services to children, commissioned a detailed discussion of the strategies and structures for interagency collaboration (Melaville and Blank 1991). As a result of these discussions, the following elements were identified as essential to a comprehensive service-delivery program:

- Easy access to a wide array of prevention, treatment, and support services
- Techniques to ensure that appropriate services are received and adjusted to meet the changing needs of children and families
- A focus on the whole family
- Agency efforts to empower families within an atmosphere of mutual respect
- An emphasis on improved outcomes for children and families (p. 36)

Establishing collaborative interagency relationships is not easy. In fact, it's incredibly difficult. Most agencies are bureaucracies that have little or no incentive to alter their practices, coordinate with other bureaucracies, or share resources. In practice these behaviors might actually be punished, with reduced budgets or reduced authority for the agency. Policy-making bodies will need to create new rules that support or mandate cooperation and client-centered service provision. Otherwise, it is unlikely most agencies will put the energy necessary into solving the problems that inevitably develop when large, complex, bureaucratic organizations attempt to work together.

This is not to say that some well-meaning (or desperate) agencies are not already moving voluntarily in this direction. There is evidence to suggest that such discussions are beginning to occur voluntarily, particularly in large urban areas. Summarized below are Melaville and Blank's (1991) guidelines for those who undertake interagency planning designed to create client-centered service-delivery systems:

Involve all key players. This includes representatives from all levels of each organization, as well as the clients whose lives will be affected.

Choose a realistic strategy. Agreeing to coordinate existing services provides a good starting point. After cooperation is an established norm, true collaboration can develop. Small successes can breed larger successes.

Establish a shared vision. "Cooperative ventures are based on a recognition of shared clients. Collaborative partnerships must create a shared vision of better outcomes for the children and families they both serve" as the starting point for interaction (p. 37).

Agree to disagree in the process. Conflict is likely, particularly as the relationship between agencies moves from the realm of general principles to specific programs. Conflict surfacing and resolution mechanisms need to be in place before major problems surface.

Make promises you can keep. Set attainable objectives, especially in the beginning, to create momentum and a sense of accomplishment. "At the same time, sufficiently ambitious long-term goals will ensure that momentum is maintained" (p. 37).

"Keep your eye on the prize." It is easy for collaborative initiatives to become bogged down in the difficulty of day-to-day operations and disagreements. It is important to refocus continually on the reasons for collaboration. Often someone outside of the direct service community who is committed to the goals of the initiative and able to attract the attention of key players can help ensure that people remain focused on the original purposes of the partnership.

Build ownership at all levels. The commitment to the success of the project must extend to all levels of all agencies involved. Involve as many different people as possible in planning from the earliest moment possible, and keep all staff informed regularly. Cross-agency training can be particularly valuable to enable staff to learn new skills, communicate perceptions, and share information.

Avoid "red herrings." Partners should delay the resolution of the "technical difficulties" that impede the delivery of comprehensive services to shared clients until partners have developed a shared vision and assessed the degree to which problems are the result of statute versus operating procedures subject to internal control. Most problems result not from statutory limitations, but from current patterns of behavior which can be changed. Such patterns should not be allowed to sidetrack the project.

Institutionalize change. "If changes in programming, referral arrangements, co-location agreements, and other initiatives are to endure, both service delivery and system level efforts will need facilities, staff, and a continuing source of financial support. Participants must incorporate partnership objectives into their own institutional mandates and budgets and earmark" permanent resources to keep joint efforts going. (p. 37).

Publicize your success. "Partnerships must demonstrate the ability to improve outcomes for children and families and express their success" in terms of dollars saved, current and future, and social benefit achieved. "Well-publicized results that consistently meet reasonable objectives will go far to attract the funding necessary to replicate and expand innovation" (p. 37).

Once partnerships are formed, there is still the matter of engaging the client with the service providers. Achieving this may require a reassessment of how best to reach clients. Social-service agencies and schools alike are realizing that clients do not come easily or willingly to environments they feel are hostile and alienating. Parents of many at-risk youth, in particular, have not necessarily had positive experiences with governmental institutions generally, and schools particularly. As a strategy to deal with this gap between home and school, the home visit is reemerging as a strategy to bridge the gap between institution and person, and to provide services where they are needed. This simple approach has proved highly effective.

Home visits are "one of the most promising vehicles we have" to make a positive impact on parents' and children's lives, according to Edward F. Zigler, the Sterling Professor of Psychology and the director of the Bush Center in Child Development and Social Policy at Yale University (cited in Cohen, October 16, 1991, p.24). Howard A. Davidson, the current chairman of the U.S. Advisory Board on Child Abuse, stated that home visits offer a "non-intrusive" way to support young families; they constitute "the best-studied prevention program in terms of its proven impact" (cited in Cohen).

Such strategies help overcome the advantage that middle-class families have when interacting with schools. These families tend to be more positively oriented toward schooling and to have had more positive experiences while in school. They are also more able to influence decisions and more likely to understand how the system operates. The parents of those who use social services have few of these advantages. Davies (1991a) describes the responsibility school people have to establish more opportunities for the voice of these parents to be heard:

School administrators and teachers must take the initiative and reach out to "hard to reach" parents and to devise a wide variety of ways for them to participate. This means having appropriately prepared and sensitive school representatives go into homes to meet with families, having some meetings outside of the school in settings less intimidating and more accessible to many parents, using natural and informal settings to reach and talk with parents (churches, markets, social centers), preparing materials in other languages in the case of people whose English proficiency is weak, and scheduling activities that are attuned to the constituents being sought. But, the key point is that for many parents who are poor and from minority and immigrant groups, the initiative has to come from the school, and a diverse and persistent strategy is needed to break down barriers and establish trust. (p. 94)

For educators, accustomed to meeting parents at the school during times convenient to the educator, the idea of visiting parents at their homes at times most convenient for parents is a novel concept. Many schools that conduct home visits view them as more valuable than traditional parent-teacher conferences, because they are opportunities to break through some of the barriers between home and school. Such visits are already being employed by other social-service agencies, such as health and welfare programs, and it would seem to be possible to integrate educational services into home visits through careful inter-agency coordination and support in many areas. Home visits also help teachers to develop a better understanding of the needs of individual students by observing firsthand the environment in which the students live.

Not all home visits need be conducted by teachers. The Schools Reaching Out project, developed by the Institute for Responsive Education, helped sponsor the development of a "home visitor" program at Ellis School in Boston, one of its demonstration elementary schools (Davies 1991b). The program recruited and trained four women who were residents of the community and had experience in community work such as adult education, counseling, or the care and education of young children. These women were paid $10 an hour to visit four or five families. In all, the program reached about seventy-five families.

During these visits the home visitors provided information about school expectations, curriculum, rules, and requirements. They dispensed advice and materials to enable parents to support their children's schoolwork, and to encourage parents to read regularly to their children. They provided information on and referrals to other agencies that provided assistance in areas such as housing, health services, summer camps, and child rearing. They listened to the concerns of families regarding schooling and learned about their interests, then communicated this information to teachers. The home visitors discussed with teachers how to deal with parents' questions regarding homework and foster children's language development (Davies 1991b).

The goal of all these activities is to create schools where the needs of the student as client become the key force for the coordination of services offered by various agencies now operating in isolation from one another. The goal is not just to offer programs to those in need of support and assistance, but to ensure that clients are more successful members of society as a result of the programs and services offered. In this sense, all the agencies providing services to children will be judged in terms of outcomes (functional human beings), rather than processes (number and variety of programs), as was discussed earlier in the context of student learning.

NEW EXPECTATIONS FOR PARENTAL INVOLVEMENT

The relationship between parents and schools is evolving as well, as educators come to recognize the critical importance of active parental involvement if students are to achieve at higher levels. Epstein (Brandt, October 1989) outlines five types of parent involvement that have been familiar to educators and parents alike:

Type 1: The basic obligations of parents to ensure children's health and safety; to parent and raise the child in a manner that prepares them for school; to supervise, discipline and guide; and to build positive home conditions that support school learning and appropriate behavior.

Type 2: The basic obligations of the school to communicate with the home about school programs and the child's progress, including memos, notices, report cards, and conferences. The form, frequency, and quality of these communications greatly affect the ability of parents to understand and fulfill their role successfully.

Type 3: Parent involvement at schools, including volunteering, attending events, participating in workshops or programs for their own education and training.

Type 4: Parent involvement in learning activities at home such as responding to the child's need for help, initiating activities to help the child learn, assisting the child on learning activities that are coordinated with the child's classwork.

Type 5: Parent involvement in governance and advocacy in ways such as decision-making roles in groups such as PTA/PTO, committees, advisory councils, and other groups at the building and district level, and as community activists monitoring the school and working for school improvement. (Summarized from Brandt, October 1989, p. 25)

These five types of involvement represent the traditional range of participation by parents. Davies (1991b) suggests there may be three common themes present in the new programs for parent involvement being put forth by many different scholars and researchers, including Comer, Levin, Epstein, Rich, Seeley, Zigler, Kagan, Weiss, and Cochran. These three common themes are as follows:

1. *Providing success for all children.* All children can learn and can achieve school success. None should be labeled as likely failures because of the social, economic, or racial characteristics of their families or communities.

2. *Serving the whole child.* Social, emotional, physical, and academic growth and development are inextricably linked. To foster cognitive and academic development, all other facets of development must also be addressed by schools, by families, and by other institutions that affect the child.

3. *Sharing responsibility.* The social, emotional, physical, and academic development of the child is a shared and overlapping responsibility of the school, the family, and other community agencies and institutions. In order to promote the social and academic development of children, the key institutions must change their practices and their relationships with one another. (p. 377)

There is considerable evidence that as this involvement increases, so does student success (Henderson 1987, Mortimore and Sammons 1987). Parental involvement comes to be much more than bake sales and PTA meetings. Parents can be effective partners only when they know what is happening in schools, know what is expected of them, and know how to provide the requested support. In return, schools can expect to be more willing to listen to parents' concerns and to involve them in decisions about their children's educational program.

Many school districts are engaged in attempts to redefine the role of parents. Chrispeels (1991) describes the rationale for and development of policies in San Diego that seek to enhance parental involvement, with particular attention to the needs of those not typically involved in education:

In many instances, however, administrators' and teachers' low expectations for and negative attitudes toward low-income or non-English-speaking children and their parents have prevented the development and implementation of well-designed programs [of parental involvement]....

In early 1988 the [San Diego City Schools] established a task force to explore ways in which parent involvement could be strengthened in the district.... The policy.... [developed by the task force] outlines a multifaceted definition of parent involvement. The board [of education] commits itself to:

- involve parents as partners in school governance, including shared decision making and advisory functions;

- establish effective two-way communication with all parents, respecting the diversity and differing needs of families;

- develop strategies and programmatic structures at schools to enable parents to participate actively in their children's education;

- provide support and coordination for school staff and parents to implement and sustain appropriate parent involvement from kindergarten through grade 12; and

- use schools to connect students and families with community resources that provide educational enrichment and support. (pp. 368-69)

One implication of a stronger partnership with parents that is often overlooked is the school's responsibility to ensure that *all* teachers are highly competent and care about children. As parents spend more time in schools and communicate with their children and the children's teacher about the educational program, they become informed and formidable critics of educational practice. The mediocrity tolerated by some school systems will be severely challenged if parents are spending more time in schools and participating in the education of their children. Fear of increased complaints from parents about insensitive or incompetent teachers, or ineffective instructional practices, causes some administrators to discourage parents from becoming more involved in schools. Such an attitude is unacceptable because it insulates teachers, administrators, and school systems from accountability for performance.

Family involvement is particularly beneficial in schools serving low-income populations. The Accelerated Schools program, developed by Henry Levin of Stanford University (Chenowith 1991; Rothman, October 30, 1991), emphasizes parent involvement as crucial to improved student performance. Webster Elementary School, in San Francisco, has successfully implemented the Accelerated Schools approach. The school strives to make parents feel welcome, helps them work toward high school equivalency diplomas, and even hires some parents as paraprofessionals. Enhanced communication between home and school has helped reduce student discipline problems (Rothman, October 30, 1991; Seeley 1989).

The philosophy of the Accelerated Schools is counter to the trend in American society of delegating functions to government that has prevailed over the past 150 years. Services such as fire, police, sanitation, public health, welfare, and child care have all come to be responsibilities of government, not of individuals or groups of citizens. In this "delegation model" (Seeley 1989), citizens fulfill their responsibility by paying taxes. Political office-holders and paid officials are then held accountable. This model may work well enough in other areas, such as police and fire protection, provided the community is supportive and engages in preventative behaviors. However, in education the model has serious flaws:

> Over the years, the model has become institutionalized in the roles, relationships, and mind-sets not only of school staffs but of parents, students, and citizens as well. As a result, efforts by school leaders to involve parents frequently meet with resistance. Parents often signal, subconsciously or overtly, that they don't have to be involved because the job has been delegated to the schools, just as they don't have to be involved in putting out fires once the fire department has been given that job. Schools staffs, for their part, often do not see parent involvement as part of their professional role and, indeed, can quite justifiably see it as an interference with the jobs that have been delegated to them. (Seeley 1989, p. 46)

The Accelerated Schools program seeks to counteract this model by establishing the principle that parental involvement is essential to the success of the school. Parental involvement is a necessity, not a luxury. It is not the specific activities that are the key to achieving this goal as much as the ability of the staff and parents to create what they jointly see as a collaborative community learning center.

A closer, more open relationship with the communities in which schools are embedded appears to be essential, inevitable, and desirable. This changing relationship will have a strong impact on schools, many of which continue to see themselves as insulated islands. Schools that view partnerships as opportunities rather than threats will be able to capitalize on additional resources and to redefine relationships in ways that reaffirm the school's role as the center of the community and that enable the school to fulfill its primary mission.

CHAPTER 16

TIME

Many educators are frustrated with the way time is structured in schools. The urge to redefine the temporal limits imposed on education is often particularly strong in high schools, where the multiple-period day arbitrarily divides learning into several blocks of time, each about fifty minutes long. Most discussions focus on reducing the number of daily preparations for teachers and the number of students with whom teachers must interact.

Discussions of the structure and allocation of time in education have two foci: how time is structured to facilitate learning for students; and how time can be organized or acquired to allow educators to rethink and redesign schools, and to attain the skills necessary to make such schools successful. This chapter discusses the first focal point, the structure of student learning time. The discussion of time for adults to develop and implement new models of schooling is contained in part 4.

REDESIGNING TIME IN SECONDARY SCHOOLS

An example of an innovative model for reconfiguring time in ways that offer the potential for changes in curriculum and instruction is the Copernican Plan (Carroll 1990). Designed for use at the high school level, this plan centers around the idea of "macroclasses" of differing possible lengths, from 70 to 226 minutes. It emphasizes the integration of subject matter through seminars. The curriculum would become less fragmented, since students would take fewer courses at any given time. Teachers would teach fewer classes each day, thereby reducing the number of students they see each day. One goal is to improve students' sense of belonging and to increase teachers' ability to meet students' individual needs. These benefits in turn can lead to greater student success and increased motivation.

Carroll identifies some of the benefits of restructuring time in American high schools:

Virtually every high school in the U.S. can reduce its average class size by 20%; increase the number of courses or sections it offers by 20%; reduce the total number of students with whom a teacher works each day by 60% to 80%; provide students with regularly scheduled seminars dealing with complex issues; establish a flexible, productive instructional environment that fosters effective mastery learning, as well as other practices recommended by research; get students to master 25% to 30% more information beyond what they learn in the seminars; and do all of this more or less within present levels of funding.

How? By redeploying its staff members and students so that teachers can concentrate on teaching students rather than on "covering" classes....

... The Copernican Plan proposes two alternative schedules. In the first, students enroll in *only one* four-hour class each day for a period of 30 days. (Each student would enroll in six of these classes each year, which fulfills the required 180 day school days.) In the second alternative, students enroll in *two* two-hour classes at a time for 60 days. (Each student would enroll in three of these two-course trimesters each year.) A school could schedule both 30-day and 60-day courses simultaneously, and the length of these large-block macroclasses could vary....

... The increased efficiency of the Copernican Plan frees a block of time in the afternoons that allows the Copernican high school to offer seminars that help students integrate knowledge across traditional disciplinary lines....

... A common response to the proposed schedules is that students cannot survive a two-hour lecture, much less a four-hour one. And the prevalence of that response is a major reason why the Copernican Plan is needed. Overuse of lecturing is a major problem of high school instruction. The Copernican Plan establishes conditions that foster the use of a variety of instructional approaches that are more personalized and more effective, and it stresses the importance of providing adequate support for staff members to develop these approaches....

... Under the Copernican Plan, a teacher prepares for and teaches only one or two classes at a time. Furthermore, average class size can be reduced by about 20%. This reduction in class size is made possible because teachers traditionally teach five classes for the full school year. Under the Copernican Plan, each teacher teaches *six* classes a year, thereby increasing the number of classes offered by 20%.

... However, the key advantage of the Copernican Plan, whatever the size of the class, is that the teacher deals with only a small number of students at one time and prepares for only one (or two) classes at a time. Even with *two* two-hour classes for 60 days, a teacher's daily student load drops more than 60%. The time classroom teachers typically spend preparing for five classes can be spent on planning for small groups or even for individual students within a single class. (pp. 358-62)

Wasson High School, in Colorado Springs, Colorado, has developed another strategy for restructuring time within the school day. A block scheduling system that combines time in a manner somewhat different than the Copernican Plan, but toward similar goals, was proposed and implemented in the 1990-91 school year. The schedule at Wasson includes the following key points:

A. The educational program is offered in a school day of four instructional blocks of 90 minutes in length. There is a 15 minute passing period between the two morning classes and a 10 minute passing period between the two afternoon classes. Students and staff share a 50 minute common lunch period between the morning and afternoon classes.

B. No staff member would teach more than three of the four blocks. Sophomores and juniors must take four blocks. Seniors must take a minimum of three blocks.

C. Two-semester courses under a traditional system (180 meetings in 50 minute periods) are combined into a single semester (90 meetings of 90 minutes each).

D. Semester-length classes under a traditional system are offered in quarter-length classes (nine weeks) under this proposal. Students change these classes at the end of each nine-week grading period.

E. English/Social Studies and Math/Science will be taught as blocks for two semesters by a team of two instructors per block.

F. AP courses will be expanded in length. An AP course which was formerly one semester in length will now be three quarters. Students would enroll in an elective related to the AP course during the fourth quarter.

G. Some specialty courses must meet daily during specified quarters. Band, Choir, Peer Counseling, Yearbook, and Journalism will meet daily in 90 minute blocks during the quarters their program needs mandate such a schedule.

H. Department chairs will receive some release time in the form of reduced teaching load to provide instructional leadership to the process.

I. The common lunch block of 50 minutes will provide opportunities for clubs and organizations to meet within the instructional day.

J. Assemblies can be scheduled before lunch by taking 15 minutes from each block, providing one hour for the assembly and still leaving 1 hour and 15 minutes for instruction in each block. One-quarter of the teachers will be available to supervise the assembly, since they will not be scheduled into a block at the concurrent time.

K. Under this plan departments are encouraged to explore the expanded opportunities for:

  1. Interdisciplinary teaching
  2. Interdisciplinary cooperative teaching and teacher exchanges

3. Heterogeneous grouping (Adapted from Wasson Restructuring Committee 1990)

Although a semester course meets fewer minutes than its year-long equivalent, teachers reported that they are able to teach comparable amounts of material (though they may not "cover" the same number of units they did in the past). Additional time is gained by decreasing the number of transitions and housekeeping tasks associated with beginning each class. The time available is utilized more effectively. Student involvement and attention are enhanced, and teachers and students are freer to interact. In addition, administrators and teachers reported that students seem less stressed and more able to focus. A majority of students agreed with this assessment. A majority also reported feeling better about coming to school, having fewer conflicts with teachers and fewer tardies, and believing that their grades had improved due to more frequent progress reports. Nearly 73 percent observed that teachers were using new teaching techniques. In a staff survey administered after the first year of the block schedule, teachers reported the following outcomes:

- In general, they noted an improvement in student achievement.
- They were able to provide more individualized attention and instruction to their students.
- They had implemented a variety of new teaching strategies and techniques.
- They were more willing to experiment with new assessment techniques.
- They spent more time preparing for each block class.
- Collegiality had increased.
- The time used for classroom administrative tasks had decreased.
- They felt better about the quality of their teaching.
- They made more parent contacts.
- Instructional units were less fragmented.
- Ninety-four percent would prefer to retain the block schedule.

A more radical reconceptualization of time is embodied in the Dalton Plan, an approach that has been around for generations (Edwards 1991). This method was developed in the early 1900s by Helen Parkhurst, a teacher who had experimented with the ideas of Maria Montessori and wanted to apply them to a secondary school environment. It was named the Dalton Laboratory Plan because it was first implemented at a high school in Dalton, Massachusetts, in 1921. Edwards (1991) describes this plan:

> The Dalton Plan involved a complete restructuring of the school day into subject labs, with students determining their individual daily schedules. From fifth through 12th grades..., traditional classrooms were disbanded, schedules were eliminated, bells were silenced....
>
> [The Plan] was adapted by each school to fit its particular circumstances, [and] was student-centered, self-paced, and individualized by means of monthly contracts. An efficient, easy-to-use system of charts helped students and teachers keep track of progress. Usually the mornings in a Dalton Plan school were devoted to the academic disciplines in the laboratories, while afternoons were given over to more traditional physical education and music classes and to extracurricular activities.
>
> Each academic area had one or several classrooms designated as labs. All textbooks and library books dealing with a particular subject, along with any required equipment, were kept in that subject's lab. Tables and chairs replaced desks. Teachers were assigned according to their specialties and remained in the subject labs to help students with assignments when needed, to organize small discussion groups, to counsel, and to encourage....
>
> Central to the Dalton Plan were teacher-designed contracts that outlined activities geared not only to learning basic skills and concepts, but also to independent thinking and creativity.... All students completed activities to ensure a grasp of the basics, but they could then choose which other tasks and activities they wished to pursue. The more they undertook and the better they performed, the higher their evaluations.
>
> Each morning, with guidance from their homeroom teachers, the students selected which contracts they wished to work on and proceeded to those laboratories. They were required to remain at least an hour in a chosen lab, but they were then free to move to another or to stay longer. There were no 50-minute classes, no bells signaling a mass migration of students. Students could finish one month's subject contract completely before beginning others, or they could work on each contract piecemeal. If students completed work on all their contracts before the month was over, they could return to their favorite labs and do more, or they could request the next month's contract and move ahead. To ensure learning in all disciplines, students could not get a new contract in any one subject until all the others were satisfactorily completed. Those who fell behind because of illness, personal or family crises, vacations, difficulty with a subject, or excessive absenteeism simply continued working on the month's contracts until they were completed and then received the next set. (p. 399)

Middle schools, in particular, are implementing approaches that create blocks of time by having groups of teachers and students stay together for more than one period. The blocks create opportunities for these teachers to tailor time to the needs of the learning experiences they design. In such a model, one hundred students might each have the same teachers in the same order (periods 1-4) for the same subjects (language arts, science, social studies, art). Assuming forty-five-minute periods, the four teachers would have three hours in which to vary the amount of time each spent with students on any given day. They could also meet with larger or smaller groups of students each day. In other words, some days one teacher might take most of the students for some activity while the other three were free to work with small groups or individual students for an extended time.

Although block scheduling is by no means new (see, for example, Vars 1984), it can be a valuable tool to enable faculties to achieve a number of goals simultaneously. Common planning time can be developed for teachers who work together in blocks. Teachers can discuss the problems and needs of individual students, since they are likely to know them better and more able to modify practices to meet student needs or cope with the unique needs of particular children.

The potential of block scheduling may still be underdeveloped. Teachers may not take advantage of the opportunities inherent in the restructuring of time, because of either the difficulty of finding the time to integrate their practices or the lack of desire to surrender their autonomy to a team. Planning to work together to achieve common goals for students is not a simple task, and most teachers do not have professional experiences with collaborative planning that prepare them for the intensive involvement and interaction that occur under a truly integrated block program.

EXTENDING THE SCHOOL YEAR

The notion of abandoning the agricultural calendar and extending the amount of time students attend school has been mentioned frequently in recent years (Barrett 1990, Pipho 1990). However, such suggestions are more often vaguely defined statements of intent than clearly defined, well-reasoned policy initiatives. The implications of an extended school year are profound, both in terms of the fiscal resources needed to accomplish this change, and in terms of the implications for social traditions surrounding family vacations and economic enterprises built around the availability of the young during the summer.

Oregon recently enacted one of the most sweeping educational reform packages in the nation, referred to as the "Mega-Education Reform Bill" when it moved through the Legislature. It is now known by its more prosaic but still ambitious title, the Oregon Educational Act for the 21st Century. This multifaceted act contains many recommendations for changes in schooling, some of which are discussed in chapter 13, Learning Environment. The act increases the number of days in the school year to 185 days by 1996, to 200 days by the year 200, and to 220 days by 2010. Skeptics point out that this portion of the bill was enacted without companion funding authorization and therefore may not be implemented. Passage of the act does suggest, however, that the state plans to engage in a serious discussion regarding the amount of time students should spend at school each year. Most troubling to observers is the lack of guarantees that anything different will happen during the additional days. Little will be accomplished if a student experiences failure for 220 days a year instead of 180.

The call to extend the school year is often based on the notion that children in other nations are spending more time in school and, as a result, are learning more than American students. It is often stated that Asian students spend 240 days a year in school. However, as Stevenson and Stigler (1992) point out, such statistics do not take into account that students attend only half-days on Saturdays, that recesses may last as much as five times longer than they do in American schools, that lunch periods can extend an hour and a half, and that many activities identified in American schools as afterschool activities may take place within the school day.

> So although Asian children spend more time at school than American children, the difference in the amount of academic instruction is not so profound as the more general statistics imply.

> Perhaps more important than the total amount of time spent in school is the way in which this time is distributed throughout the year. In contrast to the two-day weekends and long summer vacations that provide discontinuities in the American school year, time flows more or less continuously in Chinese and Japanese schools. School vacations in Asia are shorter and spaced more evenly throughout the year. Learning is an unceasing process, maintained by the momentum developed during regular classes....

> ... Throughout vacation periods, clubs and activity groups continue to meet, children may continue to receive homework assignments from their teachers, and new academic projects are begun. In these ways Asian students do have a longer "school" year, but much of the additional time is not spent in the regular classroom. (Stevenson and Stigler, pp. 143-44)

Initial efforts to extend the school year may have to focus on the groups most in need of the extra time: students who require additional learning opportunities and teachers who need time to develop new resources and techniques. It may not be cost effective or economically feasible for all teachers and students to attend school for a longer time, but it may be possible to phase in the concept gradually by first focusing on the needs of those students who will benefit most from carefully constructed programs utilizing extended instructional time. Perhaps the results from these initial applications will support the use of additional time to develop students individually, not simply to present more content to all. Another potential benefit of gradual implementation of a lengthened school year is professional development of teachers. An extended schedule can provide opportunities for many more teachers to engage in retraining to an extent not currently possible through inservice conducted during the regular school year.

The year-round school is another strategy that provides additional instructional time for those students who need it and gives teachers more opportunities for professional development. The year-round school is not a new concept in areas where overcrowding has forced educators to accommodate more students in existing school buildings. In year-round schools, students usually attend three quarters out of four, or a total of approximately 180 days annually (Ballinger 1988).

With some modification, models developed for year-round school programs that have been implemented successfully throughout the nation could guide the transition to a longer school year. Such a transition could make teacher retraining easier, since teachers could be paid during their "off" track to participate in training. They would also have a ready-made "laboratory" in which to practice their new skills and techniques without the pressure of a full teaching load, since "regular" school would be in session, and the teacher would already know many of the students.

Beyond these approaches to extending the school year, some schools are experimenting with extending the school day, from early morning to late evening, to reflect changing realities of students' lives and to become in larger measure community centers. The unfortunate reality is that the need for custodial care for children has continued to increase during the past two decades, and there is every indication that the trend will continue through the next decade. More children are in need of custodial care for two primary reasons: the increased participation by women (many of whom are single mothers) in the labor force, and the breakup of traditional community and of extended and nuclear family structures.

While many educators resist the notion of becoming more involved in custodial care, it appears that there are few other institutions prepared to meet this need, and that meeting this need provides continued institutional legitimacy to schools. To extend care beyond the boundaries of the school day requires interagency coordination, since schools do not have the resources to do so alone. However, school buildings represent an underutilized resource in most communities. Extending the amount of time they are available for children will not only help improve education for these children, but also can strengthen the sense of community that surrounds the school.

CAUTION: CHANGE IN THE ENABLING VARIABLES IS NOT NECESSARILY RESTRUCTURING

Time is often the first variable examined by high schools when the idea of restructuring is raised. It is attractive because it appears to offer a "quick fix" that leaves the content of instruction fairly intact. A coalition of faculty supportive of some sort of change in the arrangement of time can often be built. However, teachers may join this coalition for widely varying reasons. Some of the reasons may be more related to easing the working conditions for the adults than to improving learning conditions for the children.

This is not to say that such investigations of alternative schedules are without merit; quite the contrary. At the same time, it is important to foreshadow here a series of issues related to the process of restructuring, issues that are discussed at greater length in part 4. One key issue to keep in mind when considering change in any of the enabling variables (learning environment, technology, school-community relations, and time) is that specific programmatic responses must be considered in relation to broader organizational goals or purposes, generally stated in the form of mission and vision. These overarching statements of purpose help provide a framework within which specific actions or programs might be considered. Making sure that programmatic changes, such as a revised schedule, are tied to the school's vision helps prevent the spread of "projectitis" and the subsequent failure of the project if coalition members cease to support the innovation.

One of the problems with most of the approaches to modifying the allocation, organization, or amount of time devoted to instruction is that such changes are unlikely to make much difference so long as learning continues to be conceived of in terms of hours spent on a topic or in a course. This traditional conception of learning will always engender pressures to return to standardized and uniform application of time to learning tasks. And such pressure is understandable. As long as teachers think of their subjects as being independent from one another, and think of learning as being the exposure of students to material for a specified period, they will demand their "fair share." Moving to performance-based, outcome-based systems can help to break the constraints imposed by rigid structures of time. The concept of outcomes was introduced in a previous chapter, and outcome-based education will be discussed in more detail in chapter 25.

We have now come to the end of the four dimensions of educational restructuring that make up the subcategory of enabling variables. The common thread present in much of the discussion of these enabling variables (chapters 13-16) is the goal of recreating schools as communities. Almost all the changes being proposed, particularly in the areas of learning environment, school-community relations, and time, are geared toward humanizing and personalizing the interactions that occur within schools and between people inside and outside of schools. Even technology is being conceptualized as a tool to enhance the social and cooperative dimensions of learning in addition to its role as a tool for solitary study.

Changes in these enabling variables, then, support the transformation of the learning environment into a place where students take responsibility for their learning, are assisted by many adults and other children, have strong feelings of affiliation with the school and the people in it, know what is expected of them, and are actively engaged in achieving the outcomes used to frame and assess their learning.

The supporting variables, which follow in chapters 17-20, help establish and define the organizational context within which this learning takes place. They can be critically important because that context can either support or inhibit the ability of adults and children to bring about the changes in learning described up to this point.

CHAPTER 17

GOVERNANCE

Governance and three other dimensions—teacher leadership, personnel, and working relationships—set limits on and define potentialities for change in educational practices, rather than directly causing changes within classrooms. For this reason, these four dimensions are classified as *supporting variables* in contrast with the central variables discussed in chapters 9-12 (outcomes, curriculum, instruction, and assessment) and the enabling variables in chapters 13-16 (learning environment, technology, school-community relations, and time).

Ideally, schools would begin their restructuring efforts by making changes in the core dimensions that constitute the central variables. Then they would examine the learning context as represented by the enabling variables to align that context with the changes occurring in the central variables. While such a process was being conducted, the supporting variables of governance, teacher leadership, personnel, and working relationships would be modified in ways that would allow or support the achievement of the goals being pursued through the central and enabling variables. In practice, change almost never occurs in such a nice, logical sequence. Many, perhaps most, efforts at school restructuring start with or are defined as changes in the dimension of governance, usually in the form of decentralized decision-making.

Often schools begin with projects in the area of governance or perhaps teacher leadership or working relationships, proceeding on the belief that once organizational parameters have been altered, substantive change will follow. Although such alterations may facilitate and support changes in curriculum and instruction, it appears that they rarely cause change in these core dimensions. There is a danger that all the energy for restructuring will be directed toward projects related to these supporting variables, with little left to address fundamental issues of practice more closely related to the classroom and children.

TWO STRATEGIES FOR CHANGE

Change efforts in the governance of schools can be grouped into two general categories. One type attempts to decentralize power to school sites to enable those closest to the process of teaching and learning to solve the problems they identify; the other attempts to create external competition through programs of choice to compel fundamental change in education and to challenge the monopoly held by the public schools.

Changes in the first category come under names such as site-based management, decentralized decision-making, site-based decision-making, and participatory decision-making. All refer to greater decision-making authority and responsibility at the school site; these changes redefine power relationships within school districts.

Changes that fall into the second category are generally referred to under the heading of "choice." Included are mild forms that allow greater choice within a school or district for students and parents; policy initiatives and pilot programs designed to allow interdistrict movement of students, generally attached to some mechanism that causes funding to follow the student to whatever school he or she chooses to attend; charter schools that combine elements of both decentralized decision-making and choice; and more radical programs that allow unlimited options for parents within and outside the public school system.

There is a linkage between these two strategies for changing schools, according to Hill and Bonan (1991), who state that "the ultimate accountability mechanism for a system of distinctive site-managed schools is parental choice."

Each of these two strategies will be discussed in general terms, with a consideration of the policy implications and assumptions of each. We will also look at some examples of the application of these concepts through state policy and school-site experiments.

DECENTRALIZED, PARTICIPATORY DECISION-MAKING

As mentioned earlier, the perception people have regarding their relationship to large institutions in society may be changing. More people expect to be involved to a greater degree in decisions that affect their lives. Challenges faced by organizations are becoming so complex that most solutions require those closest to problems to be actively involved in developing and implementing responses. However, involving people in decision-making has its own set of difficulties. As educators move to involve more stakeholders in decision-making, they are beginning to wrestle with those issues and the tensions and tradeoffs that accompany changes in power relationships. The redistribution of power in organizations is rarely accomplished without stress and conflict. Participatory decision-making, site-based management, and their variants are certainly no exception in this regard. As popular as these approaches have been, both among educators and legislators, it appears that they must be designed and implemented with great care if they are to have an effect on student learning.

Wohlstetter and Odden (1992) suggest it is time to rethink school-based management. Their review of the research on school decentralization leads them to conclude "that school-based management (a) is everywhere and nowhere, (b) comes in a variety of forms, (c) is created without clear goals or real accountability, and (d) exists in a state/district policy context that often gives mixed signals to schools" (pp. 530-31).

> The surveys by Clune and White (1988) and Malen et al. (1990) concluded that school systems all over the country are involved in SBM. However, when programs are analyzed, the general conclusion is that the extent of decision-making responsibility devolved to the school is limited; consequently, site teachers and administrators have little to manage, particularly with respect to budget, personnel, and curriculum strategies (Clune & White, 1988; Malen & Ogawa, 1988; Wohlstetter and Buffett, 1992). Thus many studies conclude that SBM has not been much of a change because nothing real has been decentralized—SBM is everywhere and nowhere....
>
> ... Although SBM is used as a generic term for a range of decentralization activities, there are three very specific forms of SBM, yet few studies differentiate among them.... One SBM governance model, "community control," shifts power from professional educators and the board of education to parent and community groups not previously involved in school governance. Thus lay persons, not the professional hierarchy, are in control and accountability is directed outward toward the community (Ornstein, 1974, 1983). The current reform strategy in Chicago, Illinois is an example of this model....
>
> A second SBM model, "administrative decentralization" (Ornstein, 1974), features teacher control by delegating decision making down the ranks of the professional hierarchy to building-level educators. Thus individual schools, typically through site councils where teachers have the majority, are empowered to make some decisions formerly made by the central administration. In Los Angeles, California, for example, local school leadership councils have between 6 and 16 members (depending on the level and size of the school) and half of the council seats are reserved for teachers....
>
> A third SBM model features "principal control" and, in contrast to the other two forms of decentralization, may or may not have a site council. In Edmonton, Canada, for example, district policy stipulates that principals are responsible for constructing the school budget "in consultation" with staff, parents, and community members, but the principals are not required

to establish site councils and much of the consultation is conducted informally on an ad hoc basis (Wohlstetter & Buffett, 1992)....

... [R]esearch to date suggests that each form of SBM faces different obstacles and experiences different measures of success. Some SBM models of the past, particularly the New York City decentralization model of the 1970s, put the community in control; however, the general feeling is that New York City schools have not improved with the devolution of power from the central office to lower-level organizations (Fantini & Gittell, 1973; Zimet, 1973)....

Other than being justified rhetorically as a means to improve schools, SBM plans rarely entail specific learning goals for students or have accountability mechanisms that assess SBM with respect to those goals or organizational improvements (Wohlstetter & Buffett, 1992). Rather, SBM's impact is focused mostly on teachers and administrators....

... Wohlstetter and Buffett (1992) found that district-initiated SBM programs often ran afoul of state rules and regulations and that state-initiated SBM reforms, even when implemented by some schools, often ran afoul of district rules and regulations. State-initiated SBM also can run into problems when districts and superintendents do not support it and/or do not have complementary policies. As a result, site teachers and administrators get mixed signals or contradictory support from different levels of the policy system. Both are a hindrance to real school-based decision making. (Wohlstetter and Odden, pp. 531-36)

Hill and Bonan (1991), in a study of five school districts where site-based management had been employed extensively, conclude that simply involving more people in decision-making is unlikely to lead to improved student learning outcomes unless it is viewed as being of central importance and considerable time and support are given to nurturing its success. Hill and Bonan view site-based management as a systemwide reform, requiring central-office administrators, principals, and teachers to rethink their roles. Site-based management "cannot function simply as a new way of conducting labor-management relations or increasing teacher job satisfaction.... [S]ite management must focus on instruction, not on labor-management tensions."

These two authors also emphasize that new accountability methods should accompany increased decision-making responsibility: "Site-based management makes school staff, not the central office, accountable for school performance." They suggest it may take schools two to three years to redefine roles and focus energies on instructional issues. As schools evolve, they will develop distinctive characters, goals, and operating styles. Ultimately, Hill and Bonan contend, parental choice will guarantee accountability in a site-managed school system.

Malen, Ogawa, and Kranz (1990a), in a review of nearly 200 documents describing current and previous attempts to use site-based management in the United States, Canada, and Australia, conclude that "site-based management in most instances does not achieve its stated objectives." They found that site participants rarely addressed issues of central importance to schools: "Teachers and parents frequently characterize the subjects councils and committees consider as 'routine,' 'blasé,' 'trivial' or peripheral'." The councils busied themselves implementing district directives or tending to the operation of the building. The control exerted by principals limited the amount of teacher (or parental) involvement in decision-making. Councils rarely received the technical assistance, information, training, or funds necessary to function successfully. Malen and others conclude that "there is little evidence that site-based management improves student achievement."

PARTICIPATION FOR WHAT PURPOSE?

When educators consider strategies for increasing stakeholder participation in decision-making, they might benefit by asking one question first: Why are we doing this? Research on teacher involvement in decision-making in particular (S. Conley 1991) seems to indicate that such involvement in and of itself does not necessarily lead to improved organizational outcomes:

> Do students actually learn more or drop out less in a more participatory school environment?... [T]he indirect benefits of participation received by employees (e.g., satisfaction) provide an unpersuasive rationale for participation in many organizations, because the benefits of participation are likely to be viewed by managers as one-sided (Shedd, 1987). (S. Conley 1991, p. 230)

Processes for teacher participation in decision-making have yet to resolve problems that arise in determining what decisions teachers want to make. There is evidence (Bridges 1967; Mohrman, Cooke, and Mohrman 1978; Maeroff, November 1988) to suggest that teachers are not currently involved in decisions related to teaching and classroom conditions, despite the fact they have shown more interest in "operational decisions pertaining to direct student instruction than to strategic school administration"; "teachers appear to feel most deprived in decisions... that regulate the boundary between the classroom and the organization" (S. Conley 1991, p. 236).

Teachers want to be involved in decisions that they perceive as contributing to their ability to do their jobs more effectively. When teachers can be made to feel more in control of the conditions of their work environment, their sense of personal efficacy is enhanced (Fuller and others 1982, Lanier and Sedlak 1989, Rosenholtz 1989b). For most teachers, this sense of personal efficacy is a critically important contributor to the decisions they make and the behaviors they demonstrate. If teachers do not feel they can educate students successfully, they act one way; if they feel they can influence the conditions affecting success, they act another way. Herein lies one of the key potentialities of teacher involvement in decision-making: enhanced teacher efficacy.

How might teacher involvement in decision-making be promoted in ways that are meaningful to teachers and toward ends that are valuable to the organization? S. Conley (1991) suggests that

> rather than simply assuming that established forms of participation are not working, the question becomes, What are the specific advantages and disadvantages of these forms? That is, to what degree have more conventional participation forms offered teachers opportunities for involvement in school decisions? (p. 245)

How do traditional decision-making structures, such as departmental organization, teacher teams, grade-level meetings, and various standing and ad hoc committees function? What are their defects? Is the problem in the structure or in its implementation? The ways in which administrators support and facilitate involvement can be a critical factor in determining the degree of validity teachers ascribe to the process (Corcoran 1987).

ALTERNATIVE CONCEPTS OF POWER

New governance structures are being developed and employed in many schools around the nation (see, for example, Ayers 1991; Clinchy 1989; D. Conley, March 1991; Dentler and others 1987). These structures will not automatically solve the problems of broad-based participation in decision-making. S. Conley (1991) provides insight into the underlying cause of the tensions this process creates:

> New forms of participation, such as school governance structures (Malen & Ogawa, 1988), appear to be generating uneasiness among teachers and administrators as both parties reassess their respective roles (Lieberman, [May] 1988). Apprehension may be partially due to a failure to distinguish between two critical dimensions of power: authority and influence.... Authority deals with final decision-making power, referring to the ability of an organizational member to say yes or no to a particular decision. Authority stems from the legal right to make decisions governing others; for example, principals have the authority to assign students and teachers to classes, and teachers have the (de facto) authority to implement instruction (Bacharach & Mitchell, 1987). Influence, by contrast, stems from the capacity to shape decisions through informal or nonauthoritative means, including personal characteristics (e.g., charisma), expertise, informal opportunity, and resources (Bacharach & Lawler, 1980). (S. Conley 1991, p. 253)

Although the distinction between authority and influence is a useful one, there are perhaps additional ways to think about how power might be distributed and managed in organizations. Dunlap and Goldman (1991) describe an alternative concept—facilitative power—and describe its use in schools. This representation of power relations parallels S. Conley's analysis in many important respects. However, it employs different language and images to describe power relationships:

> Facilitative power reflects a process that, by creating or sustaining favorable conditions, allows subordinates to enhance their individual and collective performance. If dominance is power *over* someone, facilitative power is power manifested *through* someone—more like Clegg's (1989) images of electrical or ecological circuits of power than like the ability to break or smash something by force.
>
> In schools, we see administrators exercising facilitative power when they engage in any or all of four relatively distinct activities. First, they help to arrange material resources that provide support for educational activities. Second, they select and manage people who can work together effectively, paying attention to both the skills and the personalities that comprise the mix. They may also provide training for, and modeling of, collaborative behaviors. Third, they supervise and monitor activities, not to exercise hierarchical control, but to stress feedback and reinforcement and to make suggestions. Fourth, they provide networks for activities, adding members to groups, linking groups to activities elsewhere, helping groups to "go public" with activities, and diffusing new ideas. In short, administrators use facilitative power to work *through* others rather than to exercise power *over* them. (Dunlap and Goldman 1991, pp. 13-14, emphasis in original)

In this concept of facilitative power, administrators (and teachers) create the organizational conditions for certain ends to be pursued. They work with and through people to achieve outcomes valued by members in the organization. New governance structures may be more likely to succeed if they are accompanied by new ways of thinking about power. There is nothing magical about a structure. At best, it increases the likelihood that certain things may occur, but a structural change guarantees nothing. If, at the same time, the players within the system rethink their relationships and, if possible, their conceptions of power, new structures can have remarkable effects.

CHARTER SCHOOLS: BRIDGE BETWEEN SITE-BASED DECISION-MAKING AND CHOICE

The logical extension of decentralization is the notion of Education by Charter (Budde 1989). In this method, teachers in effect become independent contractors within the school district. The board of education sets the procedures for establishing and evaluating educational charters, and the central administration provides certain services to all charters, such as payroll and planning. Groups of teachers petition the school district to sign an "Educational Charter" that authorizes the teachers to create and provide a complete educational program for students—in essence, their own school—within certain legal and policy parameters established by the school board. They receive funding equal to the district per-pupil allocation minus administrative and other fixed costs. The teacher team has complete discretion in organizing the educational program and in determining how money is spent. Obviously, to sustain such a program economically, the teachers need to be able to attract enough students.

Minnesota is one state that has enacted a law allowing both public and private schools to receive charters.

> Under the charter-schools measure passed by the legislature last May, school boards can authorize one or more licensed teachers to create new public schools that would be free from most current rules and regulations. The law also enables existing private or public schools to become charter schools....
>
> Such schools must meet state standards for what students should know, and may not screen students, charge tuition, or have a religious affiliation. The law allows up to eight such schools statewide.
>
> But the charter schools are to be educationally, financially, and legally independent: able to hire and fire their employees, devise their budgets, and develop their curriculum. Each school must be run by a board of directors, a majority of whose members are licensed teachers. (Olson, November 27, 1991, p. 18)

In September 1992, California became the second state to allow charter schools (Olson, September 30, 1992). The California measure allows for up to one hundred such schools to be established, providing many more opportunities than the Minnesota program, with its limit of eight schools. Furthermore, the California law allows a district to convert all its schools to charter status. The measure was introduced at least in part to head off support for a private-school voucher initiative scheduled for the 1994 election. The voucher proposal would give parents the right to choose to send their children to public, private, or parochial schools at taxpayer expense.

Charter schools amount to choice within the public schools. In effect, they combine a controlled voucher plan with incentives to stimulate the development of new responses and solutions to many of the ills that beset education—solutions that might not be possible in current public schools with their structural and political barriers to fundamental change. Charter schools provide a middle ground between no choice and an unrestricted voucher plan, which would allow parents to abandon the public schools and take their vouchers wherever they chose.

A request to establish a charter school is initiated by a petition. At least 10 percent of the teachers in a district or 50 percent of the teachers in a single school must sign the petition. The school board then reviews the proposal. If approved, the school is granted a charter to operate for five years, with five-year renewals. Schools are exempt from most state regulations. They must, however, specify their educational program, the outcomes students will be expected to meet, and how progress toward achieving these goals will be measured. The California law contains provisions to ensure that basic equity issues are addressed for students; however, teachers' rights to remain part of a local bargaining unit are not maintained, raising the concerns of the teachers' unions. Charter schools can set admission criteria, but the racial and ethnic composition of the school has to reflect the student population of the district. If the local board of education denies a request for a charter twice, the decision can be appealed to the county board of education.

Charter-school legislation has been or is being considered in other states such as Colorado, Connecticut, Florida, Massachusetts, New Jersey, Pennsylvania, and Tennessee. It remains to be seen whether the Minnesota and California experiments will lead to the creation of new educational environments, or will simply recreate isolated versions of the existing public school system. The charter-school model does offer the potential for creating communities where people feel they have chosen to be there, and where those people can define themselves and organize their schools on the basis of distinct value and belief systems regarding education, thereby counteracting the bland bureaucratic sameness of most American schools.

There is obvious danger in allowing schools to reflect different beliefs and values through their instructional programs. A key challenge will be to see whether such schools will operate within the mainstream of the American value system to the degree that taxpayers will not object to their monies going to support the education that takes place in those schools. An additional challenge will be to see if such a system can be reconciled with the traditional collective-bargaining model of labor-management relations present in most districts.

SCHOOL CHOICE: THE ULTIMATE CHANGE IN GOVERNANCE

The next step along the continuum of decentralization and restructured governance of public education is school choice that extends beyond the public schools to include private and parochial schools, and in some extreme cases, home schooling. Chubb and Moe (1990, 1991) argue for this more radical and unrestricted form of choice. On the basis of their studies of private schools, they conclude that schools outside the public system may perform better and that parents should have a chance to choose between the two.

They argue that market forces must be allowed to shape schools to a greater degree. "We believe that the fundamental causes of poor academic performance are not to be found in the schools, but rather in the institutions by which the schools have traditionally been governed" (Chubb and Moe 1991, p. 18).

They identify three basic issues that must be addressed for education to improve: the relationship between school organization and student achievement, the conditions that promote or inhibit desirable forms of organization, and how these conditions are affected by their institutional settings. The key to making schools effective lies in "unleashing the productive potential already present in the schools and their personnel. It rests with granting them the autonomy to do what they do best" (Chubb and Moe 1991, p. 20). This autonomy is achieved by freeing schools from external control as embodied in the central bureaucracy, to the maximum extent possible.

Chubb and Moe argue not simply for site-based management in public schools, however. The forces of bureaucracy are too strong within any public educational system, they contend. The pressure of the market place is the only way to guarantee freedom from stifling bureaucracy. "The system [must be] built on decentralization, competition, and choice."

They challenge states to create a new system of public education based on the market principles of parental choice and school competition. The properties of that system are summarized below:

- The state sets minimum criteria and charters any group that can meet the minimum criteria.
- The state will monitor enrollment and distribute public monies accordingly.
- The system of school finance will continue to be determined and controlled by the state.
- Scholarships will be available for at-risk students to make them attractive clients.
- Each student can attend any chartered school, with state funding following the student.

- Every effort will be made to provide tax-supported transportation to all students who need it.
- The state will provide a Parent Information Center to help parents choose among schools.
- The application process to schools must be equitable.
- Each school must have complete autonomy to determine its governance structure and internal organizational structure.
- The state will hold schools accountable for meeting the criteria set out in their charters, and for adherence to applicable laws.
- The state will not hold schools accountable for student achievement or other dimensions that call for assessments of the quality of school performance. This is the function of the market place.

The Bush Administration, through its promotion of the New American Schools Development Corporation (NASDC), sought to lay the groundwork for greater school choice by sponsoring the development of new "break the mold" schools. NASDC promoted private as well as public models and actively supported the development of partnerships between groups not previously involved in public education.

Chris Whittle, through Whittle Communication Corporation, has proposed to develop a string of schools intended to compete with public schools ("Whittle To Spend Millions on 'State of the Art' Schools" 1991; Walsh, May 22, 1991). Whittle Communication will seek $2.5 to $3 billion in capital to open about two-hundred private schools in major urban areas across the nation that would incorporate the innovations developed by a special research team. By the year 2010, Whittle expects to be serving as many as two million pupils at one thousand campuses.

The schools are to be developed by a team of educators and others and will adhere to these four design criteria:

- provide a significantly improved education for no more than the current cost per pupil in public schools
- be capable of demonstrating improved results
- select students randomly from a pool of applicants
- in non-choice areas of the nation, provide 20 percent of all participating students with full scholarships ("Whittle To Spend Millions..." 1991, p. 4)

Activities such as the NASDC design-development process and the Whittle project indicate that there may be more alternatives to traditional public schools, even if these two projects themselves do not ultimately succeed. The existence of numerous alternative models is one of the prerequisites for any program of choice to have a real chance of succeeding politically. Right now there are few genuine alternatives to public schools other than parochial schools and private schools, which in almost all cases function in ways that are nearly identical to public schools. Most people are hesitant to send their children to a school with religious beliefs different than their own, therefore limiting these schools as true competition to public schools in many cases. Moreover, private schools tend to be out of the reach financially or physically (or socially) of most families.

If new options become available, options that are nonsectarian, accessible, and affordable, it is much more conceivable that the proportion of families that choose to send their children to nonpublic schools will increase. Every parent with a child in a school outside the public system becomes a natural constituent for unrestricted school choice. Therefore, projects such as the New American Schools and the Edison Project and others that may occur are important to watch, not so much for their potential impact on the public educational system, nor for the students they may pull away from public schools, but for the constituency they create for choice and for the models they establish as viable alternatives to the existing system. The parents of students who attend such schools can be a more powerful voice with policy-makers than those who promote the funding of religious schools with tax monies, an idea that will never be exceedingly popular, or those who send their children to expensive, elite schools, for whom there may be little sympathy among lawmakers to provide any financial benefits.

There certainly are some key issues that appear time and time again in this policy debate. Martin (1991) contends legislators and policy-makers are "trading the known for the unknown" when they mandate programs of school choice. I have summarized below Martin's ten recommendations about choice programs, which express the concerns many educators and policy-makers have regarding this approach.

1. *Choice programs must be well planned.* Careful attention must be paid both to family freedom as well as school improvement and educational equity.

2. *Choice programs must have equitable admission standards.* Quasi-private schools cannot be allowed to skim off the most easily-educated students, leaving the rest for the public system.

3. *Choice programs must inform parents of the ramifications of their choices.* Parent information programs must be developed with consideration of the social and economic background of the parents who will be receiving the information.

4. *Choice programs cannot guarantee that educational quality will increase.* There is no compelling evidence at this point to confirm that choice leads to better education.

5. *Choice programs must be but one part of the total reform process in education.* Overall issues of program quality and of community involvement in education must be addressed, rather than simply relying on choice to solve all educational problems.

6. *Choice programs must view the increasing racial diversity of America as a strength on which to build a world-class educational enterprise.* These programs cannot become vehicles for greater segregation and social sorting. They must actively promote the valuing of diversity if the nation is to survive.

7. *Choice programs must assure citizens their rightful role in the governance and accountability of educational programs.* Safeguards must be developed to guarantee parental involvement, even if parents are dispersed over a wide geographical area. Present protections, such as privacy laws and the civil rights of students, must be maintained.

8. *"Experimental" choice programs must begin collecting solid and hard evidence that will demonstrate their successes and failures so that the citizenry can learn from the experiments.* As the new initiatives being developed by state legislatures, the federal government, and private entrepreneurs begin to come on line, adequate requirements that they demonstrate the impact of these programs must be adopted and enforced.

9. *Developers of choice programs must confront the financial implications of greater options for parents and students.* Choice programs are not low-cost strategies for school improvement. Are the dollars being allocated to them better off being spent to strengthen and improve the existing system, or develop a new one? The reality of the cost of choice must be acknowledged.

10. *Choices will be limited in a choice program.* There is a limit to the amount of information students and parents can and will process to make a choice. More options do not necessarily lead to better decisions beyond a certain point.

These caveats notwithstanding, policy-makers have not been shy recently in attempting programs of choice. Many states, including Minnesota, Wisconsin, and Massachusetts, have launched limited experiments with choice. Nathan (1989) describes five basic types of school choice plans where choice is limited to the public system: local, program development, specialty school, open enrollment, and postsecondary option.

Local: Plans offered by local public school districts include "magnets, schools within schools, and/or alternative programs from which families select" (p. 53). Numerous urban districts have developed magnet schools as a means by which to enhance choice and promote integration. Historically, however, some of these have tended to become elite through selective examination requirements. The challenge is to devise magnets that are able to compete successfully and that guarantee access to a wide range of students.

Program Development: In these plans, "states provide funds explicitly to help school districts plan and develop different kinds of public school options" (p. 53).

Specialty School: "Statewide or regional magnet schools, drawing from several districts, are funded by cooperating districts or directly from the state" (p. 53). Minnesota, Colorado, and Oregon have laws with provisions that offer students a second chance through area learning centers, second-chance sites, or alternative learning centers.

Open Enrollment: These plans allow students to "move across district lines under certain circumstances without permission of the district in which they live" (p. 53). Some districts, such as St. Louis and Milwaukee, use this as a strategy to promote desegregation within a metropolitan area. In other states, such as Massachusetts, this approach is being utilized as means to pressure districts to improve or face loss of students.

Postsecondary Options: Students taking advantage of these plans "may attend post-secondary programs with state and/or local funds paying their tuition and fees; families not in the district decide whether to participate" (p. 53). Minnesota, for example, allows public school juniors and seniors to attend colleges, universities, and vocational schools with state funds following them.

The effectiveness of programs that give parents more choices within the public schools is still being determined. Many have only been in existence for a year or two. However, even in this brief time, some relatively dramatic changes can be seen. Walsh (October 28, 1992) states that

> public open-enrollment programs are gaining in popularity among parents and students.
>
> Three states that established open-enrollment programs in the past few years have reported dramatic increases this fall in the number of students choosing to attend schools outside their districts.
>
> In Massachusetts, the number of students participating in the school-choice program has tripled since last year, from 921 to more than 2,800 this year.

In Iowa, more than 7,500 students have opted to attend public schools outside their home districts, up almost 50 percent over last year, while Nebraska's program has seen a 75 percent increase this fall. (p. 12)

Boyer (1992), in a report sponsored by the Carnegie Foundation for the Advancement of Teaching, concludes that claims about the benefits of choice programs "greatly outdistance the evidence." The report, *School Choice,* states that 70 percent of parents with children in public school have no desire to send their children to any other school, public or private. One reason is the distances most students would have to travel to reach a school in a neighboring district. The survey found that in those states with choice programs, fewer than 2 percent of eligible parents are participating. The report concludes that parents tend to use these choice programs for other than academic reasons. No significant educational gains can be attributed to these programs at this time, the report states. Specifically, the limited Milwaukee experiment is pointed to as an example of a program that has not achieved the desired results:

> Most private schools involved in the program, which took effect in 1990, thus far have failed to report academic results—let alone demonstrate gains. And the small-scale experiment has failed to spark broader improvements in the school system. (Olson, October 28, 1992, p. 12)

The report does find some more successful choice programs within school districts. These programs, which enable all children and parents to participate, help revitalize schools, empower teachers and principals, and stimulate parents to consider which program is best suited to their children. It mentions Montclair, New Jersey; Cambridge, Massachusetts; and District 4 in East Harlem, New York City, as examples.

Boyer recommends that choice be used to supplement, but not supplant, neighborhood schools, and he recommends the creation of choice within schools, as well. He offers the following recommendations for the development of effective choice programs:

- Programs should not be arbitrarily imposed. Parents must be actively engaged in the planning and be well informed about the alternatives available to them.
- Transportation must be provided to students who need it.
- No statewide choice program should be established until a series of essential requirements, such as equitable funding, have been met, and all existing programs should be held to the same standards. (Olson, October 28, 1992, p. 12)

The relative merits of choice as a tool to restructure schools continue to be hotly debated. Reactions to the Boyer report were swift and strong. Advocates of choice, such as Terry Moe and Joe Nathan, reacted strongly to criticisms of choice contained in the report. Moe accused Boyer of engaging in a "smear job," while Nathan contended that the report contained "64 significant misstatements of fact or distortions in one chapter" (Olson, November 4, 1992). At the same time, Richard Rothstein, a research associate at the Economic Policy Institute in Washington, D.C., said that the report "confirms what most people who've studied the issue have observed. And that is that there's no reason to believe that choice in itself will be a force for improving schools" (Olson, November 4, 1992).

In all likelihood, policy-makers will continue to consider more substantial programs of choice over the next several years. It appears equally likely that such proposals will appear on state ballots, as well. Their potential impact will be far-reaching, yet their effectiveness has yet to be demonstrated. Public educators should be ready to explain why they should not be subject to the same type of competition prevalent in the rest of the economic system, and how they are offering appropriate choices within the existing system.

In the final analysis, the greatest impact on public schools from programs of choice may not come so much from the actual adoption of them as from the threat of adoption. This may provide more of a lever or motivator to cause teachers, administrators, and board members to look more seriously at the need to accommodate the desires of parents for greater control over their children's education, or at least the option to have some effect or influence on the way in which their children are educated. Choice (or the threat of choice) may be the external force that galvanizes some schools or districts to take action to improve their instructional programs and to think of parents and students as customers and clients who want their needs and goals to be considered to a greater degree than they are now. If programs of choice have this effect alone, they will have been a powerful influence on school restructuring.

IS DECENTRALIZATION THE 'MAGIC BULLET' TO SCHOOL RESTRUCTURING?

All these strategies for changing governance have one common assumption: Decentralization of decision-making and responsibility will lead to improved academic outcomes, whether such decentralization is achieved by instituting a new structure of authority within the existing system (site-based decision-making) or by decentralizing education as a system (choice). It is an assumption that resonates well with policy-makers, who look at the private sector and the political arena and see examples of this trend all around them.

In education, there is little evidence that wholesale decentralization for its own sake will necessarily or automatically lead to improved learning outcomes. What is absent from almost every plan for decentralizing decision-making is a concomitant increase in accountability to accompany enhanced authority to make decisions. Such accountability is critical to making decentralization work.

Decentralization of authority without accountability to produce some agreed-upon, observable outcomes can cause problems if those who make the decisions focus on personal agendas and quality-of-teacher-worklife issues. Cetron and Gayle (1991) forecast that "all community stakeholders will continue to demand more involvement in decisions, but will have little knowledge about what should be done to restructure." Decentralization and involvement without focus, agreement on desirable outcomes, vision, and clear accountability to produce results are unlikely to succeed as the sole strategy to restructure education.

In the private sector, decentralization can be linked to clear outcomes, generally expressed as "the bottom line." Such clarity is seldom present in education. There are many possible ways to increase accountability, particularly once a state, district, or school agrees upon the outcomes and assessments that will be employed to gauge student learning. Accountability in such an environment directly relates decisions made by adults to the effects such decisions have on children's learning. If the decisions are having no effect or a negative effect, there is little reason to allow such an educational environment to function without scrutiny or intervention. If, on the other hand, a school is showing success, there is a strong rationale to enhance its method of decision-making, or certainly to refrain from intervening in governance issues.

Kirst (1991) notes that "school-based management is often seen as equivalent to restructuring, rather than a component of the overall plan." Malen and Ogawa's (1988) study of site councils in Salt Lake City schools indicates that even though highly favorable arrangements existed to help ensure the success of these councils, "teachers and parents did not wield significant influence on significant issues in [key] decision areas." A report on the Boston school-based management plan concludes that "school-based management in Boston has not significantly altered instruction and has not shifted real authority to the schools" (Olson, September 25, 1991). In other words, simply creating new decision-making structures is no guarantee of restructuring. Involvement in decision-making can be an important component of a comprehensive strategy to help students succeed, but it is only one component.

Success, it should be noted, must be defined differently for each school. There is a "value added" aspect of education that is not captured well by a blind comparison of test scores. The performance of a school in an affluent neighborhood with strong parental support and a rich experience base for students might better be compared, at least on some important dimensions, with other similar schools rather than with all schools. Likewise, schools with large numbers of students who require additional resources or pose unique challenges can make a case to be compared with other schools with similar student populations, and with their own performance over time, in addition to performance in relation to the norm. Such comparisons, however, do not in any way imply acceptance of the disparities between schools for the rich and schools for the poor. The comparisons are merely an additional tool to understand all schools better and to improve their performance by identifying effective practices and consistently poor performers. These comparisons allow the effects of decision-making to be gauged more accurately. Such principles apply both to strategies of participatory decision-making present in public schools and to programs of choice outside the public schools.

There is little evidence that decentralization as the first (or only) element in a program of school restructuring is a successful strategy. Changes in governance may be critical to restructuring when they occur along with other activities designed to enhance student learning, and when they function to support this goal. In other words, changes in governance appear to hold the greatest promise as means to ends, not ends in themselves.

CHAPTER 18

TEACHER LEADERSHIP

T he teacher's role is likely to change in significant ways if restructuring occurs. Changes implied in the literature on restructuring include greater responsibilities for teachers and greater decision-making authority over a range of factors affecting the teaching-learning process. In short, the success of most strategies for restructuring assume or require greater teacher professionalism. Teachers are expected to take on more decision-making responsibility both inside and outside the classroom, as well as to demonstrate the ability to shape instruction and the learning environment in many important ways.

The implications of such changes, both for the culture of schools and the role of teacher, are profound. Professionalism implies a "client-oriented and knowledge-based" view of practice (Darling-Hammond 1990), which may not be the norm in many schools currently. Moving from a bureaucratic to a professional conception of teaching requires schools to change their views of "the nature of learning, the characteristics of learners, and the requirements for effective teaching" (Darling-Hammond 1990, p. 27). This is unlikely to happen without changes in the leadership roles teachers exercise within schools.

This chapter explores the rationale for greater teacher leadership, some of the implications of such a role change, and examples of ways in which school districts are creating new leadership roles for teachers.

WHY DEVELOP TEACHER LEADERSHIP?

Development of teacher leadership, like any other activity or program initiated to restructure schools, should have a clear goal and purpose related ultimately to student learning outcomes. New teacher roles or titles should not be created simply as morale-boosters or "feel good" activities that serve primarily as ends in themselves.

There are many valid reasons for pursuing teacher leadership as a component of a strategy for school restructuring. The current literature on school improvement and restructuring is replete with calls for teacher empowerment and leadership. Some advocate teacher leadership as a means to achieve greater application of democratic principles of participation (Bolin 1989; Lieberman, February 1988; Louis 1992; Schmuck and Schmuck 1992), to enhance teacher satisfaction (McClure 1988), to build professionalism (Moses and Whitaker 1990; Brandt, May 1989), to increase the capacity for organizational change (Maeroff, March 1988), and even to improve the efficiency of schools (Darling-Hammond 1990).

Development of teacher leadership can be thought of as having the potential to address all these goals. However, of all these possible applications, teacher leadership might be most valuable as a means to enhance the professional growth and development of teachers, and as a means to revitalize their teaching and their interactions with their colleagues.

Devaney (1987) offers insight into teachers' perceptions of their motivation and satisfaction; in the following paragraphs, she summarizes research on the importance of professional development for teachers:

> During 1985 Milbrey W. McLaughlin and her colleagues at Stanford University conducted in-depth interviews of 85 San Francisco Bay Area teachers of widely diverse experience and work settings, both elementary and secondary. They sought teachers' testimony on the sources of satisfaction and effectiveness in their work. One of the things they found out is that "the central career concern for teachers is professional development, not promotion." Sylvia Yee, one of the researchers writes: "... For a majority of teachers, career development resides not in external advancement structures, but in opportunities for professional development."

> When they speak about professional development, Yee says, teachers value not the typical school district inservice training, but rather "getting teachers to come together and share ideas and thoughts" in informal but rigorous ways over extended periods of time— "a combination of sharing information, observing other teachers, offering and receiving collegial feedback, and cooperative problem solving...."

> Rosenholtz writes [that] three factors—"task autonomy," certainty about their capability to help students learn, and learning opportunities for themselves—are strongly linked to teachers' intent to stay in teaching.

> Rosenholtz also identified factors in the organization and management of those schools in which teachers said they had many and varied opportunities to learn to improve their work. The conditions that characterize a "learning enriched" school, she found, are "deliberate, collaborative goal setting" by the principal and the faculty together; teacher evaluation that gives frequent situation-specific feedback on the basis of clear criteria developed with teachers; teachers' agreement with each other about what is important in teaching; and collaboration among teachers—"the ease

with which teachers request and offer advice and assistance to colleagues." (pp. 9-11)

Teacher-leadership opportunities can be powerful motivators for teachers if they are not linked explicitly to external structures that might imply promotion, such as career ladders or administrative positions. Little's (1990) examination of the "mentoring phenomenon" indicates the difficulties teachers face when they and their duties as mentors are perceived to be external to the school, rather than an integral part of it:

> Ambiguity and conflict surrounding role definition have been greatest where mentor roles remain unlinked to any larger picture, where norms are unfavorable to professional growth or career mobility, and where teachers have been left to "invent their roles as they went along."

Devaney (1987) mentions the norms that prevail within teaching (norms of conformity, competition, scarcity, isolation, and egalitarianism), the power these norms have as constraints on teacher behavior, and how teacher leaders can violate these norms, either inadvertently or deliberately. Most schools have cultures where teachers are united by their sense of personal powerlessness. They react by demonstrating a "proletarian solidarity against authority" (Devaney 1987). Tacit agreements regarding competition and performance exist so that no one "stands out" to threaten other teachers. In fact, some teachers known for their excellence will shun public recognition for fear of offending their peers. Scarcity norms evidence themselves in the reaction aroused when one teacher gains access to resources not available to all teachers. A release day, a computer, or additional supplies given to one teacher, however deserving, can create tension. Isolation is perhaps the most deeply ingrained norm in public education. In some districts isolation is formally institutionalized through contracts that require administrators to receive advance permission from teachers before entering their classrooms. Programs of teacher leadership frequently confront and challenge these norms.

There have been two basic schools of thought regarding approaches to the creation of teacher-leadership roles. One has focused on developing formal programs such as mentor teachers or career ladders. These programs have the advantage of having institutional legitimacy and, frequently, resources in the form of time and money attached to them. They have the disadvantage of not being adaptable to the unique needs of a school, and of failing to capitalize on the skills, interests, and personalities of staff members within a building. They may also have problems achieving legitimacy with teachers, who may not have been involved in their design or may not agree with the selection criteria or the ways in which the criteria are applied. Sometimes such formal programs are successful, but in other cases they are not. Little (1990) estimates that the mentor relationship in the California Mentor Teacher Program "appears to fail at least as often as it succeeds."

An alternative is to develop teacher leadership on an ad hoc basis. This method identifies interests and abilities of staff members and matches them with the leadership needs of the school. Training and resources are then tailored to the development of the individual. Legitimacy is enhanced if others already view the person as competent in the area where he or she is assigned leadership responsibilities (Little 1988). Devaney (1987) calls this the "light socket" approach to creation of leadership positions. It opens up a wide variety of roles, limited only by the needs of the school and the abilities of the staff.

There is evidence that principals in schools that are having some success restructuring are creating the conditions within which the traditional norms of teaching can be challenged and altered and diverse teacher-leadership roles can be created. Teachers link their personal and professional development with the restructuring process. This combination can be a powerful motivator for teacher involvement in organizational change (Goldman, Dunlap, and Conley 1991). Clearly the "light socket" approach has limitations, since it is dependent on a supportive principal and a culture within the school that allows or supports teacher participation in leadership roles, whereas externally imposed programs can get around these factors. On the other hand, the externally imposed programs encounter severe difficulty when they are implemented into hostile environments. Therefore, the creation of teacher-leadership opportunities may well depend in nearly all cases on the conditions present in individual school buildings.

CREATING A RANGE OF OPTIONS FOR TEACHER LEADERSHIP

This section discusses the types of roles for teachers that might be available within a school as vehicles for the development of their leadership. It suggests a combination of the two methods discussed previously. Some of the leadership options are more formal programs that generally exist in a framework broader than the individual school; many more are merely opportunities that can be presented to or developed with individuals or small groups of teachers. In combination, these options offer a broad range of leadership-development opportunities that can infuse the school culture and be available to all teachers in some form or another.

There seems to be an assumption in many schools that leadership cannot be exercised until someone has been a teacher for a long time. When less-experienced teachers attempt to exert leadership, the reaction is often less than overwhelmingly positive. This norm tends to discourage teachers early in their careers from developing their leadership abilities, or at least it dissuades them from viewing leadership as something integral to the role of teacher.

An alternative is to develop teachers' leadership systematically throughout their careers. Teachers can experience different types of leadership at different points in their careers. The following examples serve to illustrate the types of roles in which teachers might be involved over time:

Club sponsor/coach/student leadership advisor. New teachers frequently have responsibilities that they demonstrate in working with students. Rarely is this considered a form of teacher leadership or a forum for the development of the neophyte teacher's leadership skills. This is a missed opportunity to develop future teacher leaders.

Protégé to a mentor. While the leadership implications may not be immediately apparent, they become clearer if it is understood that by understanding the protégé role, the teacher is better able to understand the mentor role. Additionally, the protégé's leadership skills can be encouraged and developed by the mentor. Someone who has been mentored becomes a stronger candidate to serve as a successful mentor to someone in the next generation of teachers. (For a more detailed discussion of the protégé's role, see Krupp 1987.)

Peer observer/peer coach. All teachers could conceivably benefit from this role throughout their careers, though it may be of most value earlier in the career path, since it helps teachers to learn to accept and value help from colleagues and to communicate with other teachers about problems of practice. These roles provide many opportunities for substantive conversations about teaching, and they help alleviate the norms of privacy and conformity. In addition, many well-developed programs already exist and are available to be implemented. (For a discussion of peer coaching, see: Anastos and Ancowitz 1987, Garmston 1987, Hall and McKeen 1989, Joyce and Showers 1987, Munro and Elliott 1987, Phillips and Glickman 1991, Servatius and Young 1985, Showers 1984.)

Chair or member of committee or site council. There are numerous ad hoc and standing committees in school districts and buildings. Participation is often seen as a duty (or punishment). In addition, many states have mandated or districts have developed site councils as a dimension of decentralized decision-making. If these committees or councils begin to have genuine power, and if teachers are well matched to roles and are provided adequate training, such work can provide opportunities for teachers to develop and apply new skills in relatively controlled situations. As they gain experience, participants can grow into more formal leadership roles, such as chairing a committee or council. Assuming such roles also allows teachers to begin to develop broader perspectives on the organization—and their role in the organization—and to experience differing conceptions of power. As teachers become empowered to a greater degree, they begin to perceive their ability to influence the conditions of teaching. Leadership in this sense serves both to increase job satisfaction and to improve learning outcomes.

Department (or division) chair/coordinator. The organizational structure of secondary schools in particular is beginning to change in some schools. They are moving from traditional discipline-based departments to divisions or houses or teams, sometimes interdisciplinary in nature. At the same time, the role of department chair is also changing. The traditional role of department chair has rarely been seen as a way to develop teacher leadership. Rather, people in these positions often were expected to take a conserving posture—make certain their department did not lose resources or the principal did not do anything detrimental to them. Many of the tasks were clerical in nature.

The reshaping of the role of department chair holds great potential for creating new leadership opportunities. Since most secondary schools already commit resources to this role, it is one of the few existing legitimized leadership roles for teachers. This level of leadership can be a natural next step, in many cases, for teachers who have been leading ad hoc school improvement efforts and committees. However, for them to succeed, the duties of the department chair will need to contain a greater emphasis on school improvement and restructuring, curriculum improvement, instructional quality, and interdisciplinary relations. The people in these roles can have a significant impact on instructional practice if they are given appropriate skills and support (Acheson and Smith 1986). The expectations for the department chair should be considered in relation to the resources (in the form of release time or stipend) already devoted to it. Schools may want to ask the question: Are we getting our money's worth—in school improvement and teacher-leadership development—from this role in return for the leadership and services being provided for it?

Lead teacher. Devaney (1987) proposes a new role—that of lead teacher. This leadership role is tied much more closely to teachers' perceived needs and is designed to help them fulfill those needs. Lead teachers are neither administrators nor classroom teachers. While they retain their ties to the classroom, they are freed part-time to assist in the professional growth of their colleagues and to coordinate decision-making among a subgroup of the faculty. The lead teacher provides teachers with the following services:

- More time to prepare for and attend to individual students' unique learning needs
- More frequent, practical feedback—both affirmation and correction—on teaching technique and classroom organization and management
- Immediate, constructive help for teaching problems
- More relevant and stimulating opportunities for professional improvement—from observations of each others' teaching within the school to instruction provided outside
- Informal, continuing exchanges with other teachers about what they have learned from experience as well as new information they have garnered, and about new materials or projects they can develop together for their own classrooms or for the whole school
- A voice in the school's organization, course of study, school day, schedule, budget, student policies, and plans for improvement (p. 16)

Berry and Ginsberg (1990) present a similar argument for lead teachers and suggest that, "like the manager of managers in other professional organizations, the lead teacher will guide and influence the activities of other teachers and serve as a catalyst for the decisions other teachers make that affect student performance most directly" (p. 618). They see the creation of lead teachers as a bargain of sorts:

> In exchange for even greater regulation of *teachers* through more rigorous and more professional teacher preparation, certification, and selection procedures, there will be less regulation of *teaching*. Policy makers will generate fewer rules regarding what is to be taught, how it is to be taught, and when it is to be taught. In essence, all professions whose members must use discretion and judgment in meeting the unique needs of clients have struck such a bargain with society: the profession guarantees the competence of its members in exchange for retaining its control over the structure of work and the standards of practice. (p. 618)

Berry and Ginsberg acknowledge that there is some risk in creating differentiated roles among teachers, but they believe such differentiation can be legitimated "if the working environment provides frequent opportunities for cooperation and interaction between lead teachers and their teams." They believe that lead teachers should have a more active and direct role in improving instruction. Lead teachers should be engaged in:

1. classroom teaching
2. mentoring and coaching other teachers

3. appraising the performance of other teachers

4. professional development

5. peer reviews of school practice

6. building-level decision making (p. 618)

Lead teachers might be employed at all levels, but elementary schools (and middle-level schools that have instituted interdisciplinary teams) seem more likely to utilize this role.

Association representative. Rarely are the leaders of the teachers' association or the building representatives of the association seen as potential leaders, yet they can influence a faculty toward embracing or rejecting any given proposal and can set the tone for the building. Administrators might be well advised to attempt to understand what needs this role fulfills for the people who occupy it.

There is no reason why the leadership skills of these people should not be developed systematically. If association representatives have good communication skills, know how to apply techniques for dispute resolution, understand the processes of school improvement and change, and have a broader picture of the organization and their role in it, they are only likely to use these skills in a fashion that encourages interaction between the association and the administration. They may also become interested in other leadership positions; if so, they may be more equipped than most other teachers to fill those roles in a competent manner. When teachers can move between leadership roles in the association and in the school, feelings of disenfranchisement and alienation can be alleviated.

Teacher researcher. Some teachers have no desire to lead anyone else or to be involved in a committee. They may, however, be willing to contribute to school improvement and restructuring efforts by gathering data about particular school practices. Some cynical teachers can be enticed (or challenged) to contribute by examining their beliefs about education (for example, statements made at faculty meetings: "the parents don't support us"; "all the kids have jobs and can't do home-work"; "we give kids every chance to succeed"; "the halls are out of control"). These teachers can be commissioned to collect data to prove or disprove the stated hypothesis. This type of research does not require extensive methodological training, but merely a commitment to intellectual honesty combined with appropriate data collection and analysis techniques. Such information also has high credibility with faculties, since it is collected within the school by peers. (For a discussion of teacher as researcher, see, for example, Bracey 1991, Sagor 1991.)

Staff developer. Since the early eighties, the number of teachers who have assumed some staff-development duties has skyrocketed. This movement grew initially through the efforts of Madeline Hunter and those who have been trained to teach her materials. Subsequently a number of others such as David and Roger Johnson (cooperative learning) and Bernice McCarthy (learning styles) developed "training of trainer" programs to accompany their materials and training on specific instructional techniques. Many teachers became staff developers to teach "Elements of Instruction," cooperative learning, or learning styles to other teachers.

Since the initial work of Hunter, the role of teacher as staff developer has become much more complex. Many who began as instructional trainers have since become more like organization-development consultants, assisting the change process within a school or building. Still others organize peer-coaching and collegial-sharing activities. This role is appealing and revitalizing for many teachers at midcareer; it has been implemented in numerous forms by districts throughout the country.

Teachers can serve in at least two kinds of roles as staff developers. One is the inbuilding staff developer, who helps teachers implement techniques learned from experts while continuing to teach part-time. This teacher is released from teaching for a fixed time. The other is the staff-development consultant, who works with teachers from many different buildings and has expertise and training in a variety of areas and techniques. The staff-development consultant often retains the status of teacher and does not become an administrator. Titles such as Teacher on Special Assignment signify the unique status of the role. It is a role whose status can be ambiguous, particularly in cases where these people work closely with administrators in the planning of staff-development activities and in the implementation of particular instructional programs. In such cases, they may come to be seen as "quasi-administrators."

Noble (1987) describes some of the issues that arise when teachers are taken from the classroom and given the larger, more liberating perspective on teaching, learning, and schooling that the role of staff-development trainer offers:

> Teachers who serve as staff development trainers are usually enthusiastic, dedicated learners themselves, whose attitudes toward growth make them strong, positive models for their students. Yet, if our experiences in Greece are typical, these strong teachers may be the very ones who will then be drawn away from classrooms as a result of their involvement in staff development. Does this mean that we shouldn't let good teachers become an integral part of the staff development training process because they may be on an inexorable course **away** from direct student contact? We have no definitive answer, only impressions and ideas....
>
> First, teachers who also serve as staff development trainers could be encouraged to have the "best of both worlds" by lightening their class loads

or by making them part-time teachers, perhaps using job sharing strategies. A second idea, perhaps the one with the strongest implications for job satisfaction on both fronts, is to capitalize on the teacher/trainers' strengths in their own buildings. As trainers in a program to increase effective instruction who are also skilled in clinical supervision, teachers could have the unique opportunity to also take the role of coaches to their schools' principals. By serving as a "peer" observer and coach, the trainer can help bring about real change and improvement in the principals' instructional supervision skills. (p. 31, emphasis in original)

(For a more detailed discussion of this role, see: Bertani and others 1987, Leggett and Hoyle 1987, Marks 1983, Moye and Rodgers 1987, Tallerico 1987, Wu 1987.)

Curriculum developer. Teachers have traditionally implemented curriculum, not developed it. They have developed activities to support curriculum that has been developed elsewhere, or written objectives against which curriculum adoptions can be judged, but the curriculum itself was the product of a publisher or a large curriculum-development operation, such as a university project. With the advent of information technologies such as CD-ROM, video, and electronic databases and networks, teachers can gather enough information to be able to assemble a sophisticated curriculum program in a relatively short time. By using scanners, desktop publishing programs, and laser printers, they can quickly produce sophisticated products. Even the cost of mastering custom CD-ROM disks is not beyond the means of most districts.

What teachers lack most is training in curriculum development as a conceptual task and the time to work on such projects. If teachers are provided training, time (available in the summer), and access to technology, they will be able to produce high-quality curriculum in much less time and for less cost than is currently the case. If school restructuring succeeds in effecting change in the core functions of teaching, this kind of internal curriculum development will become more prevalent in school districts.

Educational entrepreneur. To break the bounds of conformity, and to encourage free thinkers to remain in education, new leadership roles, such as educational entrepreneur, can be developed. The educational entrepreneur experiments with new techniques, develops new programs, taps new markets, and develops new relationships inside and outside the school. Many schools restrict this type of activity to special student populations, believing such approaches are fine with at-risk or special education students, but are not appropriate for the general student body.

Educational entrepreneurs need to have institutional authorization to compete with the traditional system, to put pressure on the rest of the school to equal their performance and results. Rather than being seen as fringe players, these innovators could be placed in positions where their efforts could be modeled and emulated by other, more cautious mainstream teachers.

Reflective practitioner. No school moves very far without someone with a vision, a sense of what could be. This vision has to be developed somewhere, and it has to be spread throughout the school via some mechanism. The role of reflective practitioner is one that may be sought after by teachers who like to dream, explore, imagine, analyze. Teachers in this role lead discussions of books and articles, take the data generated by the teacher researchers and consider implications for the school, or question basic assumptions and practices in the school. They provide leadership and support for new ideas and promote examination of existing assumptions.

Schön (1989) describes this process as reflection-in-action, the ability of professionals to analyze and "self-correct" while engaged in the act of teaching. It requires teachers to be highly aware of the processes of teaching, to be capable of observing what is occurring and of analyzing what they observe or conclude. They also need to be able to reflect upon their reflection-in-action:

> There are times—when people get stuck and want to get unstuck, or want to help someone else learn to do something, or want to build on their own spontaneous artistry—when people also reflect *on* their reflection-in-action. Then people become observers of their own on-the-spot experiments, reflect on what they observe, and try to describe their knowing, their inquiry, and their change in view. They give themselves reason and try to make explicit the reason*ing* they have produced without having had to take thought. (Schon, pp. 204-5, emphasis in original)

Sullivan (1987) describes a program designed to increase the amount of professional reading and discussion in which staff at a pilot site engaged. Release time from classes was provided for thirteen teachers to engage in conversations with one another and with faculty from a local university along with state educational leaders. Coverage of classes was obtained by having university faculty alternate between substituting for the teachers one month, then participating in the discussions the next.

The experience appeared to be particularly valuable for beginning teachers, but also served as a tool for building collegiality among all participants. There were indications that the seminars led to enhanced educational practices in classrooms. Teachers occupied a variety of leadership roles throughout the process. Beginning teachers were able to interact as peers with their more experienced colleagues. The tone of faculty meetings became more professional. Teachers, through enhanced professional knowledge and interaction, came to exert more leadership and act in more professional ways. (For additional discussion of this role, see: Schön 1989, 1988, and 1983.)

Administrative intern. Administration is another avenue for teacher leadership. Many teachers are unsure of their interest in an administrative position and need an opportunity to assume the role briefly, in a controlled manner, to determine if they are truly interested in pursuing full-time administrative positions. Such internships may be brief (1-3 days of shadowing, attending meetings with the administrator, and so forth) or extended (an entire year in which the intern is in charge in the administrator's absence). They may be coordinated with an administrative certification program or independent of such a program. Such opportunities may require limited release time or be accomplished on the teacher's own time. Many more opportunities of this nature can be made available to teachers within existing budgets and administrative structures.

Mentor. Teachers can serve as mentors at almost any point after they have mastered the art, craft, and science of teaching. Usually if this is going to occur, it occurs somewhere between five and ten years into a teacher's career. The role of mentor has been studied in some depth (Galvez-Hjornevik 1986, Gray and Gray 1985, Huffman and Leak 1986, Kram 1983, Little 1990, Stroble and Cooper 1988, Zimpher and Rieger 1988, Krupp 1987). The conclusions, in general, are that this relationship can be valuable, but it is not automatically so. Mentor relationships need to evolve, and there needs to be a good match between mentor and protégé in terms of personality styles. In schools where a culture of growth and support is created—where norms of isolation, conformity, and egalitarianism are not overbearing—mentor relationships can flourish. Where these norms are dominating, it is difficult for one teacher to offer support and advice to another.

Teacher leadership, as conceived in this chapter, is multidimensional, encompassing various roles and activities throughout a career. The intent is not to limit the definition of leadership to administrative responsibilities. New conceptions of power require new theories of leadership, for teachers and administrators. Anything teachers can do to facilitate change and improvement in ways in which they interact with their colleagues has the potential for being a leadership role. The more opportunities of this nature teachers have, the more potential a school has to become a "learning organization" (Senge 1990) with the internal capacity to take control of its improvement and evolution.

CHAPTER 19

PERSONNEL

Who is qualified to be a teacher? How should the human resources present in a building be deployed to maximize student learning? These two questions are of central importance to schools undergoing restructuring. Traditionally, the only person deemed capable of teaching a class has been an adult with a teaching certificate. This constricting definition is being reexamined. At the same time, the ways in which adults are used to support the education of young people are also being reconsidered. The use of support staff and paraprofessionals is being examined. More flexible ways of contracting for services are already in place in many districts. The roles of counselors, special-education teachers, Chapter 1 teachers, teachers of the gifted and talented, and those involved in other pullout programs, along with administrators, are being rethought in an effort to provide support to those students who need it. Both of these potential areas of change—in the definition of teacher and the role of support staff—are politically volatile, yet necessary to confront, given the labor-intensive nature of education.

Along the same lines, the performance expectations of teachers and the necessity that essentially all teachers must be able to meet the more demanding needs of today's students require an overhaul of the hiring and evaluation procedures employed with nontenured teachers. The teachers coming in to education over the next few years will need to adapt rapidly to a changing profession over the course of their careers. This chapter examines these issues, beginning with a reconsideration of the role of the certified teacher as the sole legitimate source of student learning.

CREATING NEW DEFINITIONS OF TEACHER

As teaching becomes more professional in nature, and as teachers acquire new responsibilities and skills required by their changing roles, it will become increasingly necessary to examine the assumption that the certified teacher is the only person in the school building capable of teaching students. As long as teaching is defined as something that can only be done by someone with a certificate, little progress will be made in dealing with the "twin towers" present in most teacher contract negotiations—higher salaries and lower class sizes. It is clear that with the present resource base it will be impossible to make significant progress on both issues simultaneously. However, it may be possible if the roles and responsibilities of school personnel are reexamined, and if state policies and regulations are modified.

Shanker (1990) discusses the difficulty of solving education's problems solely by raising teachers' salaries:

> Our schools need to add several thousand dollars to each teacher's salary to begin to bridge the gap between the education "industry" and the private sector. However, it takes only quick calculations to demonstrate that this is not likely to happen. Since we have 2.2 million teachers, every thousand dollar increase means a $2.2 billion increase in the nationwide education budget. If we took an average competitive professional salary to be about $35,000, and added pension and Social Security costs, we would face a staggering $30 billion beyond what we now spend for education. The largest federal education program, Chapter 1, has an annual budget of about $3 billion. Therefore, when we speak of increases to make teachers' salaries competitive with other professions, we're talking about a huge sum that is unlikely to be allocated to just one item in the overall education budget....
>
> ... Here's the bottom line: Though the reform movement has brought about significant and long-delayed improvements in teachers' salaries, it is unlikely that the new levels alone will offer sufficient incentives to enable us to restaff our schools as they are now structured with the caliber and quantity of candidates that we need for the twenty-first century. (p. 357)

Shanker continues by discussing the other solution offered by many— lower class size:

> In short, a substantial reform of class size would still leave us with slightly better but essentially not very good working conditions, and, most important, probably no significant change in education quality.
>
> ... [T]he numbers just don't add up for such an improvement. A 20 percent cut in class size would mean an equal increase in staff and education budget—a huge and utterly unrealistic increase for one item. And if, by some magic, the money were there, it is unlikely that we could begin to find that number of extra teachers because of the demographic facts of life. (p. 358)

How, then, should educational reform and improvement be approached if increased teacher salaries and reduced class sizes are not the solution? Shanker suggests that part of the solution lies in greater flexibility in the staffing of schools:

In a restructured school, teachers will need to be able to call on paraprofessionals, undergraduate "interns," and/or peer tutors. Our schools will need to form alliances with private industry that can "lend-out" short-term staff, particularly in such shortage areas as math and the sciences. We will have to explore a variety of staffing strategies if we want to break away from the rigidity of the prevailing system. (p. 360)

It might be considered unusual that the president of the second-largest teachers' union would advocate allowing more noncertified people to work with children in schools, but Shanker explains that there is little choice (cited in Sparks 1991). The existing pool of certified teachers would simply not be large enough to meet the demand if large-scale educational improvement is carried out. Enhanced career options for many groups, particularly women, have caused a decrease in the number of talented people choosing education as a career. This trend is not likely to change, particularly given demographic trends that suggest a shortage in college-educated workers generally by the late 1990s.

Shanker describes potential roles that may be created in schools and how these positions would affect teacher salary and class size:

There might be more adults, but they wouldn't all be called teachers. We could use something like a hospital model in which we might have roles comparable to that of nurse, technician, general practitioner, specialist, and so forth. There would be more adults in the schools, but only some of them would earn more money. The salary issue will not be solved unless we have a different staffing structure.... That's also true of class size.... The same thing is true with trying to provide teachers more time for professional growth.

All of this means that the only way we can realize the traditional aspirations of teachers and their unions and professional associations is by moving to staff differentiation, team teaching, the use of technology, and other things like that. (cited in Sparks 1991, p. 3)

In Wisconsin, for example, a wide-ranging report containing many proposals for school improvement suggested permitting school districts to obtain waivers to allow them to hire "teachers in private practice" ("Thompson Endorses Hiring Private-Practice Teachers," February 13, 1991). The waivers would give schools greater flexibility in staffing to meet student needs better.

Many states experimented with alternative routes to certification and with the use of noncertified teachers throughout the 1980s in a series of programs. The issue in the 1990s may go beyond these early pilots to question at a more basic level exactly what it is that a certified teacher brings to the classroom that other adults do not, and how a variety of adults with different degrees of education, training, and specific knowledge can be employed to meet the needs of children in the most cost-effective manner possible.

NEW CONCEPTIONS OF THE PARAPROFESSIONAL'S ROLE

Public schools currently lack the type of salary and role differentiation present in some other professions. For example, there are roles and career paths for highly trained paraprofessionals in the medical and legal professions that are absent in education. Although the term *paraprofessional* is used by some school districts to refer to classroom aides, the roles to which it is applied are not comparable in terms of training and responsibility to paraprofessionals found in other fields. Restructuring may provide opportunities to experiment with a wider range of roles.

Some early experimentation has already occurred in Dade County, Florida, and Baltimore, Maryland, where Educational Alternatives Incorporated (EAI) secured contracts to manage public schools. Part of their plan involves using "instructional interns" in place of the traditional paraprofessionals. Schmidt (1992) describes the distinction between the two:

> The paraprofessionals...typically have high school diplomas and perhaps a few college credits, and work at union-negotiated wages starting at about $7 per hour and averaging about $10 per hour.
>
> The interns, on the other hand, are required to have college degrees, but need not have any experience in education. They are paid about $7 per hour, and receive no benefits. (p. 19)

Initial reactions by paraprofessionals have not been positive to the idea that they would be replaced by more highly educated personnel who would be paid less. Educational Alternatives would use the savings in cost to place an intern in each classroom. The assumption is that the intern is "far better prepared to help run a classroom" (Schmidt 1992) than the paraprofessionals, and that placing these interns within classrooms will have more of an impact on student learning than many of the tasks performed by paraprofessionals outside the classroom.

Conlin (1991) and Bradley (1990) describe how this technique is being applied at South Pointe Elementary School in Dade County, Florida. At South Pointe, many more adults with various degrees of training and skill are being matched with student needs. As a result, the school is meeting students' needs while simultaneously achieving greater economic efficiency. The goal is to lower pupil-teacher ratios in the range of 12-to-1 by pairing veteran teachers with more junior teachers who might be a trained paraprofessional or instructional intern, a recent graduate of a teacher-education program, or an intern from a local university. Under such a plan, traditional positions such as counselor and librarian are eliminated. Principals and lead teachers decide if the school wants specialists in fields such as music, art, and physical education, who are usually assigned to elementary schools, or whether those resources should go to reducing class size across the board by hiring more instructional interns.

For this role to succeed, school districts have to be committed to continuing the professional development of these employees. They might be among the first personnel to adopt new teaching strategies. It would be important to be able to move these paraprofessionals around much more easily than is possible with certified teachers, who often have protection in their contracts against forced transfer. The ability to move paraprofessionals within a district would give administrators the ability to concentrate resources in a particular area or school for a limited time to address particular problems. Paraprofessionals could help buildings with "unhealthy" cultures to develop new norms and procedures, and they could help invigorate veteran staff by offering support, energy, and enthusiasm.

This role might also serve as a training ground and screening mechanism for those interested in entering teaching. It would be possible to identify those with potential to become excellent teachers, and to encourage their development. The conferring of a teaching certificate could be based more on the demonstration of mastery of a complex set of skills and behaviors, rather than on completion of coursework and a structured field experience.

THE CHANGING ROLE OF CERTIFIED SUPPORT STAFF

The deployment of support personnel is an issue of increasing interest to educators involved in restructuring. While pupil-teacher ratios have gone down in absolute terms during the past twenty years, the ratio of students to teachers in regular classrooms has not decreased nearly as much. The overall decrease has been caused mostly by the addition of specialists during the past twenty years who work with small numbers of children or who have no teaching responsibilities. This group includes counselors, special education teachers, Chapter 1 teachers, talented and gifted personnel, and various teachers on special assignment in nonclassroom roles.

More and more schools are beginning to assess the effectiveness of the deployment of these professionals outside the classroom. Often there are governmental regulations that seem to block changes, and yet some schools are beginning to challenge these by integrating support staff into classrooms, or by reducing overall pupil-teacher ratios by assigning all certified staff some teaching responsibilities. This strategy has its dangers, particularly if careful thought is not given to the needs of special student populations. It has, however, in some cases led to lower class sizes in which the needs of all students can be addressed more directly, leading to improved student learning outcomes for those students.

Central Park East Secondary School in New York is one example of a school that decided to concentrate all its resources on the basic literacy and socialization needs of its students. The school was able to reduce class sizes to more manageable levels by assigning responsibility for literacy and socialization issues in some form to all adults and by eliminating as many special or pullout programs as possible.

Another response to the need for additional flexibility in the allocation of human resources in schools may be the use of more part-time and specialized employees, a practice increasingly common in the private sector. Variations on career ladders for teachers offer still another option: A neophyte might begin his or her career in education as an apprentice, later become tenured, and eventually be able to attain master teacher status.

Enhanced flexibility in personnel assignments and roles will be increasingly important in schools that redefine their purpose and direction, their curriculum and instructional program, and their learning environment. Such schools will need to have more adult-child interaction and allow some specialization of teacher roles to emerge. The ability to staff schools with a variety of adults in a variety of roles will become ever more important.

ENHANCING THE PERFORMANCE OF NEWLY HIRED TEACHERS

Restructured schools are likely to demand teachers with high skill levels, positive attitudes toward change, and the ability to work collaboratively. More attention to hiring practices and to evaluation prior to granting tenure are two inexpensive ways districts can begin to upgrade the quality of their personnel in support of school restructuring. Candidates hired for vacant positions should match the philosophy of the school where they are to work, understand and believe in the vision, and be committed to demonstrating both personal growth and flexibility, understanding that they may be asked to adapt their skills and roles frequently throughout their teaching career. This is a far cry from the situation today, where some teachers may become upset if asked to move from one classroom to another, let alone add new instructional skills or teach in a different educational setting.

Evaluation of nontenured teachers may not seem like an important restructuring strategy until one realizes that a teacher, after receiving tenure, is likely to remain in the school for a generation or more. The ability of schools to adapt to changes in the next century is being determined by the processes employed and decisions made by those granting tenure to teachers today. In this context, it is apparent that more attention should be paid to the growth, development, and evaluation of nontenured teachers. The following suggestions pertain to hiring and tenure practices and development of nontenured teachers.*

Develop comprehensive hiring procedures that include evidence of previous teaching competence. In this era of the video camera, it is not unreasonable to ask candidates to provide a video of themselves in a classroom setting. Ten minutes of videotape can reveal more than hours of interviews.

In the absence of a video, asking candidates to view a video of a teaching situation and describe what was done well and what might need to be changed can be highly informative. In Berliner's research, different conclusions were reached by novices, postulants, and master teachers as they viewed teaching situations (Brandt 1986).

Ensuring that a comprehensive reference check is undertaken before a contract is extended should be insisted upon in all cases. Anecdotal information from administrators indicates that when established procedures were bypassed or performed in a cursory manner, problems often occurred later.

Develop a mentor program for all new hires. The mentor program should allow visits by the mentor to the new teacher's classroom. This can help the new teacher adjust quickly to the expectations of the school and the community. The mentor should not be expected to deal with serious performance problems, but can help the new teacher avoid developing habits that can lead to difficulties later. A mentor program is valuable because it allows beginning teachers to receive frequent high-quality feedback on their performance (Peterson 1990).

School districts and states have already put considerable effort into developing mentor programs for teachers. This experience can be drawn upon by other districts interested in developing mentor programs.

Provide teachers in their first year of employment with an extended contract. Have new teachers report to school a week before other

---

* The following paragraphs have been adapted from Conley, David T. "Eight Steps to Improved Teacher Remediation." *NASSP Bulletin* 75, 536 (September 1991): 26-41.

teachers, not just to decorate their bulletin boards, but to learn about the district's performance standards and expectations, evaluation procedures, and sources of help and assistance. Have them meet with their mentor on a regular basis. Expect them to videotape their lessons and discuss them with others. Provide them with some release time to see other teachers in action. Give them a day or two at the end of the first year to reflect and develop a plan of action to pursue over the summer and into the coming school year. Demonstrate to them that they are in a culture that supports and values excellence.

Be certain to observe all new hires in the classroom during the first week of school. In many schools there is an unwritten agreement between principals and teachers that principals will not be in classrooms during the first several weeks, to allow the teachers to "get things settled down." While formal observations may be inappropriate during the first days of school, Emmer and Evertson's research (Emmer and others 1980, Evertson and Emmer 1982, Evertson and Harris 1992) has demonstrated that most management problems develop as a result of teacher behaviors during the first weeks of school. It is much easier to identify problems as they are developing than to try to undo them after they are firmly established.

Don't grant tenure to mediocre teachers. Allow only excellent teachers to achieve tenure or permanent employment status. This is stated as a goal in many districts. In practice, however, it is often the exception rather than the rule. Following the recommendations that have preceded will help ensure that teachers who are being considered for tenure have been thoroughly scrutinized as well as supported and nurtured. Allowing a teacher to gain tenure may be one of the single most important responsibilities that an administrator has. It should be treated as such.

One of the key ingredients required to make restructuring succeed is a caring adult, one who wants to work with young people. No training program or new educational structure can transform all teachers into caring people. At the same time, the types of changes discussed here have the capacity to make schools places where there are more adults who genuinely care about children. Staffing schools with adults who care about kids is as important as any of the more spectacular changes being considered.

CHAPTER 20

WORKING RELATIONSHIPS

Many of the ideas and trends discussed in the preceding eleven chapters—on topics from learning outcomes to personnel—have broad implications for the codification of working relationships within the school district as embodied by the contract. This chapter examines the relationship between educational restructuring and labor-management relations.

The first three sections trace the evolution of collective bargaining in education from its roots in industrial trade unionism, examine the transition to a focus on teachers' professionalism, and ask whether conflict can be avoided. Then, the next section looks at how the restructuring movement is putting pressure on both management and unions to change their roles and relationships. The final section describes collaborative strategies that are offering new models for working relationships.

ROOTS IN INDUSTRIAL UNIONISM

The current model of working relationships is based on principles of trade unionism honed in the 1930s in the industrial sector of the economy. From the midsixties to the end of the seventies, these principles were applied effectively to schools, if increases in wages and improvements in working conditions are used as indicators of success. By the midseventies, however, the limits of this model of labor relations began to become evident. The percentage of district budgets allotted to total employee compensation reached the 80 to 90 percent range in many cases. There was little room for improvement in the arena of wages and benefits, the so-called "bread and butter" issues. Unions shifted their attention to issues related to working conditions such as length of the work day, amount of preparation time, specific teacher duties, policies for assignment, transfer and reduction-in-force, grievance procedures, and, ultimately, class size.

Unions made significant gains in negotiating working conditions in the seventies and, according to Goldschmidt and Stuart (1986), on through the mideighties. More contracts contained specific language defining and delimiting how teachers were to be treated, and what administrators could and could not do. Goldschmidt and Painter (1987-88) argue that this process actually began as early as the sixties: "Over time, teachers and school boards have increasingly discussed and agreed to contract provisions that determine important educational policies (e.g., curriculum, student placement, teacher assignment, retention and development)" (p. 18, see also Perry and Wildman 1970).

Emphasis on working conditions and compensation issues varies in negotiations in the 1990s depending on the financial condition of the school district. When less money is available, the emphasis shifts to working conditions. It appears less likely that gains as significant as those in the seventies can be made by teachers' unions in either of these areas. In fact, Goldschmidt and Painter (1987-88) cite Cresswell and Spargo (1980) to suggest that the wage increases teachers attained as a result of collective bargaining in the 1970s might have been as low as 1 percent to 8 percent more than what they might have expected to gain if they had not engaged in collective bargaining. Other studies cited similar ranges (Lipsky 1982, Cooper 1982). If large wage gains cannot be expected as a result of collective bargaining and the application of the industrial trade union model to education, the motivation for shifting the emphasis of bargaining to policy issues becomes even more evident.

Both labor and management appear to have settled into roles that have become familiar, almost comfortable when approaching one another across the negotiating table. The rituals of collective bargaining are practiced with great predictability, and the outcomes can often be foreseen before the process begins. The amount of money is finite and fairly well fixed in its distribution before talks begin. Negotiation of compensation is focused on a fixed pie where more and more of the elements are already locked into place and cannot be redistributed. The area most attractive for bargaining is the domain of educational policy as manifested in terms of specific working conditions.

Collective bargaining provisions related to policy (class size limitations, transfer policies, and so forth) are highly visible and must be enforced with uniformity. This uniformity results in reduced adaptability and runs counter to the image of school districts as loosely coupled systems (Stuart and Goldschmidt 1986, Pitner and Goldschmidt 1987).

> When negotiators fix educational policy choices for the term of an agreement, they void or minimize traditionally available opportunities for individual teachers and administrators to exercise alternative professional or political judgment. A reduction in autonomous behavior has a potentially significant impact on the organization of schools (Meyer and Rowan 1978;

Weick 1976). (Goldschmidt and Stuart 1986, p. 357)

The net effect of the shift in the emphasis of bargaining to working conditions may have been to reduce the adaptability and flexibility present within educational organizations. The contractualization of working conditions reduces the capacity of administrators and principals more specifically to respond and adapt to shifting conditions, resources, and expectations for public education (Goldschmidt, Bowers, and Stuart 1984; Goldschmidt and Stuart 1986).

Because most contracts are based on the notion that all teachers are one class of workers and should be treated in the most uniform manner possible, settlements that focus on working conditions may also inhibit the ability of individual school buildings governed by site councils to develop nonstandardized solutions or procedures they deem best for their situation. Goldschmidt and Stuart (1986) emphasize how such procedures have already tended to immobilize administrators, particularly principals, and have created the conditions for greater centralization of decision-making in school districts that codify working conditions in the contract:

> As school districts set criteria for staff selection, assignment, and transfer, establish processes for student assignment and discipline, and employ specialists to manage the contract and ensure compliance with its mandates, the discretion of the school administrator closest to the operation of each school building is sharply reduced in favor of the central office....
>
> Taken together, the effects of centralization and specialization are to fix administrative behavior. In the same way that a contractually mandated curriculum establishes a necessary minimum offering, the legal requirement to comply with provisions of a contract dictates some of what administrators must do and cannot do. As a result, both the organizational structure and the work roles and responsibilities of individuals within the organization change to accommodate the special interests and processes in collective bargaining. (p. 358)

This loss of flexibility would not be as much of a concern if today's schools were not under such pressure to adapt. The codification of working conditions would serve a useful purpose in stable environments and could be very desirable, particularly if there was widespread agreement about what constituted effective educational practice. This does not seem to be the case currently.

Schools appear to be in a period when the capacity to adapt rapidly to changing conditions, populations, expectations, and resources available may be a key characteristic for survival. Even in many of the districts involved early in restructuring, there has been a tendency to incorporate restructuring procedures into the master agreement, often severely limiting the potential effectiveness of such activities. The parties have chosen this course because they continue to think in terms of traditional collective-bargaining models as the vehicle for expressing all agreements and resolving all conflicts.

The industrial trade union mindset is a powerful mental model present in many, perhaps most, school districts. It stands unquestioned as the basis for relations between and among teachers, administrators, and boards of education. These basic tenets and assumptions may be coming under examination as educators struggle with the distinction between unionism and professionalism.

UNIONISM VS. PROFESSIONALISM

Has collective bargaining led to a greater sense of professionalism on the part of teachers, since they can now influence the conditions under which they work? Or has it encouraged teachers to think of themselves as laborers who have little responsibility for the ultimate outcome of their teaching activities? These questions have been debated among those who study the phenomenon (Kerchner and Mitchell 1986, Lieberman 1980, McDonnell and Pascal 1988).

Teachers' unions, or *professional associations* as most prefer to be called, have gained mastery of collective bargaining, grievances, arbitration, fact-finding, strikes, and all other manifestations of the trade-union model of labor relations. Management and boards of education, after a slow start reacting to collective bargaining in the seventies, caught on to the new rules of the game and became versed in these methods as well. Although many school board members and central-office administrators complain bitterly about collective bargaining, most appear comfortable with the predictable patterns, cycles, rituals, and roles of the collective-bargaining process and of traditional trade-union labor-management relations. Public education has only recently institutionalized the exact model of labor relations that the industrial sector is currently seeking to redefine.

Why did education choose to adopt the industrial model of labor relations when the goals and processes of education are so different from those of a factory? Shedd and Bacharach (1991) suggest that it is the structure of management and the prevailing logic educational managers employ in their administration of schools that predetermined this choice:

> Teachers and their unions adopted factory union strategies because the administrators and school boards they faced insisted on acting like factory managers. Indeed, one of the basic reasons so many teachers chose to join

unions was that the prevailing logic of education management was itself patterned on the industrial model (Cole 1969; Callahan 1962). The structures, processes, and myths of industrial unionism complemented and in some ways even supported the top-down managerial ideology that existed in most school systems when teacher unions first won recognition, just as they fit the factory management systems of the 1930s. If there are grounds— and there are—for believing that unions and employers in public education are now in the process of inventing a new form of collective bargaining, it is because that management ideology itself is under serious attack. (p. 177)

Kerchner and Mitchell (1986) and Johnson (1987) argue that education is in the process of adapting collective bargaining to its unique needs and structure. It is likely, they say, that much of the emphasis in bargaining will be on policy issues, as teachers' unions come to perceive control over working conditions as a focal point that responds to teachers' desires to be perceived as professionals. Meanwhile, the process itself remains consistent with many aspects of the trade-union approach to organizational relations. Whether this focus on policy issues will occur, particularly in the face of tight fiscal times where unions tend to become more confrontational around bread-and-butter issues of salaries and benefits, remains to be seen.

Shedd and Bacharach (1991) speculate about the path that an evolution of collective bargaining in school districts might take. If collective bargaining is indeed undergoing a major change from a traditional labor-union model to one specifically adapted to public education, they say,

> then it is possible that the seemingly contradictory evidence of bargaining effects may be drawn from school systems at different points in such a transition. The evidence that collective bargaining has produced rigidity, centralization, diminished supervisory authority, and a "laboring" conception of the teacher's role may be drawn from settings where a traditional (industrial) model of collective bargaining continues to predominate. The evidence that bargaining has produced increased flexibility, responsiveness to public concerns, respect for the leadership role of building principals, and teacher involvement in professional decision making may reflect labor-management relationships in settings where the parties have made the transition to a newer form of collective decision making. The evidence of increased conflict and bitterness in education bargaining may be characteristic of relationships in transition between these two approaches, as one party struggles to reconstruct the labor-management relationship along lines that the other refuses to accept.

The basic outlines of this argument are sound. It is well documented in the general research on industrial relations that the parties to collective bargaining relationships tend to adopt substantive and procedural rules that reflect the characteristics of their particular industry (Dunlop, 1958; Kochan,

1980). It is equally well documented that the most serious conflicts in labor-management relations tend to occur when one or the other party attempts to change the structures and processes of bargaining itself (Weber, 1964; Chamberlain and Kuhn, 1965). There are good reasons to believe that school managers and teacher unions are, in fact, creating a new set of rules to govern their relationships—a set of rules uniquely tailored to their particular environment. (p. 167)

This analysis suggests that schools may be in the period of greatest danger as they attempt to make the transition from the known to the unknown; significant conflict is most likely when roles are being redefined. What is the goal? How should unions function if their relationship changes?

CAN CONFLICT BE AVOIDED?

The current model is premised on confrontation and potential conflict, not collaboration, as its primary method for resolving differences. Many of the new visions of the union's role are really restatements of the old role with conflict reduced. Shedd and Bacharach (1991) describe the characteristics of this new vision:

Rather than being adversarial and concerned with preserving their own power, the new unions will be cooperative and nonconfrontational. Rather than opposing efforts to improve the quality of teaching, they will actually assume responsibility for the quality and quantity of their members' efforts. Rather than negotiating rules that restrict flexibility, they will look for ways to relax restrictions on both teachers and administrators. Rather than insisting that teachers' rights and benefits be allocated equally or else on the basis of seniority, they will insist that the responsibility and compensation of teachers be differentiated, ordered hierarchically, and allocated on the basis of professional competence. (p. 168)

But can conflict be eliminated from labor relations in school districts? Is this even a reasonable goal? Or is conflict an inherent part of the relationship among teachers, administrators, and boards of education? Shedd and Bacharach (1991) suggest that this may not be an either-or question, that the goal may not be to eliminate all conflict, but to employ strategies that allow new sources of conflict to be identified and resolved:

The argument that conflict and lack of cooperation are defining characteristics of traditional labor-management relations—as opposed to particular labor-management relationships— is open to serious challenge, and the conviction that cooperativeness will be a defining characteristic of the new labor-management relations in public education is probably misleading as well. A bargaining system tailored to the markets, work processes, and management systems of public education undoubtedly will remove some of the present sources of conflict in teacher bargaining. But such a system will almost certainly expose other sources of conflict that until recently have been sheltered behind assertions of management prerogatives and union indifference. (p. 169)

RESTRUCTURING REQUIRES FLEXIBILITY

Where school restructuring is occurring, it is putting pressure on the negotiated agreement and on traditional management relationships. Districts are having to learn how to make exceptions or unique accommodations to allow greater flexibility for individual teachers or school sites to function more independently within the framework of a collective-bargaining agreement. In districts that are restructuring, schools need to be able to request waivers from the contract. Decision-making and rule interpretation may become decentralized and idiosyncratic. Individual faculties and faculty members often chafe under rules designed to protect workers from the arbitrary actions of management, particularly when the distinctions between labor and management have become less clear.

In these situations teachers are ready to take greater responsibility for their working conditions, to operate in a more professional relationship, and to abandon the security of the contract as they negotiate the rapids of change. They may have less interest in a model whose fundamental premises are that all members of the organization with the same job title should be treated in the same manner and that they should act in solidarity when dealing with management. This uniformity conflicts with the needs and desires of some to determine for themselves issues such as the hours they work, subjects they teach, responsibilities they have, and decisions they make.

There will probably continue to be a role for elements of traditional collective-bargaining models in school districts, particularly related to wages and benefits. The area where bargaining strategies may undergo change is in how working conditions are included in contracts and how such decisions are made by individual school sites. This is where most systems need greater flexibility, and where teachers are beginning to exert influence as site-based management and participatory decision-making are implemented in schools. Teacher involvement in decisions related to working conditions (schedule, budget allocation, class size, teaching loads, and so forth) causes difficulties for the traditional trade union model of labor-management relations. How does one teacher file a grievance against a decision made by a group of teachers? Who is the target of the grievance? Who is a teacher and who is an administrator? These issues are as troublesome for management as they may be for teacher representatives.

Concrete issues such as these are beginning to emerge. For example, Minnesota's charter school program ran into opposition from the state teachers' association, which was concerned that teachers in charter schools might not be certified (Olson, November 27, 1991).

ISSUES RAISED BY SCHOOL-SITE COUNCILS

Changes in governance structures, particularly the addition of mechanisms such as site-based school councils, capture the attention and interest of teachers' organizations, as they attempt to ensure that the interests of their members are properly represented on such councils.

Unions' desire for representation on site councils raises a fundamental issue: Do council members represent organizations, or do they serve as "leaders" acting as "people of good will" charged with solving the school's problems by means of their collective perceptions? In other words, does the parent represent the PTA; the school secretary, the classified employees union; the teachers, the teachers' union; the principal, the principals' association and the central administration; and so forth for the purpose of interacting within the parameters of a contract? Or do they represent diverse viewpoints with the primary goal of creating a more effective learning environment for children? Do site councils serve to address issues related to the working conditions of adults independent from or in close relation to the learning needs of children?

This issue is often unresolved when such councils are formed. The distinction can be crucial. Councils that represent formal constituent groups may do little more than serve as a form of shop steward meeting. No decisions will likely be made without referring to the contract, returning to poll members, or consulting superiors for guidance or interpretation of the group's policy on an issue. These groups seem handicapped in their ability to help a school develop new visions and solutions to complex problems. They reflect the old assumptions and fears about labor relations. They may serve primarily to maintain the status quo and allow the school to function more smoothly within existing rule-and-authority systems.

On the other hand, school-site councils that do not follow these restrictions find themselves in uncharted waters. They serve at the pleasure of their peers, with little guidance regarding their authority and charge. Principals often feel threatened by such groups (Hallinger,

Murphy, and Hausman 1991), and there are few precedents to instruct participants when they are thrust into new and unfamiliar roles. These councils can threaten the very existence of the union, particularly if they are able to address issues of working conditions. If each school can create its own working conditions, the master contract is limited primarily to issues of compensation and benefits. Indeed, tight financial times are creating situations where there is considerably less room for negotiation even of compensation issues, thereby further restricting the union's role. Will unions be willing to cede control over policy issues to such bodies at a time when those very issues may help rally the membership to support the union? And will the central administration want to lose control to site councils?

REDEFINITION OF ROLES

Restructuring seems to be more successful in situations where some trust between "management" and "labor" can be developed. The process of developing trust starts on a small scale and builds on each success to allow greater risk-taking on both sides. Districts that are redefining working relationships are often doing so gradually, with each side demonstrating its intent in controlled situations. For example, the two parties may form joint labor-management committees to address issues not specified in the contract. When such committees exist and function successfully, both sides may be more willing to leave many provisions out of the contract, to be discussed and resolved jointly as issues arise. In essence, the bargaining process continues constantly throughout the period of the contract, with as many issues as possible being resolved as they arise. This continuous process can help to decrease the number of issues to be addressed during formal bargaining.

Most school districts see the need to redefine the role of the professional association as one key dimension of its restructuring strategy. At the same time, they will benefit by redefining the role of management, as well. So long as school systems organize themselves using turn-of-the-century private-sector models, such as Taylor's notions of scientific management and bureaucracy, they will invite teacher responses based on this model. If treated like laborers, teachers will act like laborers within an industrial-management model. Not only must unions change, but management must change in step. Rarely can the union be expected to take the initiative. It is generally up to management, both boards of education and administrators, to rethink their philosophies of organization and of employee relations as a first step toward new bargaining models.

Top-down, or hierarchical, management models are comfortable to many, both teachers and administrators. Movement away from such structures is threatening to those who have learned how to survive and prosper within such a system. School systems, however, may not actually function best as top-down systems that can be directed or controlled centrally:

> The top-down strategies that have ostensibly guided school management have never made more than partial sense in public education and have never been strictly observed. At one moment teachers are treated like workers on an assembly line, at another like bureaucrats executing general directives, at still another like independent professionals who are expected to figure out for themselves what it is they should be doing. (Shedd and Bacharach 1991, pp. 179-80)

New models imply more teacher participation and involvement in decision-making on issues central to teaching and to the design of learning experiences and environments. They imply fundamentally different relations between administrators and teachers, but also among teachers themselves. The primary purpose for this change is not simply to satisfy the needs one group has for power and control over the other, but to create an organizational environment that is more adaptable and effective in responding to changing goals and heightened expectations for accountability. School districts that cannot meet student needs and improve student learning will receive ever greater scrutiny and will not automatically receive more money. This one factor alone may engender greater cooperation and collaboration among traditionally adversarial groups in education.

Is there a future for teachers' unions in a new, more collaborative educational environment? Will teachers' unions disappear if top-down management practices cease? Or will such changes create a power vacuum into which unions will step? Perhaps none of these will occur. However, teachers' unions are in a position to redefine their roles if such changes in management philosophy take place. They are uniquely different from industrial unions and can exploit the fact that teachers are both workers and managers in a real sense:

> Teacher unions may be threatened by the demise of top-down management strategies, but they are also in a good position to take advantage of that demise.... [P]ressing for collective teacher involvement in school and district decision making offers the possibility of overcoming the split between union and professional factions within their own organizations by shifting the focus of thinking about professional issues away from individual autonomy. Perhaps most important, such a shift might allow teacher unions to finally take advantage of a source of potential influence (or, to

put the matter more bluntly, a source of power) that industrial union principles have always required them to overlook: Their members, as individuals, already manage much of what goes on in most school systems. (Shedd and Bacharach 1991, pp. 182-83)

Both management and unions are going to change their roles and relationships, in all probability, as public education adapts itself for the twenty-first century. While the distinction between the two groups is unlikely to disappear, and in fact the distinction can serve a useful purpose in helping areas of conflict to surface and be resolved, the evidence suggests that schools will become more collaborative work environments, where teachers are both workers and managers, and principals are facilitators and organizers, not merely bosses. This transition to a more collaborative model will be challenging for school districts steeped in the culture of industrial models of management and labor relations.

COLLABORATIVE BARGAINING AND POLICY TRUST AGREEMENTS

Two early manifestations of this transition in bargaining are collaborative bargaining and policy trust agreements. Both are attempts to develop new methods to solve old problems within a context that suggests new relationships between management and labor. Each is discussed briefly with some examples of its application in school districts.

COLLABORATIVE BARGAINING

Several techniques have been attempted over the past several years to make traditional collective bargaining less confrontational. Smith, Ball, and Liontos (1990) use the term *collaborative bargaining* to describe a variety of experiments in bargaining that seek to move beyond the limits of collective bargaining. They distinguish between traditional collective bargaining and collaborative bargaining:

Collaborative bargaining is not an alternative *to* collective bargaining, but rather is an alternative *form* of collective bargaining. Just as there are many different methods of traditional adversarial bargaining..., there are many varieties of collaboration being instituted by school districts and teacher unions.... Some districts, particularly those in big cities, are finding, how ever, that collaboration is not only a worthwhile end in itself, but an extraordinarily effective means to achieve a higher end: school reform. The district and union leaders in these cities are using collaborative bargaining as a vehicle to initiate school-based management, mentor teacher programs, performance accountability mechanisms, and other reforms. (pp. 2, 4)

There are common elements as well as widespread variation in the ways in which collaborative bargaining is developed and practiced in districts throughout the country. At the heart of the approach is the idea that bargaining should ultimately be a win-win proposition. Many issues can be addressed outside the traditional collective-bargaining sessions by teams of teachers and administrators who understand the problem being addressed much better than members of negotiating teams who may be dealing with several dozen issues simultaneously. Furthermore, most collaborative-bargaining models include provisions for continued discussions throughout the period of the contract, and even the reopening of specific sections of the contract if changes need to be made before the contract expires. The idea is that the contract continuously evolves based on the needs of the organization and its constituent groups. Issues do not pile up awaiting formal bargaining sessions. When bargaining occurs, it is focused on fewer issues that can then be addressed more directly and conscientiously.

Smith and others (1990) provide examples of how collaborative bargaining was developed and practiced in a number of school districts:

Glenbard [Illinois] established a steering committee of school board and union representatives to research the win/win negotiating system and draw up a list of benefits and drawbacks. Among the advantages of win/win bargaining that the committee found were contract settlements with slightly higher teacher salaries (approximately 1/2 of 1 percent higher), increased union cooperation with school boards, and improved teacher morale.

In February 1987, the steering committee outlined a negotiation schedule. It was to begin in April with an all-day session at which both sides would put contract issues on the bargaining table....

Once issues were on the table, a committee of board and union leaders met in a followup session to divide the issues into two categories: issues to be negotiated formally (such as salaries) and issues to be resolved through less formal talks between board and union members. Subcommittees, formed to focus on specific issues, met two evenings per week. On the final session day, teacher salaries were still being negotiated and the session stretched to sixteen tension-filled hours before the contract was signed. The Glenbard attempt at win/win bargaining was termed a success: A contract had been signed three months before the old one expired, and the district enjoyed improved teacher morale and board/union cooperation in 1988. (p. 28)

Warwick Valley Central School District, New York, had only recently emerged from a period of intense contract negotiations conducted by third-party union and board negotiators. The sessions had dragged out over sixteen months. The district decided to develop a process that encouraged frank discussion and debate and that discouraged confrontation and posturing:

> Their attention landed on the only successful feature of the previous contract negotiations: a joint committee that had researched and made a recommendation on stipends for staff who perform cocurricular activities. The joint committee process had worked so smoothly that the district decided to negotiate the entire new contract on the basis of recommendations from joint committees.
>
> Tagged a "good faith experiment," the process included an agenda committee (comprising the school board president, another board member, the president and vice president of the teacher union, and the superintendent), which established the timetable and some basic guidelines. The agenda committee...was also charged with reviewing and, if necessary, discarding negotiations items, under the agreement that a few small committees would concentrate on a few genuinely important issues. Limiting the agenda was credited with making the new process work by helping board members and teachers define priorities. Ten items, including teacher salary, were the maximum number that could be introduced.
>
> Once the agenda was set, four committees each containing two or three teachers and at least one board member went to work. Joint committees reported back to the agenda committee, which strove to include at least portions of each committee's recommendations in the contract, written up at the table by the board attorney. The three-year contract, ratified overwhelmingly by union and board, was put together in a timely manner without confrontation and disruption of the educational process. (Smith and others 1990, pp. 29-30)

POLICY TRUST AGREEMENTS

Policy trust agreements are another mechanism by which collaboration can be promoted and problems can be anticipated and addressed outside the formal bargaining process. In California the Policy Analysis for California Education worked with twelve districts to put policy trust agreements into place. The goal, as Smith and others (1990) explain, was to

> develop new forms of school organization and new patterns of relationships among teachers and school administrators and to expand the range of labor/management discussions from technical, procedural work rules to the essence of educational policy....
>
> ...[A] policy trust agreement "is a written compact between a school district and its teachers, as represented by their union" [Koppich and Kerchner 1990]. Its purpose is "to specify educational problems of joint concern to teachers and school managers and to establish mechanisms for

working on these problems." The trust agreement encourages a sharing of decision-making responsibility between teachers and school administrators, thereby altering the traditional, hierarchical authority relationships in the school district.

Trust agreements are not considered to be alternatives to collective bargaining, but a process to strengthen teacher responsibility in innovative programs that tend to fall outside the scope of the collective bargaining agreement. Nor are trust agreements intended primarily as devices to reduce conflict....

... Trust agreements differ from collective bargaining contracts both in their conceptions of work activities and in their procedures for implementation and problem resolution. Contracts "seek to specify *rules,*" says [Douglas] Mitchell, whereas "trust agreements develop shared *goals.* This difference is extraordinarily important." Rules mandate behavior and delineate employee rights, then they hold the parties accountable for not wavering from mandated actions. By contrast, "the goals specified in a trust agreement define the *purposes* of teaching work activities and identify the *resources* to be used in pursuing those purposes."

In other words, trust agreements encourage teachers and administrators to cooperate in deciding what needs to be done. The emphasis is on joint planning rather than on accountability. (pp. 33-34)

GUIDELINES FOR BEGINNING TO COLLABORATE

While collaborative bargaining and policy trust agreements are concepts that are still evolving, there is much that can be learned from them and from the experiences of districts that develop and employ these strategies. It may be that in some districts (perhaps most) there will be a period where the bargaining moves a step or two toward collaboration, then back toward traditional methods. The transition may take time and patience, and the final result may bear little resemblance to early efforts.

Some lessons have been learned from those districts that have been involved in experimenting with collaborative bargaining. Smith and others (1990) offer the following guidelines for those interested in pursuing collaborative bargaining along with those who might choose to incorporate aspects of collaboration into their collective-bargaining process:

Before Bargaining:

- Consider holding an informal forum where representatives of all interested groups can openly discuss previous conflicts and frustrations.
- Build mutual trust.

- Conduct an inclusive forum to discuss past bargaining failures and possibilities for future efforts.
- Jointly research the alternative methods of negotiating contracts and resolving problems.
- Enhance communication and negotiation skills.
- Establish a timetable and some basic guidelines for the process, including an "escape clause" that will allow you to return to traditional collective bargaining.
- Form an agenda committee and limit the agenda to essential issues.
- Choose team members wisely.
- Remember that communication is crucial.

During Bargaining:
- Meet in comfortable, informal surroundings.
- Have patience.
- Don't try to accomplish everything at the bargaining table.
- Carefully and cooperatively approach the issue of salaries.
- Keep communications open.
- Keep information flowing.
- Negotiate with a spirit of problem-solving.
- Maintain good community relations.

After Bargaining:
- Publicize the gains that collaborative bargaining has achieved.
- Maintain union leaders' legitimacy in the eyes of their members.
- Keep a tickler file of problems encountered in negotiations and in administering the current contract.
- Ascertain that agreements are being honored.
- Set up joint committees to handle issues.
- Keep the bargaining continuous.
- Keep staff updated. (Excerpted from pp. 51-59)

This dimension of restructuring (working relationships), though discussed last, is particularly important because breakdowns in working relationships between teachers and school district management may serve to constrict much of what is possible in the other eleven dimensions. Changes in working relationships manifested in a master contract are unlikely in themselves to cause restructuring, but an inability to rethink these relationships will surely slow and perhaps derail the process. New forms of bargaining and other strategies may point the way for school districts that seek to move away from the industrial union model of labor relations. These changes in bargaining and labor relations only serve to signal more fundamental changes in power relations within school systems.

THE IMPORTANCE OF FACULTY COLLABORATION

This discussion of collaboration in the context of working relationships suggests the opportunities and difficulties schools face as they begin to rethink fundamental practices and relationships. In a restructuring school, the principle of collaboration extends beyond contract negotiation to relationships throughout the organization.

Schools are no better than their teachers. True educational improvement is much more difficult, some would say impossible, if teachers do not participate in and take ownership of its goals and processes. Teachers must be involved, their opinions respected, their power acknowledged. Private-sector companies have recognized similar principles as they sought in the 1980s to improve productivity and increase adaptability and quality. Once again, as at the turn of this century, there are lessons educators can learn from the private sector. Hopefully, they can adapt rather than mimic private-sector practices. What they learn from the private sector can help guide models of greater collaboration in school districts, but the basic principle of collaboration itself is perhaps the most important focal point.

Many of the specific changes and programs discussed in the chapters on the twelve dimensions of restructuring are based on the premise that teachers, administrators, and others would be willing to work together to a much greater degree than exists today in most schools. These types of changes, if they are to occur, require that teachers forgo their autonomy and isolation and embrace collaborative behaviors and structures. Collaboration, in turn, will demand new leadership styles and new skills from all involved in schooling. Perhaps educational reformers underestimate the ramifications of the greater collaboration that must occur for schools to succeed at restructuring.

Education, like many other aspects of postindustrial society, has become too complex to be conducted successfully by isolated specialists. The future lies down the road of mutual interdependence, of teamwork among adults and children, of human capital development, of enhanced interpersonal skills, of inclusive leadership approaches and styles, and of organizations that resemble living organisms more than inert structures.

CHAPTER 21

DISCONTINUOUS RESTRUCTURING

The various projects and programs described in the preceding twelve chapters are attempts to restructure education incrementally. An alternative to these incremental changes is the notion of reinventing education through discontinuous change. The distinction between these two different approaches to organizational change was first discussed in the Introduction, pages 9-11.

Incremental change is based on the assumption that the organization is in control of its relationship with the external environment and can dictate the rate and nature of internal organizational adaptation. Administrators can develop new policies and procedures in a timely fashion to enable them to do better that which they have been doing. Discontinuous change implies the opposite: The organization is swept along by external forces that shape internal responses and adaptations. Change is rapid and not necessarily evolutionary. Managers and leaders in this environment find their frames of reference and world views shattered. They are called on to reinvent the organization.

Educators who follow the discontinuous route to restructuring step outside the existing system and build new approaches to education from the ground up. Generally, this means they must develop a new school from scratch or create radically new ways of thinking about schooling in its entirety.

An example of discontinuous change in the private sector is General Motors' attempt to create an entirely new way to design and build automobiles, a new company within a company. The Saturn project, which GM initiated in 1985, was an attempt to rethink automobile design, production, and sales by learning from the Japanese, among others, and applying these lessons to the American automobile manufacturing industry. In launching Saturn, GM acknowledged it was unlikely to adapt incrementally to the challenges it faced from abroad. Another model was needed to provide a contrast within the company between how things were always done, and how they could be done. The Saturn automobile is a result of GM's experiment in discontinuous restructuring.

As will be discussed later, discontinuous change is not without its problems. In the case of the Saturn project, GM has been learning a variety of lessons that are informative to those in any organization attempting to change or adapt radically. Educators who contemplate the type of change necessary to transform schools, while still ostensibly remaining part of the public school system, have their own lessons to learn.

SOME EXAMPLES

Within public education there have been few attempts at discontinuous restructuring. Most change of this nature has been restricted to alternative schools, where its effects have been isolated from the mainstream of schooling. After a period of intense activity in the late sixties and early seventies, most of these radically discontinuous models faded or were absorbed into the larger system.

FOUR NEW MODELS OF EDUCATION

Recently, a new generation of schools has arisen that are not necessarily identified as alternatives in the sixties sense, but are designed to serve as new educational models. Several of these have received considerable attention during the past several years. Among them are Chiron Middle School (O'Neil 1990); the Tessaract model as applied at South Pointe Elementary in Dade County, Florida (Bradley 1990, Conlin 1991); the Saturn School (Bennett and King 1991); and Central Park East Secondary School (Meier 1987). The Holweide School in Cologne, Germany (Ratzki 1988, Ratzki and Fisher 1989/1990), which was discussed briefly in an earlier chapter, is perhaps another example, though it has been in existence much longer than any of the American examples.

The four American schools represent a radical departure from traditional assumptions about public schooling in this country, even though they remain within the system and enroll a representative cross-section of pupils and spend about the same amount of money per pupil per year as existing schools. They all have the advantage of having started "from scratch"; therefore they have been able to structure their educational program so that it expressly supports their vision of education. (The importance of vision in school restructuring is discussed in greater detail in part 4.) These schools have been able to make decisions regarding practices on almost all the twelve dimensions discussed in the previous section.

What these four schools provide is not a cookie-cutter model to be implemented by others, but lessons regarding the challenges that exist for those attempting fundamental change. Other educators can also learn from the vision of education present in each program. These lessons endure in their value and use to all educators.

One of the purposes that schools such as these can fulfill is to serve as lighthouses for the other 15,500 school districts in America. They suggest different ways in which education can be structured and delivered, and they provide valuable lessons on the implementation of such ideas.

It is interesting to note that visitors to these schools may come away somewhat disappointed when they do not instantly witness radically different behavior or attitudes, particularly by students, or when they do not instantaneously comprehend the purpose of a particular activity or environment. While changes in the physical environment and structural elements such as the daily schedule can be more readily observed, the differences in the ways learning occurs are often subtle and discernible only over a long time. Students, teachers, and parents have to unlearn old expectations, behaviors, and assumptions. New strategies must be constantly questioned, examined, and refined. Often this process is not readily apparent to the casual observer, who may leave disappointed that he or she did not witness educational "nirvana."

Rather than holding these schools (and similar schools that are emerging) to unrealistic standards and expectations, it is more fruitful to view these radically restructured schools as "laboratories" in which new approaches can be observed, examined, and debated. They should not be considered "model schools" to be emulated or replicated in slavish detail, but rather viewed as "think tanks" that can help mainstream educators reexamine their assumptions about schooling. Since educators often need to see new approaches in practice before they are willing to try them in their own schools, these schools can serve a valuable, though limited, role in the process of school restructuring by allowing mainstream educators to see different visions of education in operation. The structure and functioning of these schools and others like them have been described in detail by other writers, so will not be repeated here.*

---

* In addition to the intext citations accompanying each school, the reader is referred to David (1991); David and others (1990); Toch (1991); Toch and Cooper (1990) and the Center on Organization and Restructuring of Schools, University of Wisconsin, Madison, for additional discussion of schools involved in attempts at discontinuous restructuring.

THE EDISON PROJECT

Other harbingers of discontinuous change in education are appearing as well. One example is the Whittle Corporation's plans to develop 200 for-profit schools around the nation ("Whittle To Spend Millions..." 1991; Walsh, May 22, 1991). Whittle Communications will seek $2.5 to $3 billion in capital to open these schools in major urban areas across the nation by fall 1996. These schools will incorporate innovations developed by a special research team charged with designing new educational environments. The entire undertaking goes under the name of the Edison Project. By the year 2010, Whittle expects to be serving as many as two million pupils at one-thousand campuses.

These schools will adhere to the following criteria:

- Provide a significantly improved education for no more than the current cost per pupil in public schools.

- Be capable of demonstrating improved results.

- Select students randomly from a pool of applicants.

- In nonchoice areas of the nation, provide 20 percent of all participating students with full scholarships.

The schools will serve children in day care through those in high school. To keep costs down, Whittle proposes having students work in the schools; for example, they will serve food in the cafeteria, help care for children in the day care center, or assist teachers. These would be paid positions. "Having a job in school will be part of school," he said. Technology will be employed extensively in the form of electronic multimedia learning systems ("Whittle To Spend Millions..." 1991).

Whittle's for-profit motive separates him from most others attempting restructuring. His goals are far different from the typical private school, which is often designed simply to do what the public schools do, only to do it more "effectively." There is considerable speculation that Whittle's schools could serve as product-development laboratories and, eventually, as markets for educational products such as textbooks, curriculum materials, food services, transportation, financial management, even staff development. The public funds present in schools could provide the basis for considerable private enterprise. In other words, the nonprofit portion of schools could feed a for-profit element. Most public educators are uncomfortable with such ideas.

NEW AMERICAN SCHOOLS DEVELOPMENT CORPORATION

Another interesting attempt at second-order change, this one also at the national level, has been the New American Schools Development

Corporation, launched by former President Bush with the guidance of former Secretary of Education Lamar Alexander. The New American Schools Development Corporation was described by President Bush in a speech given at the White House on April 18, 1991:

> I'm delighted to announce today that America's business leaders... will create the New American Schools Development Corporation—a private-sector research and development fund of at least $150 million to generate innovation in education.
>
> This fund offers an open-end challenge to the dreamers and the doers eager to reinvent—eager to reinvigorate our schools. With the results of this design in hand, I will urge Congress to provide $1 million in start-up funds for each of the 535 New American Schools—at least one in every congressional district—and have them up and running by 1996....
>
> ... We ask only two things of these architects of our New American Schools: that their students meet the new national standards for the five core subjects and that outside of the costs of the initial research and development, the schools operate on a budget comparable to conventional schools. The architects of the New American Schools should break the mold. Build for the next century. Reinvent—literally start from scratch and reinvent the American school. No question should be off limits, no answers automatically assumed. We're not after one single solution for every school. We're interested in finding every way to make schools better. (U.S. Department of Education 1991, pp. 54-55)

The New American Schools Development Corporation held a competition in fall 1991 and spring 1992 to solicit designs for these "break the mold" schools. The results from this competition were announced in July 1992 before the change in administrations. Of 686 proposals submitted, 11 design teams were selected and provided funding "to pursue their visions of radically different and more productive schools" (Olson, August 5, 1992). These schools are supposed to represent another attempt at second-order, or discontinuous, change. While it will take several years or more to tell how (or whether) these projects will develop, it is clear that they represent one more attempt to create national models that demonstrate fundamentally different ways of educating young people. Because of the way these schools are being developed, they will not have to confront as many of the obstacles faced by existing schools that are attempting to transform themselves.

An examination of the recipients of the awards suggests the difficulty of discontinuous change. Olson (August 5, 1992) describes some of the problems that arose in finding truly revolutionary new ideas and designs:

> Most striking is the lack of educational outsiders in a competition intended to spark innovative ideas from a broad array of businesses, communities, and interest groups.

Although private corporations, civic groups, and others are all members of design teams, the lead players typically have a long and sustained involvement in education reform....

... "My concern was that they'd go for flaky, and they've gone for solid," said Robert E. Slavin, a Johns Hopkins University researcher and the project director of one of the award-winning teams. "They're not leaning out as far as they might have"....

... Another striking feature of the award-winning designs is how many ideas they have in common, or what one observer jokingly referred to as the "new conventional wisdom."

Most of the proposals stress the use of multi-age classrooms that enable students to progress at their own pace. A number of them attempt to "personalize" education through the use of advisers, smaller groupings of students and teachers that stay together over several years, and individual learning contracts.

Teaching methods that are widely recognized as effective—such as cooperative learning and hands-on project-oriented activities—pop up in nearly every proposal. Similarly, most include a much stronger focus on character development and community service than is now present in schools. And many attempt to blur the line between in-school and out-of-school learning.

New forms of performance-based assessment, more extensive professional development for teachers, and a more flexible use of time—including longer school days and years—are also themes that run through most of the designs.

Many also focus on the development of a more integrated, articulated curriculum, including the use of interdisciplinary teaching.

And, partly in deference to the first of the national education goals—"All children in America will start school ready to learn"—nearly every proposal talks about increasing coordination between education, health, and social-service providers.

This convergence around a common set of ideas has led some observers to complain that nothing really new emerges in the designs. But others note that all of the concepts together have not been put into practice in one school before—and, particularly, not in an entire school system. (p. 47)

THE ELEVEN NEW AMERICAN SCHOOLS

A description of the programs that were funded under this competition provides insight into both new visions of education and the difficulty of truly "breaking the mold" in public education. That some, perhaps many, of these ideas sound familiar should not be surprising. The challenge may not be simply to come up with new ideas of how to structure schooling, but to implement such concepts in practice. Ultimately any school requires a student population in order to function, and parents must be convinced that they are making a prudent and responsible decision by letting their child attend the school. So perhaps it is not so surprising that even the "break the mold" schools had to use language and structures that remain familiar to many people.

Virtually all of NASDC's projects attend to school readiness, changing relationships between community and school, increased use of technology, altered school schedules and calendars, site-based management, various spins on performance assessment, teacher as guide and coach, and integration of curriculum. As Olson noted earlier, many of these ideas are fast becoming the conventional wisdom about what the next generation of schools should look like.

The following summaries present brief portraits designed to distill the four-page descriptions of these projects provided to the press by NASDC at the time the original winners were announced in July 1992. I am indebted to Mecklenburger (1992) for his summaries of these projects, which I have condensed further in the following narrative. All materials in quotes are from the original project descriptions developed by NASDC. Some changes may have occurred in these projects since that time. These limited descriptions of programs still under development should be considered illustrative of the general approaches being undertaken; more definitive and detailed descriptions presumably will be available from each program.

ATLAS Communities. ATLAS is headed by a team of educational reformers from the Ivy League, including James Comer, Howard Gardner, and Theodore Sizer. They "have joined their separate and distinct efforts and created a program for systematic and comprehensive change for all children."

They propose to establish a "clearly articulated, integrated curriculum" focused on "essential questions." Instruction will emphasize "active inquiry" and "learning by doing." Adults will serve as "teachers, mentors, and advisors" who will work closely with small numbers of students over longer periods than one year. Students will be encouraged "to regard their time in school as an opportunity to gain facility and joy in communicating with other individuals."

The structure and governance of the project will be managed by teams, including a "Planning and Management Team of teachers, parents, school counselors, students of high school age, and a school principal" along with a Community Health Team of teachers, special educators, parents, psychologists, social workers, and nurses. "Problem solving will be collaborative and largely done by consensus."

Technology will be used "to enrich curriculum, assessment and adult development activities." And there will be a system known as

ACE, the ATLAS Community Exchange, "to facilitate communication among all participants within and across sites and organizations."

ATLAS will serve grades pre-K through 12 in urban, suburban, and rural communities.

Bensenville Community. Bensenville, Illinois, intends to "create an environment where the entire community serves as a campus" so that students learn in many settings and the school becomes a lifelong learning center. The watchwords of the project are "active learning," "teacher as facilitator," "higher-order thinking skills," "relevance," and "hands-on learning." The curriculum will be performance-based and evaluated through "performance portfolios rather than the traditional completion of tests, credits and assignment of grades."

Teacher preparation will be restructured through a partnership with Illinois State University. Schooling will become year-round, scheduling will be "flexible," and coursework will be "cross-disciplinary." There will be a governing body "consisting of parents, business leaders, government officials, educators, and other citizens." The project makes extensive use of technology, replacing the teacher's desk with an Electronic Teaching Center (ETC) that can handle an array of administrative and reporting functions. Laser discs, VCRs, and a large-screen television will be readily available for instructional use. Voice mail will facilitate home/school communication, and a satellite will bring in external resources. The use of technology will increase as schools become more experienced in its use.

Assessment will be overhauled in many ways to be able to describe student progress in terms of three levels of achievement: exceeds, meets, or does not meet world-class standards. New reporting systems that include local press and community meetings, among other things, will be created.

Audrey Cohen College. This project operates on the premise that "students learn best when they can see the connection between what they are learning and the real world" and "when they see that what they have learned in school can make a positive change in the community." From seven to thirty schools in Arizona, California, Illinois, Mississippi, New York City, and Washington D.C. will take part. The design team includes Audrey Cohen, the president and founder of the college that bears her name, and people associated primarily with museums, foundations, and national organizations, along with some school-based educators and business people.

Each semester students study a "major purpose" that has "two components: a substantive body of knowledge and a socially important thrust." Students apply what they learn. Curriculum is described as "integrated," "related," and "comprehensive." The core subjects relate to each semester's purpose, and each "comprehensive, complementary, and action-oriented" course is organized around "dimensions" (perspectives from which knowledge is examined) and results in "constructive action outside of school."

Families, organizations, and individuals in the community will "become resources for learning," so a major responsibility of some teachers and of principals is to identify, marshal, and build relationships with these groups.

Adults are classified as "teachers" and "master teachers." Children will use technology to gather and analyze information. Types of technology include audio, video, photography, interactive multimedia, and telecommunications.

New assessment strategies form a major focus. These designs will be "based on a description of the kind of person whom the program intends to graduate."

Community Learning Centers of Minnesota. This project utilizes Minnesota's charter school law that allows teachers to "contract with school boards to begin a school with the understanding that students will meet agreed-upon standards for improvement." Three initial sites include St. Cloud, North Branch, and Rothsay. These districts are "partners" in the project, but the intent is to serve preschools through high schools in a range of districts throughout Minnesota. These centers operate in an adjunct relationship to local school districts.

The project will establish competency-based education, "learning meaningful to students," "interdisciplinary curriculum," "community service activities," "active and experiential learning," and "projects and cooperative learning methods to stimulate multiple intelligences."

Site councils composed of "elected stakeholders" oversee governance. Accountability is also enforced via a contract between the Community Learning Center and the school district. The council will be a management, not a curriculum, group.

Assessment combines quantitative and qualitative measures of performance. The role of the teacher is assumed to be that of a professional who will "design curricula, arrange staff training, supervise paraprofessional personnel, review peer performance, oversee the purchase and use of technology, and ensure that assessments of learning results are available to stakeholders."

In addition to school districts, the project lists as partners Incentives, Inc; Cray Research Foundation; the Urban Coalition; the St. Paul branch of the NAACP; the William Norris Institute; and the Center for School Change, a part of the Humphrey Institute of Public Affairs at the University of Minnesota.

The Co-NECT School. This project is headed by noneducators, the Boston-based consulting organization of Bolt Beranak and Newman, and is based on the premise that certain technologies can "create a communications environment in which broader, deeper, and stronger learning occurs." The project focuses on innercity youth, including those at-risk, and aspires to serve all of K-12 education, though its initial sites are K-5 and K-6 schools in Boston and Worcester, Massachusetts.

The curriculum focuses on math and science and teaches five core subjects as well as "self-direction, perseverance, and commitment to quality." Projects and seminars are the basis for instruction in combination with innovative assessment strategies. The project is grounded on the premise that this curriculum strategy can lead to students who are comfortable with technology, have "long-term goals" for learning, have mastered "critical work skills," and are ready for life and work.

The fundamental organizing structure for the school is the concept of community. The school features "self-managing clusters" of perhaps six teachers and one hundred students who would stay together for several years. Clusters would address both learning and social needs. They are supported by "a flexible and open computer-based communications network that connects all school community members" with one another and provides them access to a rich array of local, national, and global learning resources and tools. Computers, multimedia, and interactive video will be "pervasive."

There are six additional partners: Apple Computer; NYNEX; Lotus Development Corporation; the Massachusetts Corporation for Education Telecommunications; Earthwatch, Inc.; and the Boston College Center for the Study of Testing, Evaluation, and Educational Policy.

Expeditionary Learning. This project, led by Outward Bound, USA, applies some of the experience, premises, and language of the Outward Bound program to the operation of entire schools. The project will work with all grade levels and will set up one new charter school and work with existing schools in Portland, Maine; Boston; New York City; Decatur, Georgia; and Douglas County, Colorado.

The program's organizers believe that children learn to think by being taken through "programmatically related voyages and adventures." Schools will be "vibrant and interesting communities" in which adults, who may be "expedition guides" or "leaders," work with youngsters in multiage groupings of eight to twelve students called "watches" (a nautical term for crew members on duty). Watches, in turn, are clustered into crews of eighteen to twenty-five members each.

A rigorous "world-class curriculum," the International Baccalaureate, will provide an academic structure, but it will be "intertwined" with the rest of the program.

Various expeditions may be experiential, intellectual, or "service." A "senior service expedition"— based on the premise that you should "teach what you love to teach; share what you love to share; test your readiness to do the unknown"—will be required for graduation.

"To attain a diploma, students complete prerequisites, carry out an approved senior service expedition, and pass the International Baccalaureate examination. A student may do this at his or her own pace." The use of technology is not showcased in this project, though it is noted that "computer studies" is a part of the mathematics curriculum.

Outward Bound has six partners: the Academy for Educational Development; Educators for Social Responsibility; Facing History, Facing Ourselves; the Harvard Outward Bound Project; Project Adventure; and TERC (the developers of the National Geographic Kids Network).

Los Angeles Learning Centers. This project proposes to pilot concepts at two innercity sites that break all the rules. One site will be new, built "from scratch." The other will be a cluster comprising a high school and its feeder schools, selected by application. Some 3,200 students in all will participate in the project, which is a joint venture of the United Teachers of Los Angeles, the Los Angeles Unified School District, and the Los Angeles Educational Partnership, a business-led organization.

Concepts that are central to the project include the notions of "continuity," "incentives," "modeling," "nurturing," and "high expectations." The project describes each child as part of a "moving diamond," with the student as one of the facets linked with an older student, a teacher, and the student's parents or a community volunteer. The schools will be organized into three nongraded age ranges, and these "moving diamonds" will stay together for at least several years.

Teaching will be done through interdisciplinary teams; community members will carry some teaching responsibilities, freeing teachers to become learners and planners for the equivalent of one day per week. School buildings will be open eighteen hours a day, fifty weeks a year. The concept of "after school" will disappear.

Schools will employ "site-based management" and "zero-based budgeting." A school management council—composed of teachers, parents, students, and the principal—will decide about "budget, personnel, curriculum, strategic planning, discipline, community relations, and student rights." Portfolios, standardized tests, and international comparisons will be utilized to assess learner outcomes.

State-of-the-art instructional technologies will be made available to teachers, students, administrators, and parents. Transition-to-work programs will be included for uppergrade students.

In addition to the three main partners, the project has five corporate sponsors: ARCO, Bank of America, GTE California, Rockwell International, and the Times-Mirror Company.

Modern Red Schoolhouse. This project, led by former U.S. Secretary of Education William Bennett, blends the "classical education" curriculum with a healthy dose of technology. It adds the idea of "individual education contracts that bring personal accountability to schooling," to demonstrate that all students can achieve high standards. The proposal comes from the Hudson Institute in Indianapolis, and its design team includes such well-known school reformers as Dennis Doyle and Chester Finn, Jr.

Seven school districts have already begun work in this area, upon which the project will build. They include several schools in Indiana communities—including Columbus, Beech Grove, Greentown, Indianapolis, and Lawrence Township; the Charlotte-Mecklenburg Schools in North Carolina; and Kayenta Unified School District, Arizona.

The "core curriculum" is built upon the U.S. Department of Education's James Madison series, on the Department of Labor's SCANS (Secretary's Commission for Achieving Necessary Skills) Project, and on E.D. Hirsch's book *Cultural Literacy*. "Self-paced learning," defined through individual educational contracts, "will be integrated into a computer network as part of an instructional management system available to all teachers."

Schools will have differentiated instructional staff; multiage, multiyear homerooms; teacher/advisors; and flexible daily and yearly schedules. Teachers and students will choose to come to these schools after an application process. New, as yet undevised approaches to measurement will be implemented.

These Hudson Schools will "make extensive use of computers, databases, and networks," including "electronic bulletin boards, community-access TV, and a school-specific database." Community agencies and parents will be enlisted to prepare students for school and to assist at-risk youth.

National Alliance for Restructuring Education. This project is designed to extend, coordinate, and provide technical assistance to work already in progress in Arkansas, Kentucky, New York, Vermont, and Washington States, and to school systems in Pittsburgh, San Diego, Rochester, and White Plains, New York. It is led by Marc Tucker, president and founder of the National Center on Education and the Economy.

The project's mission is to transform American education into "an output-driven, performance-oriented system...that produces students meeting national achievement standards benchmarked to the highest in the world." The project sites provide models of how this can be accomplished by "breaking the current system, root and branch."

Key to this process is the identification of "strategies that will foster sustained public support for world-class student performance standards and the revolutionary changes in policy and practice needed to meet them," along with the outcomes that are wanted, and "good measures of progress" to determine student performance and mastery of outcomes. Schools will be connected to the curriculum and institutional resources they need. The planning, financing, and delivery of health and human services will be adapted to support learning more effectively. Education will be adapted to the principles of Total Quality Management.

One curriculum priority is to establish a growing bank of teacher-oriented research information and curriculum proposals "to serve as intellectual and practice resources." Another is to "devise the policies and practices required for an effective school-to-work program."

This project is connected to the New Standards Project, which is designing new assessment procedures; the project will contribute and draw on the work of that effort. The Apple Classrooms of Tomorrow Program will provide technical assistance for "fully integrating advanced computer-based technologies into the new curriculum."

Teacher roles will shift toward that of "students' collaborators," and principals will become "the leader and facilitator of teachers' efforts."

Partners include Apple Computer, the Center for the Study of Social Policy, the Commission on the Skills of the American Workforce, the Harvard Project on Effective Services, the Learning Research and Development Center at the University of Pittsburgh, the National Alliance of Business, the National Board for Professional Teaching Standards, the New Standards Project, the Public Agenda Foundation, and the Xerox Corporation. Prominent educational reformers such as Michael Cohen, Lauren Resnick, and Robert Glaser are also affiliated with the project.

Odyssey Project. All fifty-four schools in Gaston County, North Carolina, will be part of this project. They will become "Odyssey Learning Centers" that operate year-round, dawn-to-dusk for all students. These learning centers are divided into a series of age ranges: alpha, 0-3; beta, 3-6; gamma, 7-10; delta, 11-14; and odyssey, 15-18.

Students will be "communicators, collaborators, creative producers, critical thinkers, and concerned and confident citizens." Through use of an outcome-based system, students will move through the centers as they demonstrate mastery of designated performance outcomes, which will be assessed through a variety of quantitative and qualitative measures.

Community service will be required, and parental involvement will be encouraged in many ways, including a requirement that parents spend a certain number of hours with their child at the child's learning station.

Principals will be instructional managers and noninstructional operations managers. Health care will be coordinated with community agencies.

Roots and Wings. Noted educational researcher Robert Slavin from Johns Hopkins University directs this project, which will serve elementary students in four primarily rural, disadvantaged communities in St. Mary's County, Maryland.

The curriculum uses simulations of real-life problems and real activities related to the students' own communities. There is a strong emphasis on cooperative learning, one of Slavin's areas of expertise as a researcher. Curriculum will be integrated across disciplines, as well. The goal is to create students with a strong foundation both in basic skills ("roots") and in thinking skills, creativity, flexibility, and breadth of world view ("wings").

Roots and Wings coined the term *neverstreaming* to describe its emphasis on prevention and early intervention strategies "that are effective in keeping most students from needing long-term remedial or special education services." Accordingly, Roots and Wings "will focus on early elementary years" from birth to age 11. Family support centers at each school will combine funds and talents to integrate services such as health, mental health, and day-care programs; adult education; and assistance with food and rent.

Computer technology will be used "extensively" to support instruction through simulation and other approaches. Assessment will blend portfolios of students' work with "performance-based measures recently developed by the state of Maryland."

Unfunded Projects. Mecklenburger (1992) goes on to describe an array of projects that were not funded by the New American Schools Development Corporation. Some of these contained reconceptualizations of education that appear more radical or fundamental than those present in many of the funded proposals. Some sought to involve the entire community in the educational process in some way. Others proposed moving school outside school buildings to a much greater degree and decentralizing learning. Several were built around concepts of Total Quality Management (TQM), and proposed close partnerships among schools, other governmental units, and private corporations expert in the application of the principles of TQM. The use of technology was a centerpiece in some that had close alliances with high tech companies. For whatever reasons, these were not selected, and NASDC's "break the mold" schools that were selected will, by and large, begin by attempting to modify the mold, rather than break it, apparently.

Olson (1993), in a preview of the issues that many of these projects may have to face, identified some of the tensions that existed in the Roots and Wings project as it began its planning in rural Maryland schools:

> A walk through the halls of any of the four Roots and Wings elementary schools... suggests that for many teachers, the project will require difficult, even wrenching, changes in how they do their jobs.
>
> Although some teachers are experimenting with team teaching, cooperative learning, and multi-age grouping, others can be seen lecturing in the front of the room, or working with small groups while the other students fill out worksheets, chat with their neighbors, or gaze into space....
>
> ... Much of the fall was spent in a delicate courtship between teachers in this rural community, who are proud of their schools, and researchers from the university, who are trying to understand what they have to build on....
>
> ... [S]ome teachers remain skeptical—including several of those who have been seen as the most innovative in the past....
>
> ... [One teacher who was involved with writing the grant said] "I want to see change, but I want to take the best of St. Mary's County also. That's the frustration that we are feeling right now: how to fit in what [the researchers] have proven successful to what we already have"....
>
> ... One initial source of tension between the university scholars and some teachers was whether the Johns Hopkins approach might be too structured and rigid....
>
> ... Teachers at [one of the schools] decided to pilot the Johns Hopkins approach to beginning reading in only one classroom this year, with students who were having the most difficulty with traditional reading instruction.
>
> "Probably this school is taking a more cautious approach than the other three," [said the principal]. "We're not totally sure that Johns Hopkins has the answer in this area; but if they do, we want to use it." (pp. 12, 13)

It is too early to tell what the ultimate outcome or impact from these projects is likely to be. It is clear that many, perhaps most, of these projects will continue to have to negotiate the existing system of education to a significant degree to accomplish their aims. This inability to break away from that system illustrates both the strength and legitimacy that it retains at the psychological level as the conception of education upon which new models are built. Abandoning public educational frameworks appears to be quite difficult, even for those attempting discontinuous change.

NEXT CENTURY SCHOOLS PROGRAM

Another attempt at encouraging rapid, radical change in public schools is being sponsored by the RJR Nabisco corporation, through its Next Century Schools program, a competitive grant process that, since 1990, has awarded three-year grants of up to $750,000 to forty-four schools. These grants—awarded to individual schools, not school districts—are based on the premise that change will take place school-by-school.

The experiences of the Next Century Schools illustrate the difficulty of changing one school while leaving the school system intact. Schools have encountered a range of difficulties: unexpected delays in ordering equipment caused by problems with district accounting procedures, lack of support when key central-office administrators left, and staff turnover when teachers who approved a grant proposal that would have required them to work in the summer promptly transferred to other schools once the grant was funded, citing inability to work during summers (Sommerfeld 1992).

These schools are attempting to implement many ideas similar to those being proposed by New American Schools Development Corporation (NASDC) award recipients. In fact, the Next Century Schools are widely seen as a prototype for the NASDC process.

One grant recipient, New Stanley Elementary School in Kansas City, Kansas, has extended the school year to 205 days organized in four 10- or 11-week quarters, separated by 1-week vacations. Teachers now work 226 days and use the 1-week student vacation times as opportunities for planning and development. Classes are also dismissed at 1:15 p.m. every Wednesday to allow for staff development. Teachers have rewritten the entire curriculum into an outcome-based format. Groups of fifty or sixty students stay with the same team of three teachers for three years. Decisions are made by a site-based team that controls curriculum, hiring, and instructional materials. Adult literacy and computer classes are offered for parents and community. The school has $250,000 a year available to support these efforts (Sommerfeld 1992).

Other grant recipients are combining many of the ideas presented earlier in the discussion of incremental restructuring. They are using the money to buy the time necessary to plan and reconstruct current practice.

These schools and projects are places where educators can go and see what is possible. In that sense schools that "break the mold" may support and augment efforts at incremental restructuring. These two types of change may be much more complementary than they would appear at first glance.

THREATS TO CHANGE

The examples of incremental and discontinuous change presented here serve to illustrate the possibilities for new methods and structures of education. These examples also suggest the profound difficulties associated with change in public education. Throughout this book I have questioned whether schools can remake themselves in an incremental fashion (see the Introduction to part 3 and the beginning of chapter 8). A closer look at discontinuous responses suggests that they are not automatically the answer to transforming public education, either. A careful examination of discontinuous attempts at educational restructuring reveals a whole new set of issues and problems that must be addressed.

One problem that has been evident in the Saturn experiment at GM is that the lessons learned within the new or experimental environment are not always embraced and implemented by the rest of the organization. Instead of viewing the innovative unit as an asset, other more traditional parts of the organization come to perceive it as the problem. The supposed successes in the innovative unit are explained away, as differences between that environment and the traditional environment are identified and amplified. "That's fine for them, but it will never work here," or "Sure, they can do it: Look at all the _____ they have, and all the _____ they don't have" (fill in the blanks with the appropriate words depending on the particular organizational environment). The very successes of the innovative environment threaten the existing order. The impulse to continue in the familiar way is strong, as is the desire to protect existing turf, access to resources, and power relationships, for those who have something to lose.

Beyond this limitation, there lies a more fundamental question: Can public schools be transformed by any means, incremental or discontinuous, or are they destined to operate within a predictable, identifiable range of practices? This is a question that is seldom asked by educational reformers or policy-makers, who assume that good ideas combined with effective implementation strategies are the key ingredients to educational reform or restructuring. There is considerable evidence that attempts at discontinuous restructuring within public school systems remain under constant pressure and threat from the bureaucratic structure of the district and from supposed colleagues at other schools. Will the institutional inertia present within all large bureaucratic organizations, but particularly strong in those without clear outputs, success measures, or accountability mechanisms, ultimately overwhelm all efforts, incremental and discontinuous, and leave the public with an educational system changed in only superficial ways?

Or is the issue obscured by considering schools solely as bureaucracies? Schools are relatively unique institutions in society, since they serve as surrogates for the family. Perhaps it is more useful to think of schools as social institutions, like the family, and not just as bureaucracies. As the family itself changes ever more profoundly, might it not be the hope of many that schools remain relatively constant? In times of rapid change people often turn to the stable institutions of a society for support and security. Churches, for example, often fulfill this role. Might the resistance or fear associated with large-scale change in schools also reflect, at least in part, a concern on the part of many, educators and noneducators alike, that another of the anchors from the world they knew was beginning to give way? The psychological difficulty of attempting discontinuous change when facing such a mindset should not be underestimated.

NEED FOR CONGRUENCE OF GOALS

Most of the activities described in part 3 focus on changing the methods of education and organizational relationships. Much of the change initiated in these areas is being conducted with only a dim view of the goals or reasons driving it. Perhaps the central issue is not merely to change the methods of education but to change the goals. Of course, all this change could reflect new goals for education that are still emerging. If this is the ultimate purpose of educational restructuring, then many different structures are likely to be suitable, depending on which new goals emerge.

In other words, many of the changes being attempted appear to be linked only loosely to any clear set of new goals, such as equity of achievement for all students, preparation for the workplace, development of functional families or communities, and so forth. The sum of these changes when implemented is often far less than the total of the parts. These disparate projects and activities seem unable to generate the type of synergy that could be expected if the school had developed greater goal congruence. Fullan points out the limitations of changes in structures and programs without a reexamination of basic purposes and goals: "Unfortunately, structural changes are easier to bring about than normative ones. If we are not careful we can easily witness a series of non-events and other superficial changes that leave the core of the problem untouched" (Fullan 1991, p. xiii)

Fullan's observation should not be surprising, since schools have rarely been able to effectively examine central issues, such as the fundamental or core goals of the institution. This limited capacity for self-examination should, perhaps, be the source of some concern, particularly if the goals for public education are, in fact, changing fundamentally: We may question whether all the change occurring in education is under the control of educators at all. They may simply be responding to vaguely perceived forces from the world external to schools without any real sense of what their new core mission or purpose is. Is it to do better what they already do, or to do something fundamentally different?

Within this dynamic lies the distinction between incremental and discontinuous approaches to change in schools: Should schools be improved through numerous projects and activities to do better what they currently do, or should they be reconfigured to reflect new purposes and goals? The final answer may come from forces outside schools and for the most part beyond the control of educators: What do parents, business and community leaders, and policy-makers believe should be the purposes and goals of education? Both incremental and discontinuous restructuring activities conducted by educators may ultimately serve more to define than to answer this question.

The remainder of this book is devoted to an examination of the processes by which schools might undertake large-scale change and the issues that arise when attempting to do so. It begins with an examination of the organizational and environmental forces arrayed against the ability of schools to change, and it continues with a presentation of some possible strategies educators are employing to address these forces.

PART 4

PROCESS

OF

RESTRUCTURING

INTRODUCTION TO PART 4

Part 3 presented the dimensions of restructuring, the general and specific activities that schools and districts identify as restructuring. To describe these dimensions is one thing; to successfully implement them in schools is an entirely different matter. In the following chapters, I consider a range of complex issues related to bringing about fundamental change in schools. Many ideas and suggestions are mentioned, but they are not intended to be a recipe that, if followed in a step-by-step fashion, will guarantee restructuring occurs successfully and without conflict. Instead, they are meant to serve as an outline of key areas that are important to consider when and where restructuring is attempted.

A large body of literature details the methods and techniques, challenges and difficulties involved in bringing about incremental improvement in educational practice (see, for example: Huberman and Miles 1984; Joyce, Hersh, and McKibbin 1983; Joyce 1991; Eisner 1988; Berman and McLaughlin 1974; Cuban 1984a and 1990; Fullan 1985; Fullan and Pomfret 1977; Goodlad 1984; Goodlad and Klein 1970; Kirst 1991; Malen, Ogawa, and Kranz 1990a; Malen and Ogawa 1988; McLaughlin and Marsh 1978; Sarason 1971 and 1990; Schmuck and Runkel 1985). It appears likely that schools involved in restructuring will face at least some, if not most, of the issues raised in this literature as they initiate changes that are in many cases much more profound than those examined in the works cited. At the same time, much of the literature on change in schools, with its focus on improving existing practice, may not be as applicable to the more fundamental changes being suggested through restructuring. The latter may result in disruption of existing management and control systems and may bring about changes in power relationships to a much greater degree than appears to occur during implementation of many of the innovations that have served as the focus for previous studies of change in education.

I will not revisit this literature in detail. Instead, I will briefly discuss several points that illustrate the difficulty faced by educators attempting to restructure schooling. My attention will focus on some of the fundamental challenges educators face when attempting basic changes in structure or practice. Early lessons of the emerging body of works on the process of restructuring are included. However, much remains to be learned regarding the phenomenon of school restructuring. Part 4, of necessity, raises issues and offers possibilities, rather than presenting prescriptions.

302

If the reader attempts to view part 4 as a cookbook, she or he may be frustrated. There is far too much complexity in human organizations for one method or technique to be successful across the range of settings that exist. Although many researchers and writers attempt to make sense of these complex institutions, the meaning they construct serves more as a lens through which to view any particular situation, rather than a complete panorama of the landscape. Part of the problem, or challenge, of understanding change in organizational settings springs from the multiplicity of lenses through which the phenomenon can be viewed. Each lens provides its own perspective; each is correct within the confines of that perspective.

In part 4, I do not attempt to present an integrated view of the process of educational restructuring. Instead, I examine a variety of points of view and attempt to link them loosely to suggest commonalities or themes that recur in discussions of the process of restructuring. There is a tendency to want to view these themes in a linear fashion: Which comes first, which second, and so forth? Unfortunately, there is little reason to believe that the complex process of fundamental change operates in such a predictable, linear manner in all, or even most, cases.

Clearly, there are lessons to be learned and approaches that work better in some settings than others. However, the observations, techniques, and strategies discussed in the coming chapters can be combined in a wide variety of configurations, and they may be utilized or initiated in many different sequences. My goal in part 4 is to provide a number of lenses to the reader and to invite their use as tools to comprehend change in schools. The responsibility to ascertain how these views blend into an overall picture of the landscape remains with the reader.

In chapter 22, I frame this discussion by considering the difficulties schools face in attempting to change. Powerful forces that make change difficult are arrayed against schools that attempt to change. Schools are not masters of their own destinies: They are creatures of the state, and of the community. They cannot do anything they please, such as redefine their customers or their product. They exist in a policy environment that sends confusing and conflicting messages regarding the goals and expectations for public education generally, and schools more specifically. They do not necessarily have control over the resources they receive, nor do they automatically receive resources in relation to their needs. They have come to be organized as bureaucracies rather than communities, making change all the more difficult.

The key players, teachers, suffer from role ambiguity; are they laborers or professionals? At the level of the school site, numerous obstacles, or pitfalls, to change exist. The reason for discussing these challenges is not to discourage those involved in or contemplating restructuring, but to inform decision-making and create a more realistic context within which planning for change can occur.

Chapter 23 examines the significance of culture, leadership, and readiness for change. I present four frames through which organizational culture can be viewed and outline the critical role of the principal in the change process. Then I turn attention to how principals can provide leadership to reshape and restructure school culture. The chapter continues with an examination of the critical role of the principal as a leader. The ways in which the principal conceptualizes power and authority have a profound effect on the way change is approached, and on the potential for collective action and ownership of the change process. Next I examine readiness for change and its importance as a factor that contributes to the probable success of restructuring activities.

Also in chapter 23, I present ten commitments to change that a staff might make, along with a series of key questions that can be used both to analyze current practices and to consider what restructuring goals a school would like to pursue. The chapter concludes with a "guidebook" on how to visit sites that are restructuring and what to look for. Site visitations can help teachers understand what restructuring looks like and how lessons can be adapted to their own setting.

Chapter 24 shifts to a consideration of the role of vision. Here I offer some prerequisites for successful vision-building; some "how to's" of vision-building, including an example of a process for vision-building; and some "visions" of education from different points of view.

In chapter 25, I describe how schools might take their next step toward restructuring, keeping in mind that in some situations this step may precede those that have come before. The first two sections in the chapter consider strategies to implement the vision, specifically Total Quality Management and outcomes-based education, two ways by which the methods and structures of education can be reconceptualized to achieve new visions.

The chapter continues with a description of how some of these principles of vision-building and implementation have been put into practice in a number of schools. Several lessons can be learned from their experiences. I conclude with a discussion of the importance of finding time for all of this to happen. I offer some suggestions based on how some schools are reorganizing to find time within their current structure, and how schools in Asian countries redefine the role of teacher to find more time within the school day for ongoing planning and improvement.

In the final chapter, I summarize emerging visions of school restructuring that are embedded within all of what has been described throughout the book. This chapter presents an integrated picture of how differently schools might look if restructuring of the type identified in this book were to take place. Finally, this chapter addresses the question, Will American schools, in fact, be able to restructure themselves successfully? I assess several factors that will determine the answer to this question in the years ahead.

CHAPTER 22

THE DIFFICULTY OF CHANGE IN EDUCATION

There is a tendency when focusing on the need for educational restructuring, and the programs that have been developed to respond to this need, to overlook, if even inadvertently, the tremendous obstacles that an average school must overcome to bring about significant change. In this chapter, I acknowledge the difficulty schools face and catalogue some of the barriers that exist. My purpose is not to discourage those considering or involved in educational restructuring, but to provide a more realistic context within which discussions of change can occur, and to acknowledge the difficulty that those who attempt change will face.

The chapter begins with a discussion of macrolevel factors affecting the ability of schools to change. These factors include the ambiguous policy and goal environment within which schools function, the problems schools face regarding finance systems, and the bureaucratic nature of schools as organizations. I then summarize some general observations by Fullan and Miles (1992) on why reform typically fails and how educators can avoid failure. Finally, I consider nine pitfalls encountered at the building level by schools engaged in restructuring.

AMBIGUOUS AND CONFUSING POLICY TOWARD EDUCATION

Much of the problem begins with the general policy environment within which public education exists. Different groups at different levels of government have shaped educational policy toward their goals with little regard to the overall effect of such policy fragmentation. Those who develop policy have often not given much thought to how it is to be implemented. Smith and O'Day (1991) argue that this tug-and-pull of policy development and implementation among federal and state governments, local school districts, special interest groups, and others creates a system where it is almost impossible to sustain systemic improvement efforts:

A fundamental barrier to developing and sustaining successful schools in the USA is the fragmented, complex, multi-layered educational policy system in which they are embedded (Cohen 1990, Furhman 1990).

This system consists of overlapping and often conflicting formal and informal policy components on the one hand and, on the other, of a myriad of contending pressures for immediate results that serve only to further disperse and drain the already fragmented energies of dedicated and well meaning school personnel. On the formal policy side, school personnel are daily confronted with mandates, guidelines, incentives, sanctions, and programs constructed by a half-dozen different federal congressional committees, at least that many federal departments and independent agencies, and the federal courts; state school administrators, legislative committees, boards, commissions and courts; regional or county offices in most states; district level administrators and school boards in 14,000 school districts...; and local school building administrators, teachers and committees of interested parents. Every level and many different agencies within levels attempt to influence the curriculum and curricular materials, teacher in-service and pre-service professional development, assessment, student policies such as attendance and promotion, and the special services that schools provide to handicapped, limited English-proficient and low-achieving students. (p. 237)

Within this policy environment, change becomes a very uncertain process. As was noted earlier, two results of this disjointed policy environment are a lack of goal congruence and, at a more fundamental level, a lack of control over the goals of the organization. This inability to focus effort, or to provide members of the organization with a clear picture of its purpose and goals, makes systematic change even more difficult. Joyce, Hersh, and McKibbin (1983) present the spectrum of possible functions or missions for public schools, all of which have legitimacy at some level and most of which have their own constituencies. These authors suggest three domains—personal, social, and academic—each of which has various goals or alternative functions:

The Personal Domain:

- Develop the self.
- Develop productive thinking capacities, including creativity, flexibility, ability to produce alternatives.
- Develop a personal meaning.
- Develop problem-solving ability and flexibility.
- Develop aesthetic capacity.
- Develop motivation to achieve.

The Social Domain:

- Enculturation—socializing students to their culture and transmitting their cultural heritage.

- Develop internationalism and social activism.
- Develop cooperative problem-solving—democratic-scientific approach, political and social activism.
- Promote nationalism.
- Improve human relations—increasing affiliation and decreasing alienation.

The Academic Domain:

- Emphasize general symbol proficiency—reading, writing, arithmetic, technical methods.
- Emphasize information from selected disciplines—history, geography, literature, etc.
- Emphasize major concepts from the disciplines.
  a. Treat broad, related fields together (social studies, language arts, science).
  b. Treat a few disciplines separately (i.e., economics, physics, history, music).
- Emphasize modes of inquiry.
  a. Treat theory building and scientific method.
  b. Treat knowledge creation within a few, selected disciplines.
- Emphasize broad, philosophical schools or problems—aesthetics, humanitarian issues, ethics. (Excerpted from pp. 252-56)

Public schools have faced the problem of comprehensiveness throughout most of this century. In a democratic society that rejects the social class system, public education is seen as a means to offer choice and opportunity to all citizens. Goal confusion is quite understandable, even desirable, if society supports the ability of schools to address multiple goals simultaneously. This ability requires resources, however. As I discuss in the next section, changes in school financing over the past two decades have not necessarily made it any easier for schools to pursue multiple goals simultaneously.

EQUITY OF FINANCE SYSTEMS

By the 1970s the systems by which schools were financed had grown to be blatantly inequitable. Reliance on local property taxes had resulted in communities with high assessments being able to tax themselves at a low rate, while their neighbors in poorer districts had to pay much more for their children to receive what in many cases was not even a comparable education. Such an arrangement had been acceptable so long as the level of common education that all citizens were expected to master was low and so long as economic opportunities were available even for those with little formal education. Equality of achievement was not a fundamental goal of the system. As it becomes socially important for essentially all students to complete much more schooling and be capable of performing at relatively high levels upon completion, the inequity of financing becomes a vital issue.

At the same time, the federal and state governments began to mandate more programs local school districts had to offer, without necessarily providing the funding necessary for their implementation. This gradual impingement on local control led local districts to demand that states fund programs they mandated. Such pressures contributed to a climate in which finance reform was more likely to take place.

Nearly every state has undergone change in school finance systems since the 1970s (Odden and Wohlstetter 1992). Rarely has the avowed goal of this reform been to improve student learning (though lip service has frequently been paid to this goal). Equity in the context of discussions of finance in the 1970s and early 1980s meant equity of taxation, not of student achievement. Education had relied heavily on property taxes, until the tax revolt that began in California in the late seventies caused state governments to shoulder more responsibility for funding education. In fact, finance reform often meant "leveling down," where higher spending districts were held in place or had their revenue reduced so that lower spending districts might receive an increase in funding. This form of equity often had the effect of decreasing resources for districts that had historically been among the more progressive within a state or region.

The development of educational finance policy is another example of the "fragmented, complex, multi-layered educational policy system" described by Smith and O'Day (1991). Odden and Wohlstetter (1992) note the increasing complexity of policy development in school finance, as evidenced by the number of different initiators and their varying goals. In the 1980s these forces were external to schools and occurred at the national, rather than state, level. They had implications for state financing of education and for school reform. Odden and Wohlstetter identify two events—the release of the report *A Nation at Risk* (U.S. Department of Education 1983) and the realization by business leaders that the nature of the work force and the definition of a well-prepared worker were changing—as catalysts for changes in funding during the eighties. Changes in school finance in the 1980s were for the purpose of improving American economic competitiveness by improving schools.

A new political quid pro quo emerged for increasing education funding. No longer would state political leaders provide money on the stump through equalization formulas and hope that local educators would use it to improve the education system. States created a variety of new fiscal incentives (Richards & Shujaa, 1989) to reward schools and districts for meeting education improvement objectives. (Odden and Wohlstetter 1992, p. 372)

In other words, increased funding began to be linked to increased performance. States launched testing programs to determine if improvement was, in fact, occurring, which led to intensified debate regarding whether the tests really were measuring what society wanted students to know and do.

It should be noted that more resources do not automatically equal more change in schools. The evidence from recently enacted school finance reform laws suggests that historically low-spending districts that receive increased funding do not necessarily initiate significant change or restructuring as a result of receiving additional funds. Other issues are addressed first. Money alone does not appear to change the basic culture or orientation toward change of a school district. If, as Odden and Wohlstetter suggest, "the economy will continue as a triggering event keeping education as a top policy issue" since "the link between education and the country's economic productivity...has become conventional wisdom for the 1990s," educators can expect to be under increasing pressure to deliver major changes and improvements in education as a result of new funding strategies. The current situation in many states indicates that such outcomes will be problematic, because of both the tightening of funding for many innovative districts and the difficulty of transforming the culture of historically low-spending districts through increased funding alone.

Further confounding the problems with funding is the bleak outlook for substantial increases in the funds available to government during the 1990s. The federal government remains first in line in its ability to raise new revenue, since any major increase it initiates automatically detracts from the ability of all 50 states and 15,500 school districts to raise taxes. The federal deficit remains a cloud that hovers over the decade, and it likely will absorb much of any increased revenue available in the public sector. Most states find their backs to the wall fiscally, with little relief in sight. Real income has not grown for the past twelve years for the vast majority of wage earners and has decreased for those with less than a college education. Managerial jobs are being trimmed, reflecting the decline in blue-collar jobs that occurred in the early eighties. Demands for increased efficiency in government continue.

Educational managers in the nineties will likely have to learn to effect change without large amounts of additional resources available to aid the process. There is evidence, particularly from nongovernmental organizations, that the crises triggered by fiscal shortfalls often precipitate large-scale change in bureaucratic organizations. Fiscal crisis can come to offer both threat and opportunity. Educational leaders will be challenged to manage looming fiscal crises in ways that lead to an improvement in the functions of their organizations, not merely a reduction in size or a retention of the status quo. This is both a tremendous opportunity and a formidable challenge.

BUREAUCRATIC NATURE OF EDUCATIONAL ORGANIZATIONS

Schools in this country began as extensions of local communities, with strong ties to the values and organizations of the communities within which they existed. Since the turn of the century, schools have become increasingly bureaucratic in nature and separated from the communities that surround them. While bureaucratic structures serve to protect schools from arbitrary and capricious interventions in their functioning, they also lessen the ability of schools to adapt and change. Bureaucracies limit communication, participation in decision-making, and comprehension by members of the organization's goals and their contribution to the achievement of those goals. Clark and Meloy (1990) describe the influence bureaucratic features have had on the organization of schools and on teachers' professional lives:

> Two...features of bureaucracy, specialization and specification, have had particularly important effects on the organization of schools. The former characteristic is designed to provide for technical expertise in the system where such expertise is required. The latter clarifies the assignment and scope of responsibility of individual employees. The technical expertise of the teacher has been defined narrowly, i.e., as a subject and/or grade specialization *in the classroom*. Broader instructional expertise, curriculum development and planning, has typically been vested in staff and line administrators from curriculum specialists to the principal. The consequences for teachers have been several. Teachers have become isolated from one another and from the principal during the school day. The autonomy of the teacher in the classroom has resulted in the restriction of the teacher's role and responsibility to the teaching-learning act. (p. 10, emphasis in original)

Decisions in bureaucracies are made based on hierarchies of authority. Each level defers to the level above it for guidance and approval. Workers continue to do what they have been authorized to do within their area of specialization and authority. Change is not initiated without permission. The hierarchical nature of the organization tends to drive out initiative, creativity, ownership, or a systems perspective. Schools come to be bureaucracies with a hierarchy that culminates with the principal:

> Bureaucracy, as an organizational form, carries with it a set of minimal unavoidable elements. Bureaucracy makes no sense without a hierarchy. The hierarchy serves two functions of the bureaucracy: official authority and specialization. The principal of a school assumes a set of specialized functions of an administrative nature in the building while simultaneously representing the point in the scalar hierarchy where the "buck stops" within the building unit. (Clark and Meloy 1990, p. 9)

Within this context people wait to be told what to do. They come to view their interests as the interests of the organization (or not to think in terms of the organization's interests at all). They have little experience participating in discussions or interactions across work groups. They are not able to design work tasks so that their efforts contribute harmoniously to those of all others involved in the same or similar process.

The bureaucratic structure of schools may be one of the most formidable barriers to be encountered when attempting to bring about system-level change in schools. In fact, it may be nearly impossible to get people to think about any other structure for organizing schooling:

> There is an overarching assumption that bureaucracy is an inevitable structural form for work organizations large or complex enough so that daily contact among all employees is impossible. Almost all school systems and the majority of schools meet this criterion. (Clark and Meloy 1990, p. 9)

Further complicating this conception of the nature of schools as organizations is the ambiguous role of teachers as both professionals and bureaucrats. Linda Darling-Hammond (1990) describes the principles of professionalism and suggests why the bureaucratic nature of schooling makes it difficult for such principles to take hold:

> Professionalism depends not on compensation or status, but on the affirmation of three principles in the conduct and governance of an occupation:
>
> 1. Knowledge is the basis for permission to practice and for decisions that are made with respect to the unique needs of clients;
>
> 2. The practitioner pledges his first concern to the welfare of the clients;
>
> 3. The profession assumes collective responsibility for the definition, transmittal and enforcement of professional standards of practice and ethics.
>
> These principles outline a view of practice that is *client-oriented* and *knowledge-based*. This view also suggests criteria and methods for accountability that are based on the competence of practitioners and their effectiveness. Currently the practice of teaching in public schools is not

organized to support these principles or modes of accountability. Instead, the bureaucratic organization of schooling and teaching requires practice that is procedure-oriented and rule-based. It enforces accountability based on the job scripts of practitioners and their compliance with task specifications. The individual needs of students are difficult to accommodate in this system. The growth of knowledge in the occupation is difficult to support and sustain. (p. 25, emphasis in original)

In such an environment, it might be added, it is also difficult for the system to change. For education to have much of a chance of evolving rapidly, issues of bureaucratic organization, hierarchical relationships, institutional inflexibility, and teacher isolation will have to be addressed. Given people's difficulty in conceiving of organizational structures other than bureaucracies, addressing these issues will be a challenge.

FAILURE VS. SUCCESS OF REFORMS

Fullan and Miles (1992) describe some of the reasons educational reforms typically fail. School personnel have a better chance of engaging in continuous improvement if they understand seven basic reasons why reform fails and consider seven propositions that could lead to success. The following paragraphs summarize Fullan and Miles's ideas in two parts, "Why Reform Fails" and "Propositions for Success." Headings and text in quotes have been taken verbatim from their article; all other text has been paraphrased.

Why Reform Fails

1. Faulty maps of change. All participants in reform have personal maps that guide their understanding of how change should (or will) unfold. These maps can be accurate or inaccurate.

2. Complex problems. Solutions are much more complex than participants often imagine. This requires a different map than for solving simple problems.

3. Symbols over substance. Reform can be as much a political as an educational process. People get involved in reform for a wide range of motives. The symbols we pick define how reform is interpreted. At the same time, change can easily become only symbolic. It is easier to have symbolic change than substantive change.

4. Impatient and superficial solutions. Many solutions are pseudosolutions. Particularly susceptible are those that focus on structural changes as the answer. They can be launched administratively with little involvement or support by teachers.

5. Misunderstanding resistance. Labeling an action or attitude as "resistance" can be unproductive since it diverts attention from real problems such as lack of technical skills, insufficient resources, or personal needs or developmental stages of individuals. Resistance can, in fact, be an authentic response that indicates concern about the well-being of children.

6. Attrition of pockets of success. Successful reforms have tended to require enormous effort and energy on the part of an individual or small group of individuals. It is very difficult to sustain this effort over time. Schools cannot stay innovative without continuing outside support that validates their efforts and allows them to be legitimized and institutionalized.

7. Misuse of knowledge about the change process. The change process cannot be reduced to a series of slogans or aphorisms. Reform is systemic and must be based on sound knowledge of change from a systems perspective.

Propositions for Success

1. Change is learning—loaded with uncertainty. Those who have the power to manipulate change must not disregard the personal change that is required of all who participate in a major change. This lack of sensitivity to the personal growth that others must undergo overlooks or denies the process that the change agent has already gone through to accommodate his or her behavior and world view to the innovation or change. "In short, anxiety, difficulties, and uncertainty are intrinsic to all successful change."

2. Change is a journey, not a blueprint. Rational planning models simply do not work in complex organizations such as schools. While such models can provide useful frameworks for organizing change efforts, implementation involves frequent departure from the constraints of a model, adaptation to local conditions and unexpected events, and a willingness to allow participants to create personal meaning out of the change. Strategy must be a flexible tool and not become an end in itself.

3. Problems are our friends. Effective responses to complex changes in organizations cannot be developed unless there is an acceptance of problems as natural, expected phenomena. There must be a willingness to confront and resolve problems, rather than to deny, ignore, or repress them. Schools that cope with problems successfully make use of coping styles that range from doing little to redesigning the system, retraining staff, or making individuals more capable of dealing with the problems they face. In fact, it appears that schools should assertively pursue problems if they wish to improve continuously.

4. Change is resource-hungry. "Every analysis of the problems of change efforts we have seen in the last decade of research and practice has concluded that time is the salient issue." Time requires additional resources in most cases. In addition to time, assistance in the form of training, coaching, consulting, coordination, and capacity-building is necessary. Such support should be present over a number of years. Schools need to become effective at "resourcing"—scanning the environment and identifying and acquiring resources by networking, negotiating, reworking, or simply grabbing them, when appropriate. It means abandoning notions of self-sufficiency or closed-systems thinking.

5. Change requires the power to manage it. Change must be managed. There appear to be several essential ingredients. Cross-role groups (teachers, department heads, administrators, parents, students) may be the most effective means of managing change. These groups need legitimacy, an explicit contract that is widely understood regarding the decisions it can make and the money it can spend. Even if such groups work well, they will still require cooperation, trust, and the ability to live with ambiguity and conflict. Power-sharing is complex and sensitive. It has an impact on the egos of all involved and tends to bring out insecurities in those "giving up" authority. When power-sharing begins at the school, it can rarely succeed if the district is not closely engaged in the process and does not accept the basic premises of power-sharing.

6. Change is systemic. Change has often meant a "project mentality," a steady stream of episodic innovations. These programs have tended to come and go without leaving much of a mark on schools. Fundamental change must involve all the main components of the system simultaneously and must focus on culture along with structure, policy, and regulations. Along with restructuring, schools may need to engage in "reculturing." They need to avoid ad hoc innovations and focus on a thoughtful combination of coordinated, integrated short-, mid-, and long-term strategies.

7. All large-scale change is implemented locally. The six previous points all suggest the obvious: change occurs only when teachers, principals, students, and others at the school site change their behavior. At the same time, the role of agencies that coordinate, assist, or direct groups of schools should not be overlooked. There is, ultimately, a symbiotic relationship between and among these different agencies when it comes to implementing educational change.

Other challenges as well face those who would transform schooling. In addition to the systems-level issues and general observations presented up to this point, several issues are more pertinent to change at the school-site level. The following section discusses these factors.

NINE PITFALLS OF SCHOOL RESTRUCTURING*

The nine pitfalls of restructuring presented here have been gleaned from a study of schools involved in Oregon's "2020" program (D. Conley, March 1991) combined with observations collected while working with individual 2020 schools on specific projects. Additional information has been provided by reports from school sites nationally that have been involved in restructuring long enough to have identified problem areas. Ethnographic research conducted at eight schools that were charter members of the Coalition of Essential Schools also corroborates many of these pitfalls (Muncey and McQuillan 1993). All these sources suggest the problems schools are encountering as they attempt the complex process of schoolwide restructuring.

Pitfall 1: Lack of a Vision. Many schools approach restructuring in a piecemeal fashion, developing a series of fragmented activities that respond to specific concerns, often those held by a vocal minority of the faculty or based on the latest trends or techniques. Kirst (1991) describes this as "project-itis."

The importance of general consensus about where the school is going and why cannot be stressed enough. The lack of "tight coupling" in schools means it is especially important for teachers to have a shared sense of purpose and direction, since so many of their decisions are made in isolation. A common mission helps align the efforts of everyone in the school toward agreed-upon ends and, as a byproduct, reduces resistance among nonbelievers who find themselves at odds with norms and goals established by their colleagues.

Pitfall 2: The Time Trap. There is never enough time in education. It is easy for a faculty to become sidetracked on one issue and spend most of their time spinning their wheels trying to resolve it. Successful schools use the vision to direct their energies toward activities that will yield changes and improvements. At the same time they acknowledge that it takes time to implement most new practices, usually several years, and that during the implementation phase there may be a time when efficiency and performance actually decrease. This period, dubbed the "implementation dip" by Fullan (1991, Fullan and Miles 1992), can be critical because it is during this time that teachers are most apt to return to former ways when new techniques do not go smoothly. Collegial

---

* This section is excerpted and adapted from: Conley, David. *Lessons from Laboratories in School Restructuring and Site-Based Decision-Making: Oregon's 2020 Schools Take Control of their Own Reform.* OSSC Bulletin Series. Eugene: Oregon School Study Council, March 1991.

support combined with awareness by change agents of how difficult it will be for some people to change seem to be key elements in helping people over the "implementation dip."

The time trap also has the tendency to burn out highly motivated people, those who emerge to fill newly created leadership roles. They become emotionally invested in the vision and work exceedingly hard to turn it into a reality. However, they are at risk of being overwhelmed by the combination of regular work responsibilities, new duties, and ongoing family obligations. Care must be exercised to ensure that these people have the time necessary to be successful, and that they are encouraged to take an occasional break. One way to accomplish this is to spread leadership roles around, using newly developing feelings of collegiality to encourage the sharing of responsibilities and tasks.

Pitfall 3: Proceeding Without the Community. It is very easy for educators to overlook the larger community when they undertake change. After all, the professionalization of education over the past fifty years has effectively created barriers against parent and community involvement and has reinforced the idea that educators "know what's best" for kids. We are finding that this must change, that schools cannot proceed without the involvement or at least tacit support of the community.

In some communities it is the parents of those students who are the current "winners" in the educational system who are the most upset about change (West, July 31, 1991). This stands to reason, though it is often overlooked when school restructuring projects are being developed. Olson (June 13, 1990) quotes one such parent:

> "We're just not about to let our children be experimented upon," said Richard Fruland, parent of a student at Parkway South High School, Manchester, Missouri. "We've got parents who feel the school is exemplary now, that it does an absolutely wonderful job of preparing children and educating them for the future. Whatever changes are needed amount to 'fine tuning'." (p. 8)

Schools undertaking restructuring must be willing to create a sense of urgency for change, both among faculty and community. Once again, the development of a vision helps people to understand why change is occurring and toward what ends. Community members should be involved in the process of vision building, and the vision should be communicated regularly to parents at meetings, through publications, and in face-to-face interchanges.

Pitfall 4: Questions of Meaning. The lack of a common definition of the term *restructuring* has been both a blessing and a curse—a blessing in that it has allowed groups as disparate as teachers' unions and school boards associations to align themselves in a common cause, at least in principle; a curse in that anyone can do almost anything and claim they are restructuring. And they have. This "anything goes" mentality has tended to devalue the term and has led many teachers to view it with a mixture of caution and cynicism.

Observations in selected 2020 schools in Oregon (Goldman, Dunlap, and Conley 1991) suggest that teachers and administrators in these schools do not spend a great deal of time debating the meaning of the term *restructuring*; these educators do believe, however, that changes must go beyond the superficial. This shared belief expands and is honed as concrete issues of practice are confronted, analyzed, and resolved. A definition of restructuring is built "on the fly" and modified the same way. One measure of the collegiality present in these schools relates to whether they have developed working definitions of important concepts through a series of formal and informal interactions over time.

Pitfall 5: Rose-Colored Glasses Syndrome. Too many schools underestimate the difficulty of bringing about substantial change of the type implied by the term *restructuring*. Particularly when restructuring is viewed as a series of projects, it is common for principals in particular to miscalculate the amount of time and energy necessary to achieve meaningful, sustained change, and the amount of resistance such a process engenders. Perhaps this is why in many schools that describe themselves as "restructured" an outsider sees no substantial change.

Pitfall 6: Governance as an End in Itself. The plethora of literature on site-based management and decentralized decision-making that appeared in the late eighties led many to believe that structural changes in decision-making alone would magically transform education, unleashing its pentup potential for improvement. This remains an unsupported assumption.

Instead, many faculties are bogged down in the minutia of participatory decision-making, without knowing why it was instituted or what purpose it is supposed to serve (Strauber, Stanley, and Wagenknecht 1990). In many cases, site-based management was a solution in search of a problem; in the absence of real reasons for teachers to make decisions, or substantial resources for them to control, these new structures focused on maintenance issues and concerns over quality of teacher work life. Changes in governance structure should be undertaken to achieve program goals that cannot be achieved with the current structure.

Pitfall 7: Measuring New Learning with Old Tools. Assessment is a difficult problem at this point in the restructuring movement. There is general agreement that the current measures of student learning are both inadequate and inappropriate for restructured educational environments with new goals and standards, and that development of new methods of assessment must be a high priority. However, it is extremely hard psychologically and practically for educators to abandon traditional testing systems. The result is that as schools attempt to recreate themselves, they continue to measure their effectiveness and success against old benchmarks and with old tools.

Development of alternative assessment technologies is proceeding under the sponsorship of a number of organizations ("Who's Who..." October 23, 1991; Rothman, March 13, 1991). Within the next several years many of these methods will be available. As they arrive online, educators will be challenged to discard the old techniques. Accomplishing this change will require extensive education of teachers and community members. Those schools actively engaged in restructuring must reconcile themselves to surviving during this phase when their programs are under the greatest scrutiny and when they lack the means to demonstrate their successes and learn from their failures.

Pitfall 8: Analysis Paralysis. One of the striking features of the current interest in school restructuring is the number of schools that have established "restructuring committees" or some other group charged with investigating this phenomenon. Many, perhaps most, of these committees are composed of teachers who are excited by the prospects for change. They read articles, discuss and debate, meet with experts and consultants, and visit other schools. They analyze their own school by conducting interviews, taking surveys, and analyzing trends. They develop a very good understanding of the issues and options associated with school restructuring.

The moment of truth arrives when it is time for the faculty to respond to the recommendations or observations of this committee. Will they act, or will they continue to study the process? Very often faculties demand more information or study before agreeing to any changes. The net result is to study the situation to death. The energy and enthusiasm for change dissipate before meaningful change is undertaken. The storm subsides and the school continues along the path of the status quo, with its rationale for *not* changing firmly intact.

Pitfall 9: Isolating the Innovators. The previous pitfall illustrates the difficulty innovators have in traditional school settings. While some are frustrated by being trapped in the "analysis loop," others are controlled by directing their energies to one program or area of the building where they are literally segregated from the rest of the faculty. This solution is seen most often in the form of schools-within-schools or special programs for at-risk students. These arrangements allow the appearance of a changed structure while leaving the core of the academic program untouched.

A strong argument can be made for using these separate programs as a sort of "research and development" environment within schools, where new ideas can be tried, refined, and modeled for the rest of the faculty. This strategy will work only in places where all faculty agree that the lessons learned in these "lab" settings will be applied to the total school program eventually. Getting such an agreement is not always easy. Most teachers are content to allow their colleagues to engage in experiments as long as they themselves are not compelled to change as a result of such experiments. If restructuring is to occur, the work of innovative, "pioneering" teachers must have an effect on the total school program eventually. If this doesn't occur, these pioneers will burn out and the traditional structure will reassert itself.

These observations on the pitfalls of restructuring represent initial, tentative conclusions. They suggest that most of what is being labeled as "restructuring" might better be categorized as "tinkering." Ultimately, restructuring is a high-risk, high-stakes activity that may be alien to public schools, most of which are not prepared to deal with rapid upheaval, reallocation of resources, redistribution of power, and reformulation of values. The early pioneers are learning these lessons.

The difficulties presented in this chapter are daunting. Is it possible to change public schools? In the next chapter, I offer some suggestions of how to make such a process comprehensible and how to develop a plan for proceeding in the face of the types of obstacles discussed previously. I examine ways to understand and perhaps influence the critically important culture of the school. Principals can have a significant effect upon the culture and practices of a school, and readiness and vision-building can be important tools for systems awareness and fundamental change in schools.

CHAPTER 23

CULTURE, LEADERSHIP, AND READINESS

Given that change in education is difficult, how can it be achieved? It's clear that schools are different in many ways from twenty, fifty, or one hundred years ago, naysayers notwithstanding. How did they change? In this chapter, I begin the discussion of how to manage systems change in education. Three important factors can be managed with considerable impact: culture, leadership, and readiness.

The discussion of school culture provides an overview of the concept and its importance in understanding the effect change has on those affected by it. I present four frames of reference through which organizations might be viewed and change might be effected.

Leadership in schools continues to revolve around the role of principal, even as the nature of the role is changing. The critical nature of this role is considered here. One of the key things a leader can do is create readiness for change—an often-overlooked dimension of the change process.

The chapter continues with two sections that offer means to help faculties assess their readiness and identify current practices and desired direction. Such activities can precede more formal attempts at vision-building. One helpful step is to visit other schools that may serve as models for restructuring.

UNDERSTANDING CULTURE AND ORGANIZATIONAL FRAMES OF REFERENCE

One of the factors that must be considered when attempting to bring about fundamental change in an institution is its culture. The process of school restructuring cannot be thought of simply in terms of changes in organizational structure, or of a proliferation of isolated projects and programs. Ultimately, it must address issues of the culture of the school. Deal (1987) explains why culture is so important as a means to understand schools as stable environments:

> Culture as a construct helps explain why classrooms and schools exhibit common and stable patterns across variable conditions. Internally, culture gives meaning to instructional activity and provides a symbolic bridge between action and results. It fuses individual identity with collective destiny. Externally, culture provides the symbolic facade that evokes faith and confidence among outsiders with a stake in education (Meyer and Rowan 1983). (Deal 1987, p. 6)

Understanding the importance and power of culture can help educational leaders attend to the needs that participants in the organization are sure to have in times of rapid change, which evokes powerful psychological responses on the part of many people:

> Looking at the problem of change through a cultural lens, we see an entirely different picture. Culture is a social invention created to give meaning to human endeavor. It provides stability, certainty, and predictability. People fear ambiguity and want assurance that they are in control of their surroundings. Culture imbues life with meaning and through symbols creates a sense of efficacy and control. Change creates existential havoc because it introduces disequilibrium, uncertainty, and makes day-to-day life chaotic and unpredictable. People understandably feel threatened and out of control when their existential pillars become shaky or are taken away.
>
> On an even more basic level, change involves existential loss (Marris 1974). People become emotionally attached to symbols and rituals, much as they do to lovers, spouses, children, and pets (Deal, 1985b). When attachments to people or objects are broken through death or departure, people experience a deep sense of loss and grief. Change creates a similar reaction....
>
> People develop attachments to values, heroes, rituals, ceremonies, stories, gossips, storytellers, priests, and other cultural players. When change alters or breaks the attachment, meaning is questioned. Often, the change deeply affects those inside the culture as well as those outside.... The existential explanation identifies the basic problems of change in educational organizations as cultural transitions. (Deal 1987, pp. 7-8)

Deal suggests that leaders must be adept at confronting the dilemmas that face organizations, not merely at solving problems. Dilemmas by their nature are insoluble. Leaders, rather than moving from problem to problem, attempt to create meaning by addressing recurring frustrations and seemingly unresolvable contradictions in ways that allow the organization to move itself forward and not remain trapped applying the same solutions over and over to problems that do not lend themselves to solution within the current cultural context of the organization:

> Leaders reframe impossible dilemmas into novel opportunities. Leaders in organizations across all sectors are confronted with many of the same issues that educators now face: (1) How do we encourage meaning and

commitment; (2) how do we deal with loss and change; and (3) how can we shape symbols that convey the essence of the enterprise to insiders and outsiders? Educational leaders must create artful ways to reweave organizational tapestries from old traditions, current realities, and future visions. This work cannot be done by clinging to old ways, emulating principles from effective schools and excellent companies, or divining futuristic images from what we imagine the next decades will be like. Rather, it takes a collective look backward, inward, and ahead—in education on the part of administrators, teachers, parents, students, and other members of a school community. It is a process of transformation akin to the one that produces a butterfly from a caterpillar—a cocoon of human experience in which past, present, and future are fused together in an organic process....

... Old practices and other losses need to be buried and commemorated. Meaningless practices and symbols need to be analyzed and revitalized. Emerging visions, dreams, and hopes need to be articulated and celebrated. These are the core tasks that will occupy educational leaders for several years to come. (Deal 1987, pp. 12, 14)

School leaders need to be capable of reading school culture if they hope to manage fundamental change successfully. Good ideas are rarely implemented simply because they make sense. Rather, schools tend to accept ideas or programs that are consistent with the existing structure, assumptions, and culture of the school, so that a school that "believes in" tracking is much more open to a program that makes tracking more effective than one that calls for the abandonment of tracking. The restructuring process calls for the critical examination of fundamental assumptions, practices, and relationships. It implies a movement from bureaucracy to community, from isolation to collaboration. Such changes are cultural changes, not just programmatic changes.

Managing culture is an imprecise process that is not easily prescribed. This process is part of the art of leadership, knowing when to do what in ways that have an impact on members of the organization:

Reading culture takes several forms: watching, sensing, listening, interpreting, using all of one's senses, and even employing intuition when necessary. First, the leader must listen to the echoes of school history....

... A principal must also listen to the key voices of the present. These people [in the informal leadership network of the school] may be thought of as cultural "players" in various dramas at the school.... [The cast of characters include:]

• Priests and priestesses—long-time residents who "minister" to the needs of the school. They take confession, preside over rituals and ceremonies, and link the school to the ways of the past;

• Storytellers—recreate the past and personify contemporary exploits through lore and informal history;

- Gossips—keep everyone current on contemporary matters of importance, as well as trivia of no special merit. They form the informal grapevine that carries information far ahead of formal channels of communication; and
- Spies, counterspies, and moles—carry on subterranean negotiations which keep informal checks and balances among various power centers in the school. Through such covert operations, much of the work of the school is transacted....

... Most important, the leader must listen for the deeper dreams and hopes the school community holds for the future....

This represents emerging energy the principal can tap and a deep belief system to which he or she can appeal when articulating what the school might become.

A principal can get an initial reading of a school by asking these key questions about the founding, traditions, building, current realities, and future dreams of the school:

- How long has the school existed?
- Why was it built, and who were the first inhabitants?
- Who had a major influence on the school's direction?
- What critical incidents occurred in the past, and how were they resolved, if at all?
- What were the preceding principals, teachers, and students like?
- What does the school's architecture convey? How is space arranged and used?
- What subcultures exist inside and outside the school?
- Who are the recognized (and unrecognized) heroes and villains of the school?
- What do people say (and think) when asked what the school stands for? What would they miss if they left?
- What events are assigned special importance?
- How is conflict typically defined? How is it handled?
- What are the key ceremonies and stories of the school?
- What do people wish for? Are there patterns to their individual dreams? (Deal and Peterson 1990, pp. 16-19)

Culture cannot be ignored. No program of change starts with a clean slate. The history of the institution must be recognized and dealt with. The current communication patterns and the implicit, unquestioned assumptions and value systems must be understood and acknowledged. The hopes and aspirations, dreams and fears for the future must be articulated and addressed. Understanding and responding to the school culture seems to be a critical dimension that has to be addressed in the development of a strategy for school restructuring and in the implementation of such a program.

Managing the change process within a cultural context is influenced by the frame of reference the leader employs when analyzing the organization. Leaders often have unconscious tendencies to apply one frame of reference through which they tend to explain all of what occurs in the organization, and within which all of their solutions operate. Bolman and Deal (1991) have suggested four frames of reference commonly employed by managers and leaders as they attempt to manage organizations and bring about changes in them:

> The structural frame... emphasizes the importance of formal roles and relationships. Structures—commonly depicted by means of organization charts—are created to fit an organization's environment and technology.... Problems arise when the structure does not fit the situation. At that point, some form of reorganization is needed to remedy the mismatch.
>
> The human resources frame... starts with the fundamental premise that organizations are inhabited by individuals who have needs, feelings, and prejudices.... From a human resources perspective, the key to effectiveness is to tailor organizations to people—to find an organizational form that enables people to get the job done while feeling good about what they are doing.
>
> The political frame... views organizations as arenas in which different interest groups compete for power and scarce resources.... Problems arise because power is concentrated in the wrong places or because it is so broadly dispersed that nothing gets done. Solutions are developed through political skill and acumen....
>
> The symbolic frame... abandons the assumptions of rationality that appear in the other frames. It treats organizations as tribes, theater, or carnivals. In this view, organizations are cultures that are propelled more by rituals, ceremonies, stories, heroes, and myths than by rules, policies, and managerial authority.... Improvements in rebuilding the expressive or spiritual side of organizations come through the use of symbol, myth, and magic.
>
> Each of these frames has its own vision or image of reality. Only when managers, consultants, and policymakers can look through all four are they likely to appreciate the depth and complexity of organizational life. (pp. 15-16)

Restructuring schools, then, is not simply the process of bringing about change in one of these frames while ignoring the others. Structural changes alone, such as forming a new committee or rewriting the role descriptions of department chairs, are not likely to be successful. Neither will activities that simply improve the quality of teacher worklife with no linkage to job performance; in other words, happier teachers are not automatically better teachers. Nor will more adept manipulation of the political system present in the school lead directly to restructuring. Political maneuvering can help or hinder progress but needs linkages to other frames, as well. Careful management of symbol systems, rituals, and myths can also contribute to successful change but does not guarantee it in isolation. However, if educators understand that change must occur to some degree in each of these frames, restructuring is more likely to occur and to transform schooling. A leader's job is to make conscious decisions that have an impact on the culture of the school in a way that makes that culture more amenable to change and more functional in its delivery of services to students.

THE CRITICAL ROLE OF THE PRINCIPAL

Principals remain a key variable in modifying school culture and guiding the change process (Dwyer 1984 and 1986, Fullan 1985, Smith and Andrews 1989). However, many principals are unable to see how they will be successful in a new organizational structure where they may not be at the center of power. Hallinger, Murphy, and Hausman (1991) report that "principals viewed the effects of restructuring on themselves almost exclusively in terms of power. They forecast new roles with fewer decisions to make by themselves leading to a loss of control and power."

Bredeson (1991) considers principals' reactions to restructuring from the perspective of role anxiety. He discusses the degree to which "role strain" caused stress among the principals he studied.

> Even under the most optimal of conditions, shifts in role and in role expectations produce varying degrees of role strain, defined... as acute affective/cognitive disturbance for an individual role holder manifested as anxiety, discomfort, uneasiness, perplexity and/or general distress....
>
> The responses to interview questions revealed that each of these principals was experiencing varying states and levels of anxiety manifested in feelings of having lost control, fear of failure, self-doubts about personal competence and ability to be successful, impatience and frustration, loss of identity, and increased feelings of uncertainty brought about by significant changes in their professional worklife. The whole notion of letting go of one set of professional functions and identities while learning others was described as risky, wearisome, and frustrating. (pp. 10-11)

One key link in restructuring may be to enable principals to see what their new roles will look like, and to help them to develop the skills necessary to be successful in these new roles. While this same recommendation also applies to teachers, it may be overlooked in the case of principals, who are expected, in many cases, to be largely responsible for their own professional growth and development. Given the ability of the principal to make or break innovations in schools, it is critical for them to see how they can be "winners" in any restructured system.

The notion of principals and teachers as fellow voyagers in this journey toward restructured schools suggests new relationships between them, as outlined in part 2. The National LEADership Network Study Group on Restructuring Schools (Mojkowski and Bamberger 1991), in its study of how to develop leaders for restructuring schools, lists twelve activities in which such leaders should engage. These activities appear to be consistent with those being practiced by principals in schools where the process of restructuring has been observed (Louis and Miles 1990; Goldman, Dunlap, and Conley 1993). Leaders, says the study group, do the following:

- *Create dissonance.* Using a variety of methods, new leaders constantly remind staff and others of the gap between the vision that they have for their children and their current actions and accomplishments. They use this dissonance to create a press for improvement.

- *Prepare for and create opportunities.* They exhibit a constructive and creative opportunism. They pursue opportunities that will move the school closer to the accomplishment of its mission and ignore those that do not.

- *Forge connections and create interdependencies.* They create new roles and relationships. They dismantle the egg-crate structure of schools and create opportunities and processes to connect teachers within and across disciplines and to connect people inside and outside of the school community to one another. By skillfully creating interdependencies, leaders create the consensus for understanding and action that is required in restructuring environments. The analogy to an orchestra leader is often employed to describe the subtle ways in which these leaders bind independent entrepreneurs to a shared vision and mission.

- *Encourage risk taking.* School people typically are uncomfortable with taking risks. Premature and arbitrary judgments too often inhibit creativity and risk taking. Leaders of restructuring schools create environments and conditions that provide increased comfort with making mistakes and learning from them. These leaders protect risk takers from premature judgments of failure.

- *Follow as well as lead.* Leaders recreate themselves throughout the organization, nurturing leadership behaviors in all staff. They lead through service rather than position, providing support and good "follow-ship" to ad hoc leaders.

- *Use information.* Administrators in restructuring environments use a wide variety of information about student and organizational performance. They are clear communicators who use multiple channels for accessing and distributing information. They create new ways to think about and measure the growth and productivity of learners and the learning process. Leaders use research and practice information to guide innovation and change. They monitor and document the implementation process.

- *Foster the long view.* Impatience is a prominent American virtue with serious side-effects. Leaders know when and how to delay judgment, tolerate and learn from interim set-backs, and invest for long-term yields. They know "when to hold them, and when to fold them," guided by their sense of mission and strategic direction. They work incrementally within a comprehensive design of restructuring, guided by their vision of learners and learning. The special requirements of restructuring—moving incrementally within a comprehensive design—require a highly skilled leader and facilitator.

- *Acquire resources.* They are particularly adept at resource acquisition and distribution and finding flexible resources through competitive grants and assistance from businesses and community organizations. They practice resource reallocation and cost containment. They have a simultaneous macro- and micro-orientation, identifying pockets of readiness and resistance and allocating resources accordingly. They find time for staff to plan and develop.

- *Negotiate for win-win outcomes.* They work constructively and creatively with teacher representatives within the collective bargaining agreement. They use the collective bargaining process to forge new professional agreements dealing with the teaching and learning process.

- *Employ change strategies.* The research on change management contains ample tools for analysis and intervention. Leaders are skilled in analyzing concerns and levels of commitment. They configure the right mix of strategies and tactics to keep new undertakings on track through all stages of an improvement effort. These leaders are change strategists, recognizing the dynamics of their organization and determining the potential for change.

- *Provide stability in change.* The elimination function (the deliberate abandonment of elements of the organization that have not worked previously) needs to be accompanied by a framework that provides stability while the changes are taking place. Restructuring leaders construct a scaffolding for the organization and its people so that they can experiment with new ideas, take risks, and dismantle some aspects of the organization without losing a sense of the overall framework in which they are working. These leaders provide order and direction in an ambiguous and uncertain environment.

- *Grow people while getting the work accomplished.* Formal staff development is only one means of developing staff and others in the school community. Often the most powerful learning is accomplished while meaningful work is being done. Leaders help staff to move, in their thinking and behavior, beyond the limits of their own experience. They create self-managing and self-learning groups and invest heavily in staff development. They identify and nurture potential leaders to ensure that the foundation for restructuring will endure beyond their tenure. (Mojkowski and Bamberger 1991, pp. 28-31)

Sagor's (1992) study of three principals who "make a difference" suggests that simply assigning more authority to principals in the absence of role redefinition is unlikely to lead to major educational improvements. Principals need to be in the business of developing a clear, unified focus, creating a common cultural perspective, and supporting a constant push for improvement.

This new style of leadership may have as its hallmark the ability of the leader to sublimate her or his ego to the collective needs and potentialities of the organization. This does not mean surrendering decision-making responsibility or adopting a laissez-faire style of leadership. It does suggest a very difficult balancing act requiring the principal to have a vision of education, but allowing that vision to be shaped and modified by others. The ultimate goal is to have one collective vision with broad ownership that incorporates elements of the principal's vision and of other members of the school community.

Sergiovanni (1990) describes this new style as *leadership by bonding*, where the leader, having aroused human potential, satisfied higher needs, and raised expectations of leader and followers, then arouses awareness and consciousness that "elevates organizational goals and purposes to the level of a shared covenant and bonds together leader and followers in a moral commitment" (p. 25). The model is one of shared commitment and vision. This can be very difficult to accomplish in environments where the principal is "in charge" and is the primary, or sole, source of direction for school improvement or change.

CREATING READINESS FOR RESTRUCTURING

Readiness is an elusive and little-examined dimension of the change process that becomes much more important as the magnitude of the change increases. Fullan (1991) reminds us that "above all planning must consider the pre-implementation issues of whether and how to start, and what readiness conditions might be essential prior to commencing."

If people are being asked to make a small change in their routines and practices, little readiness is needed. Written instructions delivered impersonally may be entirely adequate, for example. However, when the nature of the change is substantive, very different procedures are suggested. In such a context, readiness for change becomes its own independent dimension of the change process.

Many school leaders appear to misjudge and underestimate the amount of time and energy that must be spent on readiness. The leaders have already adjusted their world view and accommodated themselves to the change they are proposing. More importantly, they can see how they will succeed, or at the least survive, after the change has taken place. They can put what they are suggesting into a broader context and are comfortable that they understand most of the predictable ramifications of the decision to change. They have been able to adjust their mental model of the world to accommodate what they are proposing.

For many, perhaps most, of the people in the organization who are being asked to change, this level of awareness simply does not exist, nor can it exist without difficulty. Readiness is not achieved by simply providing information to participants and answering their questions regarding how the changes will affect them. Ultimately all participants need the opportunity to engage actively with the change process at a different, more fundamental level. They need to be given the opportunity to understand the rationale for change, the conceptual framework within which it exists. Readiness activities are those that allow participants in fundamental change to have the opportunity to reshape their mental model, their world view, to accommodate the proposed changes, and, most importantly, to understand how they will be able to survive and succeed in the new environment.

Schmidt and Finnigan (1992) discuss the difficulties and dangers of systems-level transformative change. They suggest that the leaders in an organization make certain they are prepared to develop a knowledge base in each of six key areas before they begin a transformative change process:

1. Understanding the dynamics of organizational transformation
2. Assessing your organization's readiness for change
3. Assessing your management team
4. Reviewing your own leadership style
5. Learning from other organizations' experiences
6. Getting started (p. 89)

Schmidt and Finnigan emphasize that organizations are social systems. They take input from their environment, process it, and deliver output. Systems are made up of interdependent component parts that shift or adjust to accommodate the demands of the environment but do not necessarily coordinate these adjustments. The adjustments function primarily to maintain equilibrium, or the status quo. Changes in one part affect all others in unintended, uncontrolled ways. Organizations maintain equilibrium only through the expenditure of great amounts of energy. All change requires energy. In times of rapid change, it makes sense to enable the organization to become inherently more adaptive, manipulating the flow of energy so that it does not go primarily toward a return to equilibrium, but rather toward enabling the organization to become more adaptive as one of its integral features.

Significant change is difficult in any organization, say Schmidt and Finnigan, who describe some of the factors that leaders might keep in mind when preparing change strategies:

Because changes are disruptive, many people naturally resist them. Some of the factors that must be taken into consideration are these:

• The level of dissatisfaction with the present situation

• The cost of change (short-term and long-term)

• How well people understand the proposed "future state"

• The consequences of not changing

• The clarity of the path for changing

In general, people will support a change if (1) they are convinced that the present situation is not desirable; (2) the proposed "future" is clear, sensible, and desirable; (3) the path toward the future is clear and realistic; and (4) the cost of the change is not too high....[T]his involves asking four critical questions:

• How will the people in the organization be affected by the change? What will they gain and what will they lose?

• How clearly do they see the advantages of the changed situation?

• How dissatisfied are they with the present situation?

• How prepared are they to take the first steps to bring about the change? (p. 94)

The Concerns-Based Adoption Model (Hord and others 1987) suggests seven stages of concern that teachers may go through when implementing an innovation. The research done to develop this model focused on how teachers responded to discrete educational innovations, such as a new curriculum. In that sense the model may be of less value in understanding large-scale systems change. However, there are many lessons from the CBAM model that appear to be relevant.

The first five stages—awareness concerns, informational concerns, personal concerns, management concerns, and consequences concerns—relate most directly to issues of readiness. Although in the CBAM model some of these stages of concern—most notably management and consequences—were to be addressed in the context of implementing a specific program, they are also informative of the issues that need to be addressed before any major change is undertaken. The additional two stages of the model—collaboration concerns and refocusing concerns—

while important to consider, are not directly related to readiness issues. Hord and others (1987) suggest ways to address concerns at each of the first five levels. The following statements relate specifically to readiness concerns and represent a subset of all statements offered by Hord and others.

Stage 0—Awareness Concerns

- If possible, involve teachers in discussions and decisions about the innovation and its implementation.
- Share enough information to arouse interest, but not so much that it overwhelms.
- Acknowledge that a lack of awareness is expected and reasonable, and that no questions about the innovation are foolish.
- Encourage unaware persons to talk with colleagues who know about the innovation....

Stage 1—Informational Concerns

- Provide clear and accurate information about the innovation....
- Have persons who have used the innovation in other settings visit with your teachers. Visits to user schools could also be arranged.
- Help teachers see how the innovation relates to their current practices, both in regard to similarities and differences.

Stage 2—Personal Concerns

- Legitimize the existence and expression of personal concerns....
- Use personal notes and conversations to provide encouragement and reinforce personal adequacy.
- Connect these teachers with others whose personal concerns have diminished and who will be supportive.
- Show how the innovation can be implemented sequentially rather than in one big leap [when this is possible]. It is important to establish expectations that are attainable.

Stage 3—Management Concerns

- Clarify the steps and components of the innovation....
- Provide answers that address the small specific "how-to" issues that are so often the cause of management concerns.
- Demonstrate exact and practical solutions to the logistical problems that contribute to these concerns.

Stage 4—Consequence Concerns

- Provide individuals [with concerns about consequences] with opportunities to visit other settings where the innovation is in use and to attend conferences on the topic.
- Don't overlook [individuals with consequence concerns].... Give them positive feedback and needed support.

- Share with these persons information pertaining to the innovation. (pp. 44-45)

While this model is useful as a framework within which strategies to support change can be considered more systematically and thoroughly, restructuring may not lend itself to such a linear approach to change. Much of what comprises readiness is spread among the five levels presented in the model. Consequently, several issues often must be addressed simultaneously before any consideration of a specific innovation can, or should, begin. For example, it may not be possible to answer all questions regarding the use of a new technique, such as authentic assessment, or of a new structure for time, such as block scheduling, before it is implemented. Furthermore, in some cases there are few models to observe or learn from, and some types of change cannot occur in increments; teachers must make the transition all at once if they incorporate different strategies of scheduling or grouping, for example.

The net result is that careful, predictable, staged strategies for change are of less value in such an environment. This is not to say that they are without use. The point is that much of the work necessary to ensure the success of large-scale change occurs before the innovation(s) are ever put into place. Helping participants develop a new world view and showing them how they will function effectively and successfully within this new context are key dimensions of ensuring success.

In addition to the suggestions contained in the CBAM model, there are other things school leaders can do to create readiness for change. The next section lists a set of commitments a school's faculty can make—involving both activities and attitudes—that can shape readiness in a school. These statements assume that, before launching a project or activity, it may be wise to acknowledge publicly that large-scale change is being contemplated and to spend some time getting to the point where there is acceptance of the need to change.

THE TEN COMMITMENTS: PREREQUISITES TO RESTRUCTURING

A fundamental question to be asked before restructuring activities begin is whether the school is ready to attempt such a challenging, arduous process. Many times a highly motivated leader or group of leaders within a school has pushed strongly for the school to restructure, in spite of the wishes of most staff and community members. Although there is sometimes reason to be a "voice in the wilderness," particularly in situations where staff are too self-satisfied to ever change, there is also danger. The backlash can be so strong that it delays serious self-examination of a school's assumptions and practices for several years or more. Such a backlash can even eliminate the word and concept "restructuring" from the school's collective vocabulary.

One way to avoid the possibility of actually retarding the process of change in a school is to begin by discussing prerequisites to restructuring. This method allows the faculty and community to explore the implications and to establish the ground rules before beginning the process itself. Behaviors (and memories of what was agreed upon) often change when it is time to begin to implement new programs and structures. Making a commitment as a faculty to a series of principles can help create a forum for individuals to raise concerns and fears, as well as to begin to create a sense of common purpose.

The following ten statements are derived from research on the restructuring process specifically, and on change in organizations generally. These statements might be used by a school's faculty to help determine if they are ready and willing to continue a process of fundamental self-examination. The statements, which I have dubbed the Ten Commitments, cause staff to reflect on their values, the school's culture, and the process to be followed if the school chooses to begin or continue a restructuring process. These ten statements are designed to be presented to a faculty as a whole for consideration and adoption before any comprehensive program for school restructuring is initiated.

1. We commit to using data to make decisions. Staff will employ information on current school processes and outcomes, best educational practices, and societal trends as their frame of reference when making decisions. This analysis involves identifying what is not working along with what is working. It also involves acquiring the skills necessary to collect and analyze data.

2. We commit to creating and sustaining a culture of continued self-examination, extensive and continual professional development, and experimentation. In many schools, these are optional activities. In a school undergoing restructuring, faculty must lend their support for professional growth, both in principle and practice. If a school is to reshape itself, its staff members will have to be willing to examine their current practices and to acquire new skills and techniques. An important qualification is that this commitment to self-examination and professional growth will not result in any information being used against an individual.

3. We commit to identifying deficiencies in the learning environment and accepting the challenge to help *all* learners succeed. In many schools, there is a tendency to blame the learner for his or her own problems and failures. Sometimes failure is attributed to the child's home environment or economic class, or even, perhaps unconsciously, to the child's race or sex. All these explanations end up removing the school and the teacher from a position of responsibility for the success of the student. Although many children do bring difficult, almost intractable problems to schools, these cannot be accepted as an explanation before the fact for lack of student success. The third commitment implies that everyone in the school knows that they have done everything in their power to help the student succeed before they attribute responsibility elsewhere. They must do everything possible to alter the design and practices of the school to meet the real needs of their clients before they assign blame to those clients.

4. We commit to viewing children as human beings first, students second. In the final analysis, the most vital and important activities in education are those that occur during face-to-face interactions between teachers and students. Technology, innovative schedules, governance structures, and teaching materials are only marginally relevant if the quality of the human interactions that take place in the classroom are inadequate. The ability to transmit knowledge of content alone is not considered to be adequate to fulfill the expectations of the role of teacher. A primary prerequisite of learning is that students know that teachers care about them. Will the school be willing to assess the ways in which students are treated as human beings? Is the school organized in ways that allow adults and students to interact with one another as human beings?

5. We commit to learning and employing a broad range of instructional methods and formats. If schools restructure, teaching methods will become more varied than what has been the case. Goodlad (1984) found that the vast majority of students spend the vast majority of their time in passive roles, either listening to lectures or doing seatwork. If this commitment is made, instructional techniques will be selected and employed based on the needs of learners, not on the limited range of strategies the teacher has mastered. Will teachers be ready to expand their instructional repertoires not only by attending inservice trainings, but by making the much more important commitment to put new practices into place?

6. We commit to discarding what doesn't work or is no longer relevant. This commitment is very difficult for educators to make, since discarding any program or task generally means hurting a colleague. That is why it is very important to make a distinction between the person and what they do or teach, or between the person and the program being considered for elimination. Very often the individuals who might be affected are highly skilled and dedicated; the problem is that what they do may no longer be the best use of their time or the resources allocated to the task or program in question. Thus it is important to honor the person and make it clear they are still a valued member of the organization.

Given the goal conflict and ambiguity that exist in most schools as they attempt to be all things to all people, it becomes ever more urgent for educators to agree on what no longer belongs in the curriculum or school program. If schools continue to face stable or declining resource bases and increasing expectations for performance, resource reallocation is the only viable strategy for improving educational processes and outcomes. Learning how to do this may be traumatic for educators, but if everyone understands that such a process will eventually be necessary, staff will be more aware of the importance and gravity of decisions to restructure, and will not be as surprised when such a process is initiated.

7. We commit to viewing parents and community members as equal partners in the education of children. This is a concept to which lip service is often paid. In practice, however, schools have established many structural barriers to parental participation. Are staff members willing to change this relationship and expect parents to be equal members of a team whose goal is to educate children? Particularly in situations where staff believe that more parental and community support for education is vital to their success, the commitment to include these groups, and to be more accountable to them, has to be seen as part of the bargain in getting their involvement, ownership, and participation in education.

8. We commit to creating opportunities for broad-based staff involvement in decision-making clearly focused on change. Schools cannot be restructured without the active cooperation of teachers. Although new governance structures in and of themselves cannot transform schools, it remains equally clear that schools will not change if teachers do not take ownership of and responsibility for new educational goals, methods, and structures. With this in mind, it is important for teachers to be actively involved in decisions that will change their work environment and job descriptions. This commitment assumes a genuine desire to use input in decision-making as a tool for change, not for obstruction.

9. We commit to establishing a shared vision of education within the school. Evidence that many schools lack clear purpose or direction seems to be mounting at the same time that the need for purpose and direction increases. Much of what occurs in schools is fragmented or even contradictory. Are staff willing to spend the time and make the commitment to develop some common direction that reflects shared beliefs and values about the purpose of an education? Are they willing to make decisions and judgments based on this vision first and their personal agendas second? Are they willing to focus the vision on improved student learning outcomes, however identified and defined?

10. We commit to helping adults who are threatened or challenged by changes occurring in the school. In return, all adults in the school agree to be supportive or constructively critical; no obstructionists are allowed once decisions have been made openly. It is not reasonable to ask people to change if they will be worse off as a result of their willingness to do so. Will the organization commit to providing resources for members who are at a disadvantage as a result of change? Will procedures be developed to ensure that staff will not be asked to do things or make decisions that are against their own best interests? Will those negatively affected be provided assistance? If so, the system may ask in return that after a certain point all members of the organization line up behind the new goals, purposes, programs, and structures of the school, or suggest how better to accomplish these aims.

Open, participatory decision-making (as specified in the eighth commitment) provides a forum within which concerns can and must be aired. It is not acceptable to ignore the existing decision-making structures and work against change. Setting this ground rule can help diffuse much of the passive-aggressive resistance that can sabotage educational change efforts.

KEY QUESTIONS TO FRAME RESTRUCTURING EFFORTS

After a faculty has succeeded in developing a strong sense of direction and identified where they are and where they want to be, what is the next step? All indications are that this next step varies from school to school. But in most cases it involves teachers' developing programs or projects of some sort based on the vision. This section provides examples of questions schools might ask, dimensions they should consider, and principles they might discuss as they begin to think about their vision of restructuring.

The following questions are organized around the twelve dimensions of restructuring presented in part 3. They can generate faculty discussion and analysis of current practices when a school is ready to consider taking "the next step." They suggest the areas where data might be collected regarding current practice, or where research on best available practice might be focused. They provide the framework within which a consideration of vision can take place after sufficient time for reflection on possibilities has occurred.

These questions suggest far more change than most schools can sustain. They do, however, offer a broader view of possibilities than can be generated from a brainstorming session, or from attendance at an educational restructuring conference. They are designed to cause a faculty to collect data and to test the accuracy of their assumptions before they proceed with restructuring.

Outcomes

- Are learner outcomes specified? Do they form the basis for assessment?
- Are outcomes consistent with the vision and goals of the school?
- Were outcomes developed with broad community involvement and with reference to the skills students need to succeed in the future?
- Are the outcomes a combination of intellectual processes, skills, and content knowledge that provide a clear framework within which assessment can occur?
- Are outcomes cumulative throughout a child's education—kindergarten through graduation? Are there benchmarks that suggest the acceptable range of performance at various ages?

Curriculum

- Is the content of all courses accurate and up-to-date?
- Does the curriculum prepare learners for the future or the past?
- Are facts and concepts balanced so that students integrate and apply information?
- Is the required course of study consistent with the school's vision?
- Do students have a role in determining what they learn?
- Do different social/ethnic/economic groups learn substantially different content?

Instruction

- Are students active participants in classroom activities and in choosing how they learn?
- Are individualized learner goals developed?
- Is factual information used as a tool to enhance concept development, rather than as an end in itself?
- Is information integrated across disciplines using systems concepts?

- Do real-world problems serve as a focus for instruction?
- Is instruction designed so that all students can succeed?
- Do members of different social/ethnic/economic groups work together cooperatively to solve problems and apply knowledge?

Assessment

- Is assessment an integral part of learning?
- Is assessment holistic and integrative?
- Does assessment include public demonstration?
- Are students involved in setting personal assessment goals and selecting assessment activities?
- Does assessment provide formative as well as summative data?
- Does assessment involve the application of information to solve real-world problems?
- Are a wide variety of assessment strategies employed?

Learning Environment

- Is the learner being placed at the center of the learning environment?
- Is the learning environment perceived as extending beyond the classroom? the school? the community?
- Are conceptions of grouping and organization being reexamined to determine their purpose and worth?
- Are personal relationships being stressed in the organization of the learning environment?
- Are curriculum, instruction, and assessment changing consistent with the learning environment?

Technology

- Is technology used both to transmit factual information in a structured manner and to empower learners to take control of their learning?
- Are teachers mastering technology personally?
- Is technology viewed broadly to include applications in addition to computers?
- Are there provisions for software and training when hardware is purchased?
- Are curriculum and instructional design changed in tandem with technology acquisitions?

School-Community Relations

- Are parents being included as partners in the establishment of goals for the learner?
- Are parents provided with enough information to participate as partners?
- Are the needs of parents considered in the organization of the school and in the expectations held for parents?
- Is the broader community invited to participate in specific ways?
- Is the community involved in and informed about changes in the school?

Time

- Is time being adapted to learning needs rather than vice-versa?
- Is time structured to respond to needs and realities of students' and parents' lives?
- Are staff and curriculum development preceding and accompanying changes in time?
- Are the boundaries of time being reconceptualized?

Governance

- Is decision-making participatory?
- Are decisions made in relation to a vision?
- Are existing decision-making structures modified and new structures added as necessary?
- Are changes in governance viewed as means to ends, not as ends in themselves?

Teacher Leadership

- Are new opportunities for teacher leadership being developed?
- Is training in leadership and group process provided when teachers need it?
- Are leadership opportunities offered to a wide range of teachers?

Personnel

- Is there an emphasis on excellence in the teaching staff, with no acceptance of mediocrity or tolerance of incompetence?
- Do the teachers want to be where they are? Are they excited about teaching and do they truly care about young people?

- Are people other than certified teachers becoming involved in teaching or in supporting the instructional process?
- Are the current distribution and allocation of staff within the school consistent with the school vision and mission?

Working Relationships

- Are there efforts to include the professional association as a partner in change?
- Is there exploration at the district level of alternative forms of bargaining?
- Is there agreement to leave much of the restructuring program out of the negotiated agreement, subject to specified guidelines?
- Are there good faith efforts to redefine the role of the professional association in a positive way?
- Are a variety of strategies being implemented to create collaborative working relationships throughout the organization?

LOOKING FOR MODELS BY VISITING OTHER SCHOOLS

One effective means of building readiness is to provide staff the opportunity to visit schools that are actively involved in restructuring. Sometimes these observations embolden visitors with more resolve to change their own schools; other times they leave educators wondering why they even bothered to visit the site. Such visits can give educators a better sense of how (and why) their school should change its practices, or can lead to a rejection of restructuring by teachers who participate in the visit. Without careful selection of visitation sites and proper preparation for those who visit, the value of such visits is greatly diminished.

Chenowith and Everhart (1991) suggest that visiting a restructuring school is like visiting a foreign country. "We liken the school visit to a visit to a foreign land.... [T]he practitioner is much like a tourist who is not familiar with the local customs and thus will find that a well-designed tour book is of considerable assistance." The "culture shock" that can confront visitors can be a powerful tool in enabling them to rethink the educational structure and methods within their own building.

Chenowith and Everhart offer a "guide book" for visitors that discusses the meaning, organization, and effects of change. The following summary of these three areas suggests the type of questions visitors should be asking, and the kinds of things they should be looking for as they undertake their visit to a "restructured" school:

The Meaning of Change

- *Readiness for Change:* ... Staff should want and choose to change.... [W]hat proportion of staff are dissatisfied with the previous or present situation? What proportion of staff is supportive of the restructuring effort? What proportion of the staff is willing to risk new action on behalf of the school and willing to undergo training for new skills and behaviors?

- *School Vision:* ... There should be a clear school vision.... [W]hat is the school's "formal doctrine"? What are its statements of intentions, public announcements, promises, etc.?... [A]re the principal and teachers able to articulate the school's mission and goals? Is there a shared sense of purpose?

- *Language:* ... Is staff language "received," full of slogans, generalities, and a "party-line" or is it "interpreted" and full of the staff's own words and meanings?... Do staff talk about their future actions generally and abstractly or speak more specifically and behaviorally? Is staff language full of simplistic terms or is it dense, full of terms portraying more complex relationships? Are there physical displays and representations of language such as posters and banners portraying the school's mission statement and goals?

- *Understanding:* ... Do the principal and staff understand the complexity and delicate nature of the change process? Do staff have access to specific skills and knowledge necessary for a successful implementation? Are the staff able to articulate or describe a theory of knowledge base upon which the innovation is based?

- *Early Success:* ... Are there notable examples of success? Are the principal and staff confident and do they possess a sense of efficacy and job satisfaction? Is the school staff aware of both short- and long-term objectives?

The Organizational Structure of Change

- *Organization and Governance:* ... How are decisions made and who makes them? Are there procedures and processes for problem solving and school-based inquiry? What incentives or rewards exist to encourage a change in organizational behavior?

- *Culture:* ... Is collegiality evident through mutual sharing, assistance, and joint work?... Is there fragmented individualism (traditional isolation), Balkanization (subgroups and cliques), contrived collegiality (unwanted contacts and use of scarce time), or a truly collaborative culture (deep, personal, and enduring)?... Do staff have adequate communication and group process skills? Are staff members able to work with diverse views? Are there norms of perseverance, self-disclosure, and acceptance of outside help?

- *Instruction and Curriculum:* ... Are instructional practices teacher centered or do they include opportunities for cooperative learning, peer and cross-age tutoring, and increased student responsibility? Does the curriculum present concepts in the abstract or are concepts applied to real, personal, and concrete experiences? Does the curriculum require changes in teacher organizational structure or merely permit traditional patterns to persist?

- *Feedback and Evaluation:* ... Does the school openly solicit diagnostic information from multiple sources? Does the school reflect upon its practices? Does it tend to create more questions than provide answers?

- *Support:* ... Are adequate financial and time resources available? Is there support from key administrators in the district? Is the required technical knowledge available and accessible? Are parents informed and involved? What sort of press coverage or information has the community received about the program?

The Effects of Change

- *Active Learning:* ... Do students take an active role in learning or do they largely "consume" what teachers have planned for them to do? What proportion of time are students involved in such an active framework? What are some examples of the student activities that are part of such an active framework?

- *Student-Centered Learning Agendas:* ... [D]o students help define appropriate elements of the learning agenda... participation varied and appropriate? Do students understand how to organize such agendas? What activities illustrate such student-centered agendas?

- *Positive Regard for Students as Learners:* ... Is a high degree of self-esteem evident both in and out of class? Do students evidence a healthy respect for their role as students?

- *Clarity of Role:* ... How do students define their role as students *vis a vis* teachers, administrators and others? How do students visualize the role behavior of others who are supposed to improve their own learning?

- *School Context:* ... Do learning experiences in which students are engaged show evidence of the social context within which learning is involved, or are learning experiences predicated on assumptions of students as individuals? Is there evidence of a mutually supportive learning community? (pp. 8-16)

A quick visit to a school with a reputation for restructuring can be useful if the visitor looks beyond the surface, not evaluating the program in absolute terms, but understanding the effects of the philosophy and program in relative terms. The learning process is elusive; it is difficult to observe, particularly over a short time. However, a careful visitor can learn to see beyond the immediate physical environment, be it immaculate or cluttered, beyond the "official" party line of the host, beyond any prepared written materials that extol the program in its conceptually pure form, to learn valuable lessons and glean useful ideas, both in terms of what to do and what not to do.

Learning is inherently difficult to observe; it occurs at the most unexpected times, and there is often no outward sign that it has occurred. Careful observation can strengthen an observer's confidence that he or she can discern the link between the environment and processes used with the learner and the likelihood that learning is occurring. Observers should clearly understand the outcomes the school is seeking, since these may be different from the outcomes actually observed.

Given the relative openness of schools to visits (compared to some segments of private industry where new techniques are hidden from competitors), staff at schools trying new programs and approaches have much to gain through visiting other schools. If visitors do not expect to see schools that have solved all of education's problems, but have taken a solid first step toward a new vision of teaching and learning, they will gain much. This form of dissemination is described by DiMaggio and Powell (1983) as "institutional isomorphism," the tendency for noncompetitive organizations to look to one another for solutions and to adopt approaches developed and piloted by innovators. Since schools demonstrate the characteristics of institutional isomorphism, visits to the many "lighthouse" schools making early strides in restructuring may be critical to the ultimate success of school restructuring at any given site.

This chapter has explored the importance of culture, leadership, and readiness as tools that set the stage for restructuring and that help define its possibilities and manage its development. The next chapter considers the importance of a unifying vision as a means by which the organization can focus itself to make more effective use of resources, and by which all members of the organization can begin to align their efforts toward agreed-upon goals. Vision-building in combination with the elements discussed in this chapter can serve as powerful tools to help set the stage for restructuring.

CHAPTER 24

THE ROLE OF VISION AND SOME REPRESENTATIVE VISIONS

Most of the traditional attempts to bring about change in education have required individuals to understand what they were to do for a particular innovation to succeed. As such, change has been viewed as a process of training people to equip them with new skills. In contrast, modern-day restructuring may demand that educators pursue new goals or utilize techniques that are currently foreign to them. This new dimension of change requires commitment to the end goals of the process, not merely the adoption of new methods. Such commitment is unlikely to be developed when teachers operate in isolation and have little understanding of or input into the overall goals, purposes, and direction of the school. Vision-building creates an opportunity for such involvement to occur.

This chapter examines the process of vision-building and provides two examples of broad visions or blueprints for change in education that were developed by organizations. I have chosen to offer these broad educational visions instead of visions for particular schools for two reasons.

First, it is often difficult to ascertain the full meaning of a school's vision without visiting the school or discussing it with members of the school community.

And second, the emphasis in these more general blueprints is on understanding vision as a phenomenon.

The chapter begins with a definition of *vision* and a review of some of the literature on vision, followed by some prerequisites for successful vision-building. A template or model for conducting a process of vision-building is then presented and discussed. The chapter concludes with two very different visions for school restructuring: one a description of a restructured school system, the other a series of principles that might guide a school toward radically different means and ends.

VISION-BUILDING: A POTENTIALLY POWERFUL COMPONENT OF RESTRUCTURING*

In many respects restructuring is not primarily the process of establishing new programs, as noted earlier, but of developing a new picture in the minds of many of what schooling should look like and what educators should be attempting to achieve. Such a picture generally encompasses a combination of values, beliefs, assumptions, and practices that, taken as a whole, constitute a vision of education. The term *vision* has begun to appear with increasing frequency in the literature on leadership and restructuring (Bennis and Nanus 1985, Burns 1978, Kanter 1983). There seems to be the assumption—mistaken, I believe—that everyone knows what vision is. Before a sense of vision can guide and motivate educators, school personnel must have a better understanding of what it is, how it can be developed, and what can be accomplished by its use.

Vision is not a term that is defined readily or operationalized easily. In some respects, its definition seems analogous to that of art: People may not be able to articulate what makes something art, but they recognize it when they see it. In some cases this ambiguity has led to abuse of the term and the development of a certain amount of cynicism surrounding it in some schools. At the same time, writers on the topic and educators in schools where the concept is having a positive impact on practice respond that they seem to understand more or less intuitively what a vision is.

For the purposes of this discussion, *vision* is defined as *an agreement, explicitly stated in some form, shared by a significant number of participants in an organizational unit, on a mixture of values, beliefs, purposes, and goals that serves to provide a clear reference point for members of the organizational unit to use when making decisions about their behavior in the organizational context. This vision must be clear enough to enable participants to make choices that help move the organization toward achievement of the general values, beliefs, purposes, or goals.*

Stated differently, vision seems to provide an internal compass for people in complex organizations that helps them understand more clearly how their actions relate to, or contribute to, broader organizational goals. At its best, vision and mission provide, or restore, a sense of purpose and meaning to workers for whom such a sense has been lost or never existed.

---

* This section has been excerpted and adapted from Conley, Dunlap, and Goldman (1992).

This sense of meaning can be critically important, particularly in large bureaucratic organizations, where workers come to lose sight of the purpose of their labor or contribution to larger goals and purposes. Bolman and Deal (1991) present the following assumptions regarding the search for meaning by members of organizations:

1. What is most important about any event is *not* what happened, but *what it means*.

2. Events and meanings are loosely coupled: the same events can have very different meanings for different people because of differences in the schema that they use to interpret their experience.

3. Many of the most significant events and processes in organizations are *ambiguous* or *uncertain*—it is often difficult or impossible to know what happened, why it happened, or what will happen next.

4. The greater the ambiguity and uncertainty, the harder it is to use rational approaches to analysis, problem solving, and decision-making.

5. Faced with uncertainty and ambiguity, human beings create *symbols* to resolve confusion, increase predictability, and provide direction. (Events themselves may remain illogical, random, fluid, and meaningless, but human symbols make them seem otherwise.)

6. Many organizational events and processes are important more for what they express than for what they produce: they are secular myths, rituals, ceremonies, and sagas that help people find meaning and order in their experience. (p. 244, emphasis in original)

An organizational vision, and the process of developing and renewing it, helps people to reduce uncertainty, create common understanding, and find meaning in their day-to-day actions. Considered in the light of Bolman and Deal's assumptions, vision can be viewed as a way in which members of an organization attempt to create a broader sense of meaning for their behaviors.

Vision-building in public schools is not easy. It requires time, which is often in short supply. It is frequently greeted with cynicism, since it has the appearance of being the latest educational fad. It assumes that the people participating in the vision-building process share enough common beliefs, values, and agreement regarding the goals of schooling to be able to arrive at some sort of understanding or expression of commonality. To be done correctly, it requires a great deal of preparation and work; considerable information about the school and trends in education and society generally must be collected and analyzed. And vision-building can be very threatening, particularly if the vision that develops ends up favoring certain elements of the educational program over others.

SOME PREREQUISITES FOR SUCCESSFUL VISION-BUILDING

Following are some general observations regarding prerequisites to successful vision-building (Conley, Dunlap, and Goldman 1992). They are based in part on interview data (D. Conley, March 1991) and in part on literature in the area of vision and related topics. These observations should be considered tentative and exploratory.

1. A previous history of and success with systematic school improvement efforts. Such a history seems to provide important conditions that encourage the "leap of faith" involved with undertaking vision-building. Staff have a stronger sense of personal efficacy, which leads them to believe they can influence the conditions of work and the organizational culture of their school site. Previous experience with school improvement also allows for the creation of leadership, particularly teacher leadership, and for more opportunities for teachers to develop the interpersonal skills necessary to conduct or participate in processes that require multiple human interactions, each with the potential for conflict.

The model or type of school improvement undertaken previously does not seem to be of critical importance. In fact, some sites have been involved in a variety of strategies over the past ten years. Most previous attempts at systematic improvement were regarded to have been at least partially successful.

2. A willingness to examine data in various forms and employ them in the decision-making process. Data can take many forms, including: (a) information about current practices at the school and the efficacy of those practices, such as attendance data; test results; parent, teacher, or student surveys; or observation of classroom practices; (b) journals and periodicals offering a perspective on current thinking and innovative practices in education, and on societal trends; and (c) visits to other school sites, or work sites, to learn firsthand about new techniques.

All this information feeds into the vision-building process to help overcome the tendency of educators to make decisions based on anecdotal or impressionistic information from self-proclaimed faculty "experts" or from the person who is most emotional about an issue. In addition to gathering this information, faculties have been willing to commit to employing it as a frame of reference when determining vision and mission or when setting goals.

3. Principals who were willing to share power and decision-making to some degree. An important distinction needs to be made here between schools with "heroic" leaders, who develop the vision personally and "sell" it through a variety of strategies, and those who simply create the conditions whereby others may develop the vision. It appears that both of these methods can provide the conditions necessary for a collective vision to be developed and embraced; however, in the case of the "heroic" principal, it still appears to be necessary for the principal to release ownership and allow the vision to become the staff's for it to take hold successfully. This sharing of ownership may involve changes from what the principal envisioned initially, and it may entail the use of a process different from that which the principal viewed as ideal. The willingness of principals to step aside to some degree seems to be mandatory for successful vision-building.

Fullan (1992) notes that "the current emphasis on vision in leadership... can blind leaders in a number of ways." Leaders can become committed to a particular way of doing things or a specific project or strategy in a narrow, self-defeating way that causes teacher resistance. High-powered, charismatic principals are also at risk of seeing their ideas and strategies depart shortly after they do. In both cases, Fullan cautions, "too much store is placed in the leader as solution compared to the leader as *enabler* of solutions.... The crucial question is, 'Whose vision is it?'"

4. A commitment to act upon the results of the vision-building process. Many schools are or recently have been involved in vision-building activities, at least in part as a result of the popularity of strategic planning. In many cases these visions have been developed in a vacuum; no one is certain why they are being created or for what purpose. Often these visions or missions can be seen adorning school hallways, stationery, and business cards, while having little impact on school decisions or operations.

Vision-building processes that are successful already have a clear role in the school's operation. In this case, the vision is an extension of the school's traditions of clear purpose and direction. Having a clearly identified role for the mission before the process begins raises the likelihood that the process will be successful.

5. A central office that is, at least, willing to keep out of the process and, at best, willing to support it actively. In the schools examined and in the literature, the central office is often viewed by participants in vision-building as a hindrance. While this perception clearly reflects the ambiguous power (and personal) relationships that often exist between individual educators at school sites and central administrators, it also suggests that the most important role central offices can play is to let schools know they can proceed with the process of vision-building without fear of reprisal. In addition, central-office staff can provide: (a) general districtwide vision, mission, and goals that create an arena in which the school may define its own purposes; (b) data not readily available to the sites that can help build the database upon which decisions about vision can be made; and (c) assistance with the process in those instances where central administration is perceived as a source of help and where there are people within central administration who have the technical skills to facilitate such a process.

6. An awareness of the natural tension between top-down and bottom-up planning strategies. Strategic planning in education has gained popularity during the past six years. It has been adapted from the private sector to the educational context primarily by increasing the amount of participation and the openness of the process. However, even in its modified form, it still emphasizes mission-setting and vision-building by a small team at the district level as the first step in the process. Is there an inherent conflict between centrally created visions and missions and those created at individual school sites?

In one study of schools involved in restructuring (Goldman, Dunlap, and Conley 1991), none of the schools was operating in a district with a strategic plan that served as a referent point for decision-making. Therefore, these schools did not have to confront this issue. It is interesting to speculate about what would occur if a strategic-planning process were to be introduced at the district level. How would these schools react to a mission and vision being imposed upon them after they had developed their own?

Perhaps it would make sense in some districts for all schools to begin by making a first pass at developing a vision before such work began at the district level. The results of such a process at the site level might help inform the district-level process and create greater ownership of the vision and mission that developed.

The more common practice has been for the district to develop its mission and vision, then mandate that each school examine its practices in relation to the district direction and develop its own version of the district's document. The relative effectiveness of these two possible strategies for integrating strategic planning and site-level vision-building bears further investigation, since they involve the basic relationship between centralization and decentralization in determining the direction of an organization.

SOME 'HOW TO'S' OF VISION-BUILDING

Many authors have described vision as if it exists independently of any systematic development, as if it resides in certain "enlightened" individuals (Bennis and Nanus 1985, Burns 1978, Kanter 1983, Peters 1987, Peters and Austin 1985). A gifted few may be able to synthesize their vision intuitively. However, for most organizations, and particularly for large ones with diverse members, the development of vision may need to be an explicit, deliberate process.

Numerous different strategies have been used to build visions. Indeed, it would be naive to think that a single formula or procedure could work in all situations and settings. Howard (1991) offers a nine-step process that is sufficiently general to encompass many of the key activities and steps present in most descriptions of successful vision-building. The steps of this process, which Howard developed from work he performed with Colorado schools, are grouped in four phases: readiness, data collection, vision building, and action planning and implementation. I have modified and adapted Howard's model in the following narrative.

READINESS PHASE

1. Raise awareness levels. Provide information to staff members, parents, students, key community leaders, and the superintendent's office regarding the need for schools to restructure and regarding the school's intention to follow the nine-step process. Information on the need for the school to restructure will include sources on changing economic, demographic, social/political, and technological trends, along with consideration of societal values, available resources, community structure, and so forth.

2. Develop commitment. Through the school's usual decision-making processes, develop a commitment to pursue restructuring by implementing the nine-step process. Do not label those who do not want to participate or who raise questions as "the enemy." Work to find ways to involve all staff and the community by creating many possible ways for individuals to participate.

3. Organize for change. Organize a development team to provide overall coordination and guidance. Educate team members about the restructuring process and about their specific roles in bringing about restructuring. This is a working group, not an advisory group. Develop clear procedures selecting team members, make responsibilities explicit, establish timelines and reporting procedures, and establish group norms before the committee's work begins.

DATA COLLECTION PHASE

4. Develop an information base. First, gather baseline data on quality indicators that may have a positive impact on student learning and that can be affected by restructuring. Such indicators come from sources such as archival records, surveys, self-reported behavior, classroom observation, focus groups, and interviews. Data obtained earlier in step 1 on the need to restructure can be included here as well.

Second, create an information base for developing the vision statement. Have the development team and other interested faculty identify articles, books, reports, videotapes, and other sources of information that would help teachers reconceptualize their school. Have team members and other interested faculty (including some who might have been skeptics initially) attend conferences, visit other schools, or spend time at local work sites to obtain new perspectives on student needs and teacher roles. Involve as many staff members as possible in these activities. Data should be summarized in a form readily available to all. Many opportunities should be created for the school community to consider the data and its implications.

VISION-BUILDING PHASE

5. Develop a vision statement. Have the development team do the initial work on developing a vision statement as a "set of educational specifications for the restructured school" (Howard). Components of the vision statement may include: Outcomes, Curriculum, Instruction, Assessment/Evaluation, Learning Environment, Technology, School-Community Relations, Time, Governance, Teacher Leadership, Personnel, and Working Relationships. The team also should identify implications of the vision statement for the school as it is currently structured. Implications must include an analysis of what skills and knowledge all students will be expected to possess upon completion of the course of study at the school (educational outcomes), along with suggested strategies for assessing student success in achieving these outcomes.

6. Assess faculty perceptions of the initial draft of the vision statement. Ask each faculty member to rate each element of the proposed vision statement in terms of "what is" and "what should be." This measures the extent of respondent agreement with items that are descriptors of the school's vision and a goal for the restructuring process. Allow for adequate discussion of the implications of the proposed vision. Once a vision statement has been formulated, ask each faculty member to write a personal statement identifying the implications of the proposed vision for his or her instructional practice.

7. Set priorities and identify activities to enact the vision. Convene a broad-based planning team comprised of members of the development team, other interested faculty, key community leaders, student leaders, parents, and others to identify elements that should be included in the school's action plans for realizing the vision. Refer the work of this group to the faculty and community for review before implementing its recommendations. Once again, consider these activities in relation to the skills and knowledge all students are expected to be able to demonstrate. Will these activities lead to the specified outcomes?

ACTION PLANNING AND IMPLEMENTATION PHASE

8. Develop detailed action plans, implement, monitor, and modify. Form three to six task forces roughly encompassing the twelve dimensions of restructuring. There should be at least one task force each for the central, supporting, and enabling variables. Additional task forces might concentrate on specific issues or programs within these areas or on projects that cut across all three dimensions.

9. Evaluate and report outcomes. Frequently assess and monitor the progress that is being made, both in terms of the specific projects being undertaken and changes in student learning outcomes. Be prepared to use different measures of student learning than are currently employed. Circulate this information widely and be prepared to modify your vision based on feedback. Link the information to the baseline quality indicators previously established and to the explicit student skill-and-knowledge outcomes identified throughout the process.

There are many possible variations on the process just described. Its primary elements—common to most good approaches to planning—include a review of the external environment and its probable impact on the school, an analysis of current practices and their effectiveness, a consideration of the thinking and writing on current best practice, and an orientation toward inclusive models of decision-making.

A vision statement, however well drafted, is only a starting point in a very long process. Some schools have conducted highly successful vision-building sessions but never moved beyond that point. While the process of vision-building can be, and frequently is, a means by which to increase communication and interaction among staff, it should be viewed as a means to an end, not an end in itself. In this sense, it is probably not desirable to say, as some who participate in vision-building do, that the process is more important than the product: both are important. The purpose is to create alignment of effort toward and ownership of the goals of change, not simply to improve staff relations. The next stage beyond vision-building is action toward restructuring. The following sections describe several different views of such action.

A VISION OF A RESTRUCTURED SCHOOL SYSTEM

Associated Oregon Industries and the National Association for Schools of Excellence (1992) offer a blueprint for change in America's schools. This comprehensive document contains eight "key points of action" combined with a two-year action plan designed to enable today's schools to reach international standards. These eight points suggest a framework within which the entire system of public education could be restructured. It is an example of a more specific step beyond a general vision of education, but one that still stops short of recommending or mandating specific programs or structures. The document is the result of a symposium conducted jointly by the two organizations; it is a good example of the way agendas of the private sector and of educators can overlap to produce a plan that may be acceptable to business and education communities alike.

A document such as this can serve as a resource that allows school personnel to focus their discussions on predetermined key issues. The points identified in this report cause teachers to consider the specific strategies that the business community believes public schools must adapt as they restructure. Some teachers could object to some of the statements; however, they are direct and facilitate discussion of the purposes, goals, and methods of education. The eight key points of action and the subpoints accompanying each are as follows:

1. *Business and school partnerships are needed to achieve an internationally competitive school system.*

   • Business and industry must take an active role in defining what competency levels are necessary for specific technical and professional occupations.

   • Business and schools must join in partnerships to provide work experience for students and internships for teachers.

   • Business people must sit on school advisory and board positions.

   • Business must provide resources for teaching basic entry level work force skills.

   • Businesses must provide awards to effective schools.

   • Businesses and schools must enter into technological information sharing services.

   • Businesses and schools must create transferable high school academic credit for on-the-job work experience.

   • Businesses and schools need to establish programs showing students a direct relationship between school performance and work performance.

2. *Structural changes are necessary to ensure delivery of an internationally competitive school curriculum.*

- Schools must be structured in a way that permits teachers to teach appropriate curricula.
- The length of the school year must be increased to match other industrial countries.
- The length of the school day needs to be expanded.
- Offer alternative pathways to high school graduation encompassing professional and technical education, with built-in flexibility between pathways that enables individuals to move easily between academic, technical, and professional education.
- Structure professional and technical training to prepare students for the needs of high tech industry, as well as adult life.
- Implement primary school programs that allow children to progress at their own developmental pace—such as the non-graded kindergarten through third grade concept.

3. *An integrated curriculum must be developed including these basic skills: keyboarding, data manipulation, problem solving and decision-making, systems of technology, resource management, economics of work, human relations, applied math and science, and career planning.*

- Reading, writing, listening, and speaking will be the primary focus in all content areas.
- Math areas stressed should be basic operations, logic, statistics, probability, and measurement. Algebra and geometry taught in isolation appear to be seldom used in the work force and everyday life.
- Applied science should be taught within an integrated curriculum.
- Higher-order thinking skills such as problem solving, analysis, synthesis, and evaluation should be emphasized at all levels and in all areas of instruction.
- Student work experience and apprenticeships with business and civic authorities should be required.
- The majority of instruction should focus on application and problem solving skills.
- The majority of instruction should engage students in actively using information, rather than passively receiving information.
- Students need to be taught and assessed by working together to solve problems and create solutions—much like adults do in the workplace.
- The availability of computers and emerging technologies must increase in classrooms, particularly at the middle school and high school levels.

- Curriculum for primary children must be developmentally appropriate and reflect that young children learn best through active involvement and play.

- At all grade levels basic skills should include the ability to use information systems, demonstrate personal and civic responsibility, model acceptable personal behaviors and skills, set priorities, demonstrate dexterity, work as a member of a team, reason, and use appropriate interpersonal skills.

- No textbook should be required as the sole source of meeting class requirements.

- Critical analysis and evaluation should be taught as prerequisites for entry-level work, further education, and everyday life.

- All schools must adopt Distance Learning Technologies. Using cable systems and satellites, a teacher with specific skills can instruct students who are hundreds of miles away. Many rural schools currently do this, making classes in specialized areas such as physics, foreign languages, and other professional and technical skills available to students everywhere.

4. *Effective assessment tools are needed to ensure all students have the opportunity to develop their potential to meet and exceed international education standards.*

- A wide variety of assessment techniques such as anecdotal information (portfolios), assigned class work, oral questioning, quizzes, senior projects, tests, and standardized measures must be used.

- Letter grades and standardized achievement tests must not be used to assess student performance until after the first four years of schooling.

- Teachers and administrators must be assessed by how well their students learn and perform.

5. *Parents must be involved to ensure their children receive the best education.*

- Parents must value school and school achievement, and they must encourage their children to do the same.

- Parents must monitor their children's progress at all levels.

- Parents must drastically limit the amount of television their children watch. Research concludes children who watch more than 10 hours of television a week have lower school achievement, are less creative, and have smaller vocabularies.

- Parents must read to their children frequently from a very early age.

- Parents must frequently listen to their primary children read.

- Schools should establish regular private consultations with parents to discuss progress, as well as techniques for incorporating supplementary home instruction.
- Some traditional parent involvement strategies must be continued: parent organizations, open houses, and volunteer programs.
- Parents should be members of school policy and oversight organizations.
- Parenting classes must be provided for parents and be required for high school students.
- Schools should be willing to use the skills of the adults in their community, regardless of age.

6. *Student self-esteem must be developed in an internationally competitive school system.*

- Self-esteem is built upon successfully achieving high individual standards.
- Schools must develop recognition programs that reward student achievement and effort.
- Teachers must help students build self-esteem by sincerely caring for them and guiding them toward genuine success on a daily basis.
- When students demonstrate success in international academic competition, celebrate their achievement.

7. *Teacher training and development is a critical factor in achieving an internationally competitive school system.*

- Teacher trainees must receive more on-site experiences in the working world.
- Teacher trainees should learn from master teachers. Teacher trainees must receive formal training in classroom management.
- Teacher trainees should be trained using international standards and strategies.
- Teacher trainees must successfully intern for one year with an experienced master teacher before being certified.
- Outstanding retired master teachers should be able to work with school districts to act as trainers and mentors, without jeopardizing their retirement benefits.
- Each school and school district must provide a strong staff training program based on locally assessed needs.
- Successful teachers should conduct most teacher training.
- Teaching leadership trainers should be recognized at each school.
- A rotating cadre of master teachers should be assigned for training statewide.

- Practicing teachers should be released and given paid sabbaticals for renewal training at least once every five years.
- Staff supervision should be conducted by master teachers.
- All teachers should be trained to teach writing, thinking, decision-making, and application of learning theory throughout the curriculum.
- Statewide inservice days must be provided.

8. *Foreign languages play a vital role in an internationally competitive school system.*

- A designated second language should be incorporated into all curricular areas, beginning in the primary years and continuing through high school graduation.
- Additional languages must be offered at the middle and high school levels.
- By sixth grade, students should be able to listen, write, speak, and read in a second language. (Associated Oregon Industries and National Association for Schools of Excellence 1992, pp. 8-36)

This blueprint, or vision, of a restructured school system is of interest because of its broad view of educational change. It acknowledges what many educators have been saying—that they cannot change schools alone—but it also asks much of them in return. Although this blueprint is more inclusive than what would be developed by most schools, it is indicative of a different perspective on schooling, one that suggests new ways in which schooling should be organized, and new roles for everyone with an interest, direct or indirect, in the educational process.

PRINCIPLES OF THE COALITION OF ESSENTIAL SCHOOLS

The Coalition of Essential Schools, founded in 1984 at Brown University by Theodore Sizer, has provided leadership in the school restructuring process consistently over the past decade. The coalition has grown to include over one hundred schools that follow its Common Principles. These principles are a series of general statements designed to serve as a philosophical outline within which schools then create specific programmatic responses to achieve their restructuring goals. These principles, listed below, provide yet another framework within which schools can consider their overall goals and purposes as they develop a plan for restructuring.

1. The school should focus on helping adolescents learn to use their minds well. Schools should not attempt to be "comprehensive" if such

a claim is made at the expense of the school's central intellectual purpose.

2. The school's goals should be simple: that each student master a limited number of essential skills and areas of knowledge. While these skills and areas will, to varying degrees, reflect the traditional academic disciplines, the program's design should be shaped by the intellectual and imaginative powers and competencies that students need rather than necessarily by "subjects" as conventionally defined. The aphorism "less is more" should dominate. Curricular decisions should be guided by the goal of thorough student mastery and achievement rather than by the goal of merely covering content.

3. The school's goals should apply to all students, but the means to these goals will vary from student to student. School practice should be tailor-made to meet the needs of every group or class of adolescents.

4. Teaching and learning should be personalized to the maximum possible extent. Efforts should be directed toward a goal that no teacher have direct responsibility for more than eighty students.

5. The metaphor of the school should be student-as-worker rather than teacher-as-deliverer-of-instructional-services. Accordingly, a prominent pedagogy will be coaching, to provoke students to learn how to learn and thus to teach themselves.

6. Students entering secondary school studies are those who can show competence in language and elementary mathematics. Students of traditional high school age but not yet at appropriate levels of competence will be provided intensive remedial work to assist them quickly to meet these standards. The diploma should be awarded upon a successful final demonstration of mastery for graduation—an "exhibition." This exhibition by the student of his or her grasp of the central skills and knowledge of the school's program may be jointly administered by the faculty or by higher authorities. As the diploma is awarded when earned, the school's program has no strict age grading and no system of credits earned by time spent in class. The emphasis is on the students' demonstrating that they can do important things.

7. The tone of the school should explicitly stress values of high expectation, trust, and decency. Incentives appropriate to the school's particular students and teachers should be emphasized, and parents should be treated as essential collaborators.

8. The principal and teachers should consider themselves generalists first and specialists second. Staff should expect multiple obligations and a sense of commitment to the entire school.

9. Ultimate administrative and budget targets should include, in addition to total student loads per teacher of eighty or fewer pupils, substantial time for collective planning by teachers and competitive salaries for teachers. Per-site costs should be within 10 percent of traditional

schools. Some services offered in traditional comprehensive high schools may have to be eliminated to accomplish this. (Sizer 1992, pp. 28-29)

In contrast with the blueprint for change in the preceding section, these statements focus specifically on the school as a self-contained institution and have fewer references to systems-level issues. They combine general principles and specific strategies, and thus their effect for teachers may be to make restructuring concrete. They imply rather clear commitments to changing behavior and organizational structure. These principles of the Coalition of Essential Schools serve as another example of how to move beyond a general vision toward actions that result in significant change in existing practice.

This chapter has presented a discussion of the role of vision and some means by which to develop it. Because there is much to consider when embarking upon restructuring, it is easy for schools, with their limited capacity to change, to become overwhelmed by both the content and process of rapid change. A vision can serve as a useful vehicle to frame change in ways that allow participants to sense implications without yet committing to specific programs. In times of rapid change, it is critical to have a vision in addition to show how specific programs will be undertaken.

The next chapter considers some techniques and principles for school restructuring that are emerging from schools actively engaged in restructuring activities.

CHAPTER 25

SOME TOOLS FOR TAKING THE NEXT STEPS TOWARD RESTRUCTURING

This chapter discusses some strategies and tools that seem to be helpful to schools as they take the "next steps" in restructuring. Several factors or models can be useful when considered along with issues of culture, leadership, readiness, and vision. Some of the topics discussed in this chapter include thinking of education as a system, using outcome-based education as a vehicle for changing this system, and finding the time for staff to participate in restructuring.

It is difficult to convey in a book, which is constructed in a linear fashion, the idea that the processes presented in each chapter do not necessarily follow one another sequentially in the real world. The tools presented here are useful in conjunction with the preceding topics; indeed, they may be utilized concurrently with or subsequently to activities conducted in other areas. In other words, the specific processes of change followed by schools and districts involved in restructuring appear to vary tremendously. People start where they are, playing the cards they have been dealt, and proceed as best they can. The concepts and approaches in this chapter offer some additional possibilities for ways in which the road to restructuring may be traveled.

The chapter begins with a discussion of systems thinking, the idea that changes need to be conceptualized in the context of the total system. Most educators are not accustomed to thinking in a systems fashion. I suggest that Total Quality Management is a means by which systems-level thinking can be both encouraged and translated into action. Next, outcome-based education is introduced, described, and analyzed as a framework within which systems redesign can occur. The discussion then turns to a consideration of the specific lessons learned from schools that were provided resources and support for improvement. The chapter concludes with an investigation of some ways in which time for restructuring can be obtained, acknowledging the critical importance of this factor to all restructuring activities.

SYSTEMS THINKING AND TOTAL QUALITY MANAGEMENT

As more schools experiment with fundamental change, it becomes clearer to many that they must think in terms of education as a system, not a series of independent programs and activities linked loosely through common administration. The effect of good programs can easily be nullified by neutral or unsupportive settings. Bureaucratic organizations such as schools have a notoriously difficult time focusing on the needs of the client.

One of the greatest challenges for most educators is to view their educational program through the eyes of their client, the student. What they often see is a series of disjointed, impersonal, often meaningless activities and interactions, random overlap and repetition of tasks, occurring within physically uncomfortable settings organized around arbitrary structures of time. They will also detect little concern for quality or integration. The notion of a client-centered, quality-oriented learning organization driven by systems thinking is little more than a dream for most educational institutions.

And yet this is the decade of systems thinking and quality in other segments of society. Many in the private sector have adopted these concepts as twin hallmarks for the nineties. Educators will be challenged to understand and adapt the concepts to public education, as well, in a decade where all sectors of the economy will be pushed to improve productivity, innovation, flexibility, and quality.

SENGE'S LAWS OF THE FIFTH DISCIPLINE

Senge talks of systems thinking as the "fifth discipline," which builds upon and integrates the other four disciplines: personal mastery, mental models, shared vision, and team learning. Together these five disciplines help people function together as a learning organization, capable of systems thinking. Senge (1990) describes the potential impact of the five disciplines, which he describes as *component technologies:*

> Today, I believe, five new "component technologies" are gradually converging to innovate learning organizations. Though developed separately, each will, I believe, prove critical to the others' success, just as occurs with any ensemble. Each provides a vital dimension in building organizations that can truly "learn," that can continually enhance their capacity to realize their highest aspirations. (p. 6)

Moving to systems thinking will be challenging for educators, who are accustomed to operating in relative isolation, within classrooms, programs, or school buildings. Systems solutions require a very different perspective. The following bulleted items state and summarize what Senge (1990) calls the "laws of the fifth discipline." Some examples of their application to educational organizations are also presented, as appropriate.

• *Today's problems come from yesterday's "solutions."* One solution often simply shifts the problem from one point in the system to another where it goes undetected for a time. Many pullout programs in education, for example, have fallen prey to this law.

• *The harder you push, the harder the system pushes back.* This phenomenon, what Senge calls "compensating feedback," occurs when a well-intentioned intervention causes system reactions that offset the benefit of the intervention. Class sizes may drop slightly, but teachers may have to assume other duties that offset any marginal advantage that accrues from the smaller class size.

• *Behavior grows better before it grows worse.* Many low-level interventions work in the short term, making them very attractive. However, they often lay the groundwork for more serious problems several years hence. A school that adopts all the "latest" programs without much understanding or commitment so that it looks good and helps advance the careers of those who want to look "progressive" can actually end up worse off when teachers become disenchanted with what is expected of them, or the programs have unintended effects over the long run that cancel their short-term benefits.

• *The easy way out usually leads back in.* There is a tendency to select familiar solutions to problems, whether these solutions actually solve the problem or not. Constant revision of discipline and attendance systems in the hopes of eliminating undesirable behavior and absenteeism is an example. Rather than understanding why the behaviors occur and how the system could be altered to result in more of the desired behaviors, changes in known programs seems to be much simpler and more logical.

• *The cure can be worse than the disease.* Some "solutions" are not only ineffective, they are addictive and dangerous. They can result in dependent behaviors that foster increased dependence and decreased ability of people to solve their own problems. This is called "Shifting the Burden to the Intervenor." The organization or agency becomes responsible for solving the clients' problems. For example, short-term solutions that result in parents being asked to take less responsibility for the child's education lead to a dependent relationship where parents come to expect the school to do many things it is incapable of doing. The proper role of the school and parents becomes the subject of serious misunderstandings.

• *Cause and effect are not closely related in time and space.* In complex human systems, the cause of a problem is often quite separate from the effect the problem has on the organization. In schools, problems from one grade level may not become apparent for several years. One bad secondary school teacher may be causing problems throughout the school for other faculty who have to deal with angry or disillusioned students as a result. A poor decision by a textbook selection committee has ramifications throughout the district for years.

• *Small changes can produce big results—but the areas of highest leverage are often the least obvious.* "Small, well-focused actions can sometimes produce significant, enduring improvements, if they're in the right place," Senge states. This is referred to as the principle of "leverage." The only problem is that such responses are usually not obvious to most participants in the system. "There are no simple rules for finding high-leverage changes, but there are ways of thinking that make it more likely. Learning to see underlying 'structures' rather than 'events' is a starting point.... Thinking in terms of processes of change rather than 'snapshots' is another." Schools will have to learn to solve their problems by understanding what their problems really are and by identifying high-leverage responses.

• *You can have your cake and eat it too—but not at once.* Senge observes:

> Sometimes, the knottiest dilemmas, when seen from the systems point of view, aren't dilemmas at all. They are artifacts of "snapshot" rather than "process" thinking, and appear in a whole new light once you think consciously of change over time....
>
> ... Many apparent dilemmas, such as central versus local control, and happy committed employees versus competitive labor costs, and rewarding individual achievement versus having everyone feel valued are by-products of static thinking. They only appear as rigid "either-or" choices, because we think of what is possible at a fixed point in time. (pp. 65-66)

Education may be improved if educators come to understand that many of the either-or dilemmas they create can be resolved if they are reconceptualized in the context of systems thinking. Higher salaries/ lower class size is an example of an insoluble dilemma that causes continuing frustration for those who believe the only answer is to do both simultaneously.

• *Dividing an elephant in half does not produce two small elephants.* Simply dividing an organization up into smaller units does not necessarily result in the integrity of purpose being retained. Separate schools tend over time to operate independently. People in schools rarely see the results of their work or notice how decisions they make affect others in the organization. Problems are left for others to solve or are not addressed in any systematic manner. Dividing the elephant can make it impossible to find the high-leverage points, since the system is incapable of responding as a system in any meaningful way.

• *There is no blame.* As Senge points out,

> We tend to blame outside circumstances for our problems. "Someone else"...did it to us. Systems thinking shows us that there is no outside; that you and the cause of your problems are part of a single system. The cure lies in your relationship with your "enemy." (p. 67)

Educators have become all too practiced at displacing responsibility for their performance to others in the system and those outside the system. Systems thinking demands that this response stop and that examination of the total system replace the process of ritual blame.

Systems thinking is demanding. It also implies the ability to alter the system based on feedback following its application. Most school districts are not used to thinking of themselves as systems, nor are they accustomed to system-level change. The applications of these concepts will be new for teachers and principals, who have been encouraged not to think in terms of the total system, but of their small piece of it.

TOTAL QUALITY MANAGEMENT

Total Quality Management (TQM) is one technique that encourages thinking of an organization (or process) as a system. It has been adopted widely in the manufacturing sector during the past decade and is now being applied to service-oriented organizations. Applying TQM to education may be difficult for many educators who are not accustomed to thinking in terms of "customers" or "clients," who have their own perceptions of quality. Moreover, educators may not be prepared to gather data on their current practices to determine which are functioning effectively to produce quality, which must be improved, and which must be abandoned.

Total Quality Management is many things to many people. It is as much philosophy as technique. It springs from the work of several management consultants, who have different names for their approach, including Deming's 14 points (Deming 1986) Juran's Trilogy, and Ishikawa's Thought Revolution. Bonstingl (1992) summarizes the common points among these differing perspectives into what he calls an "integral set of fundamental tenets." He calls them the Four Pillars of Total Quality Management:

1. The organization must focus, first and foremost, on its suppliers and customers. Understanding relationships among suppliers, primary and secondary customers, and workers helps teachers see the organization of the learning process from a different perspective.

2. Everyone in the organization must be dedicated to continuous improvement, personally and collectively. "The Japanese call this ethos *kaizen,* a societywide covenant of mutual help in the process of getting better and better, day by day" (Bonstingl, p. 6). Were schools to adopt this notion, they would reorganize to ensure that there were adequate time and resources for continuous improvement, that students would not be judged or graded on a bell-shaped curve that guaranteed failure for some. Self-assessment would become institutionalized.

3. The organization must be viewed as a system, and the work people do within the system must be seen as ongoing processes. Bonstingl states:

> Deming and others suggest that more than 85 percent of all the things that go wrong in any organization are directly attributable to how the organization's system and processes are set up. Individual teachers and students, then, are less to blame for failure than is the system—the seemingly immutable pattern of expectations, activities, perceptions, resource allocations, power structures, values, and the traditional school culture in general. Therefore, it is the system that deserves our greatest attention. (p. 6)

4. The success of Total Quality Management is the responsibility of top management. The implementation of TQM involves deep changes in the culture of the organization. The goal is to institutionalize TQM as a way of thinking, not a program or process.

To achieve total quality, schools will need to shift their emphasis from focusing on products alone to a consideration of the processes they employ. Rather than simply testing children to see if they know what teachers say they should, the focus moves to the processes of learning, beginning with a reconsideration of the goals of the system. Information on student performance can be used to identify areas of wide variation and to monitor performance of the system. However, care must be taken not to use data to control, motivate, reward, threaten, or judge people. Data serve to identify flaws in the system, not the individual. Responsibility for improving the system is shared by all, but it remains a primary responsibility of management personnel, who function in concert with others in the organization.

Because Total Quality Management is as much a philosophy as a program, it is being interpreted and applied in a wide variety of ways by schools. In one example the Burlington, New Jersey, Public Schools applied TQM techniques to solve a specific problem one step at a time (Abernathy and Serfass 1992). They sought to decrease high school tardiness and increase attendance. To do so, they systematically assessed the current situation by acquiring accurate, up-to-date information on the problem. Next they carefully analyzed these data to determine the root causes of the problem. Then they formulated countermeasures and solutions to the root causes that were within their control to change. They determined the potential effectiveness of each countermeasure in relationship to its feasibility. These systematic processes helped them determine the best system-level set of responses to the problem.

By way of contrast, Rees Elementary School in Utah employed the concept of quality, rather than the techniques of Total Quality Management, to make thoughtful improvements in every area of the school's operations, including communication, curriculum, and assessment (Harris 1992). Working with William Glasser and his notion of the quality school (Glasser 1990), staff considered their general philosophy of learning, their use of language, the ways they handled frustration and anger, their awareness of the basic needs of children, and other behaviors that contributed to their definition of a quality school. They employed control-theory charts, discussed quality-school bulletins, and explored the idea of quality with their students. They learned to think of quality through the eyes of their customers: students and parents. They altered assessment strategies to obtain more holistic descriptions of student performance in order to emphasize quality work. They used the concept of the school as a learning nation comprising various villages as a way to emphasize democratic discipline. Students were encouraged to solve their own problems and take responsibility for their actions.

These two different interpretations of the application of concepts of quality and quality management demonstrate the wide range of possible ways in which these principles can come to have an effect on educational practices. Quality management will require educators to reassess and reexamine their basic assumptions and practices. It is not easy to implement quality concepts and practices simply by adjusting or altering existing practices. In a quality system the efficacy of the processes is considered from the point of view of the customers served by the processes, in this case the student, parent, and community. The question asked is this: To what degree is the institution meeting the customer's definition of quality? The practices and structures of the school adjust to achieve the customers' specifications of quality. A little bit of change is not enough. Enid Brown, in an interview with Brandt (1992), emphasizes this point:

> A little bit of competition, "fairer" grading, a few customer surveys, and an Annual Quality Report are a violation of the Deming philosophy. As one of

my favorite tongue-twisters says, "A dab of Deming doesn't do it."

Transformation, as Dr. Deming describes it, is discontinuous. It means fundamental change. Transformation does not mean adapting here, fixing a little there. An individual or an organization must completely change its way of thinking. Education must be redesigned from the ground up, based on theory, profound knowledge. (p. 31)

This goal will be challenging in education where the customers have not been encouraged to become involved in specifying outcomes or levels of quality, and where students are workers as well as customers. Students, parents, and community also need to understand the concepts of quality for schools to employ these techniques to reshape current practices.

IMPLEMENTING THE VISION: OUTCOME-BASED EDUCATION

Outcome-based education can be viewed as a vehicle for systems-level change. If implemented successfully, it can lead to a reexamination and restructuring of all aspects of the school's instructional program. It has potential implications for all the dimensions of restructuring discussed in part 3. In this regard, OBE shares much with systems approaches, such as the concept of the learning organization (Senge 1990, Senge and Lannon-Kim 1991) and Total Quality Management (Deming 1986) strategies described previously. These approaches, along with OBE, involve applying systems thinking and concepts of quality to problems and improvement strategies, specifying desired outcomes, monitoring performance to determine progress toward goals, and modifying practices when goals are not being achieved.

Outcomes-based education was designed as the system-level application of mastery-learning concepts (Brandt 1992/1993). It was developed, at least in part, in reaction to research contained in documents such as the Coleman report that stated that students' socioeconomic backgrounds, rather than their experiences in schools, explained their subsequent achievement. This conclusion seemed counterintuitive to some researchers, who believed that if schools provided adequate time and proper instruction, all students could learn. Outcome-based education sought to turn time into a variable and make achievement a constant, rather than the reverse. One of the first school districts to move to this system—Johnson City, New York, in the early 1970s (Champlin 1991)—had schools define their outcomes first, then align their methods, organizational structure, and resource allocation in ways that enabled the outcomes to be achieved. The model relied on frequent measurement or assessment of student progress to determine success of both students and the educational system.

During the 1970s and into the 1980s, OBE tended to focus on students' achieving discrete cognitive tasks that could be measured by tests, most commonly criterion-referenced tests. This approach was frequently labeled *competency-based education*, and it continues to this day in some areas such as skill-based vocational training. OBE has evolved in the context of the restructuring movement into a vehicle for refocusing a school and school system on student learning and reshaping practices to achieve newly defined (or redefined) program outcomes: What will a student who leaves our program be able to *do*?

OBE has attracted the attention of a number of states that have committed to or are considering its adoption as the framework for the state's system of education. A framework of outcomes at the state level can create an environment in which local school districts are free to pursue the curriculum and instructional strategies they deem most effective to achieve the outcomes contained in the state framework. When utilized by a state in this fashion, it can serve as a vehicle both to promote local control and enhance accountability simultaneously.

PREMISES AND PRINCIPLES OF OBE

Spady (1988, 1992) identifies three basic premises and four key principles needed to create "success conditions" with OBE. The basic premises are that all students can learn, success breeds success, and schools control the conditions of success. The key principles consist of the following notions: (1) Ensure clarity of focus on outcomes of significance; (2) design down from ultimate outcomes; (3) emphasize high expectations for all to succeed; and (4) provide expanded opportunities and support for learning success.

Applying these principles, teachers clearly describe to students the outcomes they seek and the means by which success is to be demonstrated at the beginning of all courses. Students have a clear picture of where they are headed and are provided frequent feedback along the way. Teachers then employ a coaching approach, rather than simply "covering" the curriculum, to ensure that students have mastered content, concepts, and skills before moving on. Extra time and a variety of instructional approaches are the key.

Sometimes students continue to learn even after they have been tested on a concept: "Grade in pencil, not in ink." Second-chance instructional opportunities provide another avenue for student mastery of outcomes. Perhaps most important, teachers believe that all students can learn and demand that they meet high standards by means of quality work. Students are challenged and supported to achieve at higher levels through a system designed to demand success.

Nyland (1991) describes OBE as focusing on outcomes rather than inputs. He sees OBE as (1) a tool to make certain that what is known about effective instruction is applied, (2) a means to ensure that both adults and children accept responsibility for their own behavior, and (3) a way for teachers to share responsibility for student success. He divides the process into six steps: vision, knowledge, action, results, restructuring, and teams. Teaming is particularly important, since the major mission of the teacher teams is to ensure the success of students by shared planning, placement of students, and attention to discipline issues. Teachers also provide support to one another as they implement new instructional techniques and strategies designed to maximize student success.

Champlin's (1991) description of the Outcomes Driven Developmental Model of outcome-based education outlines some of the system-level changes that need to occur for this model to be implemented successfully. A district that adopts this model conforms to the following "essential components":

- Commits to best knowledge as the primary driving influence behind all decisions and actions.
- Specifies clear, observable, and measurable outcomes for every experience. These include exit learner behaviors, program outcomes, course outcomes, unit outcomes, and lesson outcomes.
- Accepts change as a normal part of living within a dynamic organization. All aspects of a school's operations are constantly reviewed and subject to change.
- Allows every member of the organization the opportunity to influence decision-making. Knowledge, rather than position, determines a person's ability to influence.
- Expects quality and excellence to be maintained at a high level, and not reduced.
- Puts in place a strenuous training and support system to assist each person to move successfully from theory to precise behaviors, skills, and attitudes necessary to make total success possible.
- Views the system in a holistic manner. Emphasizes the interconnected and interactive nature of the system; does not accept fragmentation.
- Creates an environment that satisfies needs. Each person is valued, nurtured, and given the opportunity to develop. (Adapted from Champlin 1991, p. 34)

These statements imply systems-level thinking and change in addition to specific modifications of programs and practices. Outcome-based education is not just another program; it is a new way of thinking about teaching, learning, and schooling. This point of view will be challenging for districts, particularly those that are accustomed to adopting the latest new program or approach piecemeal.

Fitzpatrick (1991) describes how one school district developed and implemented an outcome-based education approach. She describes system-level changes and demonstrates how they were translated into practice. Members of the district began by addressing three key questions: (1) Upon completion of their high school studies, what should our students know? (2) What should they be able to do? and (3) What should they feel or believe? Eleven outcome statements were developed to reflect the areas where students were to be required to demonstrate achievement. The curriculum-development process was then aligned with these eleven statements. Frameworks of learning and pathways students could follow were identified for various courses or groups of courses.

To facilitate program alignment, the district identified performance-based exit outcome indicators. These indicators provided regular information on student performance in each outcome area. Frequent formative assessment and opportunities for students to receive remediation or extra assistance when needed gave students more than one chance to succeed. Failure was a temporary setback. Grading shifted from time-based to outcome-based: A student does not necessarily receive a grade until a skill has been mastered. There remained no need to have student performance conform to a normal distribution. In fact, such a distribution became unacceptable.

Variations on the outcome-based model are appearing with ever-increasing frequency due in part to the fact that OBE is a systems approach to change. All elements of program and practice must be reviewed, reordered, and reinforced to ensure that desired outcomes are achieved. Measurement of success makes it possible to determine whether the system is meeting its goals and to identify areas in need of improvement or change.

THE CHALLENGE OF IMPLEMENTING OBE

Several challenges often surface when a decision is made to move to an outcome-based system. The idea seems so imminently sensible on its face that it can be difficult to discern problems with it, which can lead to a great deal of initial interest and appeal. However, like many other educational innovations, it can be adopted without any real change occurring in schooling. It is possible to take existing course requirements and objectives, change their names to "outcomes," and continue with essentially the same system that existed previously. Now instead of saying that students have failed a class, the teachers says that they have not yet mastered all the outcomes. The distinction is only semantic if the system has not been altered to ensure that greater student success results.

One problem is that outcome-based education is an idea that has been around for some time, and it has evolved during that time as more experience was gained with the model. Many people still associate outcome-based education with the competency-based movement of the late seventies, when in fact that is only one manifestation of the concept. In many school systems where competency-based learning was popular in the late seventies and early eighties, the distinction between competency-based and outcome-based education may be elusive.

Competency-based education represents what Spady (Brandt 1992/ 1993) describes as traditional outcomes-based education, or curriculum-based outcomes, a system that focuses on lower-level cognitive skills, uses unidimensional methods of assessment, teaches each competency in isolation, specifies the curriculum and teaching methods as well as the competencies, and does not examine seriously what is being taught before competencies are identified.

Outcome-based education, on the other hand, can be differentiated from competency-based education by (1) its inclusion of both lower- and higher-level cognitive tasks, (2) its use of broad outcomes as the framework within which teachers construct meaningful learning experiences that lead to mastery of outcomes, (3) its emphasis on mastery as demonstrated through integrated tasks or application of skills to real-world problems and settings through multidimensional methods of assessment, (4) the requirement that the content of the curriculum be questioned and examined before constructing outcomes, and (5) the necessity that subject areas and cognitive skills overlap and that instruction and assessment be integrated.

Outcome-based education, then, exists along a continuum of sorts, and Spady (1992) makes an important, perhaps critical, distinction among three possible levels of OBE—*traditional, transitional,* and *transformational*:

- *Traditional OBE* means that *existing curriculum content*, frameworks, and programs are taken as givens and are used to frame and define outcomes. Outcomes are defined from and for the curriculum, rather than the curriculum being "based on" intended outcomes and framed around broader competencies and orientations....

- *Transitional OBE* means that a vehicle exists for separating curriculum content from intended outcomes and for placing primacy on the latter. In this approach, Exit Outcomes clearly exist and are usually defined as broad, often *higher-order competencies and orientations* that cut across or exist independently of specific subject matter content and programs. These broad competencies are almost always content neutral, penetrate down to at least the course level, and often link various kinds of subject matter and concepts together in interdisciplinary curriculum and assessment designs. Content simply becomes a vehicle through which they are developed and demonstrated.

- *Transformational OBE* means that curriculum content is no longer the grounding and defining element of outcomes. Instead, outcomes are seen as *culminating Exit role performances* that include sometimes complex arrays of knowledge, competencies, and orientations and require learning demonstrations in varying role contexts.... The bottom line of Transformational OBE is that students' learning is manifested through their ability to carry out performance roles in contexts that at least simulate life situations and challenges. (p. 54, emphasis in original)

Districts about to embark on a program of outcome-based education will benefit greatly by deciding which of these three levels represents their conception of outcome-based education, and designing their process and system accordingly.

Outcome-based education can be troubled by problems that arise when attempts are made to strike a balance between the content and the processes of learning. On the one hand, how much specific information should students be expected to know? On the other hand, what general intellectual processes should they show they have mastered, regardless of the specific content knowledge they retain? The argument for traditional outcome-based (or competency-based) education was that it ensured mastery of very specific content. The argument for transformational outcomes is that specific content is only marginally relevant, that it is merely a means to an end, that students can demonstrate mastery through many different types of content knowledge, and that student learning skills and attitudes are more important.

This distinction between and relative importance of content and process are likely to engage teachers, parents, and community members in lively discussion, particularly in those places where schools adopt the transformational model and assume that "curriculum content is no longer the grounding and defining element" (Spady 1992) of the instructional program. Many people, educators and noneducators alike, become nervous when reformers begin to talk of abandoning content-knowledge measures.

While the appeal of transformational outcomes may be great to those who are believers in educational restructuring, there is often a gap in thinking between the group that formulates such outcomes and the rest of the teaching and administrative staff in the district. For a school system to refocus itself around transformational outcomes requires changes in nearly every element of its structure and culture. The creation of high level, integrated exit outcomes is only the beginning of a long and complex process. Those who engage in the creation of such outcomes should be aware of the challenges that a school district faces attempting to redesign itself around outcomes. While the development of such statements is an important activity, it is only the first, very small step in an extremely complex process.

If school districts are not cognizant of the path down which they are heading when they commit to transformational outcomes, it seems likely that they will not proceed much past the creation of a piece of paper with idealistic statements to which few can object. Little progress toward achievement of these outcomes is likely to be made.

Outcome-based education may become caught on the horns of its two extremes—specific low-level knowledge measures and overarching content-free statements—and become bogged down as the advocates of each extreme defend their positions zealously. Educators may want to give serious thought to the transitional approach and its relative merits before making any final decisions on a movement to outcomes-based education. The transitional model may appear less appealing to the more visionary, but it offers some advantages over the transformational approach for many schools.

The transitional approach allows faculty to become familiar with the concepts and key principles of outcome-based education. It permits teachers to retain their disciplinary backgrounds as a framework within which they might consider more integrated learning experiences, and it allows schools to communicate with parents in ways that may still be somewhat familiar. Critics point out that the transitional approach can leave traditional departmental structures in place, which may lead to sabotage of the approach. This is a valid concern. However, the key to implementation lies in extensive staff development, careful coaching, and a conscious commitment to integrate content and to use student performance of meaningful, complex tasks as the measure of mastery. If these supporting factors are attended to, the probability that teachers might begin to venture out from the safety of their academic disciplines (or their conceptions of the structure of knowledge) will be greatly increased. This natural process of increasing interdependence and collaboration sets the stage for the consideration of more transformational outcomes. In fact, they may develop more or less naturally as teachers reconsider the role of content knowledge in their conception of the goals of instruction.

Outcome-based education holds great promise as a tool to rethink roles, relationships, and practices in public schools. It challenges so many deeply held assumptions all at once that it is likely to be rejected initially or implemented only at a superficial level in many places. This may lead to the conclusion that it is another fad. Whether outcome-based education in its current form is implemented or not, it does seem likely that schools will be asked over time to judge their success not on the educational processes they conduct, but on the ability of their students to utilize their learning in meaningful ways. In this sense, the concept of outcome-based education is likely to remain for some time, regardless of the fate of the current OBE movement.

Outcome-based education, like Total Quality Management and systems thinking, requires a reconceptualization of the organization at a fundamental level. All three present exciting ways to move schools from classic bureaucratic structures to more dynamic, adaptable forms that are much more capable of meeting the needs of the wide range of students who are the clients of public schools. All three can be applied (or misapplied) at a superficial level at which little occurs other than the adoption of new vocabulary. Will educators be able to capture and adapt these ways of thinking about organizations to the unique conditions and structures of schools? Will there be adequate support from forces outside schools to allow this type of change to occur? There are no simple answers. These methods do represent ways by which schools can approach fundamental change in a systematic way, however challenging.

The next section turns from a general discussion of next steps to a specific analysis of the conditions present in and strategies employed by a group of schools that were provided resources to engage in extensive school improvement and restructuring activities. Key conditions that can help further the process of restructuring are identified. These conditions were observed to have been present in schools that have enjoyed success initiating and sustaining significant change. The experiences of these schools provide insight into how system-level conditions can be arranged to support school-site restructuring and how schools can exploit such conditions.

LESSONS FROM OREGON'S '2020' SCHOOLS

Goldman, Dunlap, and Conley (1991, 1993) studied selected schools that appeared to be restructuring with some success. These schools were all participants in a state-sponsored competitive grant process—known as the "2020 program"—that awarded funds for school improvement. The study identified four key conditions within the program that supported successful school-site restructuring. In these schools staff were found to be ready, the principal was supportive, some sort of common "vision" was shared, and the "system" did not get in the way.

These schools were adaptive. They were experimental. Their directions may have originally been rooted in someone else's "master plan" for reform, but they were modified again and again to meet the needs of the specific site. These school people were quite free to determine their own directions as events unfolded. They were able to develop and implement *nonstandardized solutions* to school reform.

The Oregon Legislature empowered teachers by requiring that they both write the 2020 grant proposals and administer the subsequently approved projects. These constraints encouraged the creation of an environment in which teachers and administrators could develop the skills and behaviors necessary to share decision-making responsibilities. The projects provided school staffs with real reasons to solve problems, seek consensus, and communicate.

There is clear evidence that these schools were actively involved in decision-making around the central variables of restructuring (learner outcomes, curriculum, instruction, and assessment) and that this involvement was integrally related to the success of the projects they undertook (D. Conley, March 1991). Principals and teachers in the 2020 schools appear to have developed the capacity for—and expectation of—central involvement in determining the goals and conditions of their work.

The collaborative site vision-building process forced teachers and principals to spend time sharing ideas and talking to one another about school goals. The discussion of common goals provided guidelines for decision-making that were legitimate in educators' minds and that apparently allowed principals to feel more comfortable about ceding some of their traditional areas of authority to teachers.

Facilitative leadership, especially by the principal, made significant contributions to the changes that emerged in the 2020 schools. Facilitative leadership was important because people—not reforms, not regulations, not rules—were key to achieving significant change in these schools. In these successful projects, educators shared power in ways that made greater sense to them. They operated outside the structure of traditional hierarchical power relationships.

This study also hinted that state legislatures, or even individual school districts, may be successful using small amounts of money on a competitive basis continually to encourage innovation and experimentation, a sort of ongoing "Hawthorne effect" to help support risk-taking and experimentation in schools. At the same time, unless careful attention is paid to creating the proper conditions, legislative support for site-based reform can as easily lead to doing nothing, or worse, as it can to opening the way to successful local adaptation.

This description of the 2020 schools helps integrate some of the themes presented through part 4. Issues of leadership, vision, culture, and system were addressed in these schools in ways that allowed them to change rather rapidly and successfully. This provides a glimpse at some of the conditions that need to be in place to enhance the success of schools that choose to take the "next step" on the road to restructuring.

One of the primary uses of the funds provided to these schools was to buy time. Teachers and administrators at these schools consistently described the availability of time as one of the key factors that supported their ability to restructure. The next section discusses this critical factor in more detail.

FINDING THE TIME TO RESTRUCTURE

No discussion of how to move toward restructuring would be complete without reference to the need for additional amounts of time for planning, interaction, and discussion to create vision, generation of new learning structures, and development of new instructional skills through staff training. Adequate time must be found to allow teachers to develop vision, modify and implement programs that spring from vision, and create the collegiality that is so vital for restructuring to succeed.

Since restructuring as defined in this book means *fundamental* changes in *assumptions*, *practices,* and *relationships*, it is clear that for most people this means they will need considerable time and support to examine their assumptions, change their practices, and rethink their relationships. Almost no program of restructuring allots adequate amounts of time to the examination of deeply held, unquestioned beliefs, to the painstaking development of new teaching skills and materials, and to the creation of new networks and interaction patterns necessary to support the kinds of changes in veteran professionals that are desired.

SOME COMMONLY EMPLOYED STRATEGIES TO GET MORE TIME

Some districts and schools have attempted to create additional time through a variety of strategies. Most common is the lengthening of the school day by five to ten minutes on four days to allow for early release of students on one day. This additional twenty to forty minutes can then be used by teachers to plan. As meager an amount of time as this may seem, even an arrangement such as this can help overburdened teachers find time on a regular basis to do the foundation and detail work needed to make restructuring occur.

Other schools start later in the day. One middle school begins its classes at 9:00 to allow teachers time to meet and plan each morning before school.

Block scheduling, discussed earlier, provides teachers with ninety minutes of planning time daily. The four-period day employed with block schedules means that each teacher has preparation time either first thing in the morning, the last period of the day, or on either side of a fifty-minute lunch period. The proximity to these additional periods of unscheduled time has the effect in practice of expanding the functional length of these ninety-minute preparation periods. In addition, during each period of the four-period day, one-fourth of the faculty are available to meet together. Careful and thoughtful assignment of prep periods can allow groups of teachers to meet together regularly throughout the year.

Innovative scheduling has helped some schools to create common prep periods or even to double prep periods for teachers involved in restructuring projects. In schools where schedules are freed from traditional five-day per-week class meetings, it would be possible to combine all of a teacher's prep time into one morning (or afternoon), allowing three to four hours of uninterrupted work time. Granted, it would require the teacher to rethink how this time would be used (if it became a time for marathon grading of papers, little would have been accomplished). Nevertheless, such innovative approaches offer possibilities to reclaim time that already exists in the day.

Schools where team teaching is possible and where project-centered or community-based learning is practiced offer other possibilities. When teachers are truly collaborative, they can reallocate students to free a few members of the faculty to plan. Similarly, when students are on a trip or working on a project in a structured way, parent volunteers can often help while one or more teachers are given time to work on restructuring-related activities.

Summer represents a tremendous, though problematic, opportunity. When people apply the metaphor of "rebuilding the airplane in flight" to describe school restructuring activities, they overlook the fact that the airplane is actually grounded three consecutive months out of each year. This is time when it is possible to accomplish a great deal. There are deep-seated objections to mandating all teachers to remain on campus in the summer. However, other creative strategies can be employed.

Many states require recertification credit for teachers, and most districts provide salary increases to teachers as they acquire more college credits. During any given summer many faculty members are taking classes, but their individual efforts may or may not be helping the school achieve its restructuring goals. The simple act of organizing a class that specifically addresses a school's restructuring needs can be an inexpensive technique for creating more common planning time during the summer. Attendance at summer conferences by teams of faculty members offers another low-cost, highly effective vehicle for moving restructuring forward.

Summer-school programs might offer another possibility. Such programs can be self-sufficient (or close to it) and can serve as "research and development labs" where new teaching techniques, organizational structures, assessment techniques, or uses of technology can be practiced and studied. Rather than repeating Intro to Math, these programs can be designed to attract a wide range of students, including the talented and gifted. They can be based on the fact that they are interesting and motivating to students, not that they simply offer remedial courses. Many communities have parents, children, and other governmental agencies that would be interested in such an option being available.

Many schools run into a different sort of problem when they attempt to achieve change by releasing teachers from their classes during the school year. So many teachers are out of their classrooms working on projects or visiting other sites that it seems the school is being run by substitutes. This creates anxiety for teachers and occasionally resentment by students and parents. When such a contingency can be anticipated, schools can recruit and train a group of substitutes, bringing them in (with pay) to attend beginning-of-the-year meetings where the school program is explained, having them meet students and become acquainted with the curriculum and school program, and even attending back-to-school nights so that parents become familiar with them. While there is some cost to training and preparing a team of substitutes in this fashion, the results generally outweigh the expense.

EARLY RELEASE DAYS

Early release days are common (and sometimes controversial) strategies for gaining more time for restructuring. Boards of education and parents may tend to look on such days with suspicion, assuming they are "working vacations" for staff. Several strategies help reduce this reaction. First, identify these days as far ahead as is practical and publish them frequently. Ideally, dates should be identified before school starts and reminders sent home regularly. Second, publicize and explain to parents and board members the topics and activities that form the focus for each release day. At the same time, demonstrate the linkage of these activities to school and district goals, along with their linkage to improved practice as demonstrated by research.

Third, invite parents and encourage them to attend these sessions. It takes only a few parents saying that such sessions are worthwhile to quiet the criticism of many. Fourth, keep staff on school grounds during school hours. Some teachers may find this suggestion offensive. However, nothing will cause more problems in many communities than to have several teachers seen going out to lunch on an early release day, regardless of how justifiable it is from the educators' perspective.

Fifth, make provisions for child care and activities for those families who legitimately cannot find someone to watch their children. Normally community volunteers and perhaps one or more substitute teachers who are properly certified can provide coverage in the library, gym, or other areas of the school where structured activities can be organized. With just a bit of planning, teachers can build these activities into their curriculums in a way that kids have meaningful things to do on these days.

Sixth, make arrangements with community agencies to have things to do for those kids who will leave school. Swimming pools, libraries, recreation centers, private child care providers, and anyone else offering services to children should know when you are having early release days. Many may plan special activities for students from your school, and some may even provide transportation.

Seventh, build tasks into the curriculum that students can do on release days. Various types of project-centered learning meet this criterion. Community-based internships and various service learning programs offer chances for students to be occupied productively during early release days.

Will these arrangements completely eliminate community resistance to early release days? Probably not, particularly if the school's restructuring program is not well known in the community. However, if these suggestions are followed and if energy is put into informing the community of both the need to change schools and the careful, thoughtful plan the school is following to accomplish this change and improve their children's education, such reactions can be kept to an absolute minimum. At the same time, teachers often feel less guilty about their decreased contact with students if it can be shown that the time faculty spends working on restructuring is not "wasted" by students.

TIME IN ASIAN SCHOOLS

When we compare our practices with those of other nations, our fundamental assumptions often become clearer. One common assumption of American educators is that class size should be kept as small as possible by having as many adults as possible engaged with children at any given moment. Another is that behavior management becomes more difficult as the number of students increases. Still another is that teacher planning is essentially a solitary activity.

Planning, or "prep" time, for all teachers has only been added during the past twenty to thirty years in most schools, and it is generally allocated daily in small blocks, perhaps thirty to forty-five minutes. This fragmented approach to planning all but guarantees that teachers are unable to use this time to do much other than grade papers and prepare the next lesson.

When practices in Asian schools are examined, it becomes clear that there are ways to gain large amounts of time, particularly if some of the assumptions cited above are challenged. Stevenson and Stigler (1992) describe a discussion they had with teachers in Beijing regarding teachers' workday issues:

> When we informed the Chinese teachers that American elementary school teachers are responsible for their classes all day long, with only an hour or less outside the classroom each day, they looked incredulous. How could any teacher be expected to do a good job when there is no time outside of class to prepare and correct lessons, work with individual children, consult with other teachers, and attend to all the matters that arise in a typical day at school! Beijing teachers teach no more than three hours a day, unless the teacher is a homeroom teacher, in which case the total is four hours. During the first three grades the teaching assignment includes both reading and mathematics; for the upper three grades of elementary school, teachers specialize in one of these subjects. They spend the rest of their day at school carrying out all their other responsibilities to their students and to the school. The situation is similar in Japan. According to our estimate, Japanese elementary school teachers are in charge of classes only 60 percent of the time they are at school. In fact, Japanese law limits the amount of time a teacher may spend in front of a classroom to twenty-three hours for a six-day week—no more than four hours a day.
>
> Large amounts of nonteaching time at school are available to Asian teachers for two reasons. The first is the larger class size. By having more students in each class but the same number of teachers in the school, all teachers can have a lower teaching load.... Although class sizes are large, the overall ratio of students to teachers within a school does not differ greatly from that in the United States.

The second factor increasing the time available to Japanese and Chinese teachers is the greater number of hours they spend at school each day. Teachers in Sendai, Beijing, and Taipei spent an average of 9.5, 9.7, and 9.1 hours per day, respectively, compared to only 7.3 hours for the American teachers. Asian teachers arrive at school early and stay late, which gives them time to meet together and to work with children who need extra help. Most American teachers, in contrast, arrive at school shortly before classes begin and leave not long after they end. This does not necessarily result in a shorter work week for American teachers. What it does mean is that they must devote their evenings and weekends to schoolwork. (pp. 163-64)

I expect that most American teachers would object to adopting the Asian model, but not necessarily because they would not want to spend more hours at school. American teachers, by and large, are competent and hard-working. But many *would* find it hard to let go of the notion that the best, perhaps only, solution to all educational problems is smaller class size. Teachers and parents tend to accept as dogma that smaller is better. Getting them to question this assumption and to explore alternative organizational and grouping arrangements will be quite difficult in many cases.

Part of the challenge is to get away from thinking in terms simply of smaller versus larger classes. Alternative instructional arrangements are possible, as was suggested in previous chapters. For example, children can take more responsibility for themselves and for other children. Other strategies allow different types of adults to work with groups of children in varying capacities, instead of all interaction being controlled by certified teachers.

NOTE TO SCHOOL LEADERS

This chapter has suggested some of the ways by which schools can begin to move toward fundamental change through reconceptualizing their philosophy, beliefs, goals, organization, and practices. The models and ideas presented serve to suggest possibilities and challenges. Restructuring ultimately is system-level change, and this type of change is very difficult for people who lack the conviction that it is necessary. Few people are willing to disrupt their lives without a good reason.

Up to this point in part 4, I have sought to explore the means by which school leaders can create and manage support for fundamental change based on participation by all involved. The means and methods described have in common the notion that those affected by change are unlikely to cooperate if their needs are not addressed, their perceptions not understood and acknowledged, and the means not provided to allow them to understand the big picture of educational restructuring.

Educational leaders will do best if they understand their organization well, know how to have an effect on both the macro and micro level, get broad-scale participation and ownership in change, be patient and develop readiness, utilize vision as a tool to unify effort and provide meaning, and encourage all involved to help solve problems by thinking about what they do in relation to the organization as a whole. As I have emphasized throughout, there is no one right sequence or set of activities one follows to bring about systems-level change.

The next chapter looks at restructuring from a holistic perspective. I attempt to identify contradictions present in attempts to restructure, and then I present an overview of how the various pieces of restructuring may begin to fit together.

CHAPTER 26

EMERGING VISIONS OF SCHOOL RESTRUCTURING

I n this concluding chapter, I examine some of the strands or themes of restructuring that have been visited in the previous chapters. I begin with a discussion of the contradictions present in restructuring—the opposing forces that may foster a sense of indecision or uncertainty by those who are deciding whether to embark on restructuring. These forces may also complicate the process for educators who are already actively involved in restructuring.

Following these points, attention turns to visions of restructuring that are beginning to emerge. In summary fashion, I weave the various trends and strategies that have been described throughout the book into one narrative that suggests how these pieces begin to fit together. Finally, I consider the extent to which restructuring is actually occurring in schools and school districts and reflect on the challenge posed by this level of change.

CONTRADICTIONS OF RESTRUCTURING

One of the reasons schools may have a difficult time responding to calls for fundamental change is that there are many contradictions present within the current pressures to restructure education. The following paragraphs identify and briefly discuss these contradictions. While not all these apparent contradictions may turn out to constrain restructuring, they represent a series of issues that must be confronted and resolved for the change process to move forward in many schools. They also challenge policy-makers, who need to take into account these contradictions when they develop and enact new rules and procedures that they expect schools to follow.

CONSTRUCTIVISM VS. OUTCOMES

Constructivist notions put control of learning in the hands of learners, who are invited to participate in the creation of their own personal interpretations and meaning of material. An outcome-based system expects all learners to demonstrate proficiency in certain agreed-upon areas. This contradiction becomes more apparent as children move from primary schools, where developmentally appropriate practice focuses on the learner quite naturally, to secondary educational environments, where expectations for mastery are clearly defined.

These two forces can be reconciled, but doing so will require thoughtful systems design and a commitment to allowing students to demonstrate proficiency in a wide variety of ways. It will also require integration and definition of the purposes of all levels of schooling.

NEW VISIONS OF EDUCATION VS. PROJECT PROLIFERATION

Through their attempts to develop new, comprehensive visions of education, educators are struggling to escape from the current paradigms and assumptions surrounding schooling. At the same time, however, they often initiate numerous projects before a vision is present or accepted. The result is that restructuring becomes defined as a particular project (a new schedule or curriculum or grouping strategy), rather than as a broader vision for learning within which many different projects or approaches may proliferate.

Allowing a number of projects to be developed simultaneously may be necessary in some cases to move the vision of the whole school along. Even the most frenetic attempts to jump start a vision via project development may fail, however. Many members of the school community (especially parents, students, and most teachers) may not perceive how the various pieces of the vision embodied in the projects fit together to form a new vision of education, nor how they may contribute to such a vision.

FOCUS ON ADULTS VS. FOCUS ON THE CHILD

Restructuring activities seem to divide into those that focus on the needs of adults versus those that focus on the needs of the child. This may seem an unfair distinction, and yet many of the new governance models being attempted that consume so much time and energy seem to relate only tangentially to the needs of children. This is not to say that such changes cannot or will not eventually benefit children. In the beginning at least, they are not focused primarily on the needs of children in most cases. Alternatively, many other activities or suggested changes connect directly with the evolving needs of children. It will be important to try to identify the places where the needs of adults and those of children overlap, or to create means to enhance such overlap, so that the results of restructuring are seen to benefit both.

INCREASED PROFESSIONALISM VS. INCREASED COMMUNITY INVOLVEMENT

The skill level and responsibilities of teachers will be altered radically if many of the changes in curriculum, instruction, assessment, learning environment, and teacher leadership come to pass. Teachers will have much more responsibilty to design curriculum, utilize a range of instructional techniques, assess student performance to provide feedback and reach important judgments, and employ a variety of grouping strategies. These responsibilities imply a higher level of professionalism among teachers. One of the key elements in the definition of a professional is the principle that a professional has wide discretion to make decisions and apply professional knowledge to solve problems.

The growth in teachers' professionalism may conflict with a countertrend to involve parents and the community to a greater degree in the governance of schools. Community members may feel they need to prescribe educational practice or set goals in ways that conflict with this increased professional latitude of teachers. As with other contradictions discussed previously, this is not automatically a problem if the roles of each are specified carefully and accepted by all, but the potential for misunderstanding seems great.

STABLE/DECLINING RESOURCE BASE VS. RADICALLY INCREASED EXPECTATIONS FOR STUDENT ACHIEVEMENT

The decade of the nineties is shaping up to be one where society comes to look upon schools as key in the struggle for economic competitiveness. Expectations that all students must reach a high level of intellectual functioning are becoming more pervasive. Schools are seen as the only opportunity for many to develop the new, higher skill levels necessary to participate in the work force. These ever-increasing expectations and demands for a highly educated citizenry are being promoted in the same forums where the need for fiscal frugality is also being urged. Often it is the same people who are demanding both simultaneously.

Satisfying higher expectations under these conditions is a new challenge for public schools, which are accustomed to addressing problems only when additional resources are provided to do so. This contradiction may prove to be profoundly troubling to educators, particularly

principals and teachers, the "front-line" workers, who will find it difficult or impossible to conceive of how to address problems in the absence
of significant infusions of new resources. The ability to think "outside of
the box," to conceptualize new ways to organize or reallocate resources,
is likely to be an important skill for the decade.

EMPOWERMENT VS. ACCOUNTABILITY

Two of the significant trends of school reform, decentralized decision-making and increased demands for accountability, appear to be on
a collision course. In many states and districts, schools will be empowered to make more decisions locally through school-site councils or
other vehicles. At the same time, national and state trends reflect a
continuing desire to hold schools more accountable for performance. It
will not be impossible to devise accountability systems that provide
wide latitude for local decisions, but it will be difficult; it will require
thoughtfulness, attention to details, and abandonment of the notion that
there is one right way by which to measure or judge school success.
Policy-makers do not have a very good track record of attending to such
subtleties.

Local councils are unlikely to prosper or survive if they cannot
make decisions that have substantial impact. However, will they be
willing to take responsibility in proportion to the authority they receive?
What will happen when a school fails to improve? Will the council or
the principal be held accountable? This relationship between site-level
decision-making and system-level accountability promises to provide a
source of tension for some time to come.

BUREAUCRACY VS. COMMUNITY

Most schools currently resemble bureaucratic organizations rather
than communities. In fact, much of the legislation and many of the
policies that have been put in place during the past seventy-five years
have been for the purpose of building bureaucratic safeguards into
schools, to remove them from the political arena. These safeguards have
worked well, for the most part, to provide schools some insulation from
their immediate communities.

Schools are now being challenged to function as true communities
for students (and parents) who may have no real sense of community in
their lives. They are asked to function as islands, or havens, within
neighborhoods, rich and poor, that have few of the characteristics of true

communities. Schools are expected to create environments where everyone shares some level of belief in and commitment to a vision of education that is focused on validating and developing each child as a valued individual, on creating opportunities for individuals to affiliate with the school as a community, and on enhancing the self-image and self-esteem of all members of that community.

A natural tension exists between the aspiration toward community and the rules and regulations designed to ensure protection for those who occupy roles within the system. Bureaucracies demand that all members follow the rules and procedures of the organization; they have difficulty creating a sense of community and belonging for all. This inherent tension between rule-based organizations that provide guarantees and protections for the adults and communities that meet the unique needs of their members may prove difficult to resolve.

NATIONAL/STATE/BUSINESS CONSTITUENCY FOR RESTRUCTURING VS. NO LOCAL CONSTITUENCY

The call for radical restructuring of schools can be found in magazines, on television, in national reports, at state and national legislative hearings, in corporate board rooms, and at meetings of business leaders and policy-makers. It is almost a given among these groups that the only way to revive public education is through massive, perhaps traumatic, change. Somehow the message does not seem to have been received, or perhaps believed, at the local level. While there is increasing evidence that more community members and parents are vaguely uneasy about the quality of education in their schools and that some sort of change is needed, this feeling has not crystallized into wide-scale demand for educational restructuring. In the average classroom, there is even less of a sense of urgency for change.

This contradiction between highly visible activity at state and national levels and little active connection to the local level is analogous to a storm on a lake, where the winds whip the surface waters into waves and whitecaps, but all remains calm several feet beneath the surface. If you are a passenger in a boat, your perspective on events is fundamentally different than if you are a fish in the water. Grassroots consensus for change in social institutions takes a long time to develop. Consequently, the coexistence of intense action at policy levels and little action at local levels may be a necessary phase from which emerges agreement on new goals and methods for education.

OLD MODELS FROM THE PRIVATE SECTOR VS. NEW MODELS FROM THE PRIVATE SECTOR

Many private-sector organizations that operate under the principles and techniques of scientific management, or Taylorism, are seeking to abandon them rapidly and replace them with management philosophies and practices based on worker involvement, commitment to quality, and maximum organizational flexibility and adaptability. Schools were strongly encouraged (or compelled) to adopt scientific management shortly after the turn of the century, when such practices were in vogue in the private sector.

Educators find themselves in a similar situation again. They are being asked to abandon the old practices of the private sector and to adopt the new practices of the private sector. Strategic planning and Total Quality Management are only two examples of this trend. The challenge for educators is to determine which practices from the private sector are in actuality techniques that have application to all organizations, and then to adapt and modify these techniques to the specific needs and unique structures of educational institutions.

EMERGING VISIONS OF EDUCATIONAL RESTRUCTURING

In the previous chapters of this book, I have attempted to summarize the complex, multidimensional process of educational restructuring. I have obtained most of my information from the writings of other scholars and from a few, selected school sites or districts that are investigating these issues and attempting to implement responses that translate them into practice. From these descriptions, visions of educational restructuring begin to emerge. They are more a collection of ideas than realities, more a consideration of what is possible than what may in all cases be practical; they are tested and proved in some cases, but not in others. I have intended them to be used not as a blueprint for action, but as sketches of alternatives.

Educators live in a world where possibilities are limited (or they certainly feel like they are a great deal of the time). These emerging visions of educational restructuring serve to suggest some of those possibilities that are often difficult to discern, particularly when engaged in the day-to-day functioning of the school.

It is important to restate that there is no single model of restructuring. By its very nature, and by definition, the process is adaptable to individual school sites. Indeed, one of the goals of restructuring is to create learning environments that are "closer to the customer" and, therefore, adapted to the unique needs of the student population served. The emerging trends described here merely suggest the broad outlines, the general parameters, within which the discussion of educational restructuring seems to be taking place.

Some might argue that what is being described as a vision of restructuring is not occurring anywhere in the country in an integrated fashion. While this may be true, there appears to be value in offering a "snapshot" of the current state of thinking on the topic as a tool to enable educators and community members to identify a different frame of reference within which to consider the methods and goals of schooling.

With these points in mind, I offer the following summary of emerging visions of educational restructuring. The following statements illustrate the types of thinking and action regarding a wide variety of educational concepts, topics, and practices that are occurring in many places throughout the nation. For consistency, all these descriptions are presented in the future tense, though some of the visions are already becoming reality in a few schools.*

The purposes and goals of education will be questioned. Schools will ask the questions: What is an educated person? What will our graduates look like and be able to do upon completion of their education in our schools? Outcomes and standards will be developed to provide a framework within which a variety of instructional techniques can be utilized and curricular material can be explored to help all students achieve mastery. Outcomes will move the focus from knowledge of content for its own sake to integration and application of facts and concepts to solve problems or create personal meaning.

Distinctions between subject areas in the curriculum will be reexamined at all levels. Curriculum will be redesigned so that learners can be actively involved in constructing their own meaning, rather than having the structure determined solely by the teacher (or the textbook publishing company). The content that is taught will be scrutinized as well. Is it relevant, accurate, meaningful? Is there a compelling reason for children to know the material? What role should the text occupy in the curriculum? Must the material be organized in a hierarchical fashion in which fewer students master each succeeding level, or do more integrative structures allow all students to aspire to higher levels of mastery?

---

* Several of these visions were published previously in "Some Emerging Trends in School Restructuring," by David T. Conley, *ERIC Digest,* number 67, ERIC Clearinghouse on Educational Management, January 1992.

The world around the school will become a source for curriculum. Local issues, problems, and resources will be integrated into the instructional process. The curriculum in a mountain community in Colorado may look different from the curriculum in a rural school in Indiana, or an urban school in New York. Information from around the world, now available to teachers and students via technology, will serve as the framework within which distinctly local issues can be examined and assessed. This power to create curriculum will allow for the application of principles and content that were previously taught in isolation from the world in which the student lives.

The learner will move to the center of the instructional process, not in the 1960s sense of indulging the student as individual, but as worker/client/customer/partner/participant. Students will be actively involved in constructing meaning, acknowledging the fact that they simply do not retain information nearly as well if they are not provided an opportunity to integrate and apply it in a personal way. Learning will not occur primarily in isolation from others; there will be many opportunities for social learning. Mastery can be demonstrated through application and exhibition of knowledge and skills acquired. A variety of teaching techniques will be necessary to design learning experiences that help learners create personal meaning.

Learning is expected to have utility. It may not necessarily lead directly to employment, but it has utility in the sense that it has some application, some use, some purpose. Often this will be accomplished by linking learning to the real world or by having significant learning occur outside the school.

The emphasis will be on success rather than sorting. It will not be acceptable for teachers to say, "I taught it; they had their chance to learn it—if they chose not to, that's their decision." Instructional methods will be adapted based on their actual success with children. Instructors will change to acknowledge the needs, capabilities, experiences, and unique challenges and motivations of the learner. This flexibility may lead to a substantial increase, not a decrease, in the amount of content that is taught in any given time to any given group of students.

Instruction will become more "personalized." Rather than having students simply progress through workbooks or texts at their own pace, as was the case in many individually guided education and mastery-learning programs of the late seventies and early eighties, the emphasis will be on the teacher's and students' jointly developing meaningful learning experiences. Learning in groups will become as common as learning individually. Students will set learning goals and be held accountable for them. They will learn by helping others, tutoring, providing advice, as well as by studying new material independently. Students will be actively involved in instructing one another. Learning will be personal, interactive, and developed in relation to goals; it will have utility and lead to demonstrable outcomes.

Assessment will be an integral part of the teaching/learning process, as opposed to evaluation, which stands apart from it. The purposes of assessment will be to provide more frequent feedback to students, helping them to continuously improve performance, rather than simply judging their performance at some arbitrary point. When assessing learning, educators will analyze larger and larger constellations of skills and abilities in an integrated fashion. This trend will parallel the evolution of curriculum and instructional techniques. The emphasis in assessment will be on the performance of the learner as an individual (or team member) in relation to certain predetermined standards, not necessarily in relation to the performance of other students.

If one student masters and can demonstrate certain skills, it will not be a problem that all other students can do so as well. In fact, it will be cause for celebration if all students can meet challenging performance standards. Assessment strategies that do not divide students into winners and losers will displace testing technologies such as standardized tests, which by definition must differentiate student performance so that no more than half the students taking the test are above average, no matter how high the performance in absolute terms.

The parameters of the learning environments will be redefined. All the structural boundaries of the current model will be challenged. In both elementary and secondary schools, students may stay with the same teacher or group of teachers for more than one year. Multiage groupings of varying combinations, in which learners can proceed at developmentally appropriate paces and can serve as tutors for one another, will proliferate. Tracking, in particular, will be replaced by the use of heterogeneous groups, cross-age grouping, peer tutors, and other strategies that permit a wider range of rates of learning on any given learning task. The idea that learning only occurs within four walls when twenty-five young people interact with one adult with a certificate will be replaced by models in which varying combinations of adults and children interact both within and outside the school building. Community-based learning, service learning, apprenticeships, and internships will all serve to enrich the educational options available to students.

Technology will emerge as a means to enhance the quality of the interaction between teacher and student, not as a substitute for it. In these emerging visions of education, technology will be an integral component. Its uses are still being explored. Technology may be used to provide basic skills, interface with vast information sources outside the school, enable students to develop their creativity, manage information about student performance and achievement, organize and assist teachers in their quest to serve as instructor and clerk simultaneously, and serve as a tool through which students gain greater control over their own learning.

School-community relations will be central to many new visions of education. Parents will be true partners. They will develop learning programs for students along with the teacher, participate in the classroom on a regular basis, make suggestions that will be heeded by the professionals, and take responsibility for creating an environment in the home that supports education.

The community at large will also play a new role in these emerging visions. Businesses and civic groups, local government, and social-service agencies will all have a vital role to play by offering services; coordinating their efforts with programs in the public schools; serving as volunteers and tutors; providing advice, expertise, and resources; serving as educational sites; helping teachers develop new skills and knowledge; and perceiving themselves as centrally involved in the education of the community's youth. All the services needed to help young people develop as healthy human beings will be coordinated and integrated into one site. Learning will occur in businesses and factories, offices and work sites. A much wider variety of apprenticeships and internships will be available.

Considerable experimentation will occur in the structural dimension of time. Blocks of time will be created to allow teachers to spend more time with fewer students so the teachers can facilitate more complex learning interactions. The driving force for reorganizing time will be the outcomes and the need to provide time for complex learning experiences where higher order thinking and holistic assessment can take place. The length of the school day and school year will be reexamined. Schools will extend their programs—beginning earlier in the day, continuing into the evening, meeting on Saturdays, offering more summer opportunities.

The time available for learning will vary so that achievement becomes the constant, and time the variable. The length of time each student spends in school will vary considerably based on need and interest. Extended school year programs will serve to provide more time for teachers to plan and develop new methods and materials, and to provide enriched learning experiences for selected students, not more of the same for everyone.

Decisions will be made democratically, with broad-based input. New governance structures will emerge to meet new needs; old ones will evolve to be congruent with new purposes and goals. The role of administrators will be to facilitate the development of vision and direction, to orchestrate the change process, to allocate resources in ways that help realize the vision, and to create new opportunities for teacher and community leadership to emerge. These administrators will see themselves not at the pinnacle of a pyramid, but as one node in a network that extends beyond the school itself and includes formal and informal decision-making structures. They will help direct the flow of energy throughout the network, rather than being the sole source of energy.

Choice will become a vehicle to stimulate the system to adapt and to respond to customer needs. It will serve to reinvigorate and infuse new ideas into the system. It will not be seen as the solution to all educational problems, but one strategy that, when applied thoughtfully, can yield positive results.

Teachers will serve in new decision-making roles and exert more control over the conditions of instruction in schools. They will occupy highly varied roles that are often adapted to the school and the unique strengths and interests present among faculty. These roles will allow for continuing career development while allowing teachers to remain in the classroom. The roles will stress collegiality and collaboration and cause schools to question norms of isolation for teachers. Teacher leaders will disseminate new ideas more rapidly and help create environments in which all teachers feel more safe and supported as they attempt to bring about fundamental changes in their practices.

Personnel structures will be adapted and redefined. The role of the instructional assistant or aide will be expanded or reconceptualized with an eye toward creating a new category of educator who is truly a paraprofessional, not an aide. These individuals will work with small groups, provide supplementary instruction, and supervise students, thereby allowing the teacher to devote more time and energy to executive-level tasks, such as planning and diagnosing, addressing the needs of particularly difficult or demanding students, communicating with parents, developing curriculum, and conducting and analyzing assessments. The roles of other specialized personnel, such as counselors, special education and Chapter 1 teachers, will be reexamined to determine how their efforts can best be integrated and coordinated with the work of the classroom teacher. Effective hiring and mentoring practices will ensure that newly hired staff are socialized into the culture of the school and district in a way that ensures they understand and support program vision and goals and are caring, competent educators.

Working relationships among educators will be based to a greater degree on trust and a commitment to solving problems in good faith, while the negotiated agreement will serve as a framework for these discussions. Waivers will be granted for individual school sites, and more problems will be addressed outside the contract and away from the bargaining table. While teachers' associations continue to be important, they will begin to function more as partners and operate more as a professional association than a trade union.

Rarely, if ever, will all these elements be present in a school's or district's vision of restructuring. Most applications of restructuring will encompass a subset or unique combination of these elements. Taken as a whole, the general description offered here provides a picture in broad brush strokes of the ways in which many educators, policy-makers, and others who think and write about the goals, structures, and methods of schooling are articulating their sense of how education might transform itself.

These trends suggest visions of education that echo the Progressive movement of the 1890s to 1930s in some respects, that build upon experiments in the late 1960s and early 1970s in other respects, and that have several unique qualities peculiar to the 1990s. Are they simply a rehashing of earlier reform movements? Yes, in the sense that there really is very little in education that has not been tried before. No, in the sense that many of these elements represent a refinement or reconceptualization of ideas tried earlier. However, the context in which they are being applied now is fundamentally different from that which existed the last time they were attempted. In that sense, reform is the process of matching the intervention with the needs of the system and society; some ideas that were very attractive to some people twenty, fifty, or one hundred years ago may simply not have been in synch with societal needs and values. The same strategy or philosophy reintroduced at a time when it meets a need in a new context of values and goals may suddenly be embraced rapidly and lead to success.

These visions can be interpreted as a statement of the potential for education to have increasing value and worth—to the entire community and the economic system. They tend to reflect the increased emphasis on each student as an individual. They build upon and assume teachers' increased knowledge, heightened professionalism, greater sophistication, and enhanced leadership skills. They acknowledge the need for new partnerships to emerge for education to succeed in a complex postindustrial, global society. And they suggest fundamental overhaul of curriculum, instruction, and assessment.

ARE THE VISIONS BEING IMPLEMENTED?

To what degree are these visions being actualized or implemented by educators? Preliminary evidence suggests that few schools have moved very far down the restructuring path on a broad scale, though many have developed programs or initiated projects. Lee and Smith (1992) found in a study of restructuring in 377 selected middle schools that fewer than 1 percent of the schools exhibited 13 or more of the 16 characteristics of restructuring identified by the researchers. The largest proportion of schools, 44.6 percent, had one to five restructuring characteristics. Having considered the Lee and Smith study and a study by Berends (1992), Prager (1992) concluded:

> This information indicates that, in spite of plentiful rhetoric and extensive initiatives by districts, states, and national organizations, the restructuring movement has yet to touch the mass of American schools in any significant way. Even in the most selective sample, less than half of those restructured schools are pursuing major elements of restructuring. In the larger sample, elements of restructuring are pursued much less frequently. In considering initiatives in the future, policymakers may want to consider why so few schools seem to have changed significantly in response to all the initiatives thus far. (p. 5)

It would be naive to suggest that educational restructuring will be easy to achieve, or even that it is a foregone conclusion, given the difficulty of fundamental change in education. Schools face great challenges simply confronting the existing images of education that are embedded within them. Barbara Benham Tye (1987) describes the paradoxical nature of American schooling: A decentralized national system of education with extensive local control results in schools that look remarkably similar, yet function in vastly different ways. Tye (1987) summarizes John Goodlad's Study of Schooling* in which she participated:

> Walk into a public high school in any of the 50 states, and you are likely to find yourself in familiar territory. You will not be surprised by the physical uniformity of classrooms; the overall control orientation of policy, program, and pedagogy; the general similarity of curriculum and of schedule; the reliance on test scores as measures of "success"; and the practice of tracking. I have come to think of these common characteristics of schooling as its "deep structure."
>
> Yet each school I studied as a part of the Goodlad team was also different from the others in dozens of big and little ways. The cumulative effect of these differences gave each school its particular "personality." Each of the 13 high schools was shaped by its own history, by the nature of the community of which it was a part, and by such internal factors as the quality of teacher/administrator relationships, the number and intensity of school problems, and the climate of most of its classrooms.

---

* See Goodlad (1984), B. Tye (1985), K. Tye (1985). Goodlad's findings have also been reported in numerous articles and technical reports.

This juxtaposition of concepts—the deep structure of schooling and the distinct personality of schools—can be used heuristically to think about the problems of change and resistance to change in our educational system. (p. 281)

By virtue of local control and decentralized decision-making, schools have the potential to adapt themselves to the needs of their local communities and student populations. Educators seem to operate, however, under self-imposed limitations regarding how they might best organize themselves to meet their clients' needs. Most tend to look backward and sideways, not forward, when seeking ideas and solutions. The challenge is for schools to be able to evolve by employing solutions from outside the routine and the familiar. Elmore (1991) examines the tendency of schools to adhere to a set of solutions to organizational problems that have become set in stone. He uses the analogy of the DNA molecule to suggest how ingrained and unquestioned certain thought-and-behavior patterns are:

Certain solutions—the age-grade structure, the allocation of single teachers to classroom units, the allocation of specific content to specific periods of time, etc.—have become "fixed" in the institutional structure of schools. They have become fixed, not necessarily because we know they "work," in some educational sense, although that may be true, but because they help us manage the organizational demands of mass education. For the most part, we adhere to these regularities of schooling because we have seemingly always adhered to them and they have come to be identified in the minds of students, teachers, and parents with what it means to "do school."

One way to think about these regularities of schooling is as a sort of genetic code for the organization of schools. The basic problems form a sort of template, just as the basic structure of the DNA molecule forms a template for the transmission of human characteristics. The particular set of solutions to these problems that we develop in a given school is like a genetic code for schooling, or the specific make-up of an individual DNA molecule....

... [T]he central problem of so-called "school restructuring" is how to make the genetic code of schools—the specific solutions to the problems posed by the regularities of schooling—more compatible with emerging conceptions of teaching and learning. (pp. 12-14)

The transformation, or restructuring, of public education in America is a task of Herculean proportions. Most schools have not acknowledged that there is a gap between their current organizational structure and instructional practices and the needs of society and of students. Given this apparent lack of any sense of urgency to change, it is difficult to discern how schools will transform themselves on the scale implied by restructuring. Education continues to receive mixed messages from policy-makers and community members regarding its legitimate role and goals. It is perhaps unfair, unreasonable, and unrealistic to ask educators to transform themselves in the absence of clear mandates and adequate support to do so. Very few examples can be found of organizations that change radically lacking some sort of external force or threat, generally combined with a clearly articulated internal mission and vision. Systems-level change is difficult and painful for most adults; educators are no exception.

Whether educators have the energy or interest needed to initiate and sustain restructuring remains to be seen. At present, policy-makers and the business community are continuing to press for substantive change and improvement in public education. If those outside education lose interest in educational change, this may be an ominous sign, for it may indicate that they have given up on public education as a key to economic and social survival. If policy-makers and key community leaders come to believe that the public education system is beyond repair, it will become increasingly difficult to obtain the resources, support, and involvement needed to reshape the school system.

The question may not be whether public education will change. It may be whether educators will remain in control of the process, and whether public education will continue to retain its legitimacy as the institution best equipped and positioned to socialize and educate the vast majority of young people. With this legitimacy comes the right to an exclusive claim on tax dollars. If educators are to change in the ways necessary for earnest, radical, and successful restructuring, it may be necessary for them, and especially teachers, to adopt a systems perspective, so that they can perceive their behaviors in a broader social-policy context.

Ultimately restructuring comes down to the behaviors of individual teachers and principals in particular educational settings. The success of restructuring depends on their willingness, along with the willingness of administrators, boards of education, state educational agencies, legislatures, the federal government, and especially community members, parents, and students, to accept changes in the "deep structure" of schooling and in the goals of public education. The act of listing all these constituencies starkly outlines the magnitude of the challenge. The reactions and behaviors of these constituencies over the next several years will determine the probable future of the emerging visions of educational restructuring presented here.

This book has attempted to outline a roadmap of restructuring. A roadmap presents possibilities, not inevitabilities. There are many ways to get "there" from "here." Public education may be at a crossroads, and the choices made or not made, the routes travelled or not travelled, in the next several years are likely to generate repercussions that will be felt for some time to come. It is my hope that educators and others interested in the future of public education study this roadmap carefully so that they can be assured that they have made a conscious decision of the road they wish to follow and the destination toward which they are headed.

BIBLIOGRAPHY

Many of the items in this bibliography are indexed in ERIC's monthly catalog *Resources in Education (RIE)*. Reports in *RIE* are indicated by an "ED" number. Journal articles, indexed in ERIC's companion catalog, *Current Index to Journals in Education,* are indicated by an "EJ" number.

Most items with an ED number are available from ERIC Document Reproduction Service (EDRS), 7420 Fullerton Rd., Suite 110, Springfield, VA 22153-2852.

To order from EDRS, specify the ED number, type of reproduction desired—microfiche (MF) or paper copy (PC), and number of copies. Add postage to the cost of all orders and include check or money order payable to EDRS. For credit card orders, call 1-800-443-3742.

Abernathy, Patricia, and Richard Serfass. "One District's Quality Improvement Story." *Educational Leadership* 50, 3 (November 1992): 14-17.

Acheson, Keith A., and Stuart C. Smith. *It Is Time for Principals to Share the Responsibility for Instructional Leadership with Others.* OSSC Bulletin. Eugene, Oregon: Oregon School Study Council, 1986. 30 pages. ED 267 510.

Adams County School District 14. *Graduation Requirements: Exit Outcomes.* September 16, 1991.

Akers, John. "Business Must Fill Educational Gap." *Computerworld* 24, 46 (November 12, 1990): 25.

Alameda Unified School District. "Graduate Profile." Unpublished document, 1992.

Alderman, M. Kay. "Motivation for At-Risk Students." *Educational Leadership* 48, 1 (September 1990): 27-30. EJ 413 159.

Alexander, K. L., and E. L. McDill. "Selection and Allocation Within Schools: Some Causes and Consequences of Curriculum Placement." *American Sociological Review* 41 (1976): 963-80.

American Association for the Advancement of Science. *Science for All Americans. A Project 2061 Report on Literacy Goals in Science, Mathematics, and Technology.* Washington D.C.: Author, 1989. 217 pages.

Amster, Jeanne, and others. *Investing in Our Future. The Imperatives of Education Reform and the Role of Business.* Queenstown, Maryland: Aspen Institute, 1990. 43 pages. ED 323 327.

Anastos, Joy, and Robert Ancowitz. "A Teacher-Directed Peer Coaching Project." *Educational Leadership* 45, 3 (November 1987): 40-42. EJ 367 356.

Anderson, James G. *Bureaucracy in Education.* Baltimore, Maryland: Johns Hopkins Press, 1968. 217 pages.

Anderson, R., and B. Pavan. *Nongradedness: Helping It to Happen.* Lancaster, Pennsylvania: Technomics, forthcoming.

Angus, L. "School Leadership and Educational Reform." Paper presented at the annual conference of the American Educational Research Association (New Orleans, Louisiana, April 1988).

Anrig, Gregory, and Archie E. Lapointe. "What We Know About What Students Don't Know." *Educational Leadership* 47, 3 (November 1989): 4-5, 7-9. EJ 398 941.

Applebee, Arthur; Judith Langer; and Ina Mullis. *Crossroads in American Education.* Princeton, New Jersey: National Assessment of Educational Progress and Educational Testing Service, 1989.

Associated Oregon Industries, and the National Association for Schools of Excellence. *Saving America's Children: Achieving International Standards in American Schools: A Blueprint for Change.* Portland, Oregon: MEDIAmerica, 1992.

Aurora Public Schools. *Pursing Our Commitment to Life-Long Learning.* Aurora, Colorado: Author, 1992.

Ayers, William. "Perestroika in Chicago's Schools." *Educational Leadership* 48, 8 (May 1991): 69-71. EJ 425 612.

Bacharach, Samuel, and Sharon Conley. "Uncertainty and Decisionmaking in Teaching: Implications for Managing Line Professionals." In *Schooling for Tomorrow: Directing Reform to Issues That Count,* edited by Thomas J. Sergiovanni and John H. Moore. Boston: Allyn and Bacon, 1989. 403 pages.

Bacharach, Samuel B., and Edward J. Lawler. *Power and Politics in Organizations: The Social Psychology of Conflict, Coalitions, and Bargaining.* San Francisco: Jossey-Bass, 1980. 249 pages.

Bacharach, Samuel B., and S. Mitchell. "The Generation of Practical Theory: Schools as Political Organizations." In *Handbook of Organizational Behavior,* edited by Jay W. Lorsch. Englewood Cliffs, New Jersey: Prentice-Hall, 1987. 430 pages.

Baird, L. "Big School, Small School: A Critical Examination of the Hypothesis." *Journal of Educational Psychology* 60 (1969): 253-60.

Baker, Stephen. "Mexico: A New Economic Era." *Business Week* 3187 (November 12, 1990): 102-06.

Ballinger, Charles. "Rethinking the School Calendar." *Educational Leadership* 45, 5 (February 1988): 57-61. EJ 368 830.

Barker, Roger Garlock, and Paul V. Gump. *Big School, Small School: High School Size and Student Behavior.* Stanford, California: Stanford University Press, 1964. 250 pages.

Barone, Thomas. "Assessment as Theater: Staging an Exposition." *Educational Leadership* 48, 5 (February 1991): 57-59. EJ 421 351.

Barr, Rebecca, and Robert Dreeben. "A Sociological Perspective on School Time." In *Perspectives on Instructional Time,* edited by Charles W. Fisher and David C. Berliner. New York: Longman, 1985. 357 pages.

Barr, Rebecca; Robert Dreeben; and Nonglak Wiratchai. *How Schools Work.* Chicago: University of Chicago Press, 1983. 191 pages.

Barrett, Michael J. "The Case for More School Days." *The Atlantic Monthly* 266, 5 (November 1990): 78-106.

Bates, Percy. "Desegregation: Can We Get There from Here?" *Phi Delta Kappan* 72, 1 (September 1990): 8-17. EJ 413 171.

Bauch, Jerold. "The TransParent School Model: New Technology for Parent Involvement." *Educational Leadership* 47, 2 (October 1989): 32-34. EJ 397 736.

Beane, James. "The Middle School: The Natural Home of Integrated Curriculum." *Educational Leadership* 49, 2 (October 1991): 9-13. EJ 432 772.

Beare, Hedley. "Educational Administration in the 1990s." ACEA Monograph Series No. 6. Paper presented at the annual conference of the Australian Council for Educational Administration (Armidale, New South Wales, Australia, September, 1989). 31 pages. ED 332 273.

Beck, Melinda. "The Geezer Boom, The 21st Century Family." *Newsweek Special Edition* (1990): 62.

Begle, E. G. *Ability Grouping for Mathematics Instruction: A Review of the Empirical Literature.* Stanford, California: Stanford University, Mathematics Education Study Group, 1975.

Bellah, Robert N.; Richard Madsen; William Sullivan; Ann Swidler; and Steve Tipton. *Habits of the Heart: Individualism and Commitment in American Life.* Berkeley: University of California Press, 1985. 355 pages.

Benjamin, Steve. "An Ideascape for Education: What Futurists Recommend." *Educational Leadership* 47, 1 (September 1989): 8-14.

Bennett, David, and D. Thomas King. "The Saturn School of Tomorrow." *Educational Leadership* 48, 8 (May 1991): 41-44. EJ 425 607.

Bennis, Warren, and Burt Nanus. *Leaders: The Strategies for Taking Charge.* New York: Harper & Row, 1985. 244 pages.

Berends, M. *A Description of Restructuring in Nationally Nominated Schools.* Madison: Center on Organization and Restructuring of Schools, University of Wisconsin, 1992.

Berger, Peter L., and Thomas Luckmann. *The Social Construction of Reality. A Treatise in the Sociology of Knowledge.* Garden City, New York: Doubleday, 1966. 203 pages.

Berliner, David. "Education Reform in an Era of Disinformation." Paper presented at the annual conference of the American Association of Colleges for Teacher Education, San Antonio, Texas, 1992.

Berman, P., and M. McLaughlin. *Federal Programs Supporting Educational Change.* Volume 8: "Implementing and Sustaining Innovations." Santa Monica, California: Rand Corporation, 1974.

Berman, Paul, and others. *Restructuring California Education: A Design for Public Education in the Twenty-First Century. Recommendations to the California Business Roundtable.* Berkeley: California Business Roundtable, 1988. ED 302 618.

Berry, Barnett, and Rick Ginsberg. "Creating Lead Teachers: From Policy to Implementation." *Phi Delta Kappan* 71, 8 (April 1990): 616-21. EJ 405 157.

Bertani, Albert; Linda Tafel; Jack Proctor; and Joan Vydra. "Teachers as Leaders: A District Plans for New Roles, New Directions." *Journal of Staff Development* 8, 1 (Spring 1987): 36-38. EJ 356 229.

Bloom, Allan David. *The Closing of the American Mind.* New York: Simon and Schuster, 1987. 392 pages.

Blum, Robert E., and Jocelyn A. Butler. "Managing Improvement by Profiling." *Educational Leadership* 42, 6 (March 1985): 54 58. EJ 315 262.

Bolin, Frances S. "Empowering Leadership." *Teachers College Record* 91, 1 (Fall 1989): 81-96. EJ 398 427.

Bolman, Lee G., and Terrence E. Deal. *Reframing Organizations: Artistry, Choice, and Leadership.* San Francisco: Jossey-Bass, 1991. 492 pages.

Bonstingl, John Jay. "The Quality Revolution in Education." *Educational Leadership* 50, 3 (November 1992): 4-9.

Borrell, Jerry. "America's Shame: How We've Abandoned Our Children's Future." *Macworld* 9, 9 (September 1992): 25-26, 28, 30.

Boyer, Ernest. "Civic Education for Responsible Citizens." *Educational Leadership* 48, 3 (November 1990): 4.

————. *School Choice.* Ewing, New Jersey: Carnegie Foundation for the Advancement of Teaching, 1992.

Bracey, Gerald W. "Teachers as Researchers." *Phi Delta Kappan* 72, 5 (January 1991): 404-7.

————. "The Second Bracey Report on the Condition of Public Education." *Phi Delta Kappan* 74, 2 (October 1992): 104-17.

————. "Why Can't They Be Like We Were?" *Phi Delta Kappan* 73, 2 (October 1991): 104-17.

Bradley, Ann. "In Dade County, Company Gears Up To Help District Run a Public School." *Education Week* IX, 37 (June 6, 1990): 1, 16-17.

Brandt, Ron. "On Deming and School Quality: A Conversation with Enid Brown." *Educational Leadership* 50, 3 (November 1992): 28-31.

————. "On Outcome-Based Education: A Conversation with Bill Spady." *Educational Leadership* 50, 4 (December-January 1992/1993): 66-70.

————. "On Parents and Schools: A Conversation with Joyce Epstein." *Educational Leadership* 47, 2 (October 1989): 24-27. ED 397 732.

————. "On Teacher Empowerment: A Conversation with Ann Lieberman." *Educational Leadership* 46 8 (May 1989): 23-26. EJ 388 737.

————. "On the Expert Teacher: A Conversation with David Berliner." *Educational Leadership* 44, 2 (October 1986): 4-9. EJ 342 524.

Bredeson, Paul. "Letting Go of Outlived Professional Identities: A Study of Role Transition for Principals in Restructured Schools." Paper presented at the annual conference of the American Educational Research Association, Chicago, 1991.

Brickley, Dan, and Tim Westerberg. "Restructuring a Comprehensive High School." *Educational Leadership* 47, 7 (April 1990): 28-31. EJ 405 188.

Bridge, R. Gary; Charles M. Judd; and Peter R. Moock. *The Determinants of Educational Outcomes: The Impact of Families, Peers, Teachers, and Schools.* Cambridge, Massachusetts: Ballinger, 1979. 357 pages.

Bridges, Edwin. "A Model for Shared Decision Making in the School Principalship." *Educational Administration Quarterly* 20, 3 (1967): 11-40.

Broder, David. "New Jobs Require Better-Educated Workers." *Eugene Register-Guard,* May 22, 1991: 11A.

Brooks, Jacqueline Grennon. "Teachers and Students: Constructivists Forging New Connections." *Educational Leadership* 47, 5 (February 1990): 68-71. EJ 402 402.

Brophy, Jere. "Probing the Subtleties of Subject-Matter Teaching." *Educational Leadership* 49, 7 (April 1992): 4-8. EJ 442 784.

Brophy, Jere E., and T. L. Good. "Teacher Behavior and Student Achievement." In *Handbook of Research on Teaching,* edited by Merlin C. Wittrock. New York: Macmillan, 1986. 1037 pages.

Brown, Ann, and Joseph Campione. "Fostering a Community of Learners." Forthcoming.

Bryson, John M. *Strategic Planning for Public and Nonprofit Organizations: A Guide to Strengthening and Sustaining Organizational Achievement.* San Francisco: Jossey-Bass, 1988. 311 pages.

Bryson, John M., and William D. Roering. "Initiation of Strategic Planning by Governments." *Public Administration Review* 48, 6 (November-December 1988): 995-1004.

Budde, Ray. "Education by Charter." *Phi Delta Kappan* 70, 7 (March 1989): 518-20. EJ 385 316.

Bugliarello, George. "Hyperintelligence: Humankind's Next Evolutionary Step." In *Rethinking the Curriculum: Toward an Integrated, Interdisciplinary College Education,* edited by Mary E. Clark and Sandra A. Wawrytko. New York: Greenwood Press, 1990. 272 pages.

Burns, James MacGregor. *Leadership.* New York: Harper & Row, 1978. 530 pages.

Calabrese, Raymond, and Harry Schumer. "The Effects of Service Activities on Adolescent Alienation." *Adolescence* 21, 83 (Fall 1986): 675-87. EJ 345 025.

California State Department of Education. *A Question of Thinking: A First Look at Students' Performance on Open-ended Questions in Mathematics.* Sacramento: Author, 1989. 93 pages. ED 315 289.

Callahan, Raymond E. *Education and the Cult of Efficiency: A Study of the Social Forces That Have Shaped the Administration of the Public Schools.* Chicago: University of Chicago Press, 1962. 273 pages.

Campbell, Roald Fay, and Tim L. Mazzoni. *State Policymaking for the Public Schools.* Berkeley, California: McCutchan Publishing Corporation, 1976. 466 pages.

Carlisle, E. R. "Educating for the Future." *Planning and Changing* 19, 3 (Fall 1988): 131-40. EJ 385 307.

Carnegie Corporation of New York. *Turning Points: Preparing American Youth for the 21st Century. The Report of the Task Force on Education of Young Adolescents.* Waldorf, Maryland: Carnegie Council for Adolescent Development, 1989. 106 pages. ED 312 322.

Carnegie Foundation for the Advancement of Teaching. *School Choice.* Princeton, New Jersey: Author, 1992. 129 pages.

Carnevale, Anthony. "Skills for the New World Order." *The American School Board Journal* 179, 5 (May 1992): 28-30. ED 444 346.

Carnevale, Anthony P.; Leila J. Gainer; and Ann S. Meltzer. *Workplace Basics: The Skills Employers Want.* San Francisco: Jossey-Bass, 1990. 494 pages. ED 319 979.

Carroll, Joseph M. "The Copernican Plan: Restructuring the American High School." *Phi Delta Kappan* 71, 5 (January 1990): 358-65. EJ 400 584.

Carson, C. C.; R. M. Huelskamp; and T. D. Woodall. *Perspectives on Education in America.* Third Draft. Albuquerque, New Mexico: Sandia National Laboratories, May 1991.

Carver, Sharon. "Integrating Interactive Technologies into Classrooms: The Discover Rochester Project." Paper presented at the annual conference of the American Educational Research Association, Boston, Massachusetts, April 1990.

Case, Ann Dinsmoor. "The Special Education Rescue: A Case for Systems Thinking." *Educational Leadership* 50, 2 (October 1992). 32-42.

Cetron, Marvin, and Margaret Gayle. *Educational Renaissance: Our Schools at the Turn of the Century.* New York: St. Martin's Press, 1991. 352 pages.

Cetron, M. J. ; W. Rocha; and R. Luckins. "Into the 21st Century: Long Term Trends Affecting the United States." *The Futurist* 22, 4 (1988): 29-42.

Chamberlain, Neil W., and James W. Kuhn. *Collective Bargaining.* New York: McGraw-Hill, 1965. 451 pages.

Champlin, John. "A Powerful Tool for School Transformation." *School Administrator* 48, 9 (November 1991): 34. EJ 434 409.

Cheney, Lynne V. *American Memory: A Report on the Humanities in the Nation's Public Schools.* Washington, D.C.: National Endowment for the Humanities, 1987. 29 pages.

Chenowith, Tom. "An Inquiry Approach to Staff Development in Accelerated Schools." *Journal of Staff Development* 12, 3 (Summer 1991): 34-38.

Chenowith, Tom, and Robert Everhart. "The Restructured School: How Do You Know If Something Is Happening?" Paper presented at the annual conference of the University Council on Educational Administration, Pittsburgh, Pennsylvania, October 26-28, 1991.

Chrispeels, Janet. "District Leadership in Parent Involvement: Policies and Actions in San Diego." *Phi Delta Kappan* 72, 5 (January 1991): 367-71. EJ 419 907.

Chubb, John E., and Terry M. Moe. "Schools in a Marketplace: Chubb and Moe Argue Their Bold Proposal." *School Administrator* 48, 1 (January 1991): 18, 20, 22, 25. EJ 418 223.

_____. *Politics, Markets, and America's Schools.* Washington, D.C.: Brookings Institution, 1990. ED 336 851.

Clark, Christopher, and Penelope Peterson. "Teachers' Thought Processes." In *Handbook of Research on Teaching,* edited by Merlin C. Wittrock. New York: Macmillan, 1986. 1037 pages.

Clark, D., L. Lotto, and T. Astuto. "Effective Schools and School Improvement: A Comparative Analysis of Two Lines of Inquiry." *Educational Administration Quarterly* 21, 4 (1984): 7-25.

Clark, David, and Judith Meloy. "Recanting Bureaucracy: A Democratic Structure for Leadership in Schools." In *Schools as Collaborative Cultures: Creating the Future Now,* edited by Ann Lieberman. New York: Falmer Press, 1990. 261 pages.

_____. "Renouncing Bureaucracy: A Democratic Structure for Leadership in Schools." In *Schooling for Tomorrow: Directing Reform to Issues That Count,* edited by Thomas Sergiovanni and John Moore. Boston: Allyn and Bacon, 1989. 403 pages.

Clarke, B. R. "The Role of the Principal in Mainstreaming." *British Columbia Journal of Special Education* 8 (1984): 247-55.

Clegg, Stewart R. *Frameworks of Power.* London: Sage, 1989. 297 pages.

Clinchy, Evans. "Chicago's Great Experiment Begins: Will Radical Decentralization Bring School Reform?" *Equity and Choice* 5, 3 (May 1989): 40-44. EJ 393 104.

Clune, W. H., and P. A. White. *School-Based Management: Institutional Variation, Implementation and Issues for Further Research.* New Brunswick, New Jersey: Eagleton Institute of Politics, Center for Policy Research in Education, 1988.

Clune, William H.; Paula White; and Janice Patterson. *The Implementation and Effects of High School Graduation Requirements: First Steps Toward Curricular Reform.* CPRE Research Report Series. New Brunswick, New Jersey: Center for Policy Research in Education, Rutgers University, 1989. 78 pages. ED 304 756.

Cohen, D. K. *The Classroom of State and Federal Policy.* East Lansing, School of Education, Michigan State University, 1990.

Cohen, Deborah. "Home Visits Seen as Key Strategy To Combat a Host of Childhood Woes." *Education Week* XI, 7 (October 16, 1991): 1, 24.

_____. "San Diego Agencies Join to Ensure 'New Beginnings' for Families." *Education Week* X, 18 (January 23, 1991): 1,16,17,19.

Cohen, Elizabeth G. "Continuing to Cooperate: Prerequisites for Persistence." *Phi Delta Kappan* 72, 2 (October 1990): 134-38. EJ 414 876.

Cohen, Michael. "Effective Schools: Accumulating Research Findings." *American Education* 18, 1 (January/February 1982): 13-16. EJ 259 025.

Cole, Stephen. *The Unionization of Teachers: A Case Study of UFT.* New York: Arno Press, 1969. 245 pages.

Collins, Allan. "The Role of Computer Technology in Restructuring Schools." *Phi Delta Kappan* 73, 1 (September 1991): 28-36. EJ 431 204.

Commission on the Reorganization of Secondary Education. "Cardinal Principles of Secondary Education." Bulletin 1918, 35. Washington, D.C.: U.S. Government Printing Office, 1928.

Commission on the Skills of the American Work Force. *America's Choice: High Skills or Low Wages.* Rochester, New York: National Center on Education and the Economy, 1990.

Commission on Standards for School Mathematics. *Curriculum and Evaluation Standards for School Mathematics.* Reston, Virginia: National Council of Teachers of Mathematics, 1989.

Conant, James B. *The American High School Today: A First Report to Interested Citizens.* New York: McGraw-Hill, 1959. 140 pages.

Conley, David T. "Eight Steps to Improved Teacher Remediation." *NASSP Bulletin* 75, 536 (September 1991a): 26-41. EJ 431 215.

_____. *Lessons from Laboratories in School Restructuring and Site-Based Decision-Making: Oregon's 2020 Schools Take Control of Their Own Reform.* OSSC Bulletin. Eugene, Oregon: Oregon School Study Council, March1991. 69 pages. ED 343 263.

_____. *Restructuring Schools: Educators Adapt to a Changing World.* Trends & Issues Series, Number 6. Eugene, Oregon: ERIC Clearinghouse on Educational Management, February 1991. 57 pages. ED 328 954.

_____. "Some Emerging Trends in School Restructuring." *ERIC Digest Series,* Number 67. Eugene, Oregon: ERIC Clearinghouse on Educational Management, University of Oregon, January 1992.

Conley, David T.; Diane Dunlap; and Paul Goldman. "The "Vision Thing" and School Restructuring." *OSSC Report* 32, 2 (Winter 1992): 1-8.

Conley, Sharon. "Review of Research on Teacher Participation in School Decision Making." In *Review of Research in Education,* Vol. 17, edited by Gerald Grant. Washington, D.C.: American Educational Research Association, 1991.

Conlin, Elizabeth. "Educating the Market." *Inc.* 13, 7 (1991): 62.

Conrad, Daniel, and Diane Hedin. "School-Based Community Service: What We Know from Research and Theory." *Phi Delta Kappan* 72, 10 (June 1991): 743-49. EJ 426 971.

_____. "The Impact of Experiential Education on Adolescent Development." *Child & Youth Services* 4, 3-4 (1982): 56-76. EJ 270 703.

Cook, William J. *Strategic Planning for America's Schools.* Arlington, Virginia: American Association of School Administrators, 1988. 189 pages.

Cooper, Bruce. *Collective Bargaining, Strikes, and Financial Costs in Public Education: A Comparative Review.* Eugene, Oregon: ERIC Clearinghouse on Educational Management, 1982. 136 pages. ED 215 441.

Corbett, H. Dickson. "Restructuring Schools: Toward a Definition." In *At-Risk Students and School Restructuring*, edited by Keith Kershner and John Connolly. Philadelphia: Research for Better Schools, 1991. ED 335 425.

Corcoran, T. B. "Teacher Participation in Public School Decision-Making: A Discussion Paper." Paper prepared for the Work in America Institute, 1987.

Cowan, Hilary. "Project TEACH: How Business Helps Our Schools." *Educational Leadership* 47, 2 (October 1989): 6-7. EJ 397 726.

Cremin, Lawrence A. *American Education: The Metropolitan Experience, 1876-1980.* New York: Harper & Row, 1988. 781 pages.

Cresswell, A. M., and F. Spargo. *Impacts of Collective Bargaining Policy in Elementary and Secondary Education: A Review of Research and Methodology: Recommendations for New Research.* Denver, Colorado: Education Commission of the States, 1980.

Cross, Christopher; Richard La Pointe; and Carl Jensen. "The FIRST Grants: Federal Leadership to Advance School and Family Partnerships." *Phi Delta Kappan* 72, 5 (January 1991): 383-88. EJ 419 910.

Cuban, Larry. "A Fundamental Puzzle of School Reform." *Phi Delta Kappan* 69, 5 (January 1988): 341-44. EJ 364 789.

_____. *How Teachers Taught: Constancy and Change in American Classrooms, 1890-1980.* New York: Longman, 1984a. 292 pages.

_____. "Reforming Again, Again, and Again." *Educational Researcher* 19, 1 (January-February 1990): 3-13. EJ 408 024.

_____. "School Reform by Remote Control: SB 813 in California." *Phi Delta Kappan* 66, 3 (November 1984b): 213-15. EJ 309 954.

_____. "The 'At-Risk' Label and the Problem of Urban School Reform." *Phi Delta Kappan* 70, 10 (June 1989): 780-84, 799-801. EJ 390 509.

Curriculum Task Force of the National Commission on Social Studies in the Schools. *Charting a Course: Social Studies for the 21st Century.* Washington, D.C.: National Commission on Social Studies in the Schools, November 1989.

Cushman, Kathleen. "Performances and Exhibitions: The Demonstration of Mastery." *Horace* 6, 3 (March 1990): 1-12.

_____. "Coalition of Essential Schools." *Horace* 9, 1 (September 1992).

Danielson, L. C., and G. T. Bellamy. *State Variations in Placement of Children with Handicaps in Segregated Environments.* Washington, D.C.: U.S. Office of Special Education and Rehabilitative Services, 1988. ED 300 987.

Darling-Hammond, Linda. "Educational Indicators and Enlightened Policy." *Educational Policy* 6, 3 (September 1992): 235-65.

_____. "Teacher Professionalism: Why and How?" In *Schools as Collaborative Cultures: Creating the Future Now,* edited by Ann Lieberman. New York: Falmer Press, 1990. 261 pages.

David, Jane L. "Synthesis of Research on School-Based Management." *Educational Leadership* 46, 9 (May 1989): 45-53. EJ 388 744.

_____. "What It Takes To Restructure Education." *Educational Leadership* 48, 8 (May 1991): 11-15. EJ 425 600.

David, Jane L., and others. *Restructuring in Progress: Lessons from Pioneering Districts.* Results in Education Series. Washington, D.C.: National Governors' Association, 1989. 60 pages. ED 306 633.

_____. David, Jane L., and others. *State Actions to Restructure Schools: First Steps.* Results in Education Series. Washington D.C.: National Governors' Association, 1990. 51 pages. ED 320 221.

Davies, Don. "Restructuring Schools: Increasing Parent Involvement." In *At-Risk Students and School Restructuring,* edited by Keith Kershner and John Connolly. Philadelphia: Research for Better Schools, 1991a.

_____. "Schools Reaching Out: Family, School, and Community Partnerships for Student Success." *Phi Delta Kappan* 72, 5 (January 1991b): 376-380, 382. EJ 419 909.

Deal, Terrence. "Reframing Reform." *Educational Leadership* 47, 8 (May 1990): 6-7, 9, 11-12. EJ 410 201.

_____. "The Culture of Schools." In *Leadership: Examining the Elusive,* edited by L. Sheive and M. Schoenheit. Alexandria, Virginia: Association for Superivision and Curriculum Development, 1987.

_____. "The Symbolism of Effective Schools." *Elementary School Journal* 85, 5 (May 1985): 601-20. EJ 321 407.

Deal, Terrence, and Kent Peterson. *The Principal's Role in Shaping School Culture.* Washington, D.C.: U.S. Department of Education, Office of Educational Research and Improvement, 1990.

Deming, W. Edwards. *Out of the Crisis.* Cambridge: Center for Advanced Engineering Study, Massachusetts Institute of Technology, 1986. 507 pages.

Dentler, Robert A., and others. "Decentralization in the Cleveland Public Schools: An Evaluation." *Equity and Excellence* 23, 1-2 (Spring 1987): 37-60. EJ 361 952.

Department of the Interior—Bureau of Education. *Cardinal Principles of Secondary Education.* Washington, D.C.: U.S. Government Printing Office, 1928.

Devaney, Kathleen. "The Lead Teacher: Ways to Begin." Paper prepared for the Task Force on Teaching as a Profession, Carnegie Forum on Education and the Economy, March 1987.

Dewar, J. "Grouping for Arithmetic Instruction in Sixth Grade." *Elementary School Journal* 63 (1964): 266-69.

DiMaggio, Paul J., and Walter W. Powell. "The Iron Cage Revisited: Institutional Isomorphism and Collective Rationality in Organizational Fields." *American Sociological Review* 48 (April 1983): 147-60.

Dornbusch, S., and P. Ritter. "Parents of High School Students: A Neglected Resource." *Educational Horizons* 66 (1988): 75-87.

Downey, R. G. "Difference Between Entering Freshman from Different Size High Schools." *Journal of College Student Personnel* 19 (1978): 353-58.

Doyle, Denis. "Can We Win the Brain Race with the Japanese?" *School Administrator* 48, 6 (August 1991): 16-20. EJ 429 825.

Dreeben, Roert, and Adam Gamoran. "Race, Instruction and Learning." *American Sociological Review* 51, 5 (October 1986): 660-69. EJ 344 747.

Drucker, Peter F. *The New Realities: In Government and Politics, in Economics and Business, in Society and World View.* New York: Harper & Row, 1989. 276 pages.

Dumaine, Brian. "What the Leaders of Tomorrow See." *Fortune* (July 3, 1989): 48, 50.

Dunlap, Diane, and Paul Goldman. "Rethinking Power in Schools." *Educational Administration Quarterly* 27, 1 (February 1991): 5-29. EJ 421 302.

_____. "'Power Over' versus 'Power Through': Professional-Bureaucratic Relationships in the 1990's." Paper presented at the annual conference of the University Council for Educational Administration, Phoenix, Arizona, 1989.

_____. "Power as a 'System of Authority' versus Power as a 'System of Facilitation'." Paper presented at the annual conference of the American Educational Research Association, Boston, Massachusetts, April 16-20, 1990. 25 pages. ED 325 943.

Dunlop, John T. *Industrial Relations Systems.* New York: Holt, Rinehart & Winston, 1958.

Dwyer, David C. "The Principal as Instructional Leader." *Peabody Journal of Education* 63, 1 (Fall 1986): 1-86.

_____. "The Search for Instructional Leadership: Routines and Subtleties in the Principal's Role." *Educational Leadership* 41, 5 (February 1984): 32-37. EJ 293 146.

Dwyer, David; Cathy Ringstaff; and Judy Sandholtz. "Changes in Teachers' Beliefs and Practices in Technology-Rich Classrooms." *Educational Leadership* 48, 8 (May 1991): 45-52. EJ 425 608.

Edmonds, Ronald. "Programs of School Improvement: An Overview." *Educational Leadership* 40, 3 (December 1982): 4-11. EJ 272 633.

Education Commission of the States. *Exploring Policy Options to Restructure Education.* Denver, Colorado: Author, 1991. 95 pages. ED 332 323.

Edwards, June. "To Teach Responsibility, Bring Back the Dalton Plan." *Phi Delta Kappan* 72, 5 (January 1991): 398-401. EJ 419 913.

Eisner, Elliot. "The Ecology of School Improvement." *Educational Leadership* 45, 5 (February 1988): 24-29.

Elam, Stanley, and others "The 23rd Annual Gallup Poll of the Public's Attitudes Toward the Public Schools." *Phi Delta Kappan* 73, 1 (September 1991): 41-56. EJ 431 206.

Elmer-Dewitt, Philip. "The Revolution That Fizzled." *Time* 137, 20 (May 20, 1991): 48-49.

Elmore, Richard. *Models of Restructured Schools.* East Lansing, Michigan: Center for Policy Research in Education, Michigan State University, 1988.

_____. "On Changing the Structure of Public Schools." In *Restructuring Schools: The Next Generation of Educational Reform,* edited by Richard Elmore and Associates. San Francisco: Jossey-Bass, 1990.

_____. "Teaching, Learning, and Organization: School Restructuring and the Recurring Dilemmas of Reform." Paper presented at the annual conference of the American Educational Research Association, Chicago, 1991.

Elmore, Richard F., and associates. *Restructuring Schools: The Next Generation of Educational Reform.* San Francisco: Jossey-Bass, 1990. 309 pages.

Emmer, Edmund; Carolyn Evertson; and L. Anderson. "Effective Classroom Management at the Beginning of the School Year." *Elementary School Journal* 80, 5 (1980): 219-31.

Enderwick, Peter. "Multinational Corporate Restructuring and International Competitiveness." *California Management Review* (Fall 1989): 44-58.

Epstein, Joyce, and Henry Becker. "Teachers' Reported Practices on Parent Involvement: Problems and Possibilities." *Elementary School Journal* 83, 2 (November 1982): 103-14. EJ 273 073.

Esposito, D. "Homogeneous and Heterogeneous Ability Grouping: Principal Findings and Implications for Evaluating and Designing More Effective Education Environments." *Review of Educational Research* 43 (1973): 163-79.

Evertson, Carolyn M., and Edmund Emmer. "Effective Management at the Beginning of the School Year in Junior High Classes." *Journal of Educational Psychology* 74, 4 (August 1982): 485-98. EJ 267 792.

Evertson, Carolyn M., and Alene Harris. "What We Know About Managing Classrooms." *Educational Leadership* 49, 7 (April 1992): 74-78. EJ 442 798.

Fantini, Mario, and M. Gittell. *Decentralization: Achieving Reform.* New York: Praeger, 1973.

Fantini, Mario D., and Robert L. Sinclair, Editors. *Education in School and Non-School Settings.* Chicago: University of Chicago Press, 1985. 288 pages.

Fink, Stephen. "How We Restructured Our Categorical Programs." *Educational Leadership* 50, 2 (October 1992): 42-43.

Finn, Jeremy D. "Withdrawing from School." *Review of Educational Research* 59, 2 (Summer 1989): 117-42. EJ 404 583.

Finn, Jr., Chester E. "The Biggest Reform of All." *Phi Delta Kappan* 71, 8 (April 1990): 584-92. EJ 405 151.

Fitzpatrick, Kathleen. "Restructuring to Achieve Outcomes of Significance for All Students." *Educational Leadership* 48, 8 (May 1991): 18-22. EJ 425 602.

Fogarty, Robin. "Ten Ways to Integrate Curriculum." *Educational Leadership* 49, 2 (October 1991): 61-65. EJ 432 787.

Foster, June, and Candace Julyan. "The National Geographic Kids' Network." *Science and Children* 25 (1988): 38-39.

Frymier, Jack. "Children Who Hurt, Children Who Fail." *Phi Delta Kappan* 74, 3 (November, 1992): 257-59.

Frymier, Jack, and Bruce Gansneder. "The Phi Delta Kappa Study of Students at Risk." *Phi Delta Kappan* 71, 2 (October 1989): 142-46.

Fuhrman, Susan. "Educational Policy: A New Context for Governance." *Publis: The Journal of Federalism* 17, 3 (1987): 131-43.

Fullan, Michael G. "Change Processes and Strategies at the Local Level." *The Elementary School Journal* 85, 3 (January 1985): 391-421. EJ 315 744.

_____. "Visions That Blind." *Educational Leadership* 49, 5 (February 1992): 19-20. EJ 439 278.

Fullan, Michael G., and Matthew B. Miles. "Getting Reform Right: What Works and What Doesn't." *Phi Delta Kappan* 73, 10 (June 1992): 744-52. EJ 445 727.

Fullan, Michael G., and A. Pomfret. "Research on Curriculum and Instruction Implementation." *Review of Educational Research* 47, 2 (1977): 335-97.

Fullan, Michael G., with Suzanne Stiegelbauer. *The New Meaning of Educational Change.* New York: Teachers College Press, 1991. 401 pages.

Fuller, Bruce; Ken Wood; Tamar Rapoport; and Sanford Dornbusch. "The Organizational Context of Individual Efficacy." *Review of Educational Research* 52, 1 (Spring 1982): 7-30.

Furhman, Susan. "Legislatures and Education Policy." Paper presented at the annual conference of the Eagleton Institute of Politics Symposium on the Legislature in the Twenty First Century, Williamsburg, Virginia, 1990.

Galvez-Hjornevik, Cleta. "Mentoring Among Teachers: A Review of the Literature." *Journal of Teacher Education* 37, 1 (January-February 1986): 6-11. EJ 333 692.

Gamoran, Adam. "Instructional and Institutional Effects of Ability Grouping." *Sociology of Education* 59, 4 (October 1986): 185-98. EJ 344 481.

_____. *How Tracking Affects Achievement.* Madison, Wisconsin: National Center on Effective Secondary Schools, 1990.

Gardner, Howard. *Frames of Mind: The Theory of Multiple Intelligences.* New York: Basic Books, 1983. 440 pages.

_____. "Making Schools More Like Museums." *Education Week* XI, 6 (October 9, 1991): 40.

Gardner, Howard, and Thomas Hatch. "Multiple Intelligences Go to School: Educational Implications of the Theory of Multiple Intelligences." *Educational Researcher* 18, 8 (November 1989): 4-9. EJ 408 016.

Garet, Michael., and Brian DeLany. "Students, Courses, and Stratification." *Sociology of Education* 61, 2 (April 1988): 61-77. EJ 369 605.

Garmston, R. J. "How Administrators Support Peer Coaching." *Educational Leadership* 44, 5 (February 1987): 18-26. EJ 350 642.

Gearhart, Maryle, and others. "A New Mirror for the Classroom: Using Technology to Assess the Effects of Technology on Instruction." Paper presented at the annual conference of the Apple Classroom of Tomorrow Symposium, Cupertino, California, 1990.

Giorgi, Amedeo, Editor. *Phenomenology and Psychological Research.* Pittsburgh, Pennsylvania: Duquesne University Press, 1985. 216 pages.

Giroux, Henry. A. *Teachers as Intellectuals: Toward a Critical Pedagogy of Learning.* Granby, Massachusetts: Bergin & Garvey, 1988. 249 pages.

Glasser, William. *The Quality School: Managing Students without Coercion.* New York: Harper and Row, 1990.

Glatthorn, Allan. "Restructuring Schools: Curriculm Reform." In *At-Risk Students and School Restructuring,* edited by Keith M. Kershner and John A. Connolly. Philadelphia, Pennsylvania: Research for Better Schools, Inc., 1991. 129 pages. ED 335 425.

Glickman, Carl. "Has Sam and Samantha's Time Come at Last?" *Educational Leadership* 46, 8 (May 1989): 4-9. EJ 388 734.

Goldman, Paul, and Diane Dunlap. "Reform, Restructuring, Site-Based Management, and the New Face of Power in Schools." Paper presented at the annual conference of the University Council for Educational Administration, Pittsburgh, Pennsylvania, October 26-28, 1990. 16 pages. ED 325 938.

Goldman, Paul; Diane Dunlap; and David Conley. "Administrative Facilitation and Site-Based School Reform Projects." Paper presented at the annual conference of the American Educational Research Association, Chicago, April 3-7, 1991. 32 pages. ED 332 334.

_____. "Facilitative Power and Non-Standardized Solutions to School Site Restructuring." *Educational Administration Quarterly* 92, 1 (February 1993).

Goldman, Paul, and Neil S. Smith. "Portrait of a Successful Educational Innovation: British Columbia's Program for Quality Teaching." Paper presented at the annual conference of the Canadian Society for the Study of Education, Kingston, Ontario, 1991.

Goldschmidt, S.; B. Bowers; and L. Stuart. *The Extent and Nature of Educational Policy Bargaining.* Final Report. Eugene, Oregon: Center for Educational Policy and Management, 1984. 137 pages. ED 245 406.

Goldschmidt, Steven, and Suzanne Painter. "Collective Bargaining: A Review of the Literature." *Educational Research Quarterly* 12,1 (1987-88): 10-24.

Goldschmidt, Steven, and Leland E. Stuart. "The Extent and Impact of Educational Policy Bargaining." *Industrial and Labor Relations Review* 39, 3 (April 1986): 350-60. EJ 333 925.

Goodlad, John. *A Place Called School. Prospects for the Future.* New York: McGraw-Hill, 1984. 396 pages. ED 236 137.

Goodlad, John I., and Robert H. Anderson. *The Nongraded Elementary School.* New York: Teachers College Press, 1987. 248 pages.

Goodlad, John, and F. Klein. *Looking Behind the Classroom Door.* Worthington, Ohio: Charles Jones, 1970.

Goodman, Kenneth S., and others. *Report Card on Basal Readers.* Katonah, New York: Richard C. Owen Publishers. National Council of Teachers of English, 1988. 167 pages. ED 300 794.

Gordon, Jack. "Can Business Save the Schools?" *Training* 27, 8 (August 1990): 19-27. EJ 412 651.

Gray, Kenneth. "Vocational Education in High School: A Modern Phoenix?" *Phi Delta Kappan* 72, 6 (February 1991): 437-45. EJ 421 308.

Gray, William A., and Marilynne M. Gray. "Synthesis of Research on Mentoring Beginning Teachers." *Educational Leadership* 43, 3 (November 1985): 37-43. EJ 329 580.

Greenfield, Elizabeth. "ILSs: New Emphases for the Coming Years." *Technological Horizons in Education* 19, 2 (September 1991): 10-12, 14.

Guiterrez, R., and R. Slavin. "Achievement Effects of Nongraded Elementary School: A Retrospective Review." Paper presented at the annual conference of the American Educational Research Association, San Francisco, 1992.

Guthrie, Grace Pung, and Larry F. Guthrie. "Streamlining Interagency Collaboration for Youth At Risk." *Educational Leadership* 49, 1 (September 1991): 17-22. EJ 432 685.

Guthrie, James W. "School-Based Management: The Next Needed Education Reform." *Phi Delta Kappan* 68, 4 (December 1986): 305-9. EJ 345 283.

Hall, Lena, and Ronald L. McKeen. "Increased Professionalism in the Work Environment of Teachers Through Peer Coaching." *Education* 109, 3 (1989): 310-16.

Hallinan, Maureen T. "Summary and Implications." In *The Social Context of Instruction: Group Organization and Group Processes,* edited by P. L. Peterson and others. Orlando, Florida: Academic Press, 1984. 258 pages. ED 268 075.

_____. "The Effects of Ability Grouping in Secondary Schools: A Response to Slavin's Best-Evidence Synthesis." *Review of Educational Research* 3 (1990): 501-04.

_____. "Ability Grouping and Student Learning." In *The Social Organization of Schools: New Conceptualizations of the Learning Process,* edited by Maureen Hallinan. New York: Plenum, 1987. 228 pages.

Hallinger, Philip; Joseph Murphy; and Charles Hausman. "Restructuring Schools: Principals' Perceptions of Fundamental Educational Reform." Paper presented at the annual meeting of the American Educational Research Association, Chicago, April 3-7, 1991. 42 pages. ED 334 681.

Harp, Lonnie. "Schools Urged to Revamp Instruction to Stress Workforce Skills." *Education Week* X, 40 (July 31, 1991): 11.

Harris, Melanie Fox, and R. Carl Harris. "Glasser Comes to a Rural School." *Educational Leadership* 50, 3 (November 1992): 18-21.

Hayes, Larry. "Re-Personalizing High Schools." *Phi Delta Kappan* 73, 9 (May 1992): 724.

Heath, S.B., and M.W. McLaughlin. "Policies for Children with Multiple Needs." In *Conditions of Children in California.* Berkeley, California: Policy Analysis for California Education, 1989. 780 pages. ED 316 933.

Heaviside, Sheila, and Elizabeth Farris. *Education Partnerships in Public Elementary and Secondary Schools.* Washington, D.C.: National Center for Educational Statistics, 1989. 35 pages. ED 304 789.

Hechinger, Fred M., and Grace Hechinger. "Are Schools Better in Other Countries?" *American Education* 10 (1974): 6-8.

Hedin, Diane. "Students as Teachers: A Tool for Improving School Climate and Productivity." *Social Policy* 17, 3 (Winter 1987): 42-47. EJ 355 106.

Henderson, Anne T., Editor. *The Evidence Continues to Grow: Parent Involvement Improves Student Achievement. An Annotated Bibliography.* National Committee for Citizens in Education Special Report. Columbia, Maryland: National Committee for Citizens in Education, 1987. 84 pages. ED 315 199.

Hill, Paul T., and Josephine Bonan. *Decentralization and Accountability in Public Education.* Santa Monica, California: Rand, 1991. 93 pages.

Hirsch, Eric Donald, and others. *Cultural Literacy: What Every American Needs To Know.* Boston: Houghton Mifflin, 1987. 251 pages.

Hoachlander, E. G.; P. Kaufman; and E. Wilen. "Indicators of Education and the Economy." In *Education and the Economy: Hard Questions, Hard Answers.* New York: The Institute on Education and the Economy, Teachers College, Columbia University, 1989.

Hodgkinson, Harold. "Schools Are Really Awful, Aren't They?" *Education Week* 11, 9 (October 30, 1991): 32, 25.

_____. "The Right Schools for the Right Kids." *Educational Leadership* 45, 5 (February 1988): 10-14. EJ 368 819.

_____. *The Same Client: The Demographics of Education and Service Delivery Systems.* Washington, D.C.: Institute for Educational Leadership, Center for Demographic Policy, 1989.

Hoerr, John; Leah Nathans Spiro; Larry Armstrong; and James Treece. "Culture Shock at Home: Working for a Foreign Boss." *Business Week* 3192 (December 17, 1990): 80-84.

Holland, A., and T. Andre. "Participation in Extracurricular Activities in Secondary Schools: What Is Known, What Needs To Be Known." *Review of Educational Research* 57 (1987): 437-66.

Hollister, Robinson. "Why Is Equality Growing?" *Focus* 12, 3 (Spring 1990): 28.

Hord, Shirley; William L. Rutherford; Leslie Huling-Austin; and Gene E. Hall. *Taking Charge of Change.* Alexandria, Virginia: Association for Supervision and Curriculum Development, 1987. 102 pages. ED 282 876.

Howard, Eugene. "A Nine-Step Process for Restructuring Schools." Unpublished paper, July 19, 1991.

Huber, George P. "The Nature and Design of Post-Industrial Organizations." *Management Science* 30 (1984): 928-51.

Huberman, A. Michael, and Matthew B. Miles. *Innovation Up Close: How School Improvement Works.* New York: Plenum Press, 1984. 309 pages.

Huffman, Gail, and Sarah Leak. "Beginning Teachers' Perceptions of Mentors." *Journal of Teacher Education* 37, 1 (January-February 1986): 22-25. EJ 333 695.

Huling, L. "How School Size Affects Student Participation, Alienation." *NASSP Bulletin* 64 (1980): 13-18.

Hurwitz, Sol. "Paying Attention to the Teacher." *Across the Board* 24, 11 (November 1987): 44-50.

Husen, Torsten, Editor. *International Study of Achievement in Mathematics: A Comparison of Twelve Countries.* New York: John Wiley & Sons, 1967.

Jackson, Philip W. *The Practice of Teaching.* New York: Teachers College Press, Columbia University, 1986. 159 pages. ED 271 427.

Jennings, L. "Parents as Partners: Reaching Out to Families to Help Students Learn." *Education Week* (August 1, 1990).

Johnson, David W., and Roger T. Johnson. "What to Say to Advocates for the Gifted." *Educational Leadership* 50, 2 (October 1992): 44-47.

_____. *Learning Together and Alone: Cooperative, Competitive, and Individualistic Learning.* Englewood Cliffs, New Jersey: Prentice-Hall, 1991.

Johnson, David W.; Roger T. Johnson; and E. J. Holubec. *Circles of Learning: Cooperation in the Classroom.* Edina, Minnesota: Interaction Book Company, 1986.

Johnson, Florence; Wilbur Brookover; and Walter Farrell, Jr. "The Effects of Principals', Teachers', and Students' Perceptions of Parents' Role, Interest and Expectation for Their Children's Education on Student Academic Sense of Futility." Paper presented at the annual conference of the American Educational Research Association, San Francisco, 1989.

Johnson, Susan Moore. "Can Schools Be Reformed at the Bargaining Table?" *Teachers College Record* 89, 2 (Winter 1987): 269-80. ED 366 867.

Joyce, Bruce R. "The Doors to School Improvement." *Educational Leadership* 48, 8 (May 1991): 59-62. EJ 425 610.

Joyce, Bruce R.; Richard H. Hersh; and Michael McKibbin. *The Structure of School Improvement.* New York: Longman, 1983. 290 pages. ED 228 233.

Joyce, Bruce, and Beverly Showers. "Low-Cost Arrangements for Peer-Coaching." *Journal of Staff Development* 8, 1 (Spring 1987): 22-24. EJ 356 225.

Joyce, B.; B. Showers; and C. Rolheiser-Bennett. "Staff Development and Student Learning: A Synthesis of Research on Models of Teaching." *Educational Leadership* 45, 2 (October 1987): 11-23. EJ 362 222.

Kanter, Rosabeth Moss. *Change Masters: Innovation for Productivity in the American Corporation.* New York: Simon and Schuster, 1983. 432 pages.

Kerchner, Charles T., and Douglas E. Mitchell. "Teaching Reform and Union Reform." *Elementary School Journal* 86, 4 (March 1986): 449-70. EJ 337 993.

Kierstad, R. "A Comparison and Evaluation of Two Methods of Organization for the Teaching of Reading." *Journal of Educational Research* 56 (1963): 317-21.

Kirst, Michael W. "Pitfalls to Restructuring." *EDCAL* 20, 24 (1991): 1.

_____. *Who Controls Our Schools?: American Values in Conflict.* New York: Freeman, 1984. 183 pages.

Kirst, Michael W., and Milbrey McLaughlin. "Rethinking Children's Policy." In *National Society for the Study of Education (NSSE) Yearbook.* Chicago: University of Chicago Press, 1989.

Kochan, Thomas A. *Collective Bargaining and Industrial Relations: From Theory to Policy and Practice.* Homewood, Illinois: Irwin, 1980. 523 pages.

Koppich, Julia E., and Charles T. Kerchner. *Educational Policy Trust Agreements: Connecting Labor Relations and School Reform. A Report on Year Two of the Trust Agreement Project.* Policy Paper No. PP90-2-1. Berkeley, California: Policy Analysis for California Education, 1990. 68 pages. ED 320 291.

Kram, K.E. "Phases of the Mentor Relationship." *Academy of Management Journal* 26, 4 (1983): 608-25.

Krupp, Judy-Arin. "Mentoring: A Means by Which Teachers Become Staff Developers." *Journal of Staff Development* 8, 1 (Spring 1987): 12-15. EJ 356 223.

Kulik, C. L., and J. A. Kulik. "Effects of Ability Grouping on Secondary School Students: A Meta-Analysis of Evaluation Findings." *American Educational Research Journal* 19, 3 (Fall 1982): 415-28.

Lanier, Judith, and Michael Sedlak. "Teacher Efficacy and Quality Schooling." In *Schooling for Tomorrow: Directing Reform to Issues That Count,* edited by Thomas Sergiovanni and John Moore. Boston: Allyn and Bacon, 1989. 403 pages.

Lapointe, Archie E.; Nancy Mead; and Gary Phillips. *A World of Differences. An International Assessment of Mathematics and Science.* Princeton, New Jersey: Educational Testing Service, 1989. 93 pages. ED 309 068.

Lawton, Millicent. "Youth-Service Mandate Splits Educators in Maryland." *Education Week* XI, 15 (December 11, 1991): 18.

Lee, V., and J. B. Smith. *Effects of School Restructuring on the Achievement and Engagement of Middle-Grade Students.* Madison, Wisconsin: Center on Organization and Restructuring of Schools, 1992.

Leggett, Diana, and Sharon Hoyle. "Peer Coaching: One District's Experience in Using Teachers as Staff Developers." *Journal of Staff Development* 8, 1 (Spring 1987): 16-20.

Leinhardt, Gaea. "What Research on Learning Tells Us About Teaching." *Educational Leadership* 49, 7 (April 1992): 20-25. EJ 442 787.

"Lessons from the Trenches." *U. S. News & World Report* 108, 8 (February 1990): 50.

Levinson, Eliot. "Will Technology Transform Education or Will the Schools Co-Opt Technology?" *Phi Delta Kappan* 72, 2 (October 1990): 121-26. EJ 414 874.

Lewis, Anne C. "Getting Unstuck: Curriculum as a Tool of Reform." *Phi Delta Kappan* 71, 7 (March 1990): 534-38. EJ 403 809.

_____. *Gaining Ground: The Highs and Lows of Urban Middle School Reform 1989-1991.* New York: Edna McConnell Clark Foundation, 1991. 129 pages. ED 341 742.

_____. *Restructuring America's Schools.* Arlington, Virginia: American Association of School Administrators, 1989. 249 pages. ED 314 820.

Lieberman, Ann. "Expanding the Leadership Team." *Educational Leadership* 45, 5 (February 1988): 4-8. EJ 368 818.

_____. "Teachers and Principals: Turf, Tension, and New Tasks." *Phi Delta Kappan* 69, 9 (May 1988): 948-53. EJ 370 310.

Lieberman, Ann, Editor. *Schools as Collaborative Cultures: Creating the Future Now.* Bristol, Pennsylvania: The Falmer Press, 1990. 264 pages. ED 333 064.

Lieberman, Ann, and Milbrey W. McLaughlin. "Networks for Educational Change: Powerful and Problematic." *Phi Delta Kappan* 73, 9 (May 1992): 673-77. EJ 442 877.

Lieberman, Ann, and Lynne Miller. "Restructuring Schools: What Matters and What Works." *Phi Delta Kappan* 71, 10 (June 1990): 759-63. EJ 410 181.

Lieberman, Myron C. *Public Sector Bargaining: A Policy Reappraisal.* Lexington, Massachusetts: Heath, 1980. 180 pages.

Lindblom, C.E. "The Science of 'Muddling Through'." *Public Administration Review* XX, 2 (Spring 1959): 79-88.

Liontos, Lynn Balster. "Collaboration Between Schools and Social Services." *ERIC Digest Series.* Number 48. Eugene, Oregon: ERIC Clearinghouse on Educational Management, 1990. ED 320 197.

Lipsky, D. B. "The Effect of Collective Bargaining on Teacher Pay: A Review of the Evidence." *Educational Administration Quarterly* 18, 1 (Winter 1982): 14-42. EJ 259 504.

Little, Judith Warren. "Assessing the Prospects for Teacher Leadership." In *Building a Professional Culture in Schools,* edited by Ann Lieberman. New York: Teachers College Press, Columbia University, 1988. 251 pages. ED 300 877.

_____. "Norms of Collegiality and Experimentation: Workplace Conditions of School Success." *American Educational Research Journal* 19, 3 (Fall 1982): 325-40. EJ 275 511.

_____. "The 'Mentor' Phenomenon and the Social Organization of Teaching." *Review of Research in Education* 16 (1990).

Lloyd-Jones, Richard, and Andrea A. Lunsford, Editors. *The English Coalition Conference: Democracy through Language.* Urbana, Illinois: National Council of Teachers of English, 1989. 111 pages. ED 303 815.

Louis, Karen Seashore. *Restructuring and the Problem of Teachers' Work.* Chicago: The University of Chicago Press, 1992.

Louis, Karen Seashore, and Matthew B. Miles. *Improving the Urban High School: What Works and Why.* New York: Teachers College Press, 1990. 357 pages. ED 327 623.

Love, Mary Joyce. "The Home Visit—An Irreplaceable Tool." *Educational Leadership* 47, 2 (October 1989): 29. EJ 397 734.

Luchs, Kathy. "Selected Changes in Urban High School Students after Participation in Community-Based Learning and Service Activities." Doctoral dissertation, University of Maryland, 1981.

Luckmann, Thomas, Editor. *Phenomenology and Sociology: Selected Readings.* New York: Penguin, 1978.

Lueder, Donald C. "Tennessee Parents Were Invited To Participate—and They Did." *Educational Leadership* 47, 2 (October 1989): 15-17. EJ 397 729.

Lutz, F. *Public Participation in Local School Districts.* Boston: Lexington Books, 1978.

MacDowell, Michael A. "Partnerships: Getting a Return on the Investment." *Educational Leadership* 47, 2 (October 1989): 8-11. EJ 397 727.

Maeroff, Gene I. "A Blueprint for Empowering Teachers." *Phi Delta Kappan* 69, 7 (March 1988): 472-47. EJ 368 805.

_____. "Teacher Empowerment: A Step Toward Professionalization." A "Bulletin" Special. *NASSP Bulletin* 72, 511 (November 1988): 52-54,56-60. EJ 379 966.

Malen, Betty, and Rodney T. Ogawa. "Professional-Patron Influence on Site-Based Governance Councils: A Confounding Case Study." *Educational Evaluation and Policy Analysis* 10, 4 (Winter 1988): 251-70. EJ 422 199.

Malen, Betty; Rodney Ogawa; and Jennifer Kranz. "Unfulfilled Promises." *School Administrator* 47, 2 (February 1990a): 30, 32, 53-56, 59. EJ 402 409.

_____. "What Do We Know About School-Based Management? A Case Study of the Literature—A Call for Research." In *Choice and Control in American Education,* edited by William H. Clune and John F. Witte. New York: Falmer, 1990b.

Mandel, Michael, and Aaron Bernstein. "Dispelling the Myths That Are Holding Us Back." *Business Week, Special Report* 3192 (December 17, 1990): 66-70.

Marcoulides, George A., and Ronald H. Heck. "Educational Policy Issues for the 1990s—Balancing Equity and Excellence in Implementing the Reform Agenda." *Urban Education* 25, 11 (April 1990): 55-67. EJ 407 975.

Marks, Merle B. "Teacher Leadership in Staff Development." *Educational Research Quarterly* 7, 4 (Winter 1983): 2-5. EJ 284 819.

Marris, Peter. *Loss and Change.* New York: Pantheon Books, 1974. 179 pages.

Martin, Michael. "Trading the Known for the Unknown: Warning Signs in the Debate Over Schools of Choice." *Education and Urban Society* 23, 2 (February 1991): 119-43. EJ 342 286.

Matthews, Marian. "Six Ways to Make Cooperative Learning More Effective." *Educational Leadership* 50, 2 (October 1992): 50.

Mazzoni, Tim L. "Analyzing State School Policymaking: An Arena Model." *Educational Evaluation and Policy Analysis* 13, 2 (Summer 1991): 115-38. EJ 430 688.

McClure, Robert M. "The Evolution of Shared Leadership." *Educational Leadership* 46, 3 (November 1988): 60-62. EJ 385 349.

McCune, Shirley. "Schools and Restructuring." *Policy Notes* 3, 1 (Fall 1988): 1-9.

McDaniel, Thomas. "Review of 'What Do Our 17-Year-Olds Know?' " *Educational Leadership* 47, 3 (November 1989): 99.

McDonnell, Lorraine M., and Anthony Pascal. *Teacher Unions and Educational Reform.* Santa Monica, California: Rand Corporation, 1988. 84 pages. ED 293 837.

McLaughlin, Milbrey, and D. Marsh. "Staff Development and School Change." *Teachers College Record* 80, 1 (1978): 69-94.

McNeil, Linda M. *Contradictions of Control: School Structure and School Knowledge.* New York: Routledge and Paul, 1986. 234 pages.

Meadows, B.J. "The Rewards and Risks of Shared Leadership." *Phi Delta Kappan* 71, 7 (March 1990): 545-48. EJ 403 811.

Mecklenburger, James A. "Educational Technology Is Not Enough." *Phi Delta Kappan* 72, 2 (October 1990): 104-8. EJ 414 869.

_____. "The Braking of the 'Break-the-Mold' Express." *Phi Delta Kappan* 74, 4 (December 1992): 280-89.

Meier, Deborah. "Central Park East: An Alternative Story." *Phi Delta Kappan* 68, 10 (June 1987): 753-57. EJ 355 462.

Melaville, Atelia, and Martin J. Blank. *What It Takes: Structuring Interagency Partnerships to Connect Children and Families with Comprehensive Services.* Washington, D.C.: Education and Human Services Consortium, 1991. 57 pages. ED 330 748.

Merenda, Daniel. "Partners in Education: An Old Tradition Renamed." *Educational Leadership* 47, 2 (October 1989): 4-7. EJ 397 725.

Mertens, Sally, and Sam J. Yarger. "Teaching as a Profession: Leadership, Empowerment, and Involvement." *Journal of Teacher Education* 39, 1 (January-February 1988): 32-37. EJ 374 363.

Meyer, Alan; Geoffrey Brooks; and James Goes. "Environmental Jolts and Industry Revolutions: Organizational Responses to Discontinuous Change." *Strategic Management Journal* 11 (1990): 93-110.

Meyer, John, and Brian Rowan. "The Structure of Educational Organizations." In *Dynamics of Organizational Change in Education,* edited by Victor Baldridge and Terrence Deal. Berkeley: McCutchan, 1983. 490 pages.

_____. "The Structure of Educational Organizations." In *Environments and Organizations,* edited by M. Meyer and others. San Francisco: Jossey-Bass, 1978.

Miller, Julie. "Bush Strategy Launches 'Crusade' for Education." *Education Week* X, 31 (April 24, 1991): 1, 26.

Miller, Lynne. "The Regular Education Initiative and School Reform: Lessons from the Mainstream." *Remedial and Special Education* 11, 3 (May-June 1990): 17-22, 28. EJ 414 957.

Minnesota Department of Education. *Proposed Rule for Secondary Graduation.* Minnesota: Author, April 22, 1991.

Mitchell, Douglas. "Educational Politics and Policy: The State Level." In *Handbook of Research on Educational Administration: A Project of the American Educational Research Association,* edited by N. Boyan. New York: Longman, 1988. 767 pages.

Mohrman, A. M.; R. A. Cooke; and S. A. Mohrman. "Participation in Decision Making: A Multidimensional Perspective." *Educational Administration Quarterly* 14, 1 (1978): 13-29.

Mojkowski, Charles, and Richard Bamberger, Editors. *Developing Leaders for Restructuring Schools: New Habits of Mind and Heart.* A Report of the National LEADership Network Study Group on Restructuring Schools. Washington, D.C.: Office of Educational Research and Improvement, Programs for the Improvement of Practice, 1991. 79 pages. ED 330 078.

Moorhouse, W. F. "Interclass Grouping for Reading Instruction." *Elementary School Journal* 64 (1964): 280-86.

Morgan, D. L., and D. F. Alwin. "When Less Is More: School Size and Student Social Participation." *Social Psychology Quarterly* 43 (1980): 241-52.

Morris, V. P. "An Evaluation of Pupil Achievement in a Non-graded Primary Plan After Three, and Also Five Years of Instruction." Doctoral dissertation. *Dissertation Abstracts* 29:3809A. 1969.

Mortimore, Peter, and Pam Sammons. "New Evidence on Effective Elementary Schools." *Educational Leadership* 45, 1 (September 1987): 4-8.

Moses, Monte C., and Kathryn S. Whitaker. "Ten Components for Restructuring Schools." *School Administrator* 47, 8 (September 1990): 32-34. EJ 413 141.

Moye, Jack, and Katherine M. Rodgers. "Teachers As Staff Developers: A Success Story." *Journal of Staff Development* 8, 1 (Spring 1987): 42-44. EJ 356 231.

Moynihan, Daniel Patrick. "Our Poorest Citizens—Children." *Focus* 11, 1 (Spring 1988): 5.

Muncey, Donna E., and Patrick J. McQuillan. "Preliminary Findings from a Five-Year Study of the Coalition of Essential Schools." *Phi Delta Kappan* (February 1993): 486-89.

Munro, Petra, and Jack Elliott. "Instructional Growth Through Peer Coaching." *Journal of Staff Development* 8, 1 (Spring 1987): 25-28. EJ 356 226.

Murphy, Carlene. "Lessons from a Journey into Change." *Educational Leadership* 48, 8 (May 1991): 63-67. EJ 425 611.

Murphy, Joseph. *Restructuring Schools: Capturing and Assessing the Phenomena.* New York: Teachers College Press, 1991. 131 pages.

Nancy, Perry. "How to Help America's Schools." *Fortune* 120, 14 (December 4, 1989): 137-42.

Nathan, Joe. "More Public School Choice Can Mean More Learning." *Educational Leadership* 47, 2 (October 1989): 51-55. EJ 397 743.

National Academy of Science. *Everybody Counts: A Report to the Nation on the Future of Mathematics Education.* Washington, D.C.: National Academy Press, 1989. 131 pages. ED 309 938.

National Alliance of Business. *A Blueprint for Business on Restructuring Education. A Corporate Action Package.* New York: Author, 1989. 51 pages. ED 312 486.

National Association of State Boards of Education. *Winners All: A Call for Inclusive Schools.* Alexandria, Virginia: Author, 1992.

National Business Roundtable. *The Role of Business in Education Reform: Blueprint for Action.* Report of the Business Roundtable Ad Hoc Committee on Education, 1988.

National Center for Education Statistics. *Education Partnerships in Public Elementary and Secondary Schools.* Washington, D.C.: U.S. Department of Education, Office of Research and Improvement, 1989.

National Center for Improving Science Education. *The Reform of Science Education in Elementary School.* Washington, D.C.: Author, 1989.

National Center on Education and the Economy. *America's Choice: High Skills or Low Wages! Report of the Commission on the Skills of the American Work Force.* Rochester, New York: Author, 1990. 209 pages. ED 323 297.

National Commission on Social Studies in the Schools. *Charting a Course: Social Studies for the 21st Century.* Washington, D.C.: Author, 1989. 92 pages. ED 317 450.

National Council of Teachers of Mathematics. *Curriculum and Evaluation Standards for School Mathematics.* Reston, Virginia: Author, 1989. 258 pages. ED 304 336.

National Governors' Association. *From Rhetoric to Action: State Progress in Restructuring the Education System.* Washington, D.C.: National Governors' Association, 1991. 60 pages. ED 336 831.

National Research Council. *Everyone Counts: A Report to the Nation on the Future of Mathematics Education.* Washington D.C.: Author, 1989. 114 pages.

National Science Teachers Association. *Essential Changes in Secondary Science: Scope, Sequence, and Coordination.* Washington, D.C.: Author, 1989.

Newman, Denis. "Opportunities for Research on the Organizational Impact of School Computers." *Educational Researcher* 19, 3 (April 1990): 8-13. EJ 411 284.

Newmann, Fred M. "Can Depth Replace Coverage in the High School Curriculum?" *Phi Delta Kappan* 69, 5 (January 1988): 345-48. EJ 364 790.

_____. "Linking Restructuring to Authentic Student Achievement." *Phi Delta Kappan* 72, 5 (February 1991a): 458-63. EJ 421 313.

_____. *What Is a "Restructured" School? A Framework to Clarify Means and Ends.* Issues in Restructuring Schools, Report No. 1. Madison, Wisconsin: Center on Organization and Restructuring of Schools, 1991b.

Nickle, Melinda Nixon; Fran Carter Flynt; Stephen Douglas Poynter; and James A. Rees Jr. "Does It Make a Difference If You Change Structure? School-Within-a-School." *Phi Delta Kappan* 72, 2 (October 1990): 148-52. EJ 414 879.

Noble, Donna L. "What Are the Effects of the Training Experience on Staff Development Trainers?" *Journal of Staff Development* 8, 1 (Spring 1987): 29-31. EJ 356 227.

Nyland, Larry. "One District's Journey to Success with Outcome-Based Education." *School Administrator* 48, 9 (November 1991): 29-35. EJ 434 408.

O'Neil, John. "Piecing Together the Restructuring Puzzle." *Educational Leadership* 47, 7 (April 1990): 4-10. EJ 405 184.

_____. "Preparing for the Changing Workplace." *Educational Leadership* 49, 6 (March 1992a): 6-9. EJ 441 164.

_____. "Wanted: Deep Understanding: Constructivism Posits New Conception of Learning." *ASCD Update* 34, 3 (March 1992b): 1, 4-5, 8.

Oakes, Jeannie. *Keeping Track: How Schools Structure Inequality.* New Haven, Connecticut: Yale University Press, 1985. 231 pages. ED 274 749.

_____. "Tracking in Secondary Schools: A Contextual Perspective." *Educational Psychology* 22 (1987): 129-53.

Oakes, Jeannie, and Martin Lipton. "Detracking Schools: Early Lessons from the Field." *Phi Delta Kappan* 73, 6 (February 1992): 448-54. EJ 439 294.

_____. *Making the Best of Schools: A Handbook for Parents, Teachers, and Policymakers.* New Haven, Connecticut: Yale University Press, 1990. 334 pages. ED 324 375.

Odden, Allan, and Priscilla Wohlstetter. "The Role of Agenda Setting in the Politics of School Finance: 1970-1990." *Educational Policy* 6, 4 (December 1992): 355-76.

Olson, Lynn. "Advocates React Angrily to Study Questioning Merits of Choice." *Education Week* XII, 9 (November 4, 1992): 5.

_____. "Black Community Is Frustrated over Lack of Results from Desegregation." *Education Week* X, 7 (October 17, 1990): 1,12-13.

_____. "Calif. Businessman's Drive for Choice Sparking Battle." *Education Week* XI, 3 (September 18, 1991): 1, 19.

_____. "California Is Second State To Allow Charter Schools." *Education Week* XII, 4 (September 30, 1992): 1, 23.

_____. "Claims for Choice Exceed Evidence, Carnegie Reports." *Education Week* XII, 8 (October 28, 1992): 1, 12.

_____. "Detroit Board Set To Vote on Plan 'To Empower' Schools." *Education Week* XI, 26 (March 18, 1992): 5.

_____. "11 Design Teams Are Tapped To Pursue Their Visions of 'Break the Mold' Schools." *Education Week* XI, 40 (August 5, 1992): 1, 47.

_____. "Missouri School's Reform: Getting Better or 'Messing Around with a Good Thing'?" *Education Week* IX, 38 (June 13, 1990): 1, 8.

_____. "Nation's First 'Charter' School Clears a Key Hurdle." *Education Week* XI, 13 (November 27, 1991): 18.

_____. "Parents as Partners: Redefining the Social Contract Between Families and Schools." *Education Week* IX (April 4, 1990).

_____. "Shortcomings in School-Based Management in Boston Noted." *Education Week* XI, 4 (September 25, 1991): 5.

_____. "Winning NASDC Project Takes Flight in Md." *Education Week* XII, 17 (January 20, 1993): 1, 12-13.

Oregon Department of Education. *School Improvement and Professional Development Program 1990-1991.* Guidelines. Salem: Author, 1990.

Ornstein, Allan C. "Administrative Decentralization and Community Policy: Review and Outlook." *Urban Review* 15, 1 (1983): 3-10. EJ 282 279.

_____. *Race and Politics in School/Community Organizations.* Pacific Palisades, California: Goodyear, 1974. 277 pages.

Pace, Glennellen. "Stories of Teacher-Initiated Change from Traditional to Whole-Language Literacy Instruction." *Elementary School Journal* 92, 4 (March 1992): 461-76. EJ 441 942.

Parsley, James. "Reshaping Student Learning." *School Administrator* 48, 7 (September 1991): 9, 11, 13-14. EJ 431 196.

Patriarca, Linda A., and Donna M. Kragt. "Teacher Expectations and Student Achievement: The Ghost of Christmas Future." *Curriculum Review* 25, 5-6 (May-June 1986): 48-50. EJ 339 149.

Paulson, F. Leon; Pearl Paulson; and Carol Meyer. "What Makes a Portfolio a Portfolio?" *Educational Leadership* 48, 5 (February 1991): 60-63. EJ 421 352.

Pavan, Barbara Nelson. "The Benefits of Nongraded Schools." *Educational Leadership* 50, 2 (October 1992): 22-25.

Payzant, Thomas. "To Restructure Schools, We've Changed the Way the Bureaucracy Works." *Amercian School Board Journal* 176, 10 (October 1989): 19-20. EJ 396 532.

Pea, Roy. "Distributed Intelligences and Education." In *Teaching for Understanding in the Age of Technology,* edited by David Perkins and others, forthcoming.

Pennar, Karen. "The Rich Are Richer—and America May Be the Poorer." *Business Week* 3240 (November 18, 1991): 85, 88.

Perry, C. R., and W. A. Wildman. *The Impact of Negotiations in Public Education.* Worthington, Ohio: Charles A. Jones Publishing Company, 1970.

Perry, Nancy J. "How to Help America's Schools." *Fortune* 120, 14 (December 4, 1989): 137-42.

Peshkin, Alan. *Growing Up American: Schooling and the Survival of Community.* Chicago: University of Chicago Press, 1978. 256 pages.

Peters, Thomas J. *Thriving on Chaos: Handbook for a Management Revolution.* New York: Knopf, 1987. 561 pages.

Peters, Thomas J., and Nancy Austin. *A Passion for Excellence: The Leadership Difference.* New York: Random House, 1985. 437 pages.

Peters, Thomas J., and Robert H. Waterman. *In Search of Excellence: Lessons from America's Best Run Companies.* New York: Harper & Row, 1982. 360 pages.

Peterson, Kenneth D. "Assistance and Assessment for Beginning Teachers." In *The New Handbook of Teacher Evaluation: Assessing Elementary and Secondary School Teachers,* edited by Jason Millman and Linda Darling-Hammond. Newbury Park, California: Sage, 1990. 443 pages.

Peterson, Penelope L. "Selecting Students and Services for Compensatory Education: Lessons from ApTitude-Treatment Interaction Research." In *Designs for Compensatory Education: Conference Proceedings and Papers.* Washington, D.C.: June 17-18, 1986. 49 pages. ED 293 903.

Petrie, H. G. "Reflections on the Second Wave of Reform: Restructuring the Teaching Profession." In *Educational Leadership in an Age of Reform,* edited by Stephen L. Jacobson and James A. Conway. New York: Longman, 1990. 209 pages.

Phillips, Mary D., and Carl D. Glickman. "Peer Coaching: Developmental Approach to Enhancing Teacher Thinking." *Journal of Staff Development* 12, 2 (Spring 1991): 20-25. EJ 431 946.

Pipho, Chris. "Outcomes or 'Edubabble'?" *Phi Delta Kappan* 73, 9 (May 1992): 662-63.

_____. "Time for Results." *Education Week* X, 13 (November 28, 1990): 24.

Pitner, Nancy, and Steven M. Goldschmidt. "Bargain over School Reform: California's Mentor Teacher Program." Paper presented at the annual conference of the American Educational Research Association, Washington, D. C., April 1987.

Port, Otis; Zachary Schiller; Resa King; David Woodruff; Steven Phillips; and John Carey. "A Smarter Way to Manufacture." *Business Week* 3157 (April 30, 1990): 110-16.

Prager, Karen. "Estimating the Extent of School Restructuring." *Brief to Policymakers* 4 (Fall 1992): 1, 4, 6. Center on Organization and Restructuring of Schools, Madison, Wisconsin.

Prestine, Nona. "Completing the Essential Schools Metaphor: Principal as Enabler." Paper presented at the annual conference of the American Educational Research Association, Chicago, 1991.

Provus, M. M. "Ability Grouping in Arithmetic." *Elementary School Journal* 64 (1960): 387-92.

Purkey, Stewart C., and Susan Degen. *Beyond Effective Schools to Good Schools: Some First Steps*. Eugene, Oregon: Center for Educational Policy and Management, 1985. 9 pages. ED 263 652.

Purkey, Stewart C., and Marshall S. Smith. "Effective Schools: A Review." *Elementary School Journal* 83, 4 (March 1983): 427-52. EJ 281 542.

Ratzki, Anne. "Creating a School Community: One Model of How It Can Be Done." *American Educator: The Professional Journal of the American Federation of Teachers* 12, 1 (Spring 1988): 10-17, 38-43. EJ 372 828.

Ratzki, Anne, and Angela Fisher. "Life in a Restructured School." *Educational Leadership* 47, 4 (December/January 1989-90): 46-51. EJ 400 500.

Rauth, Marilyn. "Exploring Heresy in Collective Bargaining and School Restructuring." *Phi Delta Kappan* 71, 10 (June 1990): 781-84, 788-90.

Ravitch, Diane. "Education in the 1980's: A Concern for 'Quality'." *Education Week* IX, 17 (1990): 33, 48.

Ravitch, Diane, and Chester E. Finn, Jr. *What Do Our 17-Year-Olds Know?: A Report on the First National Assessment of History and Literature*. New York: Harper & Row, 1987. 293 pages.

Rebarber, Theodor. "State Policies for School Restructuring." National Conference of State Legislatures and the Vanderbilt University Educational Excellence Network, April 1992.

Reich, Robert. "Preparing Students for Tomorrow's Economic World." In *School Reform: Making Sense of It All*, edited by S. Bacharach. Boston: Allyn and Bacon, 1990.

————. *Education and the Next Economy*. Washington, D.C.: National Education Association, 1988. 28 pages. ED 320 277.

Richards, Craig E., and Mwalimu Shujaa. *State-Sponsored School Performance Incentive Plans: A Policy Review*. New Brunswick, New Jersey: Rutgers University, Center for Policy Research in Education, 1989.

Richmond, George. *The Micro-Society School: A Real World in Miniature*. New York: Harper & Row, 1974. 285 pages.

————. "The Future School: Is Lowell Pointing Us Toward a Revolution in Education?" *Phi Delta Kappan* 71, 3 (November 1989): 232-36.

Robbins, Pam, and Pat Wolfe. "Reflections on a Hunter-Based Staff Development Project." *Educational Leadership* 44, 5 (February 1987): 56-61. EJ 350 651.

Roemer, Marjorie G. "What We Talk about When We Talk about School Reform." *Harvard Educational Review* 61, 4 (November 1991): 434-48. EJ 435 327.

Rogers, Vincent R., and Chris Stevenson. "How Do We Know What Kids Are Learning in School?" *Educational Leadership* 45, 5 (February 1988): 68-75. EJ 368 832.

Rosenholtz, Susan J. *Teachers' Workplace: The Social Organization of Schools*. White Plains, New York: Longman, 1989a. 238 pages.

————. "Workplace Conditions That Affect Teacher Quality and Commitment: Implications for Teacher Induction Programs." *The Elementary School Journal* 89, 4 (March 1989b): 421-39. EJ 387 704.

Rosenholtz, Susan, and Susan Kyle. "Teacher Isolation: Barrier to Professionalism." *American Educator* (1984): 10-15.

Rosenstock, Larry. "The Walls Come Down: The Overdue Reunification of Vocational and Academic Education." *Phi Delta Kappan* 72, 6 (February 1991): 434-36. EJ 421 307.

Rothman, Robert. "E.D. Consortium Seeks to Spur Alternative Assessments." *Education Week* X, 25 (March 13, 1991): 34.

_____. "Focus on Self-Esteem, Achievement Turns School into Showcase." *Education Week* XI, 9 (October 30, 1991): 14.

_____. "Large 'Faculty Meeting' Ushers in Pioneering Assessment in Vermont." *Education Week* X, 6 (October 10, 1990): 1, 18.

_____. "Panel Unveils Proposed Assessments To Measure Progress Toward Goals." *Education Week* XI, 28 (April 3, 1991): 1, 16, 17.

_____. "Pennsylvania Board Delays Vote on 'Learning Outcomes' Plan." *Education Week* XII, 3 (September 23, 1992): 19.

_____. "Schools Stress Speeding Up, Not Slowing Down." *Education Week* XI, 9 (October 20, 1991): 1, 15.

_____. "Study Confirms 'Fears' Regarding Commercial Tests: Low-Level Content and Pervasive Effects Found." *Education Week* XII, 7 (October 21, 1992): 1, 13.

_____. "Supply of New Assessment Methods Said Trailing Behind Strong Demand." *Education Week* X, 26 (March 20, 1991): 11.

Sagor, Richard. "Three Principals Who Make a Difference." *Educational Leadership* 49, 5 (February 1992): 13-18. EJ 439 277.

_____. "What Project LEARN Reveals about Collaborative Action Research." *Educational Leadership* 48, 6 (March 1991): 6-10. EJ 422 845.

Sarason, Seymour Bernard. *The Culture of the School and the Problem of Change.* Boston: Allyn and Bacon, 1971.

_____. *The Predictable Failure of Educational Reform: Can We Change Course Before It's Too Late?* San Francisco: Jossey-Bass, 1990. 187 pages.

Saxl, Ellen R., and others. "Help Is at Hand: New Knowledge for Teachers as Staff Developers." *Journal of Staff Development* 8, 1 (Spring 1987): 7-11. EJ 356 222.

Scardamalia, Marlene, and others. "Computer-Supported Intentional Learning Environments." *Journal of Educational Computing Research* 5, 1 (1989): 51-68. EJ 389 346.

Schaefer, W., and C. Olexa. *Tracking and Opportunity.* Scranton, Pennsylvania: Chandler, 1971.

Schlechty, Phillip. *Restructuring Schools for the 21st Century.* San Francisco: Jossey-Bass, 1990.

Schmidt, Peter. "Employees Protest Firm's Tactics at Baltimore School." *Education Week* XII, 2 (September 16, 1992): 1, 19.

Schmidt, Warren, and Jerome Finnigan. *The Race Without a Finish Line: America's Quest for Total Quality.* San Francisco: Jossey-Bass, 1992.

Schmuck, Patricia, and Richard Schmuck. *Small Schools, Big Problems.* Newbury Park, California: Corwin, 1992.

Schmuck, Richard A., and Philip J. Runkel. *Handbook of Organization Development in Schools.* Third Edition. Palo Alto, California: Mayfield Publishing Co., 1985. ED 280 178.

Schofield, Janet Ward, and David Verban. "Computer Usage in Teaching Mathematics: Issues Which Need Answers." In *Effective Mathematics Teaching. Vol. 1,* edited by Douglas Grouws and others. Reston, Virginia: National Council of Teachers of Mathematics, 1988. 261 pages. ED 297 933.

Schön, Donald A. "Coaching Reflective Teaching." In *Reflection in Teacher Education,* edited by Peter Grimmett and Gaalen L. Erickson. Vancouver, B.C.: Pacific Educational Press, 1988. 214 pages.

_____. "Professional Knowledge and Reflective Practice." In *Schooling for Tomorrow: Directing Reform to Issues That Count,* edited by Thomas J. Sergiovanni and John H. Moore. Needham Heights, Massachusetts: Allyn and Bacon, 1989. 403 pages. ED 304 774.

_____. *The Reflective Practitioner: How Professionals Think in Action.* New York: Basic Books, 1983. 374 pages.

"Schools Selected for Testing Pilot Project." *EDCAL* 21, 6 (1991): 1, 5.

Schorr, Lisbeth B. *Within Our Reach: Breaking the Cycle of Disadvantage.* New York: Anchor Press/Doubleday, 1988. 398 pages.

Secretary's Commission on Achieving Necessary Skills. *What Work Requires of Schools: A SCANS Report for America 2000.* Washington, D.C.: U.S. Department of Labor, June 1991.

Seeley, David. "A New Paradigm for Parent Involvement." *Educational Leadership* 47, 2 (October 1989): 46-48. EJ 397 741.

Segal, Troy; Del Valle; David Greising; Rena Miller; Julia Flynn; and Jane Prendergast. "Saving Our Schools: With America's Classrooms Besieged on So May Fronts, Here's How the Private Sector Can Help." *Business Week* 3283 (September 14, 1992): 70-78.

Senge, Peter M. *The Fifth Discipline: The Art and Practice of the Learning Organization.* New York: Doubleday/Currency, 1990. 424 pages.

Senge, Peter, and Colleen Lannon-Kim. "Recapturing the Spirit of Learning Through a Systems Approach." *School Administrator* 48, 9 (November 1991): 8-13.

Sergiovanni, Thomas. "Adding Value to Leadership Gets Extraordinary Results." *Educational Leadership* 47, 8 (May 1990): 23-27. EJ 410 204.

_____. "The Leadership Needs for Quality Schooling." In *Schooling for Tomorrow: Directing Reforms to Issues That Count,* edited by Thomas J. Sergiovanni and John H. Moore. Needham Heights, Massachusetts: Allyn and Bacon, 1989. ED 304 774.

Servatius, Joanna Dee, and Shareen E. Young. "Implementing the Coaching of Teaching." *Educational Leadership* 42, 7 (April 1985): 50-53. EJ 319 799.

Sewall, Gilbert T. *Necessary Lessons: Decline and Renewal in American Schools.* New York: The Free Press, 1983. 206 pages.

Shanker, Albert. "The Conditions of Teaching: Flexibility and Authority in the Classroom." In *School Reform: Making Sense of It All,* edited by S. Bacharach. Boston: Allyn and Bacon, 1990.

Sharan, Y., and S. Sharan. "Group Investigation Expands Cooperative Learning." *Educational Leadership* 47, 4 (December-January 1989-90): 17-21. EJ 400 492.

Shedd, Joseph B. *Involving Teachers in School and District Decision-Making.* Manuscript prepared for the State Education Department, the University of the State of New York, Organizational Analysis and Practice, 1987.

Shedd, Joseph B., and Samuel B. Bacharach. *Tangled Hierarchies: Teachers as Professionals and the Management of Schools.* San Francisco: Jossey-Bass, 1991. 232 pages.

Sheingold, Karen. "Restructuring for Learning with Technology: The Potential for Synergy." *Phi Delta Kappan* 73, 1 (September 1991): 17-27. EJ 431 203.

Showers, Beverly. *Peer Coaching: A Strategy for Facilitating Transfer of Training.* Eugene, Oregon: Center for Educational Policy and Management, University of Oregon, 1984. 106 pages. ED 271 849.

Silvestri, Kenneth. "Educating Parents for a Larger Role in School Improvement." *Educational Leadership* 47, 2 (October 1989): 43.

Sizer, Theodore R. "A Working Design: The Coalition of Essential Schools and Re:Learning." In *A Leader's Guide to School Restructuring: A Special Report of the NASSP Commission on Restructuring.* Reston, Virginia: National Association of Secondary School Principals, 1992. 62 pages.

_____. "No Pain, No Gain." *Educational Leadership* 48, 8 (May 1991): 32-34. EJ 425 605.

_____. *Horace's Compromise: The Dilemma of the American High School.* Boston: Houghton Mifflin, 1984. 241 pages. ED 264 171.

Skapski, M. K. "Ungraded Primary Reading Program: An Objective Evaluation." *Elementary School Journal* 61 (1960): 41-45.

Slavin, Robert E. "A Theory of School and Classroom Organization." *Educational Psychologist* 22 (1987a): 89-108.

_____. "Ability Grouping and Student Achievement in Elementary School: A Best-Evidence Synthesis." *Review of Educational Research* 57, 3 (Fall 1987b): 293-336. EJ 366 906.

_____. "Ability Grouping in Secondary Schools: A Response to Hallinan." *Review of Educational Research* 60, 3 (Fall 1990a): 505-7. EJ 417 573.

_____. "Achievement Effects of Ability Grouping in Secondary Schools: A Best-Evidence Synthesis." *Review of Educational Research* 60, 3 (1990b): 471-99. EJ 417 571.

_____. *Cooperative Learning: Theory, Research, and Practice.* Englewood Cliffs, New Jersey: Prentice-Hall, 1990c. 173 pages.

_____. "Synthesis of Research of Cooperative Learning." *Educational Leadership* 48, 5 (February 1991): 71-82. EJ 421 354.

_____. "Synthesis of Research on Grouping in Elementary and Secondary Schools." *Educational Leadership* 46, 1 (September 1988): 67-77.

_____. "The Nongraded Elementary School: Great Potential, but Keep It Simple." *Educational Leadership* 50, 2 (October 1992): 24.

Slavin, R., and N. Karweit. "Effects of Whole Class, Ability Grouped, and Individualized Instruction on Mathematics Achievement." *American Educational Research Journal* 22, 3 (Fall 1985): 351-67. EJ 321 805.

Smey-Richman, Barbara. *Teacher Expectations and Low Achieving Students.* Philadelphia: Research for Better Schools, Inc., 1989.

Smith, James F. "Ensuring the Quality of the Labor Force of the Future." *Business Economics* 26, 1 (January 1991): 18-20.

Smith, M.S., and J. O'Day. "Systemic School Reform." In *The Politics of Curriculum and Testing: The 1990 Yearbook of the Politics of Education Association,* edited by S.H. Fuhrman and B. Malen. Philadelphia: Falmer Press, 1991.

Smith, Stuart, C.; Diana Ball; and Demetri Liontos. *Working Together: The Collaborative Style of Bargaining.* Eugene, Oregon: ERIC Clearinghouse on Educational Management, 1990. 82 pages. ED 321 341.

Smith, W. M. "The Effect of Intra-Class Ability Grouping on Arithmetic Achievement in Grades Two Through Five." Doctoral dissertation. *Dissertation Abstracts International* 21: 563-64. 1960.

Smith, Wilma F., and Richard L. Andrews. *Instructional Leadership: How Principals Make a Difference.* Alexandria, Virginia: Association for Supervision and Curriculum Development, 1989. 165 pages. ED 314 826.

Sommerfeld, Meg. "RJR Nabisco Lays $30-Million Bet On 'Bottom Up' Reform Strategy." *Education Week* XI, 38 (June 10, 1992): 1, 10-11.

Sorensen, A. B. "The Organizational Differentiation of Students in Schools as an Opportunity Structure." In *The Social Organization of Schools: New Conceptualizations of the Learning Process,* edited by Maureen T. Hallinan. New York: Plenum, 1987. 228 pages.

Sorensen, A. B., and M. T. Hallinan. "Effects of Ability Grouping on Growth in Academic Achievement." *American Educational Research Journal* 23, 4 (Winter 1986): 519-42. EJ 351 742.

Spady, William. "Organizing for Results: The Basis of Authentic Restructuring and Reform." *Educational Leadership* 46, 2 (October 1988): 4-8. EJ 378 736.

_____. "Outcome-Based Education." In *A Leader's Guide to School Restructuring: A Special Report of the NASSP Commission on Restructuring.* Reston, Virginia: National Association of Secondary School Principals, 1992. 62 pages.

Sparks, Dennis. "Schools Must Be Fundamentally Restructured: An Interview with Albert Shanker." *Journal of Staff Development* 12, 3 (Summer 1991): 2-5.

Stansberry, Domenic. "Taking the Plunge." *Newmedia* (February 1993): 30-36.

Stedman, Lawrence C. "It's Time We Changed the Effective Schools Formula." *Phi Delta Kappan* 69, 3 (November 1987): 215-24. EJ 360 782.

Stevenson, Harold, and James Stigler. *The Learning Gap: Why Our Schools Are Failing and What We Can Learn from Japanese and Chinese Education.* New York: Summit Books, 1992.

Stockard, Jean, and Maralee Mayberry. *Effective Educational Environments.* Newbury Park, California: Corwin Press, 1992. 168 pages.

Strauber, Sandra K.; Sara Stanley; and Carl Wagenknecht. "Site-Based Management at Central-Hower." *Educational Leadership* 47, 7 (April 1990): 64-66. EJ 405 194.

Stroble, Elizabeth, and James Cooper. "Mentor Teachers: Coaches or Referees?" *Theory into Practice* 27, 3 (Summer 1988): 231-36. EJ 383 215.

Stuart, L. E.; S. M. Goldschmidt; with S. Painter. *Collective Bargaining in American Public Education: The First Twenty-five Years.* Eugene, Oregon: Center for Educational Policy and Management, University of Oregon, 1986.

Stuart v. School District No. 1 of the Village of Kalamazoo. 30 Mich. 69 (1874).

Sullivan, Maureen. "Staff Development through Professional Reading and Discussion." *Journal of Staff Development* 8, 1 (Spring 1987): 39-41. EJ 356 230.

"Summary of Panel Report on Measures of Progress Toward Goals." *Education Week* X, 28 (April 3, 1991): 18.

Sykes, G., and R. Elmore. "Making Schools More Manageable." In *The Politics of Reforming School Administrations,* edited by J. Hannaway and R. L. Crowson. New York: Falmer Press, 1989.

Szabo, Joan. "Do Public Schools Miss the Mark?" *Nation's Business* 78, 10 (October 1990): 37 39.

Tallerico, Kathryn. "Building Level Staff Development: A Personal Account of a Peer Helping Peers." *Journal of Staff Development* 8, 1 (Spring 1987): 32-34. EJ 356 228.

"The New Industrial Relations." *Special Report. Business Week* (May 11, 1981): 85.

Thines, G. *Phenomenology and the Science of Behavior: A Historical and Epistemological Approach*. London: Allen & Unwin, 1977.

"Thompson Endorses Hiring Private-Practice Teachers." *Education Week* X, 21 (February 13, 1991): 18.

Tinker v. Des Moines, 393 U.S. 509 (1969).

Toch, Thomas. *In the Name of Excellence*. New York: Oxford University Press, 1991. 325 pages.

Toch, Thomas, and Matthew Cooper. "Lessons from the Trenches." *U.S. News & World Report* (February 26, 1990): 50-55.

Turner, C. C., and J. M. Thrasher. *School Size Does Make a Difference*. San Diego: Institute for Educational Management, 1970.

Tyack, David B. "'Restructuring' in Historical Perspective: Tinkering Toward Utopia." *Teachers College Record* 92, 2 (Winter 1990): 170-91. EJ 422 096.

_____. *The One Best System. A History of American Urban Education*. Cambridge, Massachusetts: Harvard University Press, 1974. 353 pages.

Tye, Barbara Benham. *Multiple Realities: A Study of 13 American High Schools*. Lanham, Maryland: University Press of America, 1985.

_____. "The Deep Structure of Schooling." *Phi Delta Kappan* 69, 4 (December 1987): 281-84. EJ 363 380.

Tye, Kenneth. *The Junior High: School in Search of a Mission*. Lanham, Maryland: University Press of America, 1985.

Tyler, Ralph. "The Five Most Significant Curriculum Events of the Twentieth Century." *Educational Leadership* 44, 4 (December/January 1986/1987): 36-38.

Tyson-Bernstein, Harriet. "The Academy's Contribution to the Impoverishment of America's Textbooks." *Phi Delta Kappan* 70, 3 (November 1988): 193-98.

U.S. Department of Education. *A Nation at Risk: The Imperative for Educational Reform*. Washington, D.C.: Author, 1983.

_____. *America 2000: An Education Strategy*. Washington, D.C.: Author, 1991.

Van Horn, Carl E., Editor. *The State of the States*. Washington, D.C.: CQ Press, 1989. 235 pages.

Vars, G. F. *A Bibliography of Research on the Effectiveness of Block-Time, Core, and Interdisciplinary Team Teaching Programs*. Kent, Ohio: National Association for Core Curriculum, 1984.

Vars, Gordon. "Integrated Curriculum in Historical Perspective." *Educational Leadership* 49, 2 (October 1991): 14-15. EJ 432 773.

Viadero, Debra. "Maine's 'Common Core' Offers a Lesson in Standards." *Education Week* XI, 28 (April 1, 1992): 1, 21-23.

_____. "NASBE Endorses 'Full Inclusion' of Disabled Students." *Education Week* XII, 9 (November 4, 1992): 1, 30.

_____. "Standards Setters Search for Balance Between Excellence, Equity." *Education Week* XII, 3 (September 23, 1992): 21.

_____. "Texas Board Fines Publishers Over Error-Filled Textbooks." *Education Week* XI, 18 (January 22, 1992): 5.

Vickery, Tom Rusk. "ODDN: A Workable Model for Total School Improvement." *Educational Leadership* 47, 7 (April 1990): 67-70. EJ 405 195.

Villa, Richard, and Jacqueline Thousand. "How One District Integrated Special and General Education." *Educational Leadership* 50, 2 (October 1992): 39-41.

Walsh, Mark. "Entrepreneur Whittle Unveils Plans To Create Chain of For-Profit Schools." *Education Week* X, 35 (May 22, 1991): 1, 14.

_____. "Minnesota Mega-Mall To Include Education Facility." *Education Week* XI, 6 (October 9, 1991): 9.

_____. "N.Y.C. Choice Plan Will Open Boundaries of 800 Schools." *Education Week* XII, 3 (September 23, 1992): 5.

_____. "3 States See Dramatic Rise in Open-Enrollment Participation." *Education Week* XII, 8 (October 28, 1992): 12.

Waltner, Jean Campbell. "Learning from Scientists at Work." *Educational Leadership* 49, 6 (March 1992): 48-52. EJ 441 175.

Wanat, Carolyn. "Of Schools, Single Parents, and Surrogates." *Education Week* X, 33 (May 8, 1991): 25.

Wang, Margaret; Herbert Walberg; and Maynard Reynolds. "A Scenario for Better— Not Separate—Special Education." *Educational Leadership* 50, 2 (October 1992): 35-38.

Wang, Margaret C.; C. Reynolds; and H. J. Walberg. "Integrating the Children of the Second System." *Phi Delta Kappan* 70, 3 (November 1988): 248-51. EJ 379 984.

Wasley, Patricia A. "From Quarterback to Coach, from Actor to Director." *Educational Leadership* 48, 8 (May 1991): 35-40. EJ 425 606.

Wasson Restructuring Committee. *The Wasson Block Schedule.* Colorado Springs: Wasson High School, 1990.

Watson, Tim, and others. "The Relationship of Parents' Support to Children's School Achievement." *Child Welfare* 62 (1983): 175-80.

Watzlawick, Paul; John H. Weakland; and Richard Fisch. *Change: Principles of Problem Formation and Problem Resolution.* New York: Norton, 1974. 172 pages.

Weber, Arnold R., Editor. *The Structure of Collective Bargaining.* New York: Free Press, 1964.

Weick, Karl. "Educational Organizations as Loosely Coupled Systems." *Administrative Science Quarterly* 21, 2 (1976): 1-19.

Weisman, Jonathan. "Amid Publicity Over Declining Scores, Acclaimed Saturn School Faces Review." *Education Week* X, 40 (July 31, 1991): 12.

_____. "Business Roundtable Assessing State Progress on Reforms." *Education Week* XI, 12 (November 20, 1991): 22.

_____. "Report Cautiously Optimistic on School-Business Ties." *Education Week* X, 24 (March 6, 1991): 19.

_____. "Workforce Skills Hamper Productivity, Manufacturers Say." *Education Week* XI, 15 (December 11, 1991): 5.

West, Peter. "Parents Prove To Be the Toughest Nut to Crack in an Effort To Reform Science in Anchorage." *Education Week* X, 40 (July 31, 1991): 8-9.

_____. "Project To Reform Elementary Science Lauded." *Education Week* X, 29 (April 10, 1991): 8.

Westerberg, Tim, and Dan Brickley. "Restructuring a Comprehensive High School." *Educational Leadership* 48, 8 (May 1991): 23-26. EJ 425 603.

Wheelock, Anne. "The Case for Untracking." *Educational Leadership* 50, 2 (October 1992). 6-10.

Whelan, Carol Scott, and Charles Teddlie. "Self-Fulfilling Prophesy and Attribution of Responsibility: Is There a Causal Link to Achievement?" Paper presented at the annual conference of the American Educational Research Association, San Francisco, California, March 27-31, 1989. 27 pages. ED 323 211.

"Whittle To Spend Millions on 'State of the Art' Schools." *EDCAL* 20, 34 (1991): 1, 4.

"Who's Who in National Standards and Assessments." *Education Week* XI, 8 (October 23, 1991): 14, 15.

Wicker, A. W. "Cognitive Complexity, School Size, and Participation in School Behavior Settings: A Test of the Frequency of Interaction Hypothesis." *Journal of Educational Psychology* 60 (1969): 200-3.

————. "Undermanning, Performances, and Students' Subjective Experiences in Behavior Settings of Large and Small High Schools." *Journal of Personality and Social Psychology* 10 (1968): 255-61.

Widell, Brian. "Business Steps In." *Business Today* 28, 3 (Fall 1991): 13-23.

Wiggins, Grant. "Standards, Not Standardization: Evoking Quality Student Work." *Educational Leadership* 48, 5 (February 1991): 18-25. EJ 421 344.

————. "The Futility of Trying to Teach Everything Important." *Educational Leadership* 47, 3 (November 1989): 44-48, 57-59. EJ 398 953.

Willems, E. "Sense of Obligation to High School Activities as Related to School Size and Marginality of Students." *Child Development* 38 (1967): 1247-60.

Williams, David L., and Nancy Feyl Chavkin. "Essential Elements of Strong Parent Involvement Programs." *Educational Leadership* 47, 2 (October 1989): 18-20. EJ 397 730.

Willis, Scott. "Cooperative Learning Shows Staying Power." *ASCD Update* 34, 3 (March 1992): 1, 2.

Wirt, Frederick M., and Michael W. Kirst. *Schools in Conflict: The Politics of Education.* Berkeley, California: McCutchan Publishing Corporation, 1989. 413 pages.

"With Funds Restored, CAP Adds 'More Authentic Measures'." *EDCAL* 20, 24 (1991): 2, 5.

Wohlstetter, Priscilla, and Thomas Buffett. "Decentralizing Dollars Under School-Based Management: Have Policies Changed?" *Educational Policy* 6, 1 (March 1992): 35-54. EJ 441 096.

Wohlstetter, Priscilla, and Allan Odden. "Rethinking School-Based Management Policy and Research." *Educational Administration Quarterly* 18, 4 (November 1992): 529-49.

Wolf, Joan S., and Thomas M. Stephens. "Parent/Teacher Conferences: Finding Common Ground." *Educational Leadership* 47, 2 (October 1989): 28-31. EJ 397 733.

Wu, P.C. "Teachers as Staff Developers: Research, Opinions, and Cautions." *Journal of Staff Development* 8, 1 (Spring 1987): 4-6. EJ 356 221.

Zimet, M. *A Case Study of the Decentralization Law in New York City.* New York: Teachers College Press, 1973.

Zimmerman, Jack; Dia Norris; Jerry Kirkpatrick; Augusta Mann; and Ron Herndon. *Partners for Success: Business and Education.* Portland, Oregon: National Association for Schools of Excellence, 1990.

Zimpher, Nancy L., and Susan R. Rieger. "Mentoring Teachers: What Are the Issues?" *Theory Into Practice* 27, 3 (Summer 1988): 175-82. EJ 383 206.

At-Risk Families and Schools:
Becoming Partners

Lynn Balster Liontos • Foreword by Don Davies • 1992 • xii + 156 pages • Perfect (sew/wrap) bind • ISBN 0-86552-113-1 • $12.95

This book shows educators how to reach out to families who are poor, belong to racial /ethnic minorities, or speak a language other than English. The book contains many examples of effective programs along with Liontos's own recommendations for school boards, administrators, and teachers.

In the foreword, Don Davies calls Liontos's book "a welcome gift to all of us," in that it pulls together "various strands of theory, research, and demonstration" in order to give educators a basis for thinking about at-risk families and the roles they play in schools.

The Collaborative School:
A Work Environment for Effective Instruction

Stuart C. Smith and James J. Scott • Foreword by Roland S. Barth • 1990 • xii + 77 pages • ISBN 0-86552-092-5 • $9.00. (Copublished with NASSP.)

What are *collaborative schools*? In contrast to many schools where the adults work in isolation from one another, teachers and administrators in collaborative schools work as a team. Through such practices as mutual help, exchange of ideas, joint planning, and participation in decisions, the faculty and administrators improve their own skills and the effectiveness of their schools.

This book outlines the educational benefits of collaboration, describes a variety of collaborative practices already in use in schools, and suggests ideas for introducing those practices in other schools that wish to become more collaborative.

School Leadership: Handbook for Excellence

Edited by Stuart C. Smith and Philip K. Piele • Second Edition • 1989 • xvi + 392 pages • ISBN 0-86552-096-8 • $17.95.

This handbook suggests the knowledge, structure, and skills necessary for a leader to inspire all members of the school community to work together toward the goal of an excellent education for every student.

Rather than summarizing research findings as an end in itself, each chapter includes one or more sections that spell out implications, recommendations, or guidelines for putting knowledge into practice. The book is also, as Edwin M. Bridges says in the foreword, "highly readable."

Part 1. The Person
• Portrait of a Leader • Leadership Styles • Training and Selecting School Leaders • Two Special Cases: Women and Blacks

Part 2. The Structure
• School-Based Management • Team Management • Participative Decision-Making • School Climate

Part 3. The Skills
• Leading the Instructional Program • Leading the Instructional Staff • Communicating • Building Coalitions • Leading Meetings • Managing Time and Stress • Managing Conflict

Graying Teachers: A Report on State Pension Systems and School District Early Retirement Incentives

Frank V. Auriemma, Bruce S. Cooper, Stuart C. Smith • Foreword by Richard D. Miller • 1992 • x + 92 pages • ISBN 0-86552-118-2 • $12.50.

This report presents a complete state-by-state overview of the retirement programs available to America's teachers. In addition, case studies of early retirement incentive plans in six districts provide some useful information about how these plans work: amounts spent and saved, numbers of teachers eligible to retire early versus those who take the option, and the costs of replacing the teachers who retired.

Keith Geiger of NEA: "A timely, comprehensive, and invaluable resource."

Richard Miller of AASA: "Case studies in this book give useful data and methods for evaluating the effectiveness of various teacher retirement incentive plans."

Problem-Based Learning for Administrators

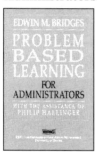

Edwin M. Bridges, with the assistance of Philip Hallinger • 1992 • xii + 164 pages • ISBN 0-86552-117-4 • $10.95.

PBL is a training strategy in which students, working in groups, take responsibility for solving professional problems. The instructor creates a hypothetical situation for the students (called a *project*) and then takes a back seat as an observer and an advisor while the students work out a solution.

Professor Bridges has spent the last five years developing, field testing, and refining PBL for use in educational management classes, and this book is the record of what he has learned. Using student essays, detailed descriptions of actual projects, data from PBL in the medical field, and his own observations, Bridges illustrates how PBL teaches leadership, management, and communication skills to administrative students.

Albert Shanker of AFT: "PROBLEM-BASED LEARNING . . . should bring a revolution to the professional development of principals."

Value Searches

Value Searches—economical, user friendly collections of ERIC resumés—are available on the following topics:
• School Restructuring
• School Choice, Vouchers, and Open Enrollment
• Parent Involvement in the Educational Process
• Instructional Leadership
• Leadership of Effective Schools
• Collegiality, Participative Decision-Making and the Collaborative School

The searches have been purged of irrelevant citations and laser printed for easy readability. The introduction to each *Value Search* lists the index terms used for the search and the time period covered—in most cases, the last five years. Instructions for using the citations, which include bibliographic information and abstracts, and for ordering copies of the complete documents and journal articles are included.

Every Value Search is updated several times each year. The price is $7.50 each (Buy 4 titles and get 1 free)

Working Together: The Collaborative Style of Bargaining

Stuart C. Smith, Diana Ball, and Demetri Liontos • Foreword by Charles Taylor Kerchner • 1990 • xii + 75 pages • ISBN 0-86552-103-4 • $7.25.

In some school districts, teacher unions and district officials are exchanging an adversarial style of labor relations for a more cooperative process that emphasizes problem-solving, mutual respect, and team involvement in the education process. This book's descriptions of collaborative bargaining practices being tried by various school districts, along with practical guidelines and pitfalls to avoid, make the volume a good starting-point for educators interested in adopting a more collaborative process.

Full payment or purchase order must accompany all orders. A handling charge ($3.00 domestic, $4.00 international) is added to all billed orders. Make checks payable to **University of Oregon/ERIC.** Address orders to ERIC/CEM, 1787 Agate Street, Eugene, OR 97403. (503) 346-5044. Fax: (503) 346-2334. Expect 6-8 weeks for delivery. (To expedite delivery, you may specify UPS for an extra charge.)